THE
BACKYARD HOMESTEAD
Book of
KITCHEN
KNOW-HOW

THE BACKYARD HOMESTEAD

Book of

KITCHEN KNOW-HOW

Field-to-Table Cooking Skills

Andrea Chesman

Storey Publishing

The mission of Storey Publishing is to serve our customers by
publishing practical information that encourages
personal independence in harmony with the environment.

Edited by Margaret Sutherland and Nancy Ringer
Art direction and book design by Mary Winkelman Velgos
Text production by Jennifer Jepson Smith
Indexed by Christine R. Lindemer, Boston Road Communications

Interior illustrations by © Elena Bulay, except for © Michael Austin: iii (chicken, plants), vi (carrot), vi and xii (oregano), vii and 146 (parsley), viii and 262 (chard leaf), 355 and 356 (plants); and © Susy Pilgrim Waters: vi and xii (Brussels sprouts plant), vii and 146 (spoon), viii and 262 (skillet)
Cover illustration by © Michael Austin
Author's photograph by Cory Byard

Storey Publishing
210 MASS MoCA Way
North Adams, MA 01247
www.storey.com

Printed in the United States by R.R. Donnelley
10 9 8 7 6 5 4 3 2 1

LIBRARY OF CONGRESS CATALOGING-IN-PUBLICATION DATA

Chesman, Andrea.
  The backyard homestead guide to kitchen know-how / by Andrea Chesman.
        pages cm
  Includes bibliographical references and index.
  ISBN 978-1-61212-204-5 (pbk. : alk. paper)
  ISBN 978-1-61212-205-2 (ebook : alk. paper) 1. Cooking (Natural foods) 2. Canning and preserving. 3. Farm produce. 4. Cooking—Equipment and supplies. I. Title.
TX741.C48 2015
641.3'02—dc23
                              2015013638

To

Alison, who supported and walked me through it

Cindy and Michael, who supported and laughed me through it

My family, who supported and helped me through it

Contents

PART 1

GETTING THE MOST FROM FRESH FOOD

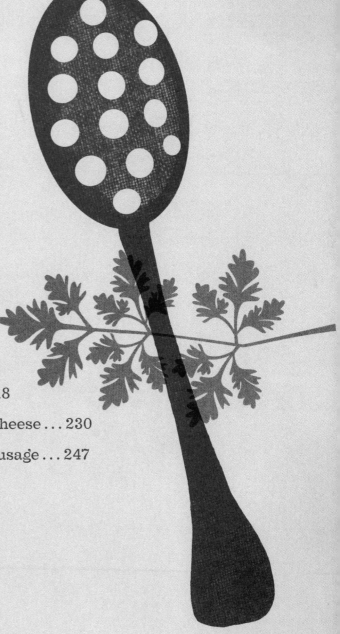

PART 2
FOOD PRESERVATION

PART 3

HOMESTEAD COOKING

Preface

I LIVE ON AN ACRE OF LAND in Ripton, Vermont, a small mountain village. I have a garden that I have at times supplemented with a community-supported agriculture (CSA) share. I make a few gallons of maple syrup every year from just five maple trees. I have harvested and preserved lots of different fruits and plenty of wild foods. And although I do not have experience with animal husbandry, I have managed to barter or buy raw milk, pastured meats, free-range eggs, and honey for most of my adult life. I have helped in a friend's annual turkey harvest, and I have received gifts of live chickens and roosters. I have cooked woodchuck, venison, frog's legs, rabbit, guinea fowl, ducks, and geese, wild and farmed. I have made omelets from duck and goose eggs. I have made pickles and jams, fresh cheeses, and butter. Some of this I have done entirely on my own. In many of my endeavors, I have been helped by my sons, Sam and Rory; my husband, Richard; and too many friends to list here.

I am grateful to live in a rural community, a community of gardeners, farmers, and homesteaders, and so I have accumulated the kitchen skills that go along with raising my own foods and living close to the land.

I came to Vermont in 1980, at the tail end of a back-to-the-land movement, along with many others in search of a more "authentic" lifestyle. Before that I had lived in a rural commune in upstate New York that disintegrated, along with many, many others. Living communally, it turns out, was pretty hard, even harder than subsisting on the land, which was pretty darn hard as it was. (Who does the dishes? Who takes care of the kids? Who takes an outside job and whose money is it anyway?)

I'm gratified to see that the back-to-the-land sensibility extends today to cities and suburban households and that food raised without chemicals is a mainstream preference.

Some of my friends make their living from working the land; many more supplement their income with day jobs. My day job has been writing cookbooks and editing other writers' cookbooks. I've been lucky to be a freelancer, lucky to be able to spend days in the kitchen when harvest or inclination drove me, and lucky to have friends who help fill in the gaps when I am in over my head.

I've raised two sons on this small homestead — one turned out to be a city boy, one a country boy. The country boy has many like-minded friends; some are lucky enough to be able to purchase land (sometimes communally, sometimes through land trusts) or access land through family. It is heartening to see all the experimenting and innovation that is the result: we are learning from each other.

My deepest thanks go to all those who helped get this book written. They include Jennifer and Spencer Blackwell of Elmer Farm; Jim Blais of Green Pasture Meats; Sam Chesman, Richard Ruane, Rory Ruane, Kate Corrigan, and Sebastian Miska of North Branch Farm & Gardens; Mac and Laurie Cox; Jane Eddy; Tonya and Adam Engst; Chris and Elaine Engst; Bay Hammond of Doolittle Farm; Kathy Harrison; Alison Joseph; Sandy Lance; Andrea Morgante; Sara Pitzer; Barbara Pleasant; Nancy Ringer; Hannah Sessions and Greg Bernhardt of Blue Ledge Farm; Rick Shappy; Judy and Will Stevens of Golden Russet Farm; Marjorie Sussman and Marian Pollack of Orb Weaver Farm; and Margaret Sutherland and all the other folks at Storey Publishing.

Introduction

A SELF-SUFFICIENT HOMESTEAD kitchen is a little different from a kitchen that is supplied from a nearby supermarket. It is a kitchen where the cooking is done from scratch using ingredients that are mostly raised or harvested nearby.

Our fruits and vegetables, though freshly harvested, may not be as pristine as supermarket produce, because we don't worry about bug bites or bruises that can be cut away, and we prize flavor and freshness over looks and long shelf life. In fact, we feel triumphant about harvesting even the damaged fruits and veggies, because we know we somehow prevailed against pernicious pests. Needless to say, our fruits and veggies are in season, and no, we don't even think to garnish a Valentine's Day chocolate dessert with fresh raspberries shipped from afar. We have a choice of meats that goes well beyond the relatively few easy-to-prepare cuts the supermarket stocks, and yes, a pig yields more than ham, tenderloin, chops, and bacon.

There's always something going on in the homestead kitchen. Kimchi may be fermenting in the cool spot under the sink. Bread may be rising on top of the refrigerator where the heat collects. In the refrigerator, salt pork may be curing, and in the slow cooker, lard or chicken fat may be rendering. Attached to one of the cupboard door handles, cheesecloth may be draining whey from cheese curds into a bowl on the counter. Yogurt may be culturing under a blanket by the woodstove or in a picnic cooler.

When you are homesteading, working in the kitchen is a never-ending journey of exploration, growth, and learning as one new skill leads to another. Just as gardening leads inevitably into preserving, maple sugaring leads to making granola — simply because you have more syrup than you need for pancakes. Raising chickens for eggs leads to making mayonnaise from scratch, and rendering lard leads to more pie baking, which leads to preserving fruit specifically for pies. And so it goes.

If my experience has taught me one thing, it is that every aspect of growing, harvesting, cooking, and preserving food is about making the best of what comes to hand. This is not the same as making do, which implies a compromise. Our home-canned tomatoes will not look as uniform as store-bought canned tomatoes, but they probably taste better. Our root cellars may not provide perfect storage conditions, but we learn that limp rutabagas make a perfectly elegant purée. A magazine or food blog may declare that certain varieties are the very best apples for pies, but the trees that came with the house yield unnamed apples, and we still make darn fine pies. We may choose to sweeten those apples with our own maple syrup even though the recipe says to use sugar. We learn to apply our best judgment to make delicious food from the raw materials we raised, bartered, or bought.

For those of us who raise much of our own food, recipes for the foods we put on the table at mealtimes should function more as guidelines than as scientific formulas. (Strict adherence to recipes for making cheeses and some preserved foods are the exceptions.) The recipes in this book provide lots of suggestions for substitutions. The vegetables in a soup or stew or salad can always be changed according to what is on hand. One fruit can be swapped in for another. Even herbs and seasonings can be altered to taste.

I've started the book with a chapter on setting up the homestead kitchen. We should all be lucky enough to work in a beautiful kitchen with an eat-in dining area, plenty of storage capacity, and lots of counter space. My own kitchen lacks everything but a wonderful view of the outside. Processed jars of vegetables and pickles spill over to the dining room because I don't have enough cupboard space, and during canning season the canners go there, too, instead of in the cupboard that is made inaccessible by recycling bins. Despite this, my kitchen functions, and yours will also when you have the equipment you need.

The book is divided into three parts: techniques for fresh foods, techniques for food preservation, and recipes. As I pulled this book together, developing new recipes and documenting old favorites, I found it hard to decide where to put certain recipes. Do the biscuits made with lard and sourdough belong with the pork chapter or the grain chapter? Does peach frozen yogurt belong in the dairy chapter or the fruit chapter? Does a granola sweetened with maple syrup belong with grains or sweeteners? It soon became obvious: our kitchens function as integrated systems where the foods we raise are put to good use in combinations that vary with the seasons. You seldom can separate one piece from another. So the third part of this book is a collection of select but (mostly) traditional recipes. There are egg dishes that can be enjoyed any time of the day, vegetable dishes that can be either side dishes or main dishes, and meat dishes specifically designed to be used interchangeably with the various types of meats and cuts you might have in your freezer.

Every single chapter included here could have been turned into a whole book. What I hope to share in this book — whether you are fully living off your land or using your gardening and husbandry skills to enrich your life — are the useful skills that will bring your harvests to the table with as much flavor and as little waste as possible. Thank you for letting me into your kitchen.

PART 1

Getting the Most from Fresh Food

Our food does not always come into the kitchen in pristine condition. What we bring into the kitchen is often dirty or otherwise not recipe ready. Vegetables have been literally just pulled from the ground and may have dirt clinging to them. Just-plucked and gutted chickens need serious rinsing. Milk is warm, and eggs have chicken poop on them.

"What do you want to do?" my son's playdate asks.

"Let's go up to the garden and see if there are any beans to eat," my son suggests.

"Then what?" the boy asks skeptically.

"Then we'll see if there are carrots, too."

And off they go to munch on dragon tongue beans, the yellow and purple variety that is delicious eaten raw, to pull baby carrots and eat those, too, with only a few swipes first on their almost-clean jeans. And to inspect some bugs, to pull apart some flowers, to climb the apple tree, to do whatever it is that boys do.

One of the pleasures of raising your own food is being in the moment. Hungry? Eat a raw bean. Thirsty? Eat a cucumber. Curious? See how many different insects you can count. In need of a mood lift? Some folks keep chickens for the sheer pleasure of watching them hunt and peck. Gardening and animal husbandry are both work and play.

Field-to-table cooking is also both work and play. Yes, there is work in getting meals on the table day after day after day. But there is also a truly enjoyable game in seeing how much you can produce and use and how little you can waste. Ideally, the kitchen is part of a circular system, not just the end of a linear progression from field to table. The most self-sufficient homesteads are ones that utilize the kitchen as a part of a mostly closed system of food production. With pigs and chickens and a compost pile, little is ever wasted, but the game is to see how well you can learn to make delicious food out of everything that comes into the kitchen. Homesteading today is not so much about subsistence as it is about quality.

Of course, everyone wants to cut down on waste. This part of the book focuses on what you need to do as the food comes into the kitchen. It focuses on fresh preparation and saves the preservation information for Part II.

CHAPTER 1

Setting Up the Homestead Kitchen

The kitchen isn't just the heart of the home; it is also the headquarters of the homestead. This is where the fruits of all your labor outside are stored, converted, used, and preserved. If you have a good setup and the right equipment, the work of transforming the food you raised into breakfast, lunch, dinner, and snack — not to mention preserving it for the future — will be much easier.

If I were designing a kitchen from scratch, I would start with a big table that could sit at least eight, preferably twelve. When you have a big table, kids can do homework and folks can visit while you cook, and it gives you a place to set down the baskets of freshly picked produce and to set aside projects you're working on. I would also design the space to include a walk-in (unheated) pantry with open shelves for canned goods and equipment only occasionally used. My spices and oils would stay cool in this pantry, and I could keep crates of winter squash and onions there, rather than upstairs in an unheated closet, as I do now. I would use the pantry to keep my ongoing vegetable ferments at a perfect temperature, at least through the winter.

I probably will never have that dream kitchen. Right now, my kitchen is too small for a table, and kids and visitors often perch on my one stool or even on the counter. My canning jars, canners, and dehydrators are stacked in a corner of the dining room during harvest season. The unenclosed porch off the kitchen that leads out to the garden is home to the grill, while the "river porch," outside my office, is where we eat during the summer and where my second refrigerator, used only during the harvest season, lives. I don't even have a dishwasher and don't know where it would go. But I make my kitchen work. We all make it work.

This chapter focuses on setting up a kitchen with the equipment and tools essential to — or extremely useful in — the homestead kitchen. You may already own much of it — the good news is that a lot of the cookware, canners, and appliances perform double duty or even triple duty in the kitchen. Single-use pieces of equipment, such as dehydrators, are covered in the specific chapters discussing the techniques that go with them.

The Big-Ticket Items

Kathy Harrison, friend and author of *Just in Case: How to Be Self-Sufficient When the Unexpected Happens*, among other books, built a screened summer kitchen in a separate outbuilding at her home in western Massachusetts. She has a two-burner propane stove and a large wash basin and still not enough counter space. (Counter space and storage are always an issue in the homestead kitchen.) She can work in her outdoor kitchen in relative comfort during the dog days of August. In typical fashion, her family constructed the kitchen from recycled parts and relied on their own labor, so the costs weren't excessive.

Even if you don't build yourself a summer kitchen, there are some big-ticket items that you will need starting out. If you buy brand-new and high-end items, you may need to spend some serious money, so shop wisely. Your needs as a backyard homesteader are not the same as those of most urban and suburban dwellers.

A Word about Stoves

If you are designing a kitchen from scratch and are looking for a conventional stove (as opposed to a woodstove), go for gas. The burners heat up faster and are easier to regulate than electric burners. An all-metal stovetop is better than one with an enamel finish. My enameled stovetop has deteriorated due to the high heat of boiling maple sap indoors, but this is just a cosmetic issue and not a functional one.

When I teach preserving workshops, I get a lot of questions about glass or ceramic stovetops. This style of stovetop is the first choice of high-end builders, but it doesn't work for home canners. If you have a glass or ceramic stovetop, you know that you are supposed to use flat-bottomed pots, including a flat-bottomed canner. Such a canner may work only if its diameter does not exceed the diameter of the burner. Check the stove's manual first. It may be possible to use a large canner on the stove, or then again it may void the warranty.

Chest vs. Upright Freezers

Chest Freezers	Upright Freezers
Less expensive	More expensive
More efficient (lower energy cost)	Less efficient (higher energy cost)
Can be difficult to access if you are short	Generally holds less per square foot
Larger footprint	Smaller footprint

Refrigerators and Freezers

You cannot have too much refrigerator and freezer space. A second refrigerator, even if you run it only for a few months a year, is invaluable at the height of the harvest season, even though you can make do with picnic coolers and ice. The second fridge is a necessity for storing milk and really, really helpful for curing and brining meat.

Freezers are necessary for storing large quantities of meat. When it comes to vegetables, most people prefer frozen to canned, so that's another reason for having at least one freezer. The freezer compartment of most refrigerators simply does not provide enough space for meat plus vegetables plus fruit.

Whether you buy a new or used freezer, you will have to choose between a chest freezer and an upright freezer. There are several factors to consider.

Using bins in either a chest or an upright freezer makes it easier to organize. If you want vegetables, you pull out the veggie bin. If you want meat, you pull out the pork or beef bin. If you have only one type of meat (beef, lamb, or pork), then consider organizing the packages by the type of cooking the cuts are best suited for, with the chops and steaks (to be grilled, pan-fried, or broiled) in one bin, the cuts for braises and stews in another, ground meat in another, fats in another, and so on. Leftovers and pre-cooked dishes go in their own bins. And while you're at it, stock up on masking tape and permanent markers. Never trust yourself to remember what a package holds even if it is in a clear plastic bag and looked so distinctive going in (I speak from hard-earned experience here).

The bins also help you rotate your stock. When you want to bring older containers or packages to the top, it's easier to rearrange a bin than to do all that finding and rearranging with the door or lid to the freezer open and leaking cold air.

It is a good idea to maintain an inventory list of the contents of the freezer. Some freezers have a surface that allows you to use dry-erase markers right on the lid or door to record your inventory. How easy is that! The difficult part is getting everyone in the house on board to maintain the system.

Small Equipment, Cookware, and Utensils

Most people already own an assortment of pots and pans, but some pieces of cookware are truly helpful for the homestead kitchen. I'm not saying you have to buy everything on the lists that follow, especially if you are just beginning to produce your own food. Just be aware of the items to keep on your wish list, and look out for good buys at yard sales, on Craigslist, and at kitchen store sales. When you are ready to take a step deeper into home-steading — say, deciding to raise your own meat birds — having the right equipment can make all the difference. You better have a very large pot to use for scalding those birds, because dry plucking is a slow process, too slow for a whole flock (and it is hard to avoid tearing the skin).

Take a long, hard look at your kitchen and see if you can solve some of your storage issues, because in the end storage can be a limiting factor, whether you are looking at root cellar capacity, freezer and refrigerator capacity, or equipment storage.

The equipment on the following list includes multi-purpose pots, appliances, and tools. They are matched with some of their potential uses. Of course, you will find other uses for these items in your day-to-day cooking. Knives and sharpening tools are covered later.

> **5-gallon stockpot.** Making big batches of stocks, soups, and stews; scalding birds to remove feathers; cooking down tomatoes and apples to make sauce; boiling down maple sap to make syrup; using as the bottom of a double boiler for cheesemaking.

Stockpots

Dutch oven

Boiling-water-bath canner

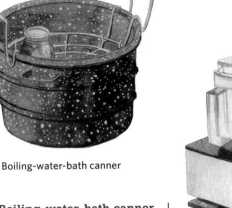

Food processor

> **2- to 3-gallon stockpot.** All of the same uses as the larger stockpot, in smaller batches, along with blanching fruits and vegetables, making jams and jellies, and culturing milk for cheese.

> **Cast-iron Dutch oven.** Long cooking of tough old birds or tough cuts of meat, rendering fat, baking beans, baking no-knead breads.

> **Boiling-water-bath canner.** Canning fruits and high-acid vegetables and sauces; culturing milk for cheese.

> **Large colander/fine-mesh strainer.** Draining and straining everything from produce to cheese to honey.

> **Large metal steaming basket.** Blanching and steaming.

> **Large-capacity bowls.** Mixing and soaking.

> **Half-sheet pans.** Roasting, baking, oven-drying.

> **Food processor.** Chopping, slicing, mixing, puréeing.

> **Digital thermometer.** Cooking birds and meat; making cheese, jams and jellies, maple syrup and apple cider syrup.

Digital thermometer

Colander

Large metal steaming basket

Large-capacity bowls

Kitchen scale

Vacuum sealer

Butter muslin

> **Kitchen scale.** Weighing produce and meats (especially important in pickling, curing, and sausage making, and helpful in determining cooking times for meats); weighing freshly ground flour for accurate baking.

> **Insulated coolers.** Keeping produce chilled after harvest; using with heat source to make yogurt.

> **Vacuum sealer.** Freezing fruits, vegetables, and meat; preserving cheese in the refrigerator; storing dried foods. Some vacuum sealers come with attachments that allow you to seal canning jars for long-term storage of dried foods, grains, and leftovers bound for the refrigerator. (This is not intended to replace either water-bath canning or pressure canning.)

> **Butter muslin or grade 90 cheesecloth.*** Making butter, cheese, and jelly; straining rendered fat; filtering honey and maple syrup.

> **Food-grade buckets, assorted sizes.** Filtering honey, collecting maple sap, curing meats, storing grains.

*Butter muslin is available wherever cheesemaking supplies are sold. Butter muslin has a thread count of 90. Most muslin sold in fabric stores has a higher thread count, meaning it is too finely woven for the uses listed here. Standard grocery-store cheesecloth is too loosely woven, but grade 90 cheesecloth is a perfect weave for kitchen uses.

Insulated cooler

Food-grade buckets

But What About . . . ?

Rice cooker. I love my rice cooker. It is a no-name brand I bought for under $20 in New York's Chinatown about 20 years ago. It is used several times a week and makes both rice and grains. I think: very handy but not absolutely necessary.

Slow cooker. It took me years to warm up to slow cookers. A Dutch oven set in a slow oven pretty much does everything a slow cooker does. The main difference is that slow cookers are generally thought to be safe to leave on entirely unattended (so you can leave the house), whereas it is considered unsafe to leave the house with the oven on. Whether or not the slow cooker saves energy is hotly debated on various websites. The slow cooker certainly doesn't heat up a kitchen the way the oven does (a minus in winter, a plus in summer). Another good use for the slow cooker: rendering fat. When you render fat, the house will be filled with the odor, which some hate and find intolerable. With an extension cord, you can render fat in the slow cooker on a porch or deck, where the odor won't offend humans (though it may attract some critters). I think: very handy but not absolutely necessary.

Blender and immersion blender. A food processor does as good a job (or better) at puréeing solids and semisolids, but is not as effective with liquids. If you make a lot of puréed soups and smoothies, you'll want a blender. An immersion blender can also be used to make butter, right in a quart mason jar. I think: pretty handy but not necessary.

Stand mixer. Great for mixing up batters and doughs. Many stand mixers have grinder attachments for making sausage. I use mine often; it is a KitchenAid that was given to my mother when she married in 1941 (amazing, right?). I think: not necessary, unless you will be grinding meat with the meat attachment.

Mandoline. A mandoline does a great job of thinly slicing vegetables, even better than a food processor, which tends to shred rather than slice. It is essential for slicing vegetables thinly for making dried veggie chips, and it comes in handy for slicing cucumbers and cabbage for pickling. The Japanese brand Benriner makes three plastic versions that sell for $25 to $75. The two more expensive versions have a wider cutting surface, which is much better for cabbage, big tomatoes, and other large items. However, as is the case for most mandolines, the hand guard is ineffective at holding the vegetables and frustrating to use; for safety, a cut-resistant glove is needed. I think: very handy but not absolutely necessary.

About the Dutch Oven

The Dutch oven is a deep pot made of heavy cast iron that comes with a tight-fitting lid. It is designed to be used on top of the stove or in the oven and can withstand very high heat. It holds its heat well and allows food to cook evenly. Some Dutch ovens are coated with enamel and some are not. They range in price from about $50 to $300.

Dutch ovens are essential for people who do a lot of cooking from scratch. Although long-cooking braises and stews can be made in a slow cooker after the food is initially browned in a skillet, it is easier to do it all in a Dutch oven, and then there is less cleanup. Dutch ovens are also great for cooking beans, incubating yogurt, and baking no-knead breads.

When choosing a Dutch oven, there are several considerations.

› **Size.** The most useful sizes are between 5½ and 7½ quarts. On the one hand, bigger is better if you regularly are cooking for crowds or like to make big batches so that you have leftovers. Bigger is also better if you want to be able to oven-braise a large bird or a tough cut of meat. On the other hand, you will get a loftier loaf if you bake your no-knead bread in a smaller Dutch oven. (I have a large one, but I wish I also had a small one for my breads.)

> **Coated or uncoated?** If the cast iron reacts to the acid (tomatoes, chiles, wine) in a braise or stew, it will impart an off-flavor. Enamel-coated Dutch ovens do not react to acids and so are definitely better for braising than uncoated ones. But they also tend to be more expensive. If your uncoated Dutch oven is very well seasoned, you can risk cooking acidic ingredients in it, but it takes patience and care to develop that seasoning of the cast iron.

> **Shape.** Dutch ovens can be oval or round. Round ones fit on the burner better and are a good shape for breads. Oval ones accommodate whole birds and rabbits better than round ones.

About the Thermometer

There are all kinds of kitchen thermometers out there, including both digital and analog (with spring-loaded dials). My preference is for a battery-operated digital thermometer with a probe connected by a long cord to the digital display. The probe and cord are heatproof; you can insert the probe into meat in the oven, set the digital display on a counter nearby, and at a glance find out the internal temperature of the roasting meat, without ever opening the oven door. I also like this thermometer because it will measure the temperature of cooking liquids (boiling sap, jams and jellies, warming milk for cheese) without steaming up the display. (When leaving it in a pot on top of the stove, you will have to rig up a way to hold the probe in the liquid, but not rest it on the bottom or side of the pot.) You can also use it to monitor the temperature of yogurt or cheese culturing in a container or the temperature inside a refrigerator.

Another feature I like on a thermometer is an alarm that sounds when the desired temperature is reached. With many temperature-sensitive processes, such as making cheese, you can set the alarm for a few degrees shy of the target, so you will be ready to remove the pot from the heat at the moment the target temperature is reached.

One thing to remember about using a probe thermometer in a roast is that the meat near the probe will cook faster than the meat farther from the probe because the metal probe conducts heat (like sticking a nail in a baking potato). So after the alarm signals that the desired temperature has been reached, test the temperature in a few spots to be sure the whole roast is at the desired temperature.

The temperature range for a good thermometer is 32°F to 392°F (0°C to 200°C), which is a wide enough range even for making candy.

The most important thing to remember about using a thermometer is to check its accuracy from time to time. Bring a pot of water to a boil and test the temperature of the boiling water. The thermometer should read about 212°F (100°C), but it will vary depending on your elevation and the atmospheric temperature. Adjust the temperature you are seeking accordingly. When making candies or maple syrup, test the thermometer that day if you want accurate results.

About the Vacuum Sealer

Do you really need one? I think: it depends. You can suck most of the air from a zippered plastic bag when the food is regularly shaped (such as a bag of peas or blueberries) just using a straw. But there is no way to suck all the air out of a bag that holds a bird. If you are freezing a lot of meats, it is a really, really good idea to use a vacuum sealer, provided you use thick plastic bags (the thinner the bag, the more air permeable it is). If you are freezing whole birds, but not meats, there are special poultry bags that shrink around the bird when immersed in heated water (see page 168).

As food freezes, moisture migrates to the surface and forms ice crystals. Over time, the food dehydrates, discolors, and loses flavor. Even with a good supermarket ziplock

---

How to Package Food with a Vacuum Sealer

The most common reason a bag will fail to seal is moisture in the sealing area. In the process of sucking out the air, moisture from the food can be drawn up to the sealing area. To prevent this from happening when you're vacuum-sealing liquid foods, freeze them first: fill your plastic bags with the food, clip the tops closed with clothespins or paper clips, and freeze in an upright position. Then seal.

① **Cut the bag and seal at one end.** If your bags are not precut, estimate the size you will need, then add 6 inches or more, depending on the thickness of the food you're sealing. Once filled, the bag must be at least 3 inches longer than what is filling it; do not try to get by with less. Cut the bag, and then use the vaccum sealer to seal it at one end.

Don't skimp on the bag length. The bag must be at least 3 inches longer than the food, taking into account the thickness of the food.

② **Fold down the edge and place the food inside.** Fold down the edge of the bag to make a 3-inch cuff. Put the food in the bag, taking care to avoid getting any food on the cuff, which would interfere with the seal.

The food you are about to seal should be as dry as possible.

③ **Seal.** Unfold the cuff on the bag, and align it across the vacuum sealer's sealing strip, with the open end of the bag tucked into the suction chamber. Close the lid, lock in place, and begin the vacuum and sealing process.

Don't forget to label the sealed package.

freezer bag, the food eventually develops freezer burn. Vacuum sealers make a big difference. Meat, poultry, and fish go from having a viable freezer life of 4 to 6 months to 1 to 2 years; fruits and vegetables go from 6 to 8 months to 2 years. Cheese in the refrigerator in a vacuum-sealed bag will last for 4 to 8 months.

Vaccum sealers are also good for sealing up dehydrated foods and anything else you want to keep dry — like important documents.

Vacuum sealers range in price from about $60 to $400 and require special plastic to use for bags. The less expensive models tend to burn out with heavy use, but it still might be more affordable in the long run to replace a less expensive one a few times than to buy an industrial-strength model (and the less expensive ones are smaller and easier to store). There are handheld units and ones that are supposed to work with ordinary supermarket plastic bags, but these have mixed reviews, and I have no experience with them.

You can buy both precut plastic bags and rolls of plastic that you can cut to any length. Some of the plastic is BPA-free, but some is not. Fruit, vegetables, and leftovers are easy to package in the precut bags, but meat and fish usually require bags cut to fit. You will probably have to order these bags and rolls of plastic online, so buy an assortment of sizes until you figure out what size works best for you.

Berries, peas, and other delicate foods should be tray-frozen first to avoid having them turned into mush by the force of the vacuum.

Knives

When it comes to knives, choose quality over quantity. That means a high-carbon stainless steel knife. The base of the blade (the tang) should extend all the way into the handle and be secured to the handle with rivets. Above all, the knife should feel sturdy and well balanced in your hand. Ceramic knives are great for slicing, but they are not heavy-duty enough for the rugged chores of a homestead kitchen (such as cutting through hard winter squash or small bones).

Although there are many, many types of specialty knives, you really only need four knives, plus a honing steel (see page 13).

> **Paring knife.** For peeling (paring) and making small cuts, such as taking the tops off root vegetables. The tip can be used for removing eyes from potatoes.

> **Slicing knife.** For carving roasts, slicing cheeses, slicing raw meat, cutting curds, cutting honeycomb, and so on.

> **Eight-inch chef's knife.** For chopping, dicing, slicing, mincing.

> **Bread knife.** The serrated edge is good for slicing not just bread but tomatoes, too.

Other Tools

> **Poultry shears.** Poultry shears and/or heavy-duty kitchen scissors are handy, particularly if you deal with poultry or rabbits a lot. In fact, if you are planning to butcher those animals, you will need shears. Shears or scissors will also be put to good use cleaning fresh-caught fish.

> **Cleavers and mallets.** A heavy-duty cleaver is necessary anytime you are cutting through bone. It is also very, very handy for cutting up hard-shelled winter squash. If you do invest in the cleaver, you will also find a soft mallet helpful for those times when you need more force than your swing allows. Sometimes your cleaver cuts into, but not all the way through, a bone or a winter squash. Tapping with the mallet will help send the blade through whatever the cleaver is stuck in.

> **Boning knife.** A boning knife does just that: removes

bones. Boning knives with flexible blades work best for poultry and fish.

When investing in good knives, consider where you will store them. Keeping knives in a drawer is a bad idea; their edges and tips will get scratched and become dull. A wooden block or wall rack is a better option.

Using Knives

Regardless of what the knife manufacturer claims, don't use the dishwasher for your good knives. The hot water, caustic detergent, and vibrating contact with other cutlery or dishes will dull fine edges, spot stainless steel, cause handle rivets to pop, and delaminate wood and most synthetic laminate handles.

A sharp knife cuts easily and is far safer to use than a dull one, which requires extra pressure. There is no such thing as a knife that never needs sharpening; with use, a knife blade will dull. Honing should be done before each use; sharpening should be done every few weeks (or more, depending on how much kitchen work you are doing).

It goes without saying that you should *always* cut on a cutting board. Don't economize on the size of your board(s). Bigger is always better.

Paring knife

Boning knife

Slicing knife

Poultry shears

Bread knife

Cleaver

Chef's knife

Rubber mallet

How to Sharpen a Knife

Many easy-to-use knife sharpeners grind away too much of the blade, so if you want to go the gadget route, check consumer reviews carefully. (Be aware that these reviews are sometimes filled with false statements generated by the manufacturers themselves.) I consider *Cook's Illustrated* to be a reliable source for product reviews. In 2011, it recommended the Chef's Choice AngleSelect 4623 manual knife sharpener, which retails for just under $30.

I rely on my son to do my knife sharpening. He points out, and rightly so, that if you can sharpen kitchen knives, you can also sharpen any tool that you need to have sharp, such as pruning shears. He sharpens knives and tools the old-fashioned way, with a whetstone. Whetstones can be made of diamond, quarried stone, or synthetic materials (the least expensive), and they may be cleaned or lubricated with either water or oil, but it is not necessary to use either. If you do use oil with your stone, use mineral oil, which is safe to consume.

① **Position the whetstone and knife.** Place the whetstone on a dampened cloth or paper towel on a flat work surface, coarse grit faceup. Hold the knife so that the cutting edge meets the stone, point-first, with the cutting edge meeting the stone at an approximate 20-degree angle. To envision this, hold the knife at a right angle to the stone, which is 90 degrees. Cut the angle in half to 45 degrees, then half again to about 22.5 degrees. Alternatively, stick a quarter-inch binder clip on the knife; this will keep the knife at the proper angle. Stabilize the blade with your other hand.

The dampened cloth keeps the stone from moving. The binder clip helps you keep the knife at a 20-degree angle.

② **Slide the knife across the stone.** Using moderate pressure, slide the blade forward and across the whetstone, covering the entire length of the blade and keeping the angle of the blade relative to the stone at a constant 20 degrees. Repeat about 10 times, then turn the knife over and give the other side of the blade 10 strokes on the whetstone.

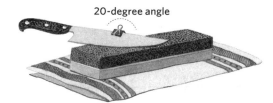

Work on the coarse side of the whetstone first, then on the fine side.

③ **Repeat on the other side of the whetstone.** Turn over the whetstone so that the fine-grit side is up. Repeat the 10 strokes at a constant 20-degree angle on each side.

④ **Finish with honing.** Finish by honing the blade on the honing steel. Rinse and wipe the blade dry to remove any metal particles.

How to Hone a Knife

If you hone your knives regularly, you won't need to sharpen them as often as you would otherwise. In fact, sharpening shortens the life span of the blade, so you want to keep your knives well honed to avoid sharpening. That said, don't work with a dull knife; it is unsafe and not fun. Hone a knife before each use to guarantee a sharp blade.

① **Steady the honing steel.** Holding the handle of your honing steel, point the steel straight down and rest its tip on a flat work surface. Hold the knife in your dominant hand, with the sharp edge of the blade touching the steel, and position the blade so that it rests at a 20-degree angle to the steel.

② **Draw the knife across the steel.** Starting with the heel of the knife (the part closest to the handle), draw the blade downward along the steel toward the counter, maintaining light pressure and pulling the handle back toward you so that the entire length of the blade, from the heel to the tip, comes in contact with the steel. As the edge of the blade makes contact with the steel, you should hear a light ringing sound. If you hear a grinding sound, either you are using too much pressure or your angle is wrong.

Get into the habit of honing your knife when you start cooking dinner each night.

③ **Alternate sides and repeat.** Repeat the same motion on the other side of the knife blade, using the opposite side of the steel. Repeat four or five times on each side. Wipe the knife with a dish towel afterward to remove any steel dust.

Sanitizing

Fear of food poisoning is at a historic high, or so it would seem when browsing topics related to food preservation on the Internet. I don't think the fear is realistic, but I do think a clean kitchen is a healthy kitchen — and some processes require extra care (handling raw meat and poultry, for example). Whenever I am doing any fermenting, cheesemaking, meat cutting,

or meat curing, I always wash my work surfaces, pots, and utensils with hot, soapy water. Then I sanitize my counters and equipment with a winemaker's "no rinse" sanitizing solution. I spray it everywhere and on everything that will be coming in contact with the food.

You can find sanitizing solution where winemaking and beer brewing supplies are sold. When used properly (follow the

manufacturer's directions), it will leave behind no taste, smell, or harmful effects and is approved for use in food preparation. Problem solved.

But do follow the manufacturer's directions for preparation, contact time to ensure sanitation (it varies between 30 seconds and 5 minutes), and shelf life. Most sanitizers need to be used on the same day they are mixed into solution with water. The sanitizing powder itself, however, keeps indefinitely. Alternatively, you can sanitize with a mild bleach solution of 1 teaspoon bleach to 1 quart water, dispensed via spray bottle. Obviously, the spray bottle you use should be dedicated to sanitation and used for nothing else in the kitchen.

The two-step soap and sanitizer process is vital, I'm told, because the soapy water brings dirt and bacteria out of microscopic crevices (think cutting boards) and breaks up oily films or residues that may protect bacteria (think plastic containers). The sanitizing solution kills any bacteria that may have been left behind. Skipping either step will allow bacteria to remain on the food preparation surface.

Planning a Garden around the Kitchen

Something to think about as you plan your garden is how you will preserve the excess vegetables you raise. If you don't have a freezer and don't like canned peas, there's no point in planting extra rows of peas. Likewise, if you don't care for pickles, there's no point in planting many cucumbers. Tomatoes are always welcome because they can be canned or frozen. Corn is acceptable as a canned vegetable (if you aren't afraid of pressure canning) and can be easily frozen.

You definitely want a say in choosing the varieties that will be planted in the garden. If you don't like to make stuffed vegetables, then don't plant round summer squash varieties. If most of your carrot crop will go into the root cellar, then select a variety that is meant to be stored — it will make a big difference after months of storage. Paste tomatoes cook down into sauce more quickly and yield more than beefsteak or cherry tomatoes. Fingerling potatoes are more work to peel and scrub than nice big russets. Sure, it's fun to experiment with oddly shaped or colored vegetables, but don't be led astray by the romance of seed catalogs.

If food self-sufficiency is important to you, give space to staple crops that keep well and yield well: white potatoes, sweet potatoes, winter squash, cabbage, and beans. Aromatic onions, garlic, shallots, and herbs may not be important sources of calories, but they are vital for making food taste good.

Over the years, I've had better luck keeping onions and garlic, but I prefer shallots for their small size and milder flavor, so I also grow them. I've experimented with a few different potato varieties and gotten swept up with the romance of fingerlings and rose and blue potatoes, but I am back to Kennebecs, a large all-purpose potato I can depend on in a short growing season. They bake and roast well and aren't fussy to wash and peel, as fingerlings are. I've fallen for Asian and Middle Eastern–type cukes because they are good picklers and they hold their quality on the vine. I think no winter squash beats a butternut for productivity, flexibility in the kitchen (peels easily and doesn't require an axe to cut in half), and storage. And, though area farmers grow wonderful heirloom tomatoes, I just can't lavish enough care on these long-season tomatoes, and so I am sticking to dependable, determinate varieties like Valley Girl and Bellstar.

CHAPTER 2

FRESH VEGETABLES
Harvesting, Handling, Cooking

Large or small, most homesteads grow a large proportion of their own vegetables for fresh eating and for preserving. And nothing beats straight-out-of-the-garden vegetables. In this chapter, you'll find a quick guide to harvesting and cooking common garden vegetables. For information on freezing, canning, drying, and pickling vegetables, see part 2. If you are in doubt about any cooking methods, see the appendix (page 334).

Harvesting

The first harvests from my first gardens were absolutely thrilling. Who knew that putting seeds in the ground would yield so easily and abundantly? I still feel that way about the first spears of asparagus that poke through the mulch each spring, the first raspberry I pop in my mouth, the first cherry tomato. But eventually, the thrill is replaced with a matter-of-fact determination to get the job done. Here are some tips to make harvest time easier.

➤ Harvest early in the morning before the sun has wilted and warmed the produce.

➤ Immediately use any bruised or less-than-perfect vegetables.

➤ Keep produce chilled on ice if you don't have refrigerator space. Replace the ice daily. (You can make ice packs in advance by partially filling plastic jugs with water and freezing.)

➤ In general, it is better to harvest regularly and keep produce chilled before preserving than to allow the veggies to overmature in the garden.

➤ Vegetables that are intended for the root cellar should be harvested as late in the fall as possible. Vegetables that can handle cold weather and are unlikely to bolt (such as kale and leeks) should be left in the garden as long as possible. Pay attention to the "days to harvest" on the seed packets, and don't plant too early if your intention is winter storage.

The wise gardener staggers plantings to avoid a glut of vegetables. If only the weather would cooperate.

Short-Term Storage

It would be great if you could harvest only as much as you needed each day, every day. Unfortunately, leaving vegetables in the garden past their prime can invite rotting, mold, disease, and bolting (going to seed). So sometimes you must harvest and store veggies until you're ready to eat or preserve them.

In general, store unwashed produce in perforated plastic bags in the vegetable crisper drawer of your refrigerator. (The A-to-Z guide that follows offers more specific advice for individual vegetables.) When the crisper drawer fills up, use the rest of the refrigerator. And when that fills up, you may want to consider adding a second refrigerator. Otherwise, be prepared to preserve small quantities throughout the summer.

When bagging up produce, make sure it is fully dry. Wet produce stored in plastic bags will rot quickly. Wrap greens in paper towels; the towels will wick away moisture and help keep the greens in better shape.

An A-to-Z Guide to Preparing Fresh Vegetables

From the garden to the kitchen to the dinner table, here are some basic guidelines for harvesting, storing, and cooking each vegetable. We all can get into a rut when it comes to preparing vegetables. For the first harvests, it's always a pleasure to enjoy the vegetables as fresh as can be, whether raw or just lightly steamed. But as the season progresses, it's time to pull out slightly more complex methods, like braising or roasting. Or consider dressing up the veggies with sauces, vinaigrettes, and drizzles; recipes for a variety of these vegetable accompaniments can be found at the end of this chapter.

The listings that follow give approximate times for most of the cooking methods for common garden vegetables, but times will vary depending on the vegetable's ripeness and size (or how finely you slice or chop it). Another important factor affecting time is how crowded the vegetables are in the pan, whether you are sautéing, steaming, boiling, frying, grilling, roasting, or stir-frying. In general, for best results, don't crowd the pan.

I've also included the best ways to preserve each vegetable in this guide. It would be wonderful if in the middle of the hot summer we could all focus only on enjoying our vegetables fresh, but the truth is that the harvest of fresh vegetables often exceeds our ability to consume them. So, even as we are preparing our vegetables fresh, some of them should be canned, pickled, dried, or frozen for long-term storage.

The "best" way to preserve any vegetable is the way that works best for you. It's all very well for me to say frozen green beans are better than canned green beans, but if you are planning to live without electricity, then freezing isn't the best way for you. I think the best way to preserve the quality of most vegetables is in a cooked dish that is then frozen, but that is based on knowing what my family likes to eat. I've also figured out how much to plant so that there isn't a surplus of vegetables I don't care to eat in their frozen, canned, or pickled state (which means only one or two zucchini plants in my garden).

For the specifics of times and temperatures, see the discussions of the particular preserving techniques in part 2.

Artichokes

> **Harvest:** Cut off plump, firm, evenly green buds with 4 inches of stem.
> **Post-harvest handling:** Store in a perforated plastic bag in the fridge for up to 7 days.
> **Prep:** For steaming, slice off the top quarter of the artichoke. Use kitchen shears to remove the sharp tips from the remaining leaves. Trim the bottoms of the stems level so that the artichokes sit upright. For braising, remove any tough outer leaves, slice in half, and trim away the choke (the inedible fuzzy center just above the tender heart).
> **Blanch:** 7 minutes (hearts)
> **Boil:** 20 to 40 minutes
> **Steam:** 20 to 40 minutes
> **Sauté or stir-fry:** Not recommended
> **Roast:** Steam, then roast for 20 minutes at 425°F (220°C).
> **Grill:** Steam, then grill for 10 minutes.
> **Braise:** Brown first, then braise for about 20 minutes.
> **Preserve:** For artichoke hearts only, blanch and then freeze. Or the hearts can be blanched, packed in olive oil, and stored in the refrigerator.
> **Comments:** Timing for blanching and cooking depends on size.

Asparagus

> **Harvest:** After the third year, when spears are at least as thick as a pencil, snap off when 6 to 8 inches tall, with tight tips.
> **Post-harvest handling:** Refrigerate upright in a little water for 4 to 6 days. The tips must stay dry.
> **Prep:** Cut off the tough ends. Leave whole or cut into 2-inch lengths.
> **Blanch:** 2 to 4 minutes
> **Boil:** 3 to 5 minutes
> **Steam:** 5 to 7 minutes
> **Sauté or stir-fry:** 3 to 5 minutes

> **Roast:** 15 minutes at 450°F (230°C)
> **Grill:** 8 minutes
> **Braise:** 8 to 12 minutes
> **Preserve:** Blanch and then freeze. Or spears can be pickled or pressure-canned.
> **Comments:** Select fat spears for roasting and grilling.

Beans, shell

> **Harvest:** Pick well-filled, crisp pods.
> **Post-harvest handling:** Store in their pods in a perforated plastic bag in the fridge for a few days. Will keep for only 1 day after shelling.
> **Prep:** With the exception of edamame (soybeans), shell before cooking.
> **Blanch:** 5 minutes
> **Boil:** 5 to 25 minutes
> **Steam:** 5 to 35 minutes
> **Sauté or stir-fry:** Not recommended
> **Roast:** Not recommended
> **Grill:** Not recommended
> **Braise:** 5 to 30 minutes
> **Preserve:** Blanch and then freeze. You can also pressure-can.
> **Comments:** Timing for cooking depends on variety. Boil edamame in their pods in heavily salted water. Fava beans should be skinned after boiling.

There's no such thing as too many fresh vegetables when you roast them. A single layer of veggies (about 2 pounds) spread out on a half-sheet pan (measuring 13 by 18 inches) will barely be enough for a family of four.

Beans, snap (flat, pole, wax)

> **Harvest:** Pick about 2 to 3 weeks after bloom, when the pods are narrow, thin, and tender.
> **Post-harvest handling:** Store dry (unwashed) in a perforated plastic bag in the fridge for up to 6 days.
> **Prep:** Snap off stem ends.
> **Blanch:** 3 minutes
> **Boil:** 3 to 4 minutes
> **Steam:** 3 to 5 minutes
> **Sauté or stir-fry:** 4 to 7 minutes
> **Roast:** 15 minutes at 450°F (230°C)
> **Grill:** 8 to 10 minutes
> **Braise:** 20 minutes
> **Preserve:** Blanch and then freeze. Or dry, pickle, or pressure-can.
> **Comments:** Roasting, grilling, and braising do wonders for larger beans, fully mature beans, and flat beans. Steaming is recommended for tender, thin, filet-type beans.

Beets

> **Harvest:** Harvest beet greens at any point by cutting 1 inch above the soil or pulling the whole plant. Roots can be harvested when they reach 1 inch in diameter, but they remain tender until they measure 3 or 4 inches.
> **Post-harvest handling:** Trim the greens from the roots, leaving about 2 inches of stems. Store the greens and roots separately, in plastic bags. The greens will keep for just a few days in the fridge. Store beet roots in a root cellar, or store them in a perforated plastic bag in the refrigerator for up to 2 weeks.
> **Prep:** Wash well. Peel roots before or after cooking.
> **Blanch:** As prep for freezing, 2 to 3 minutes for greens (not roots)
> **Boil:** 20 to 25 minutes for 2- to 3-inch roots
> **Steam:** 2 to 3 minutes for greens; 10 minutes for shredded roots

> **Sauté or stir-fry:** 4 to 8 minutes for greens; 15 minutes for shredded roots
> **Roast:** 50 to 60 minutes at 350°F (180°C) for foil-wrapped roots
> **Grill:** 15 to 20 minutes for roots sliced ¼ inch thick
> **Braise:** 20 minutes for shredded roots
> **Preserve:** Cold storage. You can also pickle or pressure-can.
> **Comments:** Harvest beets for storage as late as possible, but before the ground freezes. Beets are sometimes served raw and very thinly shredded; the beets are pretty that way but not very flavorful. Golden and candy-stripe beets have a mellower flavor than red ones.

Broccoli

> **Harvest:** Cut heads from the plant, giving the heads about 4 inches of stem, when the heads are fully formed but the buds are tightly closed. Harvest side shoots daily, to prevent bolting, while the buds are still tight.
> **Post-harvest handling:** Refrigerate in a closed plastic bag for 3 to 5 days.
> **Prep:** Place broccoli in a saltwater bath (¼ cup salt per gallon of water) for 30 minutes to remove resident cabbage worms, as needed. Remove any woody or fibrous parts of the stem. Peel the stem as needed to remove tough flesh.
> **Blanch:** 3 to 6 minutes
> **Boil:** 4 to 6 minutes
> **Steam:** 4 to 7 minutes
> **Sauté or stir-fry:** 4 to 5 minutes
> **Roast:** 20 to 25 minutes at 425°F (220°C) for two-bite-size pieces
> **Grill:** Not recommended
> **Braise:** 10 to 15 minutes
> **Preserve:** Blanch and then freeze.
> **Comments:** Briefly blanched and chilled broccoli is better than raw broccoli for serving with a dip.

Brussels sprouts

> **Harvest:** Pick when sprouts are firm and at least 1 inch in diameter; they can be left in the garden until a hard freeze. Working from the bottom of the plant up, break off any leaves 5 to 6 inches above the area harvested to direct growth to the buds. Entire plants can be harvested for storage in a root cellar.
> **Post-harvest handling:** Store in a perforated plastic bag in the refrigerator for at least 5 days.
> **Prep:** Trim away discolored leaves. Cut into halves or quarters for even cooking. Cutting an X in the base does not, contrary to popular opinion, affect the cooking time.
> **Blanch:** 6 to 8 minutes
> **Boil:** Not recommended
> **Steam:** 8 to 12 minutes
> **Sauté or stir-fry:** 3 to 6 minutes
> **Roast:** 15 minutes at 425°F (220°C) for halves
> **Grill:** 15 minutes for halves
> **Braise:** About 20 minutes
> **Preserve:** Cold storage (for about 4 weeks). Or blanch and then freeze.
> **Comments:** Roasting is probably the best way to prepare, without much risk of overcooking.

Cabbage (green, red, Savoy, Napa, Chinese)

> **Harvest:** Cut from the plant when heads are compact and firm.
> **Post-harvest handling:** Cut the head off the stem and discard the outer leaves. Store in a root cellar, or store in a plastic bag in the refrigerator for 2 to 4 weeks.
> **Prep:** Cut away any discolored leaves. Remove the core, usually by cutting the head into quarters first.
> **Blanch:** 1½ minutes shredded or sliced
> **Boil:** Not recommended
> **Steam:** 4 to 5 minutes shredded or sliced
> **Sauté or stir-fry:** 4 to 5 minutes shredded or sliced
> **Roast:** Not recommended
> **Grill:** Not recommended
> **Braise:** 15 minutes shredded or sliced
> **Preserve:** Cold storage. Can also pickle.
> **Comments:** There's no more versatile vegetable than cabbage. Finely shredded, it can be dressed in hundreds of different ways to make delicious winter salads. Sautéed or braised slowly, it makes a fine side dish that pairs well with sweet-and-sour or mustardy flavors. Stir-fried, it can form the backbone of a Chinese dish. Instead of blanching individual leaves for stuffing, a shortcut is to remove the core from the whole head, then freeze. Thaw and remove the leaves when you're ready to stuff them.

Carrots

> **Harvest:** Pick whenever big enough to be enjoyed. Harvest larger ones first (they tend to have darker tops). Can withstand a few light frosts in the ground.
> **Post-harvest handling:** Cut off the tops. Store in a root cellar or keep in a perforated plastic bag in the refrigerator for up to 4 weeks.
> **Prep:** Most people prefer to scrape off the thin skin with a vegetable peeler.
> **Blanch:** 2 to 5 minutes sliced, diced, or julienned
> **Boil:** 5 to 7 minutes for whole baby, sliced, diced, or julienned
> **Steam:** 5 to 7 minutes for whole baby, sliced, diced, or julienned
> **Sauté or stir-fry:** 5 to 8 minutes for whole baby, sliced, diced, or julienned
> **Roast:** 20 to 30 minutes at 425°F (220°C) for whole baby, sliced, diced, or julienned
> **Grill:** About 10 minutes for whole baby, sliced, diced, or julienned
> **Braise:** 15 to 20 minutes for whole baby, sliced, diced, or julienned

- **Preserve:** Cold storage. Can also be dried, blanched and frozen, or pickled.
- **Comments:** Carrots are one of the tastiest vegetables to eat raw, especially when freshly harvested. Varieties really matter; enjoy early varieties fresh, and store later-ripening varieties in the root cellar.

Cauliflower

- **Harvest:** Begin harvest when heads are 6 inches in diameter by cutting the heads off their stems. Look for firm, compact white heads, before the heads begin to separate into curds and before brown spots appear, indicating rot.
- **Post-harvest handling:** Remove outer leaves. Store in the refrigerator loosely wrapped in plastic for a few days.
- **Prep:** Cut florets off the core. Discard the leaves.
- **Blanch:** 3 to 6 minutes
- **Boil:** 4 to 6 minutes
- **Steam:** 4 to 6 minutes
- **Sauté or stir-fry:** 5 to 6 minutes
- **Roast:** 20 minutes at 450°F (230°C)
- **Grill:** Not recommended
- **Braise:** 15 to 20 minutes
- **Preserve:** Cold storage (for about 4 weeks). Can also be pickled or blanched and frozen.
- **Comments:** May be eaten raw. Colored cauliflowers retain best color when steamed.

Celery

- **Harvest:** Cut off outer stalks when long enough to enjoy. Harvest the whole stalk before the first frost.
- **Post-harvest handling:** Store in a plastic bag in the refrigerator for up to 2 weeks.
- **Prep:** Trim off root end and leaves.
- **Blanch:** 3 minutes
- **Boil:** 3 to 5 minutes
- **Steam:** 3 to 5 minutes

- **Sauté or stir-fry:** 3 to 5 minutes sliced or julienned
- **Roast:** Not recommended
- **Grill:** Not recommended
- **Braise:** 25 minutes
- **Preserve:** Blanch and then freeze. Can also be dried.
- **Comments:** The tops and wilted stalks can be stored (without being blanched) in freezer bags and added, still frozen, to the pot when you're making stock. Wilted stalks sometimes can be revived in ice water.

Celery root

- **Harvest:** For eating fresh, harvest when the roots are about 4 inches in diameter. For storage, harvest before the first frost. Trim off the tops before storing.
- **Post-harvest handling:** Store in a root cellar, or keep in a perforated plastic bag in the refrigerator for up to 2 weeks.
- **Prep:** Peel off thick skin. Slice, dice, or julienne. Drop into acidulated water (1 tablespoon lemon juice or vinegar to 2 cups water) to prevent browning.
- **Blanch:** Not recommended
- **Boil:** Not recommended
- **Steam:** 15 to 20 minutes shredded
- **Sauté or stir-fry:** 15 to 20 minutes shredded
- **Roast:** 20 to 25 minutes at 425°F (220°C)
- **Grill:** Not recommended
- **Braise:** 25 minutes
- **Preserve:** Cold storage. Can be frozen in cooked dishes.
- **Comments:** May be grated and eaten raw. Cooked, it pairs especially well with chicken.

Collard greens

- **Harvest:** Cut when the leaves are large enough to enjoy; harvest the outer leaves first. Don't cut the central bud until you are done with the harvest. Will withstand frost.

> **Post-harvest handling:** Store in a plastic bag in the refrigerator for up to 1 week.
> **Prep:** Wash well. Discard tough stems for quick cooking.
> **Blanch:** 3 minutes
> **Boil:** 2 to 3 hours for classic Southern-style greens
> **Steam:** 10 minutes for leaves cut into ribbons (without stems)
> **Sauté or stir-fry:** 10 minutes for leaves cut into ribbons (without stems)
> **Roast:** 15 minutes at 450°F (230°C) for leaves cut into ribbons (without stems)
> **Grill:** Not recommended
> **Braise:** 10 to 20 minutes for leaves cut into ribbons (without stems)
> **Preserve:** Keep in the garden for as long as possible. Can be blanched or sautéed and then frozen. Can also be dried or pressure-canned.
> **Comments:** With the tough stems removed, collards can be cooked like kale.

Corn

> **Harvest:** Corn is ready when the ear is filled at the tip, the kernels are milky when cut with a thumbnail, and the silks are browning. Pull the ear away from the stalk with a slight twist.
> **Post-harvest handling:** Keep chilled. Do not husk until you're ready to cook.
> **Prep:** Discard the husks and silks unless you're roasting the corn in its husk.
> **Blanch:** 3 minutes
> **Boil:** 3 to 5 minutes on or off the cob
> **Steam:** 4 to 5 minutes on or off the cob
> **Sauté or stir-fry:** 3 to 5 minutes for kernels
> **Roast:** 20 to 30 minutes at 500°F (260°C) for ears in the husk, 15 minutes for husked ears, or 10 to 15 minutes for kernels
> **Grill:** 20 minutes for ears in the husk; 15 to 20 minutes for husked ears

> **Braise:** About 10 minutes for kernels
> **Preserve:** Blanch kernels or cobs, then freeze. Kernels can also be dried, made into a pickled relish, or pressure-canned.
> **Comments:** Newer super-sweet varieties will keep for longer in the refrigerator than older varieties.

Cucumbers

> **Harvest:** For pickling, the smaller the better; for slicing, pick at about 6 inches unless it is a long variety. Harvest frequently to encourage continuous fruiting.
> **Post-harvest handling:** Keep cool. Store bone-dry in a plastic bag in the refrigerator for 1 to 2 weeks.
> **Prep:** Peeling is not necessary. If a cucumber is overripe, it may have a prodigious amount of seeds; cut in half vertically and scrape out the seeds with the tip of a spoon.
> **Blanch:** Not recommended
> **Boil:** Not recommended
> **Steam:** Not recommended
> **Sauté or stir-fry:** Not recommended
> **Roast:** Not recommended
> **Grill:** Not recommended
> **Braise:** Not recommended
> **Preserve:** Can be kept in a cool root cellar for 2 to 3 weeks. Or pickle them.
> **Comments:** Not recommended for cooking. Middle Eastern and Japanese types are as good for pickling as the classic pickling types, keep better in the fridge, and do not overripen as quickly on the vine.

Eggplant

> **Harvest:** Cut from the stem when the fruit is at least one-third the expected size. The skin on mature fruit is glossy; it becomes dull when overripe. Harvest frequently to encourage continued fruiting.

> **Post-harvest handling:** Do not refrigerate. The flesh browns at temperatures below 50°F (10°C). Instead, keep at room temperature for up 1 to 3 weeks, depending on variety (Asian types store better) and degree of ripeness when harvested.

> **Prep:** Leave whole for roasting, or slice or dice. Peeling is usually not necessary.

> **Blanch:** Not recommended

> **Boil:** Not recommended

> **Steam:** Not recommended

> **Sauté or stir-fry:** 8 to 10 minutes cubed or sliced

> **Roast:** 20 to 25 minutes at 400°F (200°C) for slices and cubes, or 30 to 40 minutes for whole eggplant

> **Grill:** 10 to 15 minutes for slices, or 30 to 45 minutes for whole eggplant (cover grill to intensify smoke flavor)

> **Braise:** About 20 minutes for slices and cubes

> **Preserve:** Freeze in a cooked dish. You can also dry eggplants or pickle them in vinegar, pack them in olive oil, and refrigerate.

> **Comments:** Eggplant is great when pan-fried: coat slices with seasoned flour, then an egg wash, then seasoned crumbs, and pan-fry for 10 to 14 minutes, until well browned.

Fennel

> **Harvest:** Cut at base when bulbs are full size.

> **Post-harvest handling:** Separate bulbs from fronds and store separately in perforated bags in the refrigerator. The bulbs will keep for up to 2 weeks, and the fronds for 1 to 2 weeks.

> **Prep:** Slice off the root end and stems and discard. Remove all tough or blemished layers. Cut the bulbs in half and remove the core.

> **Blanch:** Not recommended

> **Boil:** Not recommended

> **Steam:** Not recommended

> **Sauté or stir-fry:** 4 minutes for slices

> **Roast:** 15 minutes at 425°F (220°C) for slices

> **Grill:** 10 to 12 minutes for slices

> **Braise:** 20 minutes for slices

> **Preserve:** Blanch and then freeze. Can also be pickled or dried.

> **Comments:** Fennel is also delicious raw. Use the fronds for garnish.

Garlic

> **Harvest:** Pull up by hand or dig up with a garden fork when the leaves begin to die back. Wash immediately for snowy white peels. Trim away the roots and long stems.

> **Post-harvest handling:** Allow the bulbs to cure for about 2 weeks, then store in a cool, dry area, where they will keep for months.

> **Prep:** Separate the heads into individual cloves and peel. Smashing a clove with the side of a chef's knife is the easiest way to separate the skin from the clove.

> **Blanch:** Cover the cloves with fresh water and bring to a boil. Drain. Repeat 2 more times.

> **Boil:** Not recommended

> **Steam:** Not recommended

> **Sauté or stir-fry:** 30 seconds for minced

> **Roast:** 20 minutes at 350°F (180°C) for whole bulb wrapped in foil

> **Grill:** 20 to 30 minutes for whole bulb wrapped in foil, over indirect heat

> **Braise:** 20 minutes

> **Preserve:** Cold, dry storage. Can also be pickled or dried. After drying, garlic can be ground into garlic powder.

> **Comments:** Burnt garlic has a bitter flavor, so be careful when sautéing to keep the heat moderate or the time brief. Garlic scapes (the

green stems with flowers of hard-neck varieties) can be harvested and used like scallions. Save your largest bulbs for planting.

Jerusalem artichokes

> **Harvest:** Dig up late in the fall after the tops die or early in spring before the tops grow.
> **Post-harvest handling:** Store washed and bone-dry in a perforated plastic bag in the refrigerator, where the tubers will keep for up to 4 weeks.
> **Prep:** Peel. Drop into acidulated water (1 tablespoon lemon juice or vinegar to 2 cups water) to prevent browning.
> **Blanch:** Not recommended
> **Boil:** Not recommended
> **Steam:** Not recommended
> **Sauté or stir-fry:** 5 to 8 minutes for slices
> **Roast:** 15 minutes at 500°F (260°C) for slices
> **Grill:** Not recommended
> **Braise:** About 15 minutes
> **Preserve:** Cold storage. Can also be pickled.
> **Comments:** Once established, a bed of Jerusalem artichokes will always produce more than you can possibly consume.

Kale

> **Harvest:** Cut individual leaves from the bottom of the plant up to encourage the plant to continue forming new leaves. The plants can withstand frost and will remain in good condition until the temperature falls below 10°F (−12°C), so harvest as needed.
> **Post-harvest handling:** Store in a closed plastic bag in the refrigerator for up to 1 week.
> **Prep:** Strip leaves off tough stems for quick cooking.
> **Blanch:** 2 minutes
> **Boil:** 2 hours for classic Southern-style greens
> **Steam:** 8 to 10 minutes for leaves cut into ribbons (stems removed)

> **Sauté or stir-fry:** 6 to 10 minutes for leaves cut into ribbons (stems removed)
> **Roast:** 10 to 15 minutes at 450°F (230°C) for leaves cut into ribbons (stems removed)
> **Grill:** About 2 minutes per side; discard stems after grilling
> **Braise:** About 10 minutes for leaves cut into ribbons (stems removed)
> **Preserve:** Leave in the garden for as long as possible. Can be pickled, dried, or blanched and then frozen.
> **Comments:** Can be eaten raw in salads if massaged with dressing to break down the cell walls.

Kohlrabi

> **Harvest:** Cut the bulb from the root when the bulb is 2 to 3 inches in diameter.
> **Post-harvest handling:** Remove stems. Store in a plastic bag in the refrigerator for up to 2 weeks.
> **Prep:** Peel
> **Blanch:** Not recommended
> **Boil:** 10 to 15 minutes cubed
> **Steam:** 10 to 15 minutes cubed
> **Sauté or stir-fry:** 5 to 10 minutes sliced, cubed, or julienned
> **Roast:** 25 minutes at 450°F (230°C) cubed
> **Grill:** Not recommended
> **Braise:** 30 minutes
> **Preserve:** Cold storage. Can also be blanched and then frozen.
> **Comments:** Kohlrabi can be eaten raw. It tastes like a mild turnip.

Leeks

> **Harvest:** Pull as needed. When small, leeks can be chopped and used like scallions. The plants are hardy to 20°F (−7°C); they can be overwintered under a foot or more of mulch.
> **Post-harvest handling:** Will keep for a month or two in a root cellar or in a plastic bag in the fridge.
> **Prep:** Trim off the roots, slice the stalks in half vertically, and wash well. Fan out the leaves under running water to be sure all the dirt is washed out. Use only the whites and tender pale green parts.
> **Blanch:** Not recommended
> **Boil:** About 10 minutes to poach (sliced and gently simmered)
> **Steam:** About 10 minutes for slices
> **Sauté or stir-fry:** 5 minutes for slices
> **Roast:** 15 to 20 minutes at 425°F (220°C)
> **Grill:** 10 to 15 minutes for whole leeks
> **Braise:** 35 minutes for slices
> **Preserve:** Keep in the garden under mulch. Can also be dried, tray-frozen, or frozen in cooked dishes.
> **Comments:** If you need sliced leeks, you can wash them after slicing, which is easier than washing them while they're still whole. Just slice them up, then put the slices in a bowl of water, swish them around, and lift out of the water, leaving the dirt behind. The darker green parts you trim off can be saved for making stock; wash them, throw them into a bag, and store in the freezer until you're ready to use them.

Lettuce

> **Harvest:** Harvest leaf types when the leaves are large enough to enjoy, taking the leaves from the outside of the head. Harvest head types when heads are firm.
> **Post-harvest handling:** Wash well, lifting the leaves out of the soaking water. Dry well, then refrigerate in a closed plastic bag lined with paper towels. Lettuce will keep for about 1 week.
> **Prep:** Tear into bite-size pieces.
> **Blanch:** Not recommended
> **Boil:** Not recommended
> **Steam:** Not recommended
> **Sauté or stir-fry:** Not recommended
> **Roast:** Not recommended
> **Grill:** Not recommended
> **Braise:** Not recommended
> **Preserve:** Not recommended
> **Comments:** Lettuce is not recommended for cooking.

Washing Greens

This is the method to use for all leafy greens, including arugula, Asian greens (mizuna, chrysanthemum greens, Chinese broccoli, bok choy), chard, kale, lettuce, mustard greens, spinach, and turnip greens.

1. Fill a large bowl or basin with cold water.

2. Submerge the greens in the water.

3. Lift the greens out of the water and place in a colander to drain.

4. Drain the dirty water from the bowl or basin and refill with fresh cold water.

5. Repeat until the water is clean when you lift out the greens.

Okra

> **Harvest:** Cut from the stem when pods are 2 to 3 inches long.
> **Post-harvest handling:** Refrigerate bone-dry in a plastic bag in the refrigerator for up to 5 days.
> **Prep:** Leave whole or slice.
> **Blanch:** 3 to 4 minutes
> **Boil:** Not recommended
> **Steam:** Not recommended
> **Sauté or stir-fry:** 5 to 10 minutes
> **Roast:** 15 minutes at 425°F (220°C)
> **Grill:** 8 to 10 minutes
> **Braise:** 25 minutes
> **Preserve:** Blanch and then freeze. You can also dry, pickle, or pressure-can.
> **Comments:** You can also coat okra with batter or bread crumbs and deep-fry for 3 minutes in oil heated to 365°F (185°C).

Onions and shallots

> **Harvest:** Pull when the leaves have mostly all died back and the necks appear tight. When half the tops have fallen over, bend over the remaining tops by hand to speed things up. Harvest on a sunny day, if possible, to reduce the risk of mold.
> **Post-harvest handling:** Gently brush off any dirt and cure in a dry, airy place for 2 weeks. Use onions with soft necks first; they will not keep long.
> **Prep:** Peel. To peel boiling onions (also called pearl onions), place in a bowl and cover with boiling water; when the water is cool, the onions will slip out of their skins.
> **Blanch:** 1 minute
> **Boil:** 15 minutes for small boiling onions
> **Steam:** Not recommended
> **Sauté or stir-fry:** 3 to 5 minutes for slices over medium-high heat until tender; 10 to 20 minutes for slices over low heat until caramelized
> **Roast:** 20 to 30 minutes at 400°F (200°C)

> **Grill:** 10 to 15 minutes for thick slices
> **Braise:** 15 to 25 minutes for small whole onions
> **Preserve:** Cold, dry storage. Pearl onions and shallots can be pickled whole. You can also tray-freeze or dry chopped onions and shallots. After drying, onions can be ground to make onion powder.
> **Comments:** Shallots are mellower in flavor than onions. Sweet onion varieties contain more moisture and don't sauté or roast as well as other types. They also don't keep as well.

Parsnips

> **Harvest:** Dig up in the fall after at least one frost or in the spring as soon as the ground thaws.
> **Post-harvest handling:** Remove the tops. Store in a root cellar, or keep in a perforated plastic bag in the refrigerator for up to 2 weeks.
> **Prep:** Peel with a vegetable peeler. Cut into cubes or julienne.
> **Blanch:** 2 minutes
> **Boil:** 10 minutes
> **Steam:** 10 to 15 minutes
> **Sauté or stir-fry:** About 10 minutes shredded
> **Roast:** 20 minutes at 425°F (220°C)
> **Grill:** Not recommended
> **Braise:** 20 to 30 minutes
> **Preserve:** Cold storage, or leave in the garden under mulch
> **Comments:** Parsnips can be used interchangeably with other root vegetables, but they are noticeably sweeter, particularly in soups.

Peas
(green, snow, sugar snap)

> **Harvest:** Pick green peas and sugar snap peas when pods are plump but not bulging. Pick snow peas when pods are at their mature length. Harvest late in the afternoon for maximum sweetness.

> **Post-harvest handling:** Store in a perforated plastic bag in the refrigerator. Unshelled green peas will keep for 1 to 2 days, and snow peas and sugar snap peas for 5 to 7 days.

> **Prep:** Press green peas on the pod seam to pop open the pod, then strip out the peas with your thumb. For snow peas and sugar snap peas, strip the strings and blossom ends from the edible pods.

> **Blanch:** 2 to 4 minutes

> **Boil:** 2 to 4 minutes

> **Steam:** 2 to 4 minutes

> **Sauté or stir-fry:** 2 to 3 minutes

> **Roast:** Not recommended

> **Grill:** Not recommended

> **Braise:** 5 minutes

> **Preserve:** Blanch and freeze green peas and snap peas. Tray-frozen green peas will keep for 1 to 2 months. They can also be dried or pressure-canned.

> **Comments:** Snow peas and sugar snap peas are both delicious raw.

Peppers, hot (chile)
and sweet (bell)

> **Harvest:** Cut from the plant, leaving 1 inch of stem, when fruits are the desired size and color. Frequent harvesting encourages continued fruiting.

> **Post-harvest handling:** Store in a brown paper bag in the refrigerator for 1 to 2 weeks.

> **Prep:** Leave whole for roasting; otherwise slice or dice. For sweet peppers, discard seeds and veins.

> **Blanch:** 2 minutes for slices or dice

> **Boil:** Not recommended

> **Steam:** Not recommended

> **Sauté or stir-fry:** 3 to 5 minutes for slices or dice

> **Roast:** 10 to 20 minutes for whole peppers

> **Grill:** 10 to 20 minutes for whole peppers

> **Braise:** 10 to 15 minutes for slices or dice

> **Preserve:** Chiles are best dried. Both sweet and hot peppers can be roasted, peeled, and then packed in oil and refrigerated. Can also be pickled or tray-frozen.

> **Comments:** In chiles, the seeds and veins contain the heat. Leave or remove as desired. To peel, first roast the peppers, and then let them steam in a covered container or bag for 10 minutes to loosen the skins. Peel over a bowl to catch any liquids. Do not rinse; doing so will rinse away flavor.

Potatoes, sweet

> **Harvest:** Dig up when large enough to enjoy, before the first frost.

> **Post-harvest handling:** Cure for 10 days under moist conditions (such as under a tarp) at 80°F to 85°F (27°C to 29°C).

> **Prep:** Peeling is optional.

> **Blanch:** 8 to 10 minutes for cubes

> **Boil:** 10 to 15 minutes for cubes

> **Steam:** 10 to 15 minutes for cubes

> **Sauté or stir-fry:** About 10 minutes; blanch first

> **Roast:** 15 minutes at 500°F (260°C) for cubes

> **Grill:** 10 to 15 minutes for slices

> **Braise:** 35 minutes for slices or cubes

> **Preserve:** Moderately warm (50°F–60°F/ 10°–16°C), dry storage. Can also be cooked and then frozen or pressure-canned.

> **Comments:** You can also bake sweet potatoes whole for 45 to 60 minutes at 350°F (180°C).

Potatoes, white
(or red, blue, or yellow)

> **Harvest:** Dig up as soon as the tubers are large enough to enjoy. If you plan to store potatoes, wait until the plants die back and allow potatoes to cure in the ground for another week or two to harden the skins.
> **Post-harvest handling:** Brush off dirt. Cure in darkness at 50°F to 60°F (10°C to 16°C) for 14 days. Store in baskets, burlap bags, or paper bags in the dark, with good air circulation.
> **Prep:** Scrub, and remove sprouts or bad spots. Peeling is optional.
> **Blanch:** About 10 minutes
> **Boil:** 15 to 25 minutes
> **Steam:** 15 to 25 minutes for small, new potatoes
> **Sauté or stir-fry:** Blanch first, then pan-fry until browned, 10 to 20 minutes.
> **Roast:** 25 to 30 minutes at 425°F (220°C)
> **Grill:** 15 to 25 minutes for slices; 60 to 90 minutes for foil-wrapped whole potatoes
> **Braise:** About 30 minutes
> **Preserve:** Cold, dry storage. Can also be dried, frozen in cooked dishes, or pressure-canned.
> **Comments:** Russet types make the best oven fries (see page 279), baked potatoes, and mashed potatoes. Waxy types are best for potato salads. Bake whole potatoes for 60 to 90 minutes at 350°F (180°C).

Pumpkins

> **Harvest:** Pie pumpkins, not the jack-o'-lantern type. Pick when the shells harden.
> **Post-harvest handling:** Keep cool and dry. Dry storage at 50°F (10°C), as in an unheated attic or closet, is ideal.
> **Prep:** Slice off the top of the pumpkin (the stem end) or cut in half vertically. Scrape out the seeds and fibers.
> **Blanch:** Not recommended

> **Boil:** Not recommended
> **Steam:** 20 to 50 minutes for halves and pieces
> **Sauté or stir-fry:** 10 to 15 minutes for shredded flesh
> **Roast:** 45 to 60 minutes at 425°F (220°C) for halves or quarters
> **Grill:** Not recommended
> **Braise:** 30 to 45 minutes for cubes
> **Preserve:** Cold, dry storage. Cooked flesh can be puréed and then frozen or pressure-canned.
> **Comments:** After roasting, scrape out the flesh and purée for pies and other baked goods.

Radishes
(red, white, and black)

> **Harvest:** Begin harvesting when the roots are almost full size. Mature radishes become bitter and bolt rapidly.
> **Post-harvest handling:** Wash and dry. Cut off stems and leaves (which may be stir-fried). Store in a plastic bag in the refrigerator for 2 to 3 weeks.
> **Prep:** Cut off the tops and roots. Slice or leave red radishes whole; peel radishes as needed.
> **Blanch:** Not recommended
> **Boil:** 10 to 15 minutes for cubed black (German) radishes
> **Steam:** 10 to 15 minutes for cubed black (German) radishes
> **Sauté or stir-fry:** 5 to 10 minutes for diced black (German) radishes and daikon
> **Roast:** 25 minutes at 450°F (230°C) for cubed black (German) radishes and daikon
> **Grill:** Not recommended
> **Braise:** 30 minutes for cubed black radishes and daikon
> **Preserve:** Cold storage for black radishes and daikon; not recommended for red radishes.
> **Comments:** Red radishes are best raw; large black (German) radishes are similar to turnips but Spanish black radishes are mild.

Rutabagas

> **Harvest:** Dig up when roots reach the desired size.
> **Post-harvest handling:** Store in a root cellar, or keep in a perforated plastic bag in the refrigerator for up to 4 weeks.
> **Prep:** Trim off the tops and roots; peel.
> **Blanch:** Not recommended
> **Boil:** 30 minutes cubed
> **Steam:** 30 minutes cubed
> **Sauté or stir-fry:** 10 minutes shredded
> **Roast:** 25 minutes at 450°F (230°C) cubed
> **Grill:** Not recommended
> **Braise:** 30 minutes cubed
> **Preserve:** Cold storage. Can also be frozen in cooked dishes.
> **Comments:** The leaves are tasty; prepare them as you would mustard greens or turnip greens.

Salsify and scorzonera

> **Harvest:** Dig up when roots reach the desired size; you can harvest before a hard freeze or overwinter them in the ground.
> **Post-harvest handling:** Store in a root cellar, or keep in a perforated plastic bag in the refrigerator for up to 4 weeks.
> **Prep:** Trim off the tops and roots; peel. Keep in acidulated water (1 tablespoon lemon juice or vinegar to 2 cups water) if not cooking immediately.
> **Blanch:** Not recommended
> **Boil:** 30 minutes cubed
> **Steam:** 30 minutes cubed
> **Sauté or stir-fry:** 10 minutes shredded
> **Roast:** 25 minutes at 450°F (230°C) cubed
> **Grill:** Not recommended
> **Braise:** 30 minutes cubed
> **Preserve:** Cold storage, or leave in the garden under mulch. Can also be frozen in cooked dishes.
> **Comments:** Nutty and delicious but difficult to grow.

Spinach

> **Harvest:** When leaves are large enough to enjoy, cut individual outer stems or the whole plant about 1 inch above the soil. When the plant sends up a tall central stem, it is about to bolt. Spinach generally can withstand a light frost.
> **Post-harvest handling:** Wash well, lifting the leaves out of the soaking water. Dry well, then refrigerate in a closed plastic bag lined with paper towels.
> **Prep:** Pinch off any tough stems.
> **Blanch:** As prep for freezing, 30 to 60 seconds
> **Boil:** 30 to 60 seconds
> **Steam:** 3 to 5 minutes
> **Sauté or stir-fry:** 4 to 6 minutes
> **Roast:** Not recommended
> **Grill:** Not recommended
> **Braise:** 5 minutes
> **Preserve:** Blanch and then freeze. Can also be pressure-canned.
> **Comments:** After blanching, boiling, or steaming, squeeze or press the leaves to remove excess moisture.

Squash, summer (crookneck, pattypan, yellow squash, zucchini, etc.)

> **Harvest:** Cut or twist off the stem when squash are the desired size — the smaller the better.
> **Post-harvest handling:** Store in a plastic bag in the refrigerator for about 5 days.
> **Prep:** Before sautéing or stir-frying, slice, salt, and let drain for 30 minutes (optional).
> **Blanch:** As prep for freezing, 1 to 2 minutes
> **Boil:** Not recommended
> **Steam:** 4 minutes
> **Sauté or stir-fry:** 4 to 5 minutes
> **Roast:** 15 minutes at 450°F (230°C)
> **Grill:** 4 to 5 minutes
> **Braise:** 5 minutes

> **Preserve:** Freeze in a cooked dish. Can also be grated, drained, and frozen for use in baked goods. Can be pickled, but will never make a pickle as crisp as a cucumber pickle.

> **Comments:** Frequent harvest encourages more fruiting. Summer squash is a blank slate that absorbs flavors. To intensify summer squash flavor, salt slices and let drain on paper towels before cooking.

Squash, winter (acorn, buttercup, butternut, delicata, Hubbard, spaghetti, etc.)

> **Harvest:** When shells harden, before frost, cut off the vine, leaving 1 inch of stem.

> **Post-harvest handling:** Wash with a mild bleach solution and dry well. Cure in a well-ventilated area before storing in a cool, dark spot. Most winter squash will keep for 3 to 4 months.

> **Prep:** Butternut can be peeled. All winter squash are generally halved, seeded, and then cut into quarters or eighths, sliced, or chopped.

> **Blanch:** Not recommended

> **Boil:** 15 minutes for quarters or eighths

> **Steam:** 15 minutes for quarters or eighths

> **Sauté or stir-fry:** 10 minutes shredded

> **Roast:** 20 to 30 minutes at 425°F (220°C) for slices or cubes, 30 to 40 minutes for quarters or eighths, and 45 to 60 minutes for halves or wedges

> **Grill:** Not recommended

> **Braise:** 20 to 30 minutes for cubes

> **Preserve:** Dry, cold storage. Freeze or pressure-can cooked cubes and purées.

> **Comments:** Delicata has edible skin. Large Hubbard squash, which make the smoothest purées, require cutting with a cleaver and mallet, chopping with a hatchet, or dropping onto concrete to get them open. Red kuris also make smooth purées. Acorns tend to be bland and stringy compared to other varieties, though not as stringy as spaghetti squash. Because it can be peeled and therefore easily cut into cubes or shredded, butternut is the most versatile variety.

Swiss chard

> **Harvest:** When stems are large enough to enjoy, cut them about 1 inch above the soil. Harvest whole plants or individual outer leaves for continued production.

> **Post-harvest handling:** Store in a plastic bag in the refrigerator for up to 1 week.

> **Prep:** Separate the leaves from the stems to allow stems to cook slightly longer.

> **Blanch:** As prep for freezing, 3 to 4 minutes for stems, and 2 to 3 minutes for leaves

> **Boil:** 3 to 5 minutes for stems, and 3 to 4 minutes for leaves

> **Steam:** 3 to 5 minutes for stems, and 3 to 4 minutes for leaves

> **Sauté or stir-fry:** 3 to 4 minutes for stems, and 2 to 3 minutes for leaves

> **Roast:** 20 to 25 minutes for stems, and 15 minutes for leaves, both at 450°F (230°C)

> **Grill:** Not recommended

> **Braise:** 35 to 40 minutes

> **Preserve:** Keep in the garden until a hard freeze. The stems can be blanched and then frozen. The stems and leaves can be dried, frozen in cooked dishes, or sautéed and frozen.

> **Comments:** Swiss chard tastes a lot like beet greens; in fact, chard is a cultivar of beets. Use them interchangeably.

Tomatoes

> **Harvest:** Pick when fruits are firm with good color.
> **Post-harvest handling:** Store at room temperature.
> **Prep:** To skin, first blanch for 30 seconds. To seed, cut in half horizontally and squeeze out seeds.
> **Blanch:** 30 seconds
> **Boil:** Not recommended
> **Steam:** Not recommended
> **Sauté or stir-fry:** 5 to 10 minutes
> **Roast:** 2 hours at 350°F (180°C) for plum tomato halves, or 20 minutes at 425°F (220°C) for cherries and slices
> **Grill:** 2 to 4 minutes for thick slices
> **Braise:** 10 to 15 minutes
> **Preserve:** Can be frozen whole for cooking later, roasted and then frozen, or cooked into sauce or salsa and frozen. Can also be canned whole or as purées. Can be pressure-canned as a soup or sauce with meats and other vegetables. Can also be dried.
> **Comments:** Refrigeration destroys the flavor of fresh tomatoes.

Turnips, purple top

> **Harvest:** Dig up or pull when roots reach the desired size. Harvest the greens when they're large enough to enjoy.
> **Post-harvest handling:** Store in a root cellar, or keep in a perforated plastic bag in the refrigerator for up to 4 weeks. Store greens in a plastic bag in the fridge for about 5 days.
> **Prep:** Trim the top and base from the roots; peel. Remove the tough stems of the greens and treat like kale.
> **Blanch:** Not recommended
> **Boil:** 30 minutes for cubed roots
> **Steam:** 30 minutes for cubed roots; 4 minutes for greens
> **Sauté or stir-fry:** 10 minutes for shredded roots; 4 minutes for greens
> **Roast:** 25 minutes at 425°F (220°C) for cubed roots
> **Grill:** Not recommended
> **Braise:** 30 minutes for cubed roots; 10 minutes for greens
> **Preserve:** Cold storage. Can be pickled.
> **Comments:** The root flavor is mildest when freshly harvested (and if not overmature). Greens are best harvested young and will become bitter in hot weather.

Turnips, salad (hakurei)

> **Harvest:** Pull when roots reach the desired size.
> **Post-harvest handling:** Store the tops and roots separately in plastic bags in the fridge. Tops will keep for up to a week; roots for up to 2 weeks.
> **Prep:** Wash well. Trim the top and base from the roots; peel if desired.
> **Blanch:** Not recommended
> **Boil:** 10 to 15 minutes for cubed roots
> **Steam:** 10 to 15 minutes for cubed roots; 4 minutes for greens
> **Sauté or stir-fry:** 5 to 10 minutes for sliced or cubed roots; 4 minutes for greens
> **Roast:** 25 minutes at 450°F (230°C) for halved or quartered roots
> **Grill:** Not recommended
> **Braise:** 30 minutes for halved, quartered, or cubed roots; 10 minutes for greens
> **Preserve:** Can be pickled.
> **Comments:** The tops are delicious raw in salads or cooked like other greens. The roots can be cooked like regular turnips, though they're much milder in flavor, or served raw like radishes.

A kitchen doesn't have a full palette of flavors without herbs. Here's a guide to harvesting and cooking with some of the most useful culinary herbs. Most herbs are best harvested as needed, but they can be dried for use in the winter.

Rapidly growing annual herbs, especially dill and cilantro, are quick to bolt in hot weather. Here are some tips to delay bolting:

- Plant in a partly shaded spot to slow the plant's growth.

- Mulch to keep the soil cool and retain moisture. Plant in tight bunches to shade the ground, which also helps keep the soil cooler.

- To encourage leafing out rather than flower production, start harvesting leaves while the plant is still immature. Harvest repeatedly, taking one-quarter to one-third of each stem at a time.

- Pinch back flowers about 1½ to 2 inches down on the stem rather than just at the base of the flower.

Remember, bolting is natural. All plants want to produce seeds; you can't delay bolting forever, but you can stagger your planting times to spread out the growing season.

Basil

When to harvest: Cut and use the main stem just above the second set of leaves to stimulate bushy growth. Continue to harvest from the top. For best flavor, do not allow the plant to flower. The final harvest should take place before cold weather sets in.

Uses: A traditional ingredient in cuisines all over the world. Easily made into pesto (see page 35), which you can store in the fridge for about 5 days, or freeze in recipe-size batches.

Cilantro

When to harvest: Pick leaves before flowering.

Uses: Make into pesto by purée-ing with olive oil, lime juice, and zest; store in the fridge for 3 to 5 days, or freeze in recipe-size batches. Add to salsas and Mexican, Thai, and Vietnamese dishes. Cilantro doesn't take well to drying, so making pesto and freezing it is the best way to preserve its flavor.

Dill

When to harvest: Cut as soon as four or five leaves appear, cutting above the first leaf node to encourage bushier growth. Harvest whole flower heads with a few leaves attached for pickling. Let the flower heads mature to harvest for seeds.

Uses: Dill is a particularly good match for cucumber, potato, and fish dishes.

Oregano

When to harvest: Pick leaves as needed, before flowering.

Uses: Oregano is called for in many Italian dishes. It is easily dried.

Parsley, curly or flat-leaf

When to harvest: As needed, snip off stems from the outside of the plants.

Uses: Flat-leaf parsley is stronger in flavor than the curly variety. Use in soup, stocks, and sauces, or add to salads. Parsley can be harvested, stuffed into plastic bags, and frozen for use throughout the winter.

Rosemary

When to harvest: As needed, snip off the tips of the stems.

Uses: Use in soups, sauces, and stocks. Leave the stems whole and remove before serving, or strip the needles from the twigs and chop. Throw whole stems directly on coals or use stems as kabob sticks when grilling.

Sage

When to harvest: Pick leaves as needed.

Uses: Use in soups, sauces, stocks, and stuffings. Chop finely. Use sparingly.

Thyme

When to harvest: As needed, pick leaves from the top of the plant.

Uses: Strip the leaves from the woody stems. They add distinctive flavor to soups, sauces, and stews.

Making the Most of What's in Season

Vegetables can star in some easy-to-whip-together dishes. Once you have the basic techniques down, you can easily vary them according to the vegetables and seasonings you have on hand.

> **Deep-frying.** The Japanese call it *tempura*, and the Italians *fritto misto* ("mixed fry"). American cooks — particularly in the South — batter-dip and fry green beans, okra, zucchini, and cucumber pickles, but almost any vegetable lends itself to this treatment. Whatever you call it, first coat the vegetables in seasoned flour, then in batter or an egg wash, then in bread crumbs. Deep-fry at 365°F (185°C), then drain on paper towels, and serve with a sauce. Tempura is usually accompanied by a soy dipping sauce, and fritto misto by a tomato-based marinara sauce; American fried vegetables are often accompanied by either ketchup or ranch dressing. (See page 278 for a basic recipe for tempura vegetables.)

> **Braising.** We tend to think of braising as a cooking method for tough cuts of meat, but it is also a great way to enhance the flavor of a vegetable. Braising can mellow strong-tasting vegetables like collard greens and give a new flavor experience to over-familiar vegetables like zucchini and green beans. Start by creating a flavor base: sauté over low heat a little bacon or cubed smoked meat with aromatic vegetables such as finely chopped garlic, onions, carrots, celery, shallots, or any combination thereof, in oil, butter, or animal fat, such as duck fat. Or sauté a mix of curry spices, Ethiopian spices, or Mexican spices in the oil, butter, or fat. Then add the vegetables and a splash of stock, wine, coconut milk, vinegar, or water (or nothing in the case of a watery vegetable, like summer squash). Cover with a tight-fitting lid and cook over low heat for 20 minutes or up to 3 hours for Southern-style collard greens. Just before serving, season with a little salt and pepper and perhaps some fresh herbs or a splash of vinegar. If the vegetables are swimming in liquid, remove the veggies with a slotted spoon, boil the liquid vigorously to reduce to a glaze, then return the vegetables and stir until coated.

> **Gratin.** Just about every vegetable can be enjoyed baked in cream, a white sauce, or a cheese sauce, then topped with bread crumbs and sometimes more cheese. (See page 277 for a basic gratin recipe.)

> **Quiche.** Chop and blanch any vegetable, combine with cheese and eggs in a crust, and bake until the custard filling is just firm. (See page 284 for a basic quiche recipe.)

Sauces for Vegetable Side Dishes

I am a lover of vegetables and enjoy most veggies either steamed and garnished with salt or sautéed with garlic. But occasionally it is time to gild the lily, and that's when I sauce a dish of vegetables with aioli, hollandaise, cheese sauce, or pesto. These terrific and easy sauces should be part of your go-to repertoire when you want to make your vegetables irresistible.

Aioli

Makes 2½ cups

I had my first taste of aioli in Vermont at the Bread and Puppet Theater's Annual Resurrection Circus, where it was served slathered on slices of rustic bread at the "free bread store." The generosity of giving away loaves and loaves of bread is as much a message of social justice as Bread and Puppet's wordless play involving giant puppets, and equally well received.

There is nothing like aioli to brighten a platter of raw vegetables. It is also pretty terrific slathered on bread or served as a replacement for tartar sauce with seafood.

INGREDIENTS

8–10 garlic cloves

2 egg yolks, at room temperature, lightly beaten

Juice of 1 lemon

1 teaspoon Dijon mustard

1 cup extra-virgin olive oil

1 cup sunflower, canola, or other neutral-tasting vegetable oil

Salt and freshly ground black pepper

1. In a food processor fitted with a steel blade, purée the garlic. Add the egg yolks, lemon juice, and mustard, and process until smooth.

2. Combine the two oils. With the motor running, slowly pour the oil in a thin, steady stream. Continue processing until you have a thick, shiny sauce.

3. Season to taste with salt and pepper and store in the refrigerator until you are ready to use it. Remember, with the raw yolks, it is quite perishable.

Note: To make mayonnaise, simply omit the garlic from the aioli recipe.

Easy Hollandaise

Serves 6

Hollandaise is, of course, the sauce used in eggs Benedict. It is a classic with asparagus. Serve any roasted or steamed vegetable on toast and top with a poached egg (page 87) and hollandaise sauce, and you have a vegetarian dinner worthy of a special occasion.

(page 87)

INGREDIENTS

1¼ cups butter
2 egg yolks
2 tablespoons fresh lemon juice, plus more to taste
Salt and freshly ground black pepper

1. Melt the butter in a small saucepan over medium heat until foaming. Remove the pan from the heat.

2. Combine the egg yolks and lemon juice in a blender; cover and blend to combine. With the blender running, remove the lid insert and slowly pour the hot butter into the blender in a thin stream of droplets. When you come to the bottom of the saucepan, discard the milk solids. Continue to blend until a creamy sauce forms.

3. Season to taste with salt and pepper and more lemon juice, if needed. Serve immediately, if you can. You can try to keep hollandaise warm in a thermos or on top of a double boiler, but it is best to serve as soon as possible.

Basic Cheese Sauce

Makes about 2½ cups

A cheese sauce is the starting point for tons of vegetable dishes — everything from mac and cheese with veggies to a white vegetable lasagna. You can use this sauce to make a gratin (see page 277). You can also make a white vegetable lasagna with this sauce, layering sautéed or grilled summer vegetables (bell peppers, summer squash, cherry tomatoes, eggplant, green beans, spinach, broccoli, broccoli rabe) with sheets of lasagna and cheese sauce. Or use it to make macaroni and cheese, folding in blanched veggies, or diced and drained tomatoes or halved cherry tomatoes.

(see page 277)

INGREDIENTS

¼ cup butter
¼ cup all-purpose unbleached flour
2 cups milk
1–1½ cups grated cheddar, fontina, Swiss, Gruyère, or Jarlsberg cheese
Salt and freshly ground black pepper

1. Melt the butter over medium heat in a medium saucepan. Blend in the flour with a wooden spoon to make a smooth paste. Cook for 2 minutes, stirring constantly.

2. Stir in the milk, a little at a time, until the sauce is thick and smooth. Bring to a boil, stirring constantly. Stir in the cheese and cook until smooth and melted, about 2 minutes more.

3. Season to taste with salt and pepper. Serve hot.

Pesto

Makes about ⅔ cup

Pesto — the heavenly paste made from fresh basil, Parmesan cheese, olive oil, and pine nuts — is an incredibly versatile flavoring agent. It is the start of many dishes, including sautéed or grilled vegetables (especially summer vegetables such as summer squash, peppers, green beans, eggplant) plus pasta plus pesto. It is worth the space in the garden to grow as much basil as you can, so that you can make many batches of pesto to freeze and have it available year-round. This is the recipe I use.

INGREDIENTS

3 tablespoons pine nuts, almonds, or walnuts

1½ cups tightly packed fresh basil leaves

2 garlic cloves

¼ cup extra-virgin olive oil, plus additional oil for sealing the top

3 tablespoons freshly grated Parmesan cheese

Salt and freshly ground black pepper

1. To toast the nuts, put them in a dry skillet over medium heat and toast, stirring occasionally, until golden brown, 7 to 10 minutes.

2. Combine the pine nuts, basil, and garlic in a food processor fitted with a metal blade. Process until finely chopped.

3. With the motor running, add the oil through the feed tube and continue processing until you have a paste. Add the cheese, season to taste with salt and pepper, and briefly process, just until well mixed.

4. Set the pesto aside for at least 20 minutes to allow the flavors to develop, if you are going to use it the same day you make it. Otherwise, spoon the pesto into an airtight container and pour in enough oil to completely cover the pesto and exclude any air. Seal and store in the refrigerator for up to 1 week, or in the freezer for up to 6 months.

Note: If you are multiplying this recipe to make quantities of pesto for the freezer, you may want to toast the nuts in the oven. Preheat the oven to 350°F (180°C) and spread out the nuts on a baking sheet. Toast, stirring occasionally, for 10 to 15 minutes, until golden brown.

Vinaigrettes and Drizzles

Quite possibly the easiest way to dress a vegetable is with a drizzle of oil and vinegar or with a carefully blended vinaigrette, which is simply a combination of oil and vinegar, with or without additional flavorings. All through tomato season, I'll fan out sliced tomatoes on a plate, drizzle with extra-virgin olive oil, then a drizzle of balsamic or red wine vinegar, and sprinkle with salt and pepper. Sometimes the tomatoes will get a sprinkle of fresh basil, or chopped garlic, or sliced red onion, or the slices will be paired with fresh mozzarella (see page 243). Fresh sliced cucumbers, salad greens, radishes, steamed green beans, steamed baby bok choy, steamed broccoli, and blanched leeks all get the same treatment, though sometimes I go for a more Asian flavoring with a drizzle of sesame oil, soy sauce, and rice vinegar or black vinegar. Generally, I aim for equal amounts of each, but it isn't necessary to be exacting. Bottled salad dressings mystify me; they never taste as good as homemade.

Classic Vinaigrette

Makes about ¼ cup

High-quality ingredients make a difference in a combination this simple. Although the vinaigrette can be made in large quantities, and leftovers can be stored for a couple of days in the refrigerator, a vinaigrette tastes best when freshly made.

INGREDIENTS

- 1 tablespoon balsamic, red wine, white wine, or sherry vinegar
- 1 small garlic clove or shallot, minced, or 1 tablespoon minced fresh herbs
- ½ teaspoon Dijon mustard
- 3 tablespoons extra-virgin olive oil
- Salt and freshly ground black pepper

Combine the vinegar, garlic, and mustard in a small bowl. Whisk until smooth. Slowly pour in the oil, whisking constantly until the oil is fully incorporated. Season with salt and pepper. Use immediately.

Maple-Soy Vinaigrette

Makes about ¼ cup

This is my house vinaigrette. It goes with everything but is particularly well suited to be served as a drizzle over mixed roasted root vegetables.

INGREDIENTS

- 1 tablespoon balsamic vinegar
- 1 tablespoon soy sauce
- 1 tablespoon maple syrup
- 1 tablespoon extra-virgin olive oil

Combine the vinegar, soy sauce, and maple syrup in a small bowl. Whisk until smooth. Slowly pour in the oil, whisking constantly until the oil is fully incorporated. Use immediately.

Making Vegetable Soups

Whether you're looking for a hearty bowl of comfort or a quick meal that you can throw together with whatever vegetables you find in the refrigerator, soup is the answer.

Soup starts with soup stock, which can be made from vegetables (recipe follows), poultry (page 107), or beef (page 142). It is the foundation that allows the vegetables to star, so go for homemade stock when you can. Make plenty and keep a supply in the freezer.

Improvise. Soup is a very forgiving medium. So play with the flavors; add different vegetables and herbs; think hot and cold, thin and thick, hearty and light. If it happens that you keep adding ingredients until you find the perfect balance of flavors, and you find yourself with much more soup than you intended, consider it a lucky break; the leftovers freeze beautifully. Just don't forget: bread makes the meal. (See chapter 4 for more on that topic.)

Vegetable Stock

Makes 3½ to 4 quarts

Many dishes call for vegetable stock, and you may use it in place of chicken or beef stock when you're cooking for vegetarians. Vegetable stock can also be seen as a way to clean out the refrigerator of less-than-perfect vegetables. The goal, however, is to make a well-balanced pot liquor, so don't go overboard with sweet root vegetables or cabbagey cruciferous ones.

INGREDIENTS

2 carrots, 2 parsnips, or one of each
2 leeks or the tops of 4 leeks
1 large onion
1 large bunch parsley or ¼ small head green cabbage
1 fennel bulb (optional)
4 garlic cloves
1 tablespoon dried thyme
1 cup dried mushrooms
4 quarts water
1 cup dry white wine
1 tablespoon black peppercorns

1. Quarter the carrots, leeks, and onion. Combine them with the parsley, fennel (if using), garlic, thyme, and mushrooms in a large soup pot. Add the water. Cover, bring to a boil, then reduce the heat and simmer for 30 minutes.

2. Add the wine and peppercorns and continue to simmer, covered, for 10 minutes. Then remove from the heat, strain, and discard all the solids.

3. Use immediately or cool and then refrigerate. The stock will keep for about 5 days in the refrigerator or for 4 to 6 months in the freezer.

Cream of Any Vegetable Soup

Serves 4 to 6

If you were raised on canned "cream of" soup, you may be pleasantly surprised by how wonderful creamy vegetable soups can be. This version is particularly pleasing because it can be adjusted for type of vegetable and amount of dairy. The heavy cream added at the end makes the soup wonderfully rich and luxurious. Use just one type of vegetable or the flavors will be muddy.

INGREDIENTS

4 tablespoons butter

2 garlic cloves, minced

2 leeks, white and tender green parts, sliced (or substitute 1 onion, diced)

4 cups chicken stock (page 107) or vegetable stock (page 37)

¼ cup dry sherry or white wine

1 baking potato, peeled and cubed

4 cups chopped, sliced, diced, or whole vegetable (asparagus, broccoli, carrots, cauliflower, celery, celery root, corn, green peas, parsnips, rutabagas, spinach, etc.)

½ milk

½ cup heavy cream (optional)

Salt and white pepper

1. Melt the butter in a large heavy saucepan over low heat. Add the garlic and leeks and cook until softened and fragrant, about 5 minutes. Do not let the garlic color. Stir in the chicken stock and sherry. Add the potato. Bring the mixture to a boil. Reduce the heat and simmer for 15 minutes.

2. Meanwhile, steam the vegetables until tender. (Use the timings on pages 17–30, if needed.)

3. Stir in the vegetables and adjust the heat as needed so that the soup continues to simmer for another 10 to 15 minutes, until the potato is completely tender.

4. Purée the soup in batches in a blender or with an immersion blender. If you are looking for an absolutely smooth, velvety texture, strain through a fine-mesh sieve back into the saucepan.

5. Stir in the milk and cream (if using) and season to taste with salt and white pepper. Warm until heated through. Serve at once.

CHAPTER 3

FRESH FRUIT
Harvesting, Handling, Cooking

Even the smallest backyard homestead can raise fruit, and it is possible that raising fruit is even more rewarding than raising vegetables — especially in the realm of pure pleasure. Who doesn't like strawberries? And while you can find people who will tell you they don't care for broccoli, or peas, or winter squash, you rarely run across someone who doesn't enjoy a sweet, juicy, tree-ripened peach.

Many fruits are perennials; once you get the trees or plants established, they will reward you with fruit for years to come. How great is that? Of course, establishing an orchard is generally a long-term commitment, and not all fruits will thrive in all climates, even with a wide choice of varieties and cultivars. But undoubtedly there are fruits for every climate.

Just a reminder: you will be competing with critters — insect pests, birds, and four-legged creatures — that have superior senses for detecting ripe fruit. It's the rare homesteader who hasn't gone to bed planning to harvest the next day and awakened to a critter-plundered landscape.

It's important to harvest and store your fruit in the best ways possible so that you will have the tastiest fruit for fresh eating, dessert making, and preserving. Most fruits can be enjoyed out of hand — no preparation necessary. But once the novelty of the fresh fresh fruit wears off, there are still plenty of easy desserts to be made (see chapter 20). You'll also want to consider canning and freezing fruit, as well as making jams and jellies, all of which is covered in part 2.

An A-to-Z Guide to the Fruits

Here you'll find an alphabetical listing of some of the most common homestead and backyard fruits, with ideas for short-term storage and dishes you might make with an abundance of each fruit. The profiles give harvesting tips as well, but remember that fruits that are destined to become jams and jellies are best picked slightly underripe, when their pectin content is highest.

Apples

Because apples are so easy to store in a root cellar and are so long lasting, they are an ideal homestead fruit. Even if you don't have a root cellar, you can easily store apples in the form of canned or frozen applesauce, canned or frozen pie filling, frozen cider, and apple cider syrup (page 82).

> **Harvest tips:** Harvest season varies according to variety and location. When a few apples have fallen from the tree and the bottoms of the fruits are reddened (or the appropriate color), the apples should be checked for ripeness. An apple is ripe when it can be picked with a gentle lift and twist; this method helps you retain the stem for better keeping. When you bite into the apple, the flesh should taste sweet and juicy, and should not look green or starchy. The flesh at the bottom of the apple should be more yellow than green, and the seeds should be dark brown.

> **Handling and short-term storage:** Generally, the earlier a variety is ready for harvest, the less well the apple keeps; and the colder the storage, the longer the apple retains its quality. Storage temperatures of 33°F to 35°F (0.6°C to 1.6°C) are ideal: apples kept at that temperature can last for up to 6 months. Unfortunately, most refrigerators are set for about 37°F (2.7°C), and often the temperatures are higher, depending on where in the refrigerator the apples are stored, how tightly packed the refrigerator is, and how often the door is opened. Temperatures tend to be even higher in a root cellar. The best way to store apples is in perforated plastic bags in the refrigerator. Less-than-terrific apples can be made into applesauce.

> **Fresh desserts:** Apples are a favorite for baking in pies, crisps, quick breads, and coffee cakes. To make baked apples, cut the tops off the apples, remove the cores, and fill with honey, maple syrup, or brown sugar; then bake, covered, for 40 to 60 minutes. A drizzle of a caramel sauce goes well with most apple desserts.

Apricots

Apricots continue to ripen after they are harvested, meaning they get softer, but they don't get any sweeter. Only those who grow their own and allow the apricots to develop the most sugar get the very best flavor. Understand, though, that you are competing at that point with the insects, birds, and other critters who also appreciate a fully ripened apricot.

> **Harvest tips:** The apricot harvest season stretches over a few weeks, with the fruits on an individual tree ripening at different times. Apricots are ready for harvest when the skin turns from green to yellow and the fruit is starting to soften but is still firm enough to handle. They should separate easily from the twigs.

> **Handling and short-term storage:** Apricots can be kept for a short period at room temperature, or for 1 to 3 weeks in the refrigerator. Less-than-terrific apricots can be made into jam.

> **Fresh desserts:** Just about anything you can do with peaches you can also do with apricots, including pies, tarts, ice cream, and crisps and cobblers. Serve on top of biscuits (pages 331 and 332) with whipped cream to make apricot shortcake. Apricots can be dipped in chocolate, layered into yogurt, folded into whipped cream to make a fool, or sliced and arranged atop cheesecake. A drizzle of chocolate goes well with many apricot desserts.

Blueberries

Blueberries are firmer and less prone to mold than strawberries and bramble berries. They have the advantage of holding their quality on the bush and in the refrigerator longer. Another advantage of blueberries is that they can be sweetened to taste and made into jam without added pectin.

> **Harvest tips:** In general, berries don't continue to ripen once picked. A fully ripe blueberry will be uniform in color; some varieties will have a dusty bloom. The berries should release from their stems with very little effort; if you have to yank at all, it means the berries aren't fully ripe.

Handle the berries gently and pick by rolling each berry from the cluster with your thumb into the palm of your hand. When you pick this way, the berries that aren't ripe won't come loose. Harvest every couple of days.

> **Handling and short-term storage:** Chill the berries as soon after picking as possible to extend their shelf life. Store in shallow, covered containers. Do not wash until just before cooking or eating. If refrigerated in a dry condition, fresh-picked firm berries will keep for 10 to 14 days.

> **Fresh desserts:** To make a fresh sauce, crush the berries in a food processor or with a potato masher and combine with a sweetener to taste. Serve as is, or topped with whipped cream. Serve on top of a cheesecake or a fresh fruit tart. Make a berry fool by folding into whipped cream. Serve on top of biscuits (pages 331 and 332) with whipped cream to make berry shortcake. These berries are also terrific in crisps and cobblers or baked into coffee cakes or quick breads.

Bramble berries

Bramble berries include raspberries, blackberries, dewberries, and loganberries. There's a variety of these delicate berries adapted to most of the different growing regions of North America. All are highly perishable and wildly expensive at the supermarket; it makes sense to grow your own and enjoy a true abundance.

> **Harvest tips:** Harvest as soon as the berries taste sweet and show their ripe color. Bramble berries should be easy to pull off the stem; if it takes any real effort, they aren't ripe. The berries are best picked early in the morning, before they are heated by the sun. Don't pick berries while they are wet from rain, unless you are just popping them in your mouth. Wet berries mold rapidly.

> **Handling and short-term storage:** Do not wash or hull the berries until you are ready to eat or freeze them. Best-case scenario: eat them the same day you pick them. If you need to store the berries for a day or two, place them in a single layer on a towel-lined tray in the refrigerator. For more than 2 days, try puréeing them with sugar. The sugar should stave off mold for an extra couple of days, depending on how much sugar you use.

> **Fresh desserts:** The berries can be enjoyed as is or macerated (sprinkle with sugar and let sit for 30 minutes to draw out the juices; use about 1 tablespoon sugar for every 2 cups berries). Serve in a bowl plain, or topped with whipped cream. Make a berry fool by folding into whipped cream. Serve on top of biscuits (pages 331 and 332) with whipped cream to make berry shortcake. Serve on top of a fresh fruit tart or cheesecake, or use to make a fresh berry pie, crisp, or cobbler.

Cherries, sweet and tart

Sweet cherries are wonderful eaten out of hand. Tart cherries (also called pie cherries or sour cherries) are pretty sour, and most people prefer them in a pie, with plenty of sugar. It's easier to judge a ripe sweet cherry than a ripe tart cherry because the tart cherry will never taste fully ripened to the untrained taster. Once picked, a cherry will not get any more ripe.

> **Harvest tips:** Keep a close eye on the cherries. Like other stone fruits, they reach full size, then develop the sugars that make the fruit good to eat. Pick your cherries when they have developed their mature color, which varies from yellow-pink to almost black, depending on the variety. Do a taste test to determine if the cherries have reached their full flavor; the cherries should be firm but juicy and tender enough to bite into easily.

To pick, grasp each fruit by the stem near its attachment point to the branch. Lift up and twist the stem free from the branch. Try to leave the stem on the cherry; it keeps better that way. As you pick, handle the cherries gently and place in a shallow container; you don't want too much weight on them.

> **Handling and short-term storage:** As soon as the cherries come into the kitchen, put them in a small, perforated plastic bag and chill them in the refrigerator, where they will keep for at least 5 days, and up to 2 weeks if you are lucky. The small bag is to prevent bruising; if you pile the whole harvest into one bag, you will have mush on the bottom. Don't wash before chilling.

> **Fresh desserts:** For dessert, nothing beats a big bowl of sweet cherries, and serving them that way has the added advantage of not requiring pitting. Every other way you serve them, you must pit first using a cherry pitter or a sharp paring knife. Once pitted, almost any way you would enjoy a berry, you can enjoy sweet cherries. A classic dessert for both sweet and tart cherries is clafoutis (cherries baked in a pancake-like batter), and everyone loves cherries in pie, crisps, and cobblers. Chocolate and cherries — the classic combination called Black Forest — is always wonderful; Black Forest Ricotta Mousse (page 329) is proof.

Citrus fruits

Citrus fruits are perfect for warm-climate homesteaders because the harvest season is so long and the fruits keep best on the trees. There's no need to worry about harvesting at the right time, and no overabundance to deal with. And, of course, there's no reason to do anything with a citrus fruit except peel and eat. Too bad so few climates will support them.

Citrus fruits include grapefruit, kumquats, oranges, tangelos, tangerines, and mandarins. Limes and lemons, which are used mainly for flavoring, are also citrus fruits.

> **Harvest tips:** The best indicator of ripeness is taste, not color. If the fruit tastes good, it is ready to eat. But don't rush to harvest everything at once. You can keep the ripe fruits on the tree for a few months; they will usually get sweeter, and your harvest will be extended.

Harvest the fruits by cutting them off with pruning shears; pulling on a fruit is likely to damage it, which will shorten its life span.

Once you begin to harvest, pick fruit from the lower branches first, leaving the high fruit until later in the season because the lowest fruits are more likely to be damaged by frost or brown rot, a fungal disease that may splash up from the soil where it lives.

> **Handling and short-term storage:** If you must harvest extra citrus to avoid frost or because of high winds on heavy branches, you can store the fruit in the refrigerator for several weeks.

Under dry conditions at room temperature — in a bowl on the counter — the fruits will last 7 to 10 days.

When you need both citrus juice and grated zest, grate the zest before squeezing the juice. Both jobs will be easier. Before juicing citrus fruit, microwave it for 15 to 45 seconds until slightly warm to the touch, and it will yield more juice. Another trick is to roll the fruit on the counter for a few seconds to help break the cell walls.

> **Fresh desserts:** Once you get beyond the pure enjoyment of eating fresh citrus out of hand, there is the joy of juice made from the fresh fruit and sweetened if needed. The flesh doesn't lend itself to baking that much, but there are plenty of desserts made with the juice and finely grated zest, including lemon meringue pie, lemon squares, and key lime pie, not to mention pound cakes and cheese-cakes. Lemon curd is a luscious combination of butter, sugar, eggs, and lemon juice cooked until thickened. Lemon curd can be used as a spread on toast, the filling for lemon squares, or a topping for fruit desserts, ice cream, or pound cakes. It becomes an instant mousse when blended with whipped cream. Other citrus fruits can also be used to make fruit curd.

Currants, gooseberries, and jostaberries

Currants, gooseberries, and jostaberries grow well in poor soils and high elevations — places where fussier fruits won't flourish, but these berries are not as popular in the United States as they should be, probably stemming from federal and state bans on their cultivation because they are an alternate host for the white pine blister rust. The federal ban was lifted in 1966, but some states, including Massachusetts, still ban black currants and regulate the planting of red currants and gooseberries in some areas of the state. Check with your state's agriculture department to find out the status of these regulations.

If you've never heard of jostaberries, I'm not surprised. They are a hybrid between the gooseberry and the black currant. The josta-berry is two to three times the size of the red currant, nearly the size of the common goose-berry. It comes in both red and black varieties, and the best fruit set occurs when black and red jostaberries are grown together.

> **Harvest tips:** The general advice here is to harvest these berries when they are slightly underripe if you plan to preserve them as jam or jelly. At this stage the fruit has plenty of pectin. For enjoying fresh, you can harvest the berries when they are fully ripe; they will be deeply colored and soft. The fruits maintain their quality on the bush for up to 3 weeks once fully colored, so you don't need to harvest them all at once. These berries are borne in clusters and are easy to strip off the stems.

> **Handling and short-term storage:** Depending on how ripe the berries are when picked, they will keep in a covered shallow container in the refrigerator for 1 to 3 weeks. Before cooking, pull or cut off the stems and tails on both ends.

> **Fresh desserts:** The classic gooseberry dessert is a fool, made with stewed berries. Stew gooseberries, currants, and jostaberries with sugar to taste to make dessert sauces for ice cream, pound cake, or shortcakes. These berries are also good in a sauce designed to cut the richness of game or liver.

Elderberries

Where you find elderberries in the wild, chances are the seeds were spread by birds that once feasted on a homesteader's cultivated bush. The elderberry was commonly grown on early American homesteads because it produced valued medicines as well as fruit for cooked desserts, wines, and preserves. It is more common in the wild than in supermarkets because its musky flavor is not for everyone.

> **Harvest tips:** Harvest elderberry fruit when the berries have turned from green to dark purple, usually in August or September. Cut off the entire cluster with pruning shears. In the kitchen, strip the berries into a bowl (the fruit will stain your hands, clothes, and counter, so take care). Try to avoid taking the stems with the fruits.

> **Handling and short-term storage:** Keep the fruit refrigerated, and cook or process the berries as soon as possible.

> **Fresh desserts:** This is a fruit you won't enjoy fresh. Traditionally, elderberries have been made into wines, jellies, liqueurs, and syrups. You can stew elderberries with sugar to taste; serve the stewed berries folded into whipped cream or made into pies, crisps, or cobblers. Combining the elderberries with apples mellows their intense flavor.

Figs

Luscious tree-ripened figs can be produced in Zones 8 through 10 and can be grown in containers in Zone 7. These fruits are extremely perishable, which is why they are such a rarity at markets, except as dried fruits. If you are fortunate enough to live in a warm climate where fig trees flourish, enjoy your figs but don't limit yourself to desserts; figs are wonderful in salads and paired with salty cured meats and cheeses.

> **Harvest tips:** Figs won't ripen once picked; they must be allowed to ripen fully on the tree. A ripe fruit is slightly soft and starting to bend at the neck. Harvest the fruits gently to avoid bruising.

> **Handling and short-term storage:** Fresh figs do not keep well and can be stored in the refrigerator for only 2 to 3 days. They'll retain better flavor if kept out of the refrigerator, but in that case they will keep for only 1 or 2 days.

> **Fresh desserts:** Figs lend themselves to simple preparations, like broiling. Partially quarter the figs so they open like flowers, broil briefly, then drizzle with honey, mascarpone, sweetened yogurt, or sweetened crème fraîche. Or poach the whole figs gently in a sweetened, spiced syrup. Use sliced fresh figs as a topping for a fruit tart, or serve the quartered fruits on a cheese plate.

Grapes

There are three different types of grapes in common use: the European *Vitis vinifera*, which includes most of the wine grapes, and the two American natives, *V. labrusca*, which includes the Concord grape, the classic variety for grape jelly, and the southern muscadine (*V. rotundifolia*). While people do make wine from all the different types of grapes, and there are some wine hybrids that are good for table eating, generally most of the table grape cultivars are the foxy-tasting *V. labrusca* or the muscadine. *V. labrusca* cultivars tend to be most cold-hardy, while European grapes tend to do well in warm, dry, Mediterranean-type zones. But newly developed hybrids are extending the ranges of all three different types of grapes, making plenty of exceptions to the rules.

In the kitchen, grapes are pretty neatly divided into table varieties and wine varieties. Table grapes tend to be larger, with thicker pulp and thinner skins, and, of course, they are best for eating fresh and for making into jams, jellies, juice, and other preserves and desserts.

➤ **Harvest tips:** As grapes mature, the ripe color and sugar content increase and the acidity decreases, but they will not continue ripening once picked from the vine. Test a few from the tip of a cluster to see if they are ready to harvest, usually in late summer to early fall. Generally the berries at the tip of the cluster are the last to ripen. The natural bloom on the grape will become noticeable at the fully ripe stage, and the berries will become slightly less firm to the touch. Harvest the ripe clusters from each vine by cutting them off with a knife or pruning shears. After the ripe clusters are picked, the immature clusters left on the vine will continue to mature. Excessive rains during harvest may cause skins to split, so you may have to harvest earlier than is absolutely desirable if an extended period of wet weather is forecast.

➤ **Handling and short-term storage:** Grapes can be stored for up to 6 weeks in a root cellar or refrigerator, but grapes can absorb the odors of other fruits and vegetables, so keep them separate. In the root cellar, you can store the grapes in cardboard boxes or crates lined with clean, dry straw. Separate bunches with straw or sawdust. Check often for spoilage. Handle gently.

➤ **Fresh desserts:** I don't think you can improve on a fresh table grape, but many like to make grape pies, sorbets, and other frozen desserts. Generally only the flesh of muscadines is used; their skins are just too tough to chew. Table grapes pair beautifully with nuts and cheese on a cheese plate for snacks and dessert.

Melons

Unlike most other fruits, melons are annuals and grow on vines, often planted in the vegetable garden along with other cucurbits like cucumbers and winter squash. The challenge with melons is to harvest them when they are fully ripe, though honeydews and muskmelons will ripen on the kitchen counter.

➤ **Harvest tips:** Muskmelons are ripe when the rind is tan rather than green between the surface netting. Many will have a strong melon fragrance, and the surest sign that the fruit is ready is a crack that forms on the stem right near the point of attachment with the melon. This crack signals the "slip" stage, and in a few days the melon will slip off the vine with minimal pressure. If you have to work to separate the melon from the vine, chances are it is not ripe. Muskmelons are overripe when the outer skin softens, making it easily penetrable by birds and bees.

Watermelons are ripe when the curled tendril at the stem end dries and turns brown, the underside of the melon turns yellow or cream-colored, and the melon gives a deep, resonant sound when thumped. The melon's skin also becomes dull and is difficult to penetrate with a fingernail.

Honeydews and casaba melons — varieties with smooth, hard skins — must be cut from the vine. The skin of these varieties actually feels hairy when the fruit is not ripe. As the fruit matures, the skin becomes smooth and slippery and some varieties change color. When the fruit is fully ripe, the skin changes again to have a waxy feel. In addition, the blossom end should have a ripe, fruity smell. You should be able to hear seeds rattle in a ripe honeydew, and it should resonate with a hollow thump if you slap it.

> **Handling and short-term storage:** Most melons will ripen a little bit more for 2 or 3 days after they're picked. Store melons at room temperature until they are totally ripe, then refrigerate for up to a few weeks.

> **Fresh desserts:** You can't do much to improve upon the flavor of a fully ripened melon; I myself don't even try. Peeled slices or chunks make a fine addition to a cheese plate.

Pawpaws

Pawpaws break all the rules. They are basically a tropical fruit, but they're hardy from Zone 4 to Zone 7 or 8 and are found in the wild in North America. The pawpaw tree has large, lush leaves like those of an avocado tree, but it is the only temperate member of a family of tropical fruits that includes sweetsop, soursop, atemoya, and custard apples, which the fruit resembles. Sometimes called the "poor man's banana," this fruit tastes like a cross between a banana and a mango.

> **Harvest tips:** The fruit is ripe when it is deeply aromatic and soft, giving slightly when gently squeezed. Skin color, which is not a reliable indicator of ripeness, can vary from green to bright green, eventually turning black or brown. When the fruits on an individual tree begin to ripen, you'll need to harvest them at least every other day for a 1- to 2-week period.

> **Handling and short-term storage:** Pawpaws have a shelf life of 3 to 5 days at room temperature, but they will keep for 1 to 3 weeks if refrigerated.

> **Fresh desserts:** To use, spoon the soft flesh out of the skin (which isn't edible) and discard the large seeds. Use the soft pulp as you would mashed banana: in quick breads, smoothies, and cakes. It is delicious blended until smooth and folded into whipped cream.

Peaches and nectarines

Peaches and nectarines are botanically the same fruit, *Prunus persica*, with yellow or whitish flesh, a delicate aroma, and a skin that is either velvety (peaches) or smooth (nectarines) in different cultivars. Peaches and nectarines, along with cherries, plums, and apricots, are stone fruits (drupes). Cultivated peaches are divided into clingstones and freestones, depending on whether the flesh sticks to the stone or not; freestones are much, much easier to deal with in the kitchen.

> **Harvest tips:** Although different peach and nectarine varieties have different amounts of red blush, all will go from green to yellow, orange, red, or some combination thereof. When ripe, the fruit should separate easily from the twig. If it is hard to pull off the tree, it isn't ripe! Peaches and nectarines will not ripen further once removed from the tree, though they will soften.

> **Handling and short-term storage:** Fresh peaches and nectarines can be kept at room temperature for just 3 to 4 days. Refrigeration will extend their life, but not by more than a day or two. The fruits need humidity, so refrigerate them in a plastic bag. To peel peaches before cooking or baking, bring a large pot of water to a boil. Add the peaches and blanch for 30 seconds. Remove with a slotted spoon and immerse them in a bowl of cold water. The skins will slip off easily. Generally, nectarines do not need to be peeled.

> **Fresh desserts:** There is no end to the possibilities when it comes to peaches and nectarines. The fruit is terrific out of hand, but you can also slice the fruit and macerate it (sprinkle with sugar and let sit for 30 minutes to draw out the juices; use about 1 tablespoon sugar for every 2 cups slices). Serve in a bowl plain or topped with whipped cream or crème fraîche. Make a peach fool by folding it into whipped cream. Serve on top of biscuits (pages 331

and 332) with whipped cream to make peach shortcake. Serve on top of a fresh fruit tart or use to make a pie. Peaches and nectarines are also delicious made into a sorbet or ice cream. A drizzle of chocolate or caramel goes well with many peach and nectarine desserts.

Pears

Pears are often regarded as apples' poor relations, but they are really a very different type of fruit. Aside from being roughly the same size as apples and ripening around the same time, pears are different in flavor, texture, and ripening characteristics.

> **Harvest tips:** Pears actually do best when picked slightly immature because they ripen from the inside out. If you wait until the flesh just under the skin is fully ripened, the insides will be mush. Take hold of a hanging pear and twist it up into a horizontal position; a pear that's ready to be picked will readily detach from the tree.

> **Handling and short-term storage:** Freshly picked commercially grown pears are cooled down to about 30°F (−1°C), which greatly enhances their keeping quality. You can come close by quickly refrigerating your just-harvested pears. Bartlett pears need to be cooled only for a day or two, while winter pears such as Anjou, Bosc, and Comice require 2 to 6 weeks of chilling. Then remove the pears from the refrigerator to ripen as you need them. The pear has a rather limited window of time between not quite ripe and overripe. At 65°F to 75°F (18°C to 24°C), Bartlett pears will ripen in 4 to 5 days; Bosc and Comice pears will ripen in 5 to 7 days; Anjou pears will ripen in 7 to 10 days. Not surprisingly, the longer the pears have spent in cold storage, the shorter the ripening period. A pear is fully ripe when the flesh just below the stem yields evenly to gentle pressure.

> **Fresh desserts:** Pears are a favorite for poaching in fruit juice, sugar syrup, or wine (about 45 minutes for peeled, cored halves). Their sensuous curves make them a favorite for baked fruit tarts, and they can also be baked into crisps, quick breads, and coffee cakes. To make baked pears, peel, cut into halves, remove the cores, and fill with a tablespoon of chopped nuts and a sweetener or sweetened soft cheese (such as chèvre or ricotta). Bake, covered, for about 30 minutes at 350°F (180°C). A drizzle of chocolate or caramel goes well with many pear desserts.

Plums

There are basically two types of plums. European plums (dusky blue skin, green flesh) usually are freestones and are the best type for baking and making into desserts. Japanese types are often not freestones and usually more juicy; they are best for eating out of hand.

> **Harvest tips:** Although plums will have the best flavor if left to fully ripen on the tree, you can pick the fruits when they are still slightly firm and store them in a cool place to fully ripen. With blue or purple varieties, the color changes from green to greenish-blue or reddish-purple, then to dark blue or purple. In other varieties, the color proceeds from a yellowish-green to a more definite yellow or straw yellow, and then to their characteristic yellow or red. As the color increases, the flesh becomes slightly soft, especially at the tip end. You can tell when a plum is ripe by applying gentle pressure with your fingers. If the skin of the fruit feels soft, then it is ready to be picked. The plum should come off the tree easily with only a slight twist; if it clings to the stem, it isn't ripe.

> **Handling and short-term storage:** Store plums in open plastic bags in the refrigerator, where they will keep for 2 to 4 weeks.

> **Fresh desserts:** European plums make the best desserts. You can slice European plums and macerate them (sprinkle with sugar and let sit for 30 minutes to draw out the juices; use about 1 tablespoon sugar for every 2 cups slices). Serve in a bowl plain or topped with whipped cream or crème fraîche. Make a plum fool by folding into whipped cream. Serve on top of biscuits (pages 331 and 332) with whipped cream to make plum shortcake. Serve on top of a fresh fruit tart or bake in a coffee cake.

Rhubarb

Technically rhubarb is a vegetable, but it has a low enough pH to be treated as a fruit in terms of canning; plus it is most typically used in pies, dessert sauces, and crisps.

> **Harvest tips:** Rhubarb emerges early in the spring and can be harvested when the stalks are as thick as your thumb. Twist off the stalk, harvesting the outside stalks first. (To keep the plant producing stalks, cut out the seed pods as soon as they form in the center of the plant.) Before taking rhubarb into the house, cut off the leaves, which are poisonous.
> **Handling and short-term storage:** Wrap the stalks, washed or unwashed, in paper towels and store in a plastic bag in the refrigerator for up to 2 weeks.
> **Fresh desserts:** Make rhubarb sauce by slicing the stalks into 1-inch pieces, combining with a little water in a saucepan, and cooking until tender, about 30 minutes. Sweeten to taste with honey, maple syrup, or white or brown sugar. Apple pie spices (cinnamon, nutmeg, ginger, allspice) are all tasty additions. Serve as is, perhaps topped by whipped cream. Use the sauce like applesauce, or to top ice cream and other desserts. Make a rhubarb fool by folding rhubarb sauce into whipped cream. Rhubarb is classically paired with strawberries in pie, in part because strawberries lose a lot of character when baked and rhubarb has an abundance of character.

Strawberries

Strawberries are the most widely grown homestead fruit for good reason. They are delicious and productive, and establishing a bed doesn't require a long-term commitment.

> **Harvest tips:** Generally the fruit ripens about 30 days after blooming. Harvest as soon as the berries taste sweet and are their ripe color. The berries are best picked early in the morning, before they are heated by the sun. Wet berries mold rapidly, so don't pick berries while they are wet from rain — unless you are just popping them straight into your mouth.
> **Handling and short-term storage:** Do not wash or hull the berries until you are ready to eat or freeze them. Best-case scenario: eat or freeze them the same day you pick them. If you need to store the berries for a few days, place them in a

The Fruit Calendar

May to June: Rhubarb, strawberries

May to August: Apricots

May to October: Plums

June: Currants, gooseberries, jostaberries

June to July: Cherries

June to August: Blueberries, blackberries, loganberries

July to September: Peaches, nectarines, figs, melons

July to October: Raspberries

August: Early apples

September to October: Apples, grapes, pawpaws, pears

October: Late apples and pears

November to March: Citrus

single layer on a towel-lined tray in the refrigerator. To keep them for more than a few days, try puréeing the berries with sugar. The sugar should stave off mold for an extra day or so.

> **Fresh desserts:** Combine sliced strawberries with white sugar (1 tablespoon per 2 cups fruit, or more to taste) and let sit for 30 minutes to draw out the juice. Serve as is, or topped with whipped cream. Make a strawberry fool by folding into whipped cream. Serve on top of biscuits (pages 331 and 332) with whipped cream to make strawberry shortcake. Concentric circles of strawberries, pointed tips up, make a dramatic topping for a fresh fruit tart.

Fruit Desserts

Nothing equals biting into a perfect peach you grew yourself, or grabbing a handful of berries off a bush in your own backyard, or inhaling the amazing perfume of a sun-ripened strawberry. And fruit you grew yourself needs no improvement. So for most occasions, a bowl of fruit makes a perfect dessert. In the height of summer, a bowl of berries and another of whipped cream is exceptional. A platter of melon slices is the perfect way to finish a spicy meal. Or you can serve a bowl of peaches or mixed summer fruits, such as peaches, plums, and nectarines. Or it could be a bowl of apples and/or pears. If the fruit is large, offer knives with the dessert plates, so guests can cut off slices to eat.

Whatever the fruit, here are a few handling and processing tips:

> Wash all fruit under cold running water just before using.
> Once peeled, many fruits — including apples, apricots, pears, peaches, and nectarines — will darken. To prevent this, dip the fruits in a bowl of cold water mixed with

lemon juice, using 1 tablespoon lemon juice per 2 cups water.
> Overripe fruit that is soft but still tastes good can be puréed, sweetened with sugar, and frozen to use as a topping for ice cream or pancakes or as a filling for crêpes. You can also purée fruit, punch up the flavor with fruit liqueur (see page 53), and serve as a sauce. The type of fruit liqueur you use doesn't have to match the fruit you are puréeing.
> For an elegant presentation, serve fruit desserts in wine goblets, oversized martini glasses, brandy snifters, or old-fashioned glasses.

Fruit under a Blanket: Crisps, Crumbles, and Cobblers

American recipe collections are filled with variations on a single theme: fresh fruit baked under a topping made with oats (crisps and crumbles) or biscuit dough (cobblers). These simple fruit desserts are made with pantry staples and can be adapted to whatever fruit is on hand. Here's the basic formula.

The Fruit

1. For a dessert to serve six people, measure out 6 cups fresh berries, pitted cherries, or peeled and sliced apples, peaches, pears, plums, or nectarines.

2. Put the fruit in a bowl and sweeten to taste with ¼ to ½ cup white or brown sugar. Let stand for 30 minutes, then transfer the fruit to a colander set over a bowl to catch all the juice that has been pulled from the fruit.

3. Pour the collected fruit juice into a saucepan, bring to a boil, and boil until the juice is reduced to half its original volume.

The Toppings

Prepare one of the following toppings:

CRISP TOPPING #1

- ¾ cup unbleached all-purpose flour
- ¾ cup old-fashioned rolled oats
- 1 teaspoon ground cinnamon
- ½ teaspoon freshly grated nutmeg or ground ginger
- ½ teaspoon salt
- 6 tablespoons butter, diced, at room temperature
- ½ cup maple syrup, honey, apple cider syrup, or firmly packed brown sugar

Combine all the ingredients in a bowl and stir well.

CRISP TOPPING #2

- ½ cup unbleached all-purpose flour
- ½ cup crushed cookies
- ½ cup chopped nuts
- 1 teaspoon ground cinnamon
- ½ cup butter, diced, at room temperature
- ½ cup maple syrup, honey, or firmly packed brown sugar

Combine all the ingredients in a bowl and stir well.

COBBLER TOPPING

- 1 cup unbleached all-purpose flour
- 3 tablespoons sugar
- 1 teaspoon baking powder
- ½ teaspoon salt
- 4 tablespoons butter or lard, chilled and diced
- 5 tablespoons (or more) milk

Combine the flour, sugar, baking powder, and salt in a bowl. Add the butter and cut it into the flour mixture with a pastry blender or two knives. Add 5 tablespoons milk and stir with a fork until the dough comes together, adding up to 1 more tablespoon milk as needed to incorporate all the flour. Turn out onto a lightly floured work surface and knead once or twice. Pat into a round about ½ inch thick. Cut into nine rounds, each about 3 inches in diameter.

To Bake

1. Preheat the oven to 350°F (180°C). Grease an 8-inch or 9-inch square baking pan or a 9-inch or 10-inch deep pie pan.

2. Transfer the fruit from the colander to the baking pan, scraping with a silicone spatula to get all the sweet juices out. Pour the reduced juice over the fruit, again scraping the pan with the spatula.

3. Sprinkle the crisp topping over the fruit, or drop the biscuit dough rounds over the fruit. Bake for 35 to 45 minutes, until the topping is browned and the fruit juices are bubbling. Let cool slightly before serving.

Fresh Fruit Tarts

Fruit tarts are oddly greater than the sum of their parts, and the parts are quite simple: bake a pie crust (see page 333), fill with a simple creamy or chocolate layer (more on that below), top with beautifully arranged fresh fruit, and glaze with a little melted jelly.

The creamy or chocolate layer functions to hold the fruit in place. Here are some choices:

➤ Beat 4 ounces softened cream cheese with ½ cup sugar.
➤ Beat 1 cup mascarpone with ⅓ cup whipped cream and 3 tablespoons sugar.
➤ Beat ½ cup heavy cream to soft peaks, and fold in ½ cup lemon curd.
➤ Melt 3 ounces dark chocolate with 1 tablespoon butter. Pour into tart shell and let set.

Then top with concentric circles of fruit, either whole berries or sliced larger fruits.

Glaze with ⅓ cup apple or currant jelly, heated until melted. For a classic fruit tart filled with pastry cream, see page 323.

Fruit Pies

Fruit pies are tricky for the very simple reason that fruit is never consistent from variety to variety, from season to season, even from week to week. The fruit may yield too much juice because it was a wet growing season or because the fruit is overripe. The fruit may be unusually sweet, unusually dry, or unusually tart. So you can't count on carefully following a single recipe to get the same results each time. In the days when pie was considered a breakfast food, served daily, cooks didn't follow recipes; instead, they judged by taste and eye how much sweetener and how much thickener to add. You can do the same. (For the pie crust recipe, see page 333.)

Thickening the Juices in a Pie

Rose Levy Beranbaum, author of *The Pie and Pastry Bible*, has changed my method of baking pies. She recommends letting the fruit and sugar sit until the sugar pulls all the juice from the fruit (usually about 30 minutes). Then dump the fruit in a colander set over a bowl to separate the fruit and juice. Pour the juice into a saucepan and bring to a boil. Continue to boil until you have reduced the juice to about half its volume. Then add the thickener to the juice and return the juice to the fruit.

Some people prefer to use tapioca to thicken fruit juices in a pie; others prefer flour or cornstarch, which are usually readily at hand. I think a product called ClearJel is the one most likely to yield excellent results each time.

ClearJel is a modified cornstarch that has been in commercial use for more than 30 years. It has only recently become available to home cooks; you are not likely to find it at your local grocery store, but it is readily available from online and mail-order sources. It can be used for both baking and freezing (other starches lose their thickening power when frozen, which is why apple pies are often runny after freezing). ClearJel is the only thickener recommended by the U.S. Department of Agriculture (USDA) for canned pie fillings or canned vegetable relishes. It doesn't break down in the presence of acid. And it doesn't break down as the pie sits. What you see in the first slice of pie is what you will get throughout.

Tips on Using ClearJel

➤ Don't confuse ClearJel with Instant ClearJel, which is used in recipes that are never cooked. ClearJel can be spelled in a variety of ways — Clear Jel, Clearjel, Clear Gel, Cleargel — depending on the manufacturer, but all the names refer to the same basic product. Pectin products, such as Sure-Jell, are not the same thing.

➤ To prevent clumping, combine ClearJel with the sugar or other dry ingredients before adding to liquids or wet solids (like the fruit). However, if you have already combined the fruit and sugar as above, you will need to dissolve the ClearJel in a little cold water, then add it to the fruit.

➤ ClearJel will start to thicken fruit juices as soon as it is heated, but it reaches its maximum thickness upon cooling, and it resists weeping during storage.

➤ If your recipe calls for flour as a thickener, use the same amount of ClearJel, or slightly less. If the recipe calls for cornstarch or tapioca, use slightly less than double the amount of ClearJel.

➤ Fresh fruit needs slightly less ClearJel (or whatever thickener you're using) than frozen fruit.

> When cooking without a specific recipe, vary the amount of ClearJel depending on the juiciness of your fruit. For a typical 9-inch pie:

- **Apple pie:** Use 1 to 2 tablespoons of ClearJel.
- **Berry pie:** Use 3 to 5 tablespoons of ClearJel, depending on the juiciness of the fruit and whether you want the filling to be somewhat runny or very stiff.
- **Peach pie:** Use 2 to 4 tablespoons of ClearJel.

Fruit Sauces

Applesauce is a traditional favorite, but sauces can be made from other fruits, following the same basic method. Pears make a fine sauce, but with a gritty texture that some find off-putting. Rhubarb makes an excellent sauce and breaks down in the cooking process, so no puréeing is necessary. If you remove apple skins before cooking, the applesauce will be yellow; with the skins it will turn pink. The flavor is the same either way. You can also blend apples with other fruits, such as raspberries and blueberries. You can freeze a fruit sauce or can it in a boiling-water bath.

Applesauce

Makes 12 to 13 quarts per bushel (28 pounds)

This recipe scales down easily; it will take less time to cook down if you reduce the amount of apples.

INGREDIENTS

28 pounds apples, quartered
½–1 cup water, apple cider, or other fruit juice
Honey, maple syrup, brown sugar, or white sugar to taste

1. Put the apples in a large heavy pot with the water. You should have about 1 inch of liquid on the bottom — add more if needed. Cover with the lid and simmer over medium heat until very soft, stirring occasionally, 55 to 60 minutes.

2. Run the fruit through a food mill to separate out the seeds and peels.

3. Add sweetener to taste; the sweetness will vary with the tartness of the apples. Don't forget that the sweetener helps preserve the applesauce.

4. You can freeze or can the applesauce. To can in a boiling-water bath (see chapter 11), fill clean hot jars with the hot applesauce, leaving ½ inch of headspace. Process pints for 15 minutes, quarts for 20 minutes.

Note: This recipe makes a smooth sauce. If you want to peel and core your fruit before cooking, you can cook the fruit just enough to break it down, then stop cooking for a chunky sauce.

Fruit Liqueurs

Fruit liqueurs are surprisingly simple to prepare and make excellent presents for the holidays and for hostess gifts. They are served with dessert or after dessert with coffee — with or without ice. They are also used to add fruity flavor to mixed drinks and some baked goods.

Fruit liqueurs are made by steeping any juicy fruit (berries, sliced citrus, peaches, cherries) in vodka with sugar. The longer the fruit steeps, the mellower the flavor, so don't serve it before its time. It will taste better if served from a pretty bottle (don't ask me why), so investigate your options at supply houses for home winemakers. Use either screwtop or corked bottles. A colored glass is better than a clear glass because the color of the liqueur will fade over time if exposed to light.

Homemade Fruit Liqueur

Makes about 4½ cups

The quality of the vodka is not important here, so do your wallet a favor and buy an inexpensive one.

INGREDIENTS

4 cups fresh or frozen, unsweetened fruit
1 (750 ml) bottle vodka
  Spices, such as cinnamon sticks, whole allspice berries, or vanilla bean (optional)
1 cup sugar

1. Prepare the fruit by removing any stems or pits and cutting it into bite-size pieces. (Berries can be left whole.)

2. Put the fruit in a 2-quart canning jar. Add the spice, if using. Add the vodka and sugar. Stir the mixture, and cover with the lid and screwband.

3. Set the container on a shelf, away from heat or sunlight, for at least 6 weeks. Give the jar a shake occasionally. The sugar will not dissolve for a couple of days, but it will eventually.

4. To finish the liqueur, strain the mixture through butter muslin, several layers of cheesecloth, or a paper coffee filter. (Discard the fruit. Theoretically, it can be served on top of ice cream or cake or folded into whipped cream if used within 1 to 2 days, but I think it tastes too strongly of alcohol.) If the liqueur is at all cloudy, strain again using a fresh coffee filter to get a clear liquid with no cloudiness.

5. Pour into clean bottles and cap. The liqueur can be enjoyed immediately but will develop more flavor over the next few months. Fruit liqueurs will begin to lose their bright color and some flavor after 1 year, but they will not go bad because the alcohol is a preservative.

CHAPTER 4

Grains and Beans

Growing your own grain on limited acreage is high-end homesteading, and it's not for everyone. Still, there are homesteaders who do grow grains, especially for their chickens. Other homesteaders buy in bulk what they do not raise themselves. So whether you grow your own or buy from regional growers, you will want to make whole grains an integral part of your cook-it-from-scratch kitchen.

What are grains good for? Obviously, life without cookies isn't unimaginable, but beyond the standard white-flour cookies, cakes, and pies we are all so fond of, whole grains form the basis of inexpensive breakfast cereals and porridges, crackers to match homemade cheese, and artisan breads that do such a good job of mopping up the juices from slow-cooked meats. And beyond breakfast and baked goods, grains can be used to fill in the corners of a meal when meat and vegetables, or vegetables alone, won't satisfy.

Oh, and homegrown grains yield a wonderful by-product for gardeners: weed-free straw, a most excellent mulch.

Dried beans, in contrast, are easily a staple crop for homesteaders. All it takes is a growing season long enough to take a young bean through the shell stage and on to the dried stage, which equates to around 100 frost-free days for most varieties. Drying beans are not a pretty sight in the garden, but the end products are well worth it.

One of the big advantages of growing your own beans is that you can take advantage of growing different heirloom varieties and explore some new and interesting flavors. Plus these are seeds that are very easy to save. Beans don't cross-pollinate, so you don't even have to worry about separating different varieties. Just save the best and earliest-maturing seeds for next year.

All about Grains

Most of us start our days with grain: porridge, granola, pancakes. Even a breakfast of eggs usually includes toast, and there's no toast like the kind from homemade bread. Whether the grain you produce or buy is cracked, rolled, ground into flour, or just threshed and winnowed, the first issue is how to store it.

Storing Grains

Grain needs to be stored, well sealed, where it is cool, dry, and protected from rodents and insects. Depriving the grain of oxygen and heat delays rancidity; depriving it of moisture prevents mold and fungi.

There may already be insects or insect eggs in your grain; this is completely normal and even expected. Bugs aren't an issue when you buy grain in small quantities from your local natural foods store and use it quickly, before anything hatches, but for larger quantities you need to take precaution. You don't want to treat the grain with fungicides and pesticides like many grain mills do. Freezing the grain for 24 hours or heating the grain in the oven for 30 minutes at 140°F (60°C) will take care of the little critters.

Small quantities do well in sealed plastic bags in the freezer. Small quantities also do well in vacuum-sealed canning jars (see page 6), if stored away from heat and light. Four-gallon buckets with lids that seal (which metal garbage cans do not have) are good for storing large quantities, particularly if you keep them in a cool basement or an unheated attic. A 4-gallon bucket will hold about 20 pounds of grain. If the bucket is plastic, make sure it is made with (or lined with) "food-safe" plastic. (Good sources for free or inexpensive, odor-free buckets are bakeries and supermarkets, which get some of their raw materials in them.) Packets of oxygen absorbers, like those you have probably seen packaged with snack foods or crackers, are easily found online and can be put in the buckets to absorb oxygen, thereby delaying deterioration in the grain or its nutrient value.

Longevity

How long to store whole grains is a subject about which there is little agreement. According to the folks at Bob's Red Mill, you can expect whole grains to last at least 2 years. The Whole Grains Council, however, suggests that whole grains last only 4 to 6 months at room temperature and 6 to 12 months in the freezer. Factor in the freshness of your homegrown grains, and perhaps you can rely on the most optimistic shelf-life statistics, but only if you are providing optimum storage conditions in a sealed container in a dark, cool location. Once you have ground your whole grains into flour, the shelf life is diminished.

Rancidity

What does it mean when grain "goes bad"? Obviously, if it is crawling with bugs or has clumps of mold, it should be discarded. Rancidity is more subtle. The aroma and flavor of rancid grain are best described as sharp or bitter. Depending on how sensitive your nose or palate is, you may or may not notice the rancidity; in my household, my husband detects rancidity in nuts, oils, and grains well before I do.

When a grain is rancid, it means that the oils naturally occurring in the grain have broken down and formed different chemical compounds, some of which are potentially toxic and have been linked to advanced aging, neurological disorders, heart disease, and cancer. Vitamins are destroyed by rancidity. While you may be tempted to use up whole grains that are showing signs of rancidity, wishing to be frugal and thinking you can mask the bitter flavors, you will be doing everyone a favor if you compost them instead.

Heat, light, and oxygen hasten rancidity, and susceptible foods should be stored in the refrigerator or freezer, in tightly shut, opaque containers. A cool basement or attic can also be used. Containers should be dated with time of purchase or harvest.

Natural Insect Control

The last thing you want to deal with is flour weevils or pantry moths in your homegrown grain. Keeping your cupboards clean and free of crumbs or loose grains is your first line of defense. Tucking bay leaves in your grain containers and pantry shelves may provide additional defense.

Grinding Whole Grains

Some grains, such as oats, rice, and quinoa, you'll use whole. But for most baking, you need flour, and that means grinding the whole grain. You'll find that freshly ground flour has more flavor and is sweeter than previously ground flour, but it does take some work.

If you want to take the route of grinding as you go instead of buying preground flour, be aware that hand-cranked grinders take muscle and time — 8 to 10 minutes of vigorous cranking to grind 1 cup of whole grains (which is why inventive people have been known to hook up their grinders to stationary bicycles). By contrast, an electric grinder will do the same amount of work in about 1 minute, though the noise is considerable — about as loud as a tractor lawn mower.

Generally speaking, 1 cup of whole grains, such as wheat berries, will yield 1½ cups of whole-grain flour. This may seem counterintuitive, but air is introduced into the flour as the grain is ground, and this accounts for the increased volume. You then may want to sift out the bran to make white flour, in which case your yield is somewhat reduced in weight, but not in volume because more air is introduced by sifting.

To adapt tried-and-true recipes for the use of freshly ground flour, consider using weights instead of volume measures. One cup of supermarket all-purpose flour weighs about 4.25 ounces. To substitute home-ground flour, weigh out the equivalent on a kitchen scale.

One advantage of owning a grinder is that it will allow you to make cracked wheat or rye berries. You can then fold these cracked grains into bread doughs for interesting crunch and flavor, or you can make them into porridge. The "lazy" overnight method described on page 58 works well with cracked grains.

Cooking Whole Grains

Whole grains can be cooked on top of the stove to make a starchy side dish. There's nothing complicated about cooking whole grains. When in doubt, cook like pasta: boil the grains in a large pot of salted water. Indeed, you can cook any grain, including rice, this way. Many restaurants employ this method to partially cook grains, then finish the grains

Hand-grinders take time and energy. Electric grinders are more expensive and very noisy.

in a quickly cooked-to-order pilaf or risotto. However, the cooking water you drain off does contain the grain's water-soluble vitamins. The preferred method of cooking is steaming. Alternatively, you can cook the grain into a pilaf or risotto, which can be either a side dish or the main course. When cooking grains so that all the cooking liquid is absorbed, you can use either plain water, salted water, stock, or broth. When cooking rice to complement an Asian meal, I always use plain water because the stir-fry or sauce I serve with the rice will be highly seasoned and well salted, and more salt isn't desirable. When I am making a pilaf or risotto, I usually use stock (unsalted broth) to impart more flavor and add salt to taste before serving.

When cooking grains, figure that ¼ cup of uncooked grain makes ½ cup of cooked grain. In general, ½ cup cooked grains is a side-dish serving and 1 cup cooked grains plus a generous amount of vegetables and/or meat or fish is a main-dish serving.

Boiling Method

1. Bring a large pot of salted or unsalted water to a boil.

2. Add grain. There's no need to measure; just make sure there is enough room in the pot for the amount of grain you want.

3. Boil until al dente — that is, tender but not mushy. (See the chart on page 59 to gauge the approximate timing.) Drain.

Steaming Method

1. Combine 1 cup grains with 1¼ to 3 cups unsalted water, salted water, or seasoned broth in a saucepan and bring to a boil. (The amount of liquid will depend on the grain you're using; see the chart on page 59.)

2. Cover, reduce the heat to low, and simmer until all the water is absorbed and the grain is tender. (Again, see the chart on page 59 to gauge the approximate timing.)

3. Remove the lid and wipe it dry. Fluff the grain with a fork, cover again, and let it sit off the heat for 5 to 10 minutes.

Pilaf

1. Heat 3 tablespoons of any animal fat or oil in a saucepan or skillet.

2. Add spices (such as chili powder or curry powder) and finely diced aromatic vegetables (onion, celery, carrots, mushrooms, sweet peppers, chiles, and/or garlic) and sauté for 1 to 2 minutes, until fragrant. Optional: add diced or cubed meat, cooked or raw, and brown for 3 minutes.

3. Add 1 cup grains and continue to sauté until the grains are coated in oil.

4. Add 1¼ to 3 cups broth or stock and bring to a boil. (The amount of liquid will depend on the grain you're using; see the chart on page 59.) If you are making tomato rice, add the tomatoes at this point, decreasing the amount of broth or stock you are adding by the amount of liquid you can squeeze from the tomatoes.

5. Cover, reduce the heat to low, and cook until all the liquid is absorbed and the grain is tender. (Again, see the chart on page 59 to gauge the approximate timing.)

6. If you like, stir in fresh, blanched, or thawed frozen vegetables, in bite-size pieces, such as peas, green beans, Swiss chard, spinach, or broccoli. You can also stir in fresh herbs at this time. Season to taste with salt and pepper.

Risotto

1. Blanch 4 cups diced vegetables until just barely tender (see the chart on page 160 to gauge the approximate timing) and drain, or sauté in butter, animal fat, or oil until just wilted. Set aside. Optional: add diced or cubed meat or fish, cooked or raw, and brown for 3 minutes.

2. Heat 5½ cups high-quality vegetable stock (page 37) or unsalted poultry stock (page 107) and ½ cup dry white wine until simmering.

3. Heat 3 tablespoons of any animal fat or extra-virgin olive oil in a large skillet over medium-high heat. Reduce the heat to medium and add 2 minced shallots, 2 minced garlic cloves, and 2 cups arborio rice.

4. Add 1 cup of the simmering stock to the rice and stir until the liquid is mostly absorbed. Continue adding more stock, 1 cup at a time, stirring as the liquid is absorbed. It will take a total of 20 to 30 minutes for all of the liquid to be absorbed and the rice to become tender and creamy.

5. Stir in the vegetables and allow to heat through. Stir in 2 to 3 tablespoons chopped fresh herbs or pesto, 2 tablespoons butter, and ¼ to ½ cup freshly grated Parmesan cheese. Season generously with salt and pepper to taste. Serve immediately.

Lazy Overnight Method

This method only works with cracked wheat berries or steel-cut oats; it doesn't work with whole grains. Less starch is released, so the texture is less creamy and more pebble-like than regular oatmeal or cooked wheat cereal. Everyone who tastes oatmeal made this way loves it. I love it for its flavor, texture, and convenience.

1. Combine 1 cup grain with 2 to 4 cups salted water. (The amount of liquid will depend on the grain you're using; see the chart at right.)

2. Bring to a boil in a covered saucepan.

3. Turn off the heat and let it sit overnight.

4. In the morning, reheat on top of the stove or in a microwave. Store any leftovers in the refrigerator.

Tips for Cooking with Grains

> Cooking times may vary depending on the age of the grain, the variety, and the pans you're using.

> Cooking times for whole grains (such as wheat berries, unhulled barley, kamut, and spelt berries) can be reduced by soaking the grains overnight in water to cover by 2 inches. Drain and cook with fresh water.

> If the grain is not as tender as you would like when the cooking time is up, simply add more water and continue cooking. On the other hand, if the grain becomes tender before all the liquid is absorbed, simply drain the excess.

> You can cook grains in advance and store them in the refrigerator for 3 to 4 days, then reheat with a little water or stock.

> Cooked grains can form the basis of a salad, with the addition of chopped veggies and a vinaigrette dressing.

> Cooked grains, reheated with a little milk (dairy, nut, or soy) and sweetened to taste, make a delicious hot breakfast cereal.

> Everything tastes better with butter. When serving a plain grain as a side dish, be generous with butter and salt. Just as buttered rice is tastier than plain rice, buttered millet and quinoa are tastier than those same grains served plain.

Cooking Grains

Grain (1 cup)	Water or Stock	Cooking Time	Yield
Amaranth	2 cups	20–25 minutes	3 cups
Barley, hulled	3 cups	45–60 minutes	3½ cups
Buckwheat*	2 cups	20 minutes	4 cups
Bulgur	2 cups	10–12 minutes	3 cups
Cornmeal (polenta)	4 cups	25–30 minutes	2½ cups
Farro, pearled	2½ cups	25–40 minutes	3 cups
Kamut (soaked overnight)	4 cups	45–60 minutes	3 cups
Millet, hulled	2½ cups	25–30 minutes	4 cups
Oats, steel-cut	3–4 cups	20–30 minutes	3–4 cups
Quinoa	2 cups	12–15 minutes	3 cups
Rice, brown	2½ cups	25–45 minutes (varies)	3 cups
Rye berries (soaked overnight)	4 cups	45–60 minutes	3 cups
Sorghum	4 cups	25–40 minutes	3 cups
Spelt berries (soaked overnight)	4 cups	45–60 minutes	3 cups
Wheat berries (soaked overnight)	4 cups	45–60 minutes	2½ cups
Wild rice	3 cups	45–55 minutes	3½ cups

*Benefits from being cooked pilaf-style.

Making Bread

Bread is either cheap (soft, squishy supermarket loaves) or expensive (artisan bakery loaves). But it's necessary. A good loaf of bread makes a meal out of salad, soup, scrambled eggs, or just an assortment of veggies. And who doesn't crave a nice hunk of bread to sop up that last drop of gravy or tomato juices mingled with olive oil and vinegar? A stack of toast and a cup of hot cocoa takes the sting out of miserable weather and emotional storms.

When I started baking bread, I developed a sandwich loaf that pleased the household, but I am still working on my artisan loaf. The pursuit of the artisan loaf has led some bakers to extremes — like pilgrimages to France and building brick ovens in the backyard, not to mention that extensive Internet chatter. So let's just accept that the pursuit of the perfect loaf is a lifelong challenge.

What's an artisan loaf? It is basically a bread made of flour, water, salt, and either sourdough starter or yeast. It has been allowed to rise slowly, over the course of 12 to 18 hours. It has a very large crumb (lots of airholes) and a solid crust. It is baked on a stone or a baking sheet, within the generous confines of a Dutch oven, or in a baguette pan — and never in a loaf pan.

What follows is my method, tested in my household over time. There is much

Bread Is the Staff of Life

Bread can be the foundation of very simple vegetable feasts. Here are some menu ideas that begin with two slices of toast on a plate. Rub the toasted bread with a sliced clove of garlic for even more flavor.

- **Asparagus.** Steam, roast, or grill the asparagus. Place it on the toast. Top with two sunny-side-up or poached eggs (page 87). Garnish with shaved Parmesan, crumbled bacon (page 253), and hollandaise sauce (page 34) or cheese sauce (page 34).

- **Eggplant.** Brush slices of eggplant with olive oil and grill or broil until tender. Layer on toast with sliced tomatoes or tomato sauce, mozzarella (page 243), and basil.

- **Ratatouille.** Spoon ratatouille onto toast and top with two sunny-side-up or poached eggs (page 87). Garnish with shaved Parmesan.

- **Tomatoes.** Dice the tomatoes and combine with olive oil, vinegar, finely chopped basil, garlic, and salt and pepper. Let sit for at least 30 minutes before spooning onto toast with a slotted spoon. If you like, top with fresh mozzarella (page 243) or shaved Parmesan.

- **Roasted fall vegetables.** Dice any combination of root vegetables and winter squash. Toss with olive oil and roast for about 40 minutes at 425°F (220°C). Spoon onto the toast. Top with two sunny-side-up or poached eggs (page 87). Drizzle with maple syrup or a reduction of balsamic vinegar.

- **Cabbage and onion.** Thinly slice some cabbage and onion. (Note that the cabbage will wilt down, so slice more than you think you need.) Cook slowly in butter, olive oil, bacon fat, or chicken fat over medium heat until the vegetables are golden and all wilted, 15 to 20 minutes. Spoon onto the toast and top with crumbles of fresh goat cheese or other grated cheese.

- **Beans.** The Brits made beans and toast famous, and insist on Heinz pork and beans. But any nicely seasoned beans make a fine supper on toast.

written about bread baking: many fine books, much useful Internet chatter, and just as much widely disseminated myths and falsehoods. Mine is not the only way to bake, but it should help you get started on the path to a good loaf.

Sourdough Starter

Sourdough bread begins with sourdough starter, a culture of yeasts and bacteria that you will feed and nurture to keep alive. Like any other bread yeast, this starter provides leavening. I prefer sourdough over traditional bread yeasts because it also gives my breads flavor — and I don't even like classic sourdough! Or so I used to think. The name *sourdough* is a misnomer because many sourdough cultures don't taste the least bit sour. My breads don't taste at all sour until they are a few days old, and they usually are eaten far sooner than that.

Keeping a sourdough starter alive is not that demanding, though it does take up refrigerator space (in the winter, I keep mine in my root cellar). If you bake with the sourdough starter at least every 2 weeks, you can keep it alive indefinitely. And even if you don't bake that often, as long as you feed it every 2 weeks, the starter will thrive indefinitely. Unless the starter turns black, it can be revived.

Sourdough Starter

This sourdough starter can be used to add flavor and leavening to bread (page 64), pizza crusts (page 283), pancakes (page 266), waffles (page 267), biscuits (page 332), cakes, muffins, doughnuts, and crackers. You'll want a large container with a lid for storing it; I prefer a 2-quart glass canning jar with a plastic lid.

INGREDIENTS

2 cups all-purpose flour
2 teaspoons sugar
1 packet (2¼ teaspoons) active dry yeast
2 cups warm water (105°–115°F/41°–46°C)

1. Mix the flour, sugar, and yeast together in a clean 2-quart canning jar. Gradually stir in the water and mix until it forms a thick, fairly smooth batter.

2. Cover the container with a kitchen towel and set it in a warm, draft-free place, preferably at around 70°F (21°C). Temperatures above 100°F (38°C) will kill the yeast. Let sit for 2 to 5 days, stirring it once a day. The mixture should bubble as it ferments. (This will foam up quite a bit, hence the large canning jar.) The starter is ready when it develops a pleasant sour smell and looks bubbly.

3. Your starter is now ready to use. Store it in the refrigerator with the lid screwed on just lightly, so developing gases can escape. You will need to feed the starter regularly to keep it alive. (Regularly means at least every 2 weeks, but the more frequently you feed your sourdough starter, the more active it will be and the shorter the time it will need to rise in a dough.)

Ripe, bubbly starter ready for use

Feeding Your Sourdough Starter

Your starter should be fed every 12 hours if left sitting on the counter, or every time you remove some sourdough starter to bake with. If you aren't baking regularly and store your starter in the refrigerator, try to feed it once a week, but every 2 weeks should be good enough.

While the sourdough sits, yeasts and bacteria become active, digesting the starch in the sourdough and releasing carbon dioxide, alcohol, and acetic or lactic acid, depending on the bacteria that have colonized your starter. Commonly called *hooch*, alcohol and acid accumulate as a liquid layer on top of the starter. Some sources will tell you to pour off the hooch; some will tell you to pour it off only if it smells offensive. I stir mine in and think it contributes to the flavor of the bread and the texture of the dough.

Begin by stirring in the hooch; then remove about 2 cups of starter. You can use this starter to make a fresh batch of bread or another baked item, give it to a friend to start his or her own culture, feed it to your chickens or pigs, or compost it.

Replace the starter you removed with an equal amount of water plus flour — that is, 1 cup water plus 1 cup flour. Mix well. If your starter immediately becomes bubbly, just cover it and return it to the refrigerator or cool spot. If it acts sluggish, let it sit out for a few hours, and make sure it becomes active again before storing it.

Sourdough and Metals

Many older books about sourdough (and those cookbooks and Internet blogs that just repeat old myths) warn readers never to use metal utensils or metal mixing bowls with sourdough. That advice comes from before the age of stainless steel, which is fine to use with sourdough. Sourdough is corrosive, though, so it's a good idea to store it in a glass jar. I use a plastic cap on my starter jar. These are caps that fit canning jars but are meant to be used after the jar has been processed, stored, and opened. They cannot be used for canning.

Sourdough Starter Math

Most masters of sourdough will tell you to feed your starter with equal weights of water and flour, which turns out to be about ⅔ to ¾ cup of water for every 1 cup of flour. It makes a drier starter but is perfectly fine. My recipes have been developed for a looser, wetter starter. How loose? It is a somewhat ropy, gloopy, pourable batter.

Reviving a Neglected Starter

My sourdough came to me from my friend Jane Eddy, potter, artist, quilter, gardener, mother, and grandmother. She got it from Cushman Anthony in 1966 in Ann Arbor, Michigan, where her husband, Marshall, was a law student with Anthony. The sourdough, meanwhile, came to Anthony from his neighbor in Ann Arbor, who got it from his father, a fish and wildlife warden in Alaska. His father got the sourdough from his secretary, who got it from her grandfather, who was one of the original "sourdoughs" in the Klondike Gold Rush of 1896.

Along the years, Jane became lax about feeding the starter — and this will happen to you, too — but she was always able to revive it.

If your starter hasn't been fed in a while (longer than 2 weeks), wake it up by bringing it to room temperature and feeding it every 12 hours for 2 days or more, until it gets nice and bubbly again. Keep it out on the counter and feed it twice daily, removing 1 cup of starter each time. You can compost the starter you remove or use it for baking. (If the starter remains sluggish, give it a boost with a little active dry yeast.)

Once the starter is revived (active and bubbly), store it in the refrigerator and feed again within 1 week.

Growing the Gift of a Starter

If someone gives you a cup of sourdough starter, you'll need to grow it if you want to continue to use it. Feed it 1 cup of flour and 1 cup of water once a day for 2 or 3 days — without removing any, as you would if you were simply reviving your starter — and you will then have an adequate amount.

No-Knead Sourdough: One Dough, Many Forms

A few years back, a recipe from well-regarded food writer Mark Bittman and a best-selling bread book with the words *Five Minutes* in its title put no-knead breads into the consciousness of American bakers. Meanwhile, a lively Internet community has been exploring no-knead breads,

mostly under the name *artisan*, for years. No matter what you call it, these rustic loaves have a large crumb, big open holes, and a chewy texture and are about as close to a professional artisan loaf as you can get in a home kitchen with a modest amount of equipment.

I have played around with many different formulas and recipes, and I think that the flavor of the artisan loaf is lacking unless a sourdough starter is used. So this is my formula, based on the work of many others.

If you have ever made a loaf of bread that requires kneading, it may take you a while to get the hang of this style of bread making. Basically, you are making a very slack dough, one you couldn't knead if you tried.

The following recipe allows you to make a dough that is relatively easy to handle. In general, the wetter the dough, the bigger the air holes in the loaf will be. On the other hand, a drier dough is easier to handle and will rise more in the oven, making a rounder rather than a flatter loaf. You can adjust the amount of water and flour to get the consistency that suits you best. You can use up to half whole-wheat flour or rye flour instead of all white flour, but I recommend starting with white bread flour until you get some experience handling this dough.

I make the dough sometime after dinner, at night. My flour comes out of the freezer, and my starter comes out of the refrigerator or cool root cellar. (If I wanted to cut down on the rising time, I would bring both to room temperature before mixing.) I leave the dough on the kitchen counter overnight. The next day, I bake it when convenient, usually in the afternoon. The dough needs a 12- to 18-hour rise in order to develop enough flavor and a light texture. You can slow things down by letting it rise in the refrigerator for 48 hours or more. (I haven't pushed it to the limit, so I don't know what the limit is.)

My first attempts with this bread made a ciabatta (translates from the Italian as "slipper") that I baked in a preheated Dutch oven. Once I got the hang of handling the dough gently to avoid degassing it, I was making boules, nice round loaves. Instead of the Dutch oven, you can also use a preheated baking stone or baking sheet, in which case your loaf will spread out and be a ciabatta rather than a boule. You can also shape the dough into two baguettes and bake them in a baguette pan, which is perforated to encourage a crustier finish. Or you can form the dough into dinner rolls and bake on a baking sheet. There are lots of options.

STEP-BY-STEP How to Make the Basic No-Knead Bread

This is the bread that is worthy of sopping up the juices from your best grass-fed beef or pastured pork or chicken roasts and stews. Toasted, it is the reason you slaved over a hot stove to put up all those jams last summer. It makes the perfect base for serving your homemade pâtés (pages 294 and 295) and cheeses (see chapter 15). Really, no homestead is complete without great bread, and this one is a winner.

The instructions that follow call for a flexible plastic tool known as a bowl scraper. There are probably a dozen ways to improvise one (including using a silicone spatula instead), but the scraper is handy and inexpensive. It is used to coax the wet dough out of the bowl in which it rose. You want to coax the dough, not dump it, because you want the dough to retain as much gas as possible. Traditionally, artisan loafs are proofed in a woven basket called a banneton. The banneton imparts a distinct pattern on the loaf, but because my method involves letting the dough proof on parchment paper and transferring the dough still on the paper into a Dutch oven, the pattern won't be seen. Therefore, a bowl works as well as a basket.

This loaf is baked in a preheated Dutch oven. Variations follow for turning the dough into baguettes and dinner rolls.

INGREDIENTS

2 cups sourdough starter (page 61)

2 cups white bread flour

2 teaspoons salt

About ⅓ cup water

① **Mix the dough.** Pour the sourdough starter into a large bowl. Add the flour and salt. Stir until all the flour is moistened and incorporated into the dough, adding up to ⅓ cup water, as needed. The amount of water you will use won't be the same each time because the sourdough starter will be thinner or thicker depending on ambient temperatures, whether or not you stir in the hooch (I always do), the moisture content of the flour, and other variables. The mixing should take only a minute or so. The dough is finished when all the flour has been incorporated and the dough is a loose, shaggy ball. Cover with plastic wrap; the long rise will result in a dry skin on the dough if you use a towel instead of the plastic wrap.

The dough looks shaggy and wet.

② **Let rise.** Set aside to rise for 12 to 18 hours. The dough should increase in size and may develop bubbles on its surface. You can leave it at this stage to let it develop more flavor, or you can bake it.

Overnight the dough relaxes and expands in volume.

③ **Shape the loaf.** Place a bowl and a sheet of parchment paper on the counter. Spread a few tablespoons of flour on a work surface. Remove the plastic wrap from the dough and set aside. Using a bowl scraper, turn the dough out onto the floured surface . Make a very rough ball by folding in first one side of the dough, then the other side, then the top, then the bottom. This should take only a minute; don't handle the dough more than that. If the dough sticks to the work surface, use the bowl scraper to lift it up.

Fold in the top, then the bottom.

Fold in the sides.

④ **Proof the dough.** The dough will benefit from another short rise. Place the dough on the parchment paper, seam-side down. Lift up the paper and ease it into a banneton or bowl. Cover with the plastic wrap and let rise for about 30 minutes.

Proof in a parchment paper-lined bowl.

⑤ **Preheat the oven and pan.** When you are ready to bake, put a cast-iron Dutch oven in the oven and begin preheating to 500°F (260°C).

How to Make the Basic No-Knead Bread *continued*

⑥ **Transfer the dough to the pan.** When the oven is preheated, remove the Dutch oven. Remove the plastic wrap from the dough. Lift up the parchment paper that holds the dough and gently ease it into the preheated Dutch oven. With a very sharp knife, score a deep *X* in the top of the loaf. If you like, spray the dough with water to make the crust crisper. Cover the Dutch oven with the lid.

Preheated
Dutch oven

Loaf is moved still on
the parchment paper.

⑦ **Bake.** Bake for 30 minutes. Then reduce the oven temperature to 400°F (200°C) and remove the lid from the Dutch oven. Continue baking for another 20 minutes, until the bread is browned; it should register 190°F (88°C) on an instant-read thermometer.

⑧ **Cool.** Turn the bread out of the Dutch oven and let cool completely on a wire rack before slicing. (If you slice the bread while still warm, it will develop a gummy texture.)

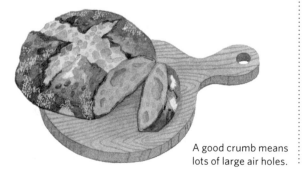

A good crumb means
lots of large air holes.

Variation: Baguettes

Same dough, different outcome. Since I lack the steam-injected ovens of commercial bakeries, I admit the crust is a bit on the soft side. But on the inside, the open texture and terrific flavor are serious compensation. A baguette pan, made of perforated metal, is designed to hold two or three baguettes and results in a superior crust, but a half-sheet pan can be used.

① **Prepare the dough and let rise.** This step is the same as for basic no-knead bread.

② **Prepare the pan.** Brush your baguette pan with oil, or spray with nonstick cooking spray, and sprinkle with cornmeal. (The dough is too wet to rely on a pan's nonstick coating.) If you aren't using a baguette pan, set out a piece of parchment paper a few inches wider than a half-sheet pan. Spread 2 to 3 table-spoons of flour on a work surface.

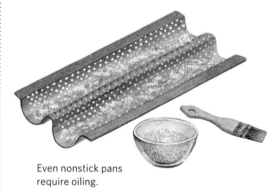

Even nonstick pans
require oiling.

③ **Shape the dough.** Remove the plastic wrap from the bowl of dough and set aside. Using a bowl scraper, coax the dough out of the bowl and onto the floured surface. Divide the dough ball in half. If the dough is very wet, sprinkle additional flour on the dough — just enough to make it possible to handle it. Take half the dough and form it into a rectangle about 16 inches long. Starting from one of the long sides, roll the dough to form a thick rope, coaxing the dough from the work surface with the bowl scraper and/or adding additional flour as needed. Transfer to the prepared pan or parchment paper, seam-side down. Do this quickly so that the dough doesn't stretch very much. Repeat with the second ball of dough, and place the rolled loaf as far as possible from the first loaf for the best air circulation. (This is possible only with a three-loaf pan.) If your loaves are not in a baguette pan, make a pleat in the middle of the parchment paper to draw the loaves a little closer. Then roll up two kitchen towels and place them on either side of the baguettes to keep them from spreading as they proof.

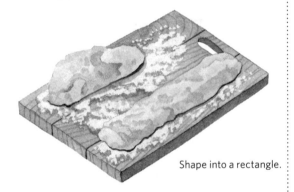

Shape into a rectangle.

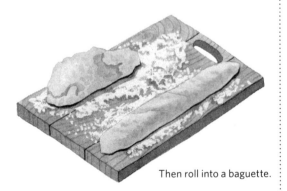

Then roll into a baguette.

④ **Proof the loaves and prepare the oven.**
Cover the loaves with the reserved plastic wrap and let rise for about 30 minutes. When you are ready to bake, put a metal roasting pan or cast-iron skillet in the bottom of the oven. (Once the bread is in the oven, you will add ice cubes to the pan to generate steam.) If you will be baking on a baking sheet, set it upside down on the middle rack in the oven. If you are baking on a baking stone, set it right side up on the middle rack of the oven. Begin preheating the oven to 500°F (260°C).

Towels prevent loaves
from spreading.

⑤ **Bake.** When the oven has preheated, prepare to start baking; the loaves will continue to rise in the oven. Measure out about 1 cup of ice cubes. Have your spray bottle handy. With a sharp knife, slash down the length of each loaf about 1 inch deep. Stick the baguette pan in the oven, or slide the parchment paper with the two loaves onto a peel

Ice creates steam.

or an upside-down baking sheet, and from there slide the parchment paper onto the upside-down baking sheet or baking stone in the middle of the oven. Throw the ice cubes into the skillet and spray water on the loaves. Quickly shut the oven door. Bake for about 20 minutes, until well browned, turning the pan midway for even baking.

⑦ **Cool.** Let cool completely on a wire rack before slicing.

Remove the loaves from the pan and cool on a wire rack.

Variation: Dinner Rolls

① **Prepare the dough.** Prepare the dough and let rise as for the basic no-knead bread.

② **Shape into rolls.** Divide the dough into 8 to 10 equal-size pieces and form each into a ball. Place seam-side down on a sheet of parchment paper.

Handle the dough as little as possible to form rolls.

③ **Preheat the oven.** Set a large baking sheet upside down on the middle rack in the oven. Preheat the oven to 500°F (260°C).

④ **Bake.** When the oven is preheated, use a pair of scissors to cut an X into the top of each roll. If you like, brush with an egg wash (1 egg beaten with 1 tablespoon milk or water) and sprinkle with poppy seeds or sesame seeds. Slide the parchment paper onto the preheated baking sheet as described for the baguettes (page 67), and bake for about 25 minutes, until browned.

Cut an X on the top of each roll with either a knife or a pair of kitchen scissors.

Granola

Homemade granola is to store-bought granola as homemade bread is to store-bought bread. Unless you can buy directly from a bakery that specializes in small-batch granola, your homemade granola will be better because it is fresher and because it is sweetened to the degree you want and baked to the doneness you want. This may take a small amount of practice and negotiation with other family members. (I like my granola a tad darker and a tad sweeter than my husband does, but mostly we get along.)

Oats form the basis of most granolas, but wheat flakes and/or barley flakes are fine to substitute for part or all of the oats. Nuts and seeds form the next greatest amount and add a lot of interest to the mix. Of course, if you are allergic to nuts, you can enjoy an entirely nut-free version; just substitute an equal amount of grain. As for types of nuts and seeds, I have a strong preference for almonds, hazelnuts, sunflower seeds, and pumpkin seeds because I think they have the best texture once toasted; I avoid walnuts and pecans. Shredded dried coconut can be part of the nuts-and-seeds component; for good or bad, it tends to be a dominating flavor. I often throw in ground or whole flaxseed and wheat

You'll find a recipe for Vanilla Nut Granola on page 265.

STEP-BY-STEP **How to Make Granola**

You'll find a recipe for Vanilla Nut Granola on page 265. The formula here is more general and will help you develop your own household-favorite granola recipe.

INGREDIENTS

5–6 cups rolled oats or other flaked grains

2 cups nuts and seeds

½–1 teaspoon salt

Spices (1 teaspoon ground cinnamon; ½ teaspoon ground ginger, ground cloves, freshly grated nutmeg, or whatever other spices you prefer)

¾ cup honey, maple syrup, or apple cider syrup (page 82)

½ cup melted coconut oil or other neutral oil, such as canola or sunflower oil

1 teaspoon vanilla extract (optional)

① **Preheat the oven and prepare the pan.** Preheat the oven to 300°F (150°C). Lightly oil a half-sheet pan or a large or shallow roasting pan, or line with parchment paper. (Using parchment paper makes cleanup easier but reduces the amount of clusters formed.)

② **Mix.** In a large bowl, combine the grains, nuts, salt, and spices. Combine the honey and oil in a small bowl, and heat in the microwave for about 1 minute, or heat by setting the bowl in a small saucepan filled with hot water and heating gently for a few minutes. When the mixture is entirely liquid and warm to the touch, stir in the vanilla (if using). Stir into the grain and nut mixture and mix well. Spread evenly in the prepared pan.

③ **Bake.** Bake, stirring occasionally, for 40 to 45 minutes, until golden. Do not let the granola become dark; stir frequently during the final 15 minutes to avoid scorching at the sides of the pan.

④ **Cool and store.** Remove from the oven. For easier cleanup, if you haven't used parchment paper, run a spatula under the mixture so that it is loose and not sticking to the pan; for more clusters, do not disturb. Allow to cool completely. Store in an airtight container. Granola will keep for a month or more, but it tastes best the first week.

germ for their nutritional contributions. I do not add dried fruit in advance. If toasted with the grains, the fruit becomes miserable, hard, stick-to-your-teeth morsels. When added after toasting, the fruit tends to dry out in storage (though not as much). It is easy to add as desired when serving.

I like to use coconut oil, which gives a faint coconut flavor to the granola, but any neutral-tasting oil works. If you skimp on the oil, the granola will be less crisp and less likely to form delicious, crunchy nuggets. For sweeteners, honey, maple syrup, and apple cider syrup (page 82) all work well. Honey has a slight edge for producing those yummy grain-and-nut clusters. To maximize the yummy clusters, do not disturb the granola as it cools on the baking sheet.

Granola without salt tastes flat to me. I love salty-sweet contrasts, so I use a good ½ teaspoon of salt per quart of granola, but you can use less. Other flavorings to consider include vanilla extract or other flavor extracts, ground cinnamon, or other sweet spices, such as ground ginger, ground cloves, or freshly grated nutmeg.

Dried Beans

Dried beans (and I include peas and lentils in this category) are a homestead staple for good reason: they provide inexpensive protein, can be enjoyed in myriad ways, and store well. A dish of dried beans cooked with a bit of meat — perhaps a tough cut that requires lots of cooking, like ham hocks or beef or pork shanks — or lavished with butter (in the case of lentils) can easily become a family favorite that you turn to often to stretch the budget, to make good use of odd cuts of meat, or simply to make a satisfying, hearty meal.

Getting Beans Ready for Storage

When the beans come into the kitchen after being threshed (separated from the pods) and winnowed (separated from the debris), they still need to be sorted. Among the good beans you will find still more debris, stones, and broken, misshapen, or otherwise unacceptable beans. This is no time to be frugal; some of those beans will have an unpleasant flavor, so the next step is sorting. Oh, and those subpar beans can be fed to livestock, as long as they aren't rotten.

The easiest way to do the sort is to lay a white sheet on your kitchen table and spread out the beans there. The sheet makes it easy to roll the beans around, allowing you to check them carefully. Divide them into two bowls — a big bowl for the good ones, a small bowl for the bad ones. If the beans are soft (bite one and see), continue drying them until they feel firm to the bite before moving them to storage.

good beans

discards

The discarded beans are broken or misshapen. Also, expect to find pebbles and other debris to discard.

Bean Storage and Preservation

Taking precautions against an insect infestation, particularly bean weevils, is a good idea, especially if you have harvested more beans than you will consume in 2 to 4 months. Give the beans 24 hours in a freezer to kill the potential pests. Alternatively, spread the beans out on a half-sheet pan in a layer less than 2 inches deep and heat for 30 minutes at the lowest setting of your oven.

Store dried beans in a dry, cool, airtight container away from sunlight. Beans are best used within 9 to 12 months of harvest. But they will last for years if needed; they will just take longer to cook. And, incidentally, if you are buying dried beans, try to buy the beans where there is a good turnover of stock, and don't buy more than you will use in a year.

Cooking Dried Beans

Dried beans benefit tremendously from a presoak; it cuts the cooking time down considerably. Lentils and split peas, however, are never presoaked. There are two methods of soaking:

> **Overnight soak.** Put the dried beans in a large bowl. Add water to cover by at least 2 inches. Leave for 8 hours,

Cooking Beans

The cooking times given here are for presoaked beans (with the exception of lentils and split peas, which require no presoaking). Figure that 1 pound of dried beans (about 2½ cups uncooked) will yield about 5½ to 6½ cups cooked. The older the beans, the longer the cooking time.

Bean	Cooking Time
Black beans	1 to 1½ hours
Black-eyed peas	30 to 45 minutes
Cannellini	1 to 1½ hours
Chickpeas	2 to 2½ hours
Cranberry beans (borlotti beans)	40 to 45 minutes
Great Northern beans	1 to 1½ hours
Kidney beans	About 1 hour
Lentils (red, brown, green)	25 to 30 minutes
Lima beans (Fordhook, baby, Christmas, butter beans)	1 to 1¼ hours
Navy beans	1 hour
Pea beans	1 hour
Pink beans	50 minutes
Pinto beans	1 to 1½ hours
Soldier beans	25 minutes
Split peas (green, yellow)	30 minutes
Soybeans	3 to 4 hours
Yellow-eye beans	30 minutes

or overnight. You can soak the beans longer, but if the kitchen temperature is warm, they will start to ferment (usually after 24 hours) and you'll have to throw them out (or feed them to livestock). Drain when you are ready to cook, and cook in fresh water.

> **Quick soak.** Put the dried beans in a stockpot. Add water to cover by at least 2 inches. Bring to a boil, cover, and boil for 10 minutes. Remove from the heat and let sit for 1 hour. Drain when you are ready to cook, and cook in fresh water.

Alternatively, if you forget to presoak, add 1 to 2 hours to your cooking time.

Tips for Cooking with Dried Beans

> To cook dried beans, soak for at least 8 hours, then drain off the soaking liquid and start cooking in fresh water.
> Enhance the flavor of your beans by cooking them with aromatic vegetables (such as onions, garlic, and celery), herbs, and spices.

> Do not cook the beans with acidic foods, such as tomatoes or wine; these will lengthen the cooking time and toughen the skin of the beans.
> Salt will not add to the cooking time. However, if you add the salt early on, be aware that as the large volume of liquid cooks down, the salt flavor will concentrate. If you salt at the end of the cooking process, you are less likely to oversalt.
> When you first bring the beans to a boil, the liquid will sometimes get quite foamy. Skim off this foam, then reduce the heat and simmer. Boiling hard tends to make the beans fall apart.
> Set the pot lid to partially cover the pot; this reduces the risk of running out of cooking liquid.
> The beans should always be covered by the cooking liquid or they will not soften properly. If too much liquid is lost to evaporation (the beans boiled too vigorously, the lid was left off, the age of the beans required additional

cooking time), add boiling water to cover the beans and continue cooking. Cold water will toughen the skin of the beans.
> Slow cookers do a good job of cooking beans.
> The cooking time in any recipe should be regarded as a guideline only; cooking times will vary depending on age of the bean, the size of the pot, and heat levels. So taste or squeeze five beans for doneness (a one-bean test may not yield an accurate result). The beans should be firm but tender throughout. Beans cook from the outside in, so be sure the cores of the beans are not hard.
> When the beans are done, immediately drain off the cooking liquid if the beans are to be used in a salad or another dish in which a firm texture is best. Otherwise, the beans will continue to cook slightly in the warm cooking liquid.

CHAPTER 5

HOMEMADE SWEETENERS:
Honey, Maple Syrup, and Apple Cider Syrup

Although it is easy enough to run to the store to buy sugar anytime you need some sweetener, it is wonderful to be able to produce what you need in that department. Depending on where you live, you may be able to harvest or make your own honey, maple syrup, boiled apple cider, or apple cider syrup.

Homegrown sweeteners are somewhat regional by nature, with maple syrup dominating in New England. Honey is more broadly made than other sweeteners but comes with its own issues, like the pests and diseases that have been decimating bee populations. And apples are grown throughout most of North America, so apple cider syrup, though more traditional in New England, is a possibility for all.

Can these syrups replace white sugar for all your baking needs? It depends on your goals. If you want to make lovely, light layer cakes, the kind you frost with buttercream, the answer is no. If you are content with rustic desserts and are especially happy with recipes that were developed in areas of the world where, say, honey was a mainstay (think baklava), then yes.

Storing Sweeteners

Though I call for storing honey, maple syrup, and cider syrup in sterilized canning jars in the step-by-step instructions that follow, these homemade sweeteners do not necessarily have to be stored in canning jars, nor is it absolutely necessary to sterilize the jars. I choose to use glass jars over plastic containers because I want to avoid possible off-flavors from the plastic. And I sterilize the jars because I want to be sure that the sweetener is not compromised by careless mishandling. Also, maple syrup and apple cider syrup will go into the jars hot; if the jars are hot also, they are likely to seal when capped, which extends the shelf life of these products. I often give these homemade sweeteners away as gifts, and I want to be sure these gifts are of the highest quality. For instructions on how to sterilize canning jars, see page 176.

Honey

If you keep bees, you have already made some basic decisions that affect what will come into the kitchen. If you planned to extract the honey, you set up the hive with wired foundations that are strong enough to withstand the mechanics of the extractor. Then you either bought a honey extractor or built one from the many plans available in beekeeping books and online. But if you planned to bring comb honey into your kitchen, you started with either an open hive or a thin, nonwired foundation. You can drain and filter comb honey (a slow process), or you can enjoy eating it by the spoonful or spread on toast or crackers. You can even cut it into small chunks and use it as a garnish. Chances are, you want both comb honey and some filtered liquid honey to bake with, serve with tea, and so on.

There are a couple of ways you can extract honey from a small amount of comb in the kitchen. But be warned! Honey attracts ants, flies, and other insects, so try to keep everything very, very, clean.

STEP-BY-STEP How to Extract Honey

A low-tech way to extract honey is the "squish and drain" method (or the "squish and spin" alternative). To go slightly higher tech, install a honey gate — a spout with an on/off lever — in a plastic bucket (it will require drilling a hole); you can dispense the filtered honey from this bucket into canning jars for storage, which will make the process much easier and neater.

EQUIPMENT

Long-bladed knife
At least 2 large shallow plastic bins
Food-safe buckets
Potato masher or other tool for breaking up the comb
Large fine-mesh strainer
Butter muslin
Clean canning jars and lids

① **Cut the comb.** Cut the comb from the frames and let the comb fall into a shallow plastic bin. Set the now-empty frame in another bucket.

② **Break it up.** Break up the comb with your hands, a potato masher, or some other tool. This will result in a pulpy, sticky mess.

Extracting honey is sticky business. The frame shown here will need something washable to lean upon. And you need somewhere to put the emptied frame.

A potato masher does a good job of breaking up the comb.

③ **Strain.** Set a fine-mesh strainer over a food-safe plastic bucket. Pour the sticky mess into the strainer and let drain. It will take about 16 hours for the honey to slowly drip into the bucket. To speed up the process, use a salad spinner to spin batches of the comb, separating the wax and honey.

If you like, you can take what remains in the strainer and heat it in a double boiler; it will separate into solid wax and some additional honey.

If ants are a problem, consider setting the receiving bucket in a sink (or bathtub) filled with several inches of water. If any ants should come scouting for the honey, they will drown instead.

It will take about 16 hours to strain the honey from the comb at room temperature. Figure that a 4-gallon bucket will hold 50 to 53 pounds of honey. Figure you will get 2½ to 3 pounds from each frame. (Honey weighs 12 pounds per gallon.)

④ **Strain again.** The strained honey will still contain bits of wax and other debris. Line a strainer with dampened butter muslin and strain again.

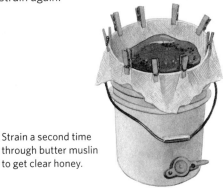

Strain a second time through butter muslin to get clear honey.

Infants and Honey

According to the U.S. Centers for Disease Control and Prevention, honey can contain the bacteria that cause infant botulism, so children under 1 year old should not be fed honey. Honey is safe for children over the age of 1.

⑤ **Store.** Fill clean jars with honey. Cap, cover, and store at room temperature. (This process is much easier if you've installed a honey gate on your collection bucket.) The honey will keep indefinitely, but like all natural products, fresh honey tastes best.

Let the honey sit in the bucket for a day or so to reduce the amount of air bubbles in it. Then fill clean canning jars with the clear honey.

Storing Honey

Honey doesn't need pasteurization and will keep indefinitely at room temperature. Indeed, heating destroys the beneficial bacteria and nutrients (and pollen) in the honey. Many people feel that the advantage of keeping bees is to produce "raw" honey that is never heated. However, most varieties of honey will eventually become solid. This crystallization is normal and does not mean the honey is bad; it can be used in the same ways that liquid honey is used. See below for a tip on how to reliquefy the honey.

Comb honey is easy to store in flat plastic containers; beekeeping supply houses sell special containers, or you can use plastic sandwich containers. You can also fill a canning jar with pieces of comb honey, topping off with liquid honey if you like.

Maple Syrup

Every year I am surprised anew by how great fresh maple syrup tastes. As terrific as pure maple syrup tastes all year long, fresh syrup is that much better. If you live in an area where sugar maples grow and the springtime weather cooperates, with freezing temperatures at night and above-freezing temperatures by day, you really don't want to miss out on one of the greatest treats of Mother Nature.

You can boil down sap to make maple syrup in your kitchen, and it isn't a bad way to get started. We put in somewhere between seven and nine taps on our maple trees and make a few gallons of syrup each year. By the end of sugaring season, we have had enough — in terms of work, in terms of maple-scented air, in terms of canning jars lining the counters. And we do make enough to meet our maple syrup needs for the year and to give some away as gifts.

We have been boiling maple sap into syrup in the kitchen for about a dozen years and have only run into a problem once: an ice dam formed on the roof above the kitchen because of extra moisture that collected during very cold weather. We weathered it. Oh, and the surface of my stove around the burner has become pitted and has lost its finish, a cosmetic issue caused by long periods of high heat. I've heard tales of wallpaper falling off walls, mold forming on painted surfaces, and the like, but I've never experienced said disasters or known anyone with firsthand experience of them. But consider yourself warned. Good ventilation — that is, a ventilation hood over the stove — will go far to prevent problems.

If you have a source of outdoor heat (a firepit, a propane burner, or a turkey fryer, as one of my friends uses), you can do the initial boiling outside and finish it indoors, where you can more easily control the temperature. This is smarter than a completely indoor operation, but then you have other issues (maintaining a fuel source and being outdoors in all sorts of weather).

Not all maple syrup tastes the same! How well you

Sweet Tips

- If your honey has crystallized, place the open jar in a saucepan of very hot water and stir every 5 minutes until the honey turns liquid.

- If you can, measure the oil in a recipe first, then use the oiled cup for the liquid sweetener. The oil will cause the sweetener to slide right out.

- When used in a salad dressing, honey, maple syrup, and apple cider syrup act as emulsifiers to keep the oil bound into the mixture.

handle the process and your sanitation practices will definitely affect the final product. But there is more to it than that. Early in the season, the sap will yield a light-colored syrup, what used to be called Fancy and is now called Grade A Light Amber by the USDA. Under the original labeling system, people might have been mistaken into thinking that Fancy syrup was superior to Grade B syrup, the darker, end-of-the-season syrup. Or that Grade B was less processed than Grade A. It's all made in exactly the same way, with the same amount of boiling.

As the season progresses, the sap yields a darker syrup, producing Grade A Medium Amber, then Grade A Dark Amber, and finally Grade B. These are the USDA terms; Canada has different names for the same colors of syrup. In Vermont (we are always the outliers), the syrup goes from Grade A: Golden Color with a Delicate Taste, to Grade A: Amber with Rich Taste to Grade A: Dark with Robust Taste, to Grade A: Very Dark with Strong Taste. The USDA calls that Grade C and won't allow it for retail sales. In Vermont, we call that grade "buddy," because you can only get it at the end of the season, as leaf buds begin to form. That is when it is time to stop. In my area, you stop before you hear spring peepers

(frogs). In between the extremes of light and buddy, the syrup will have hints of vanilla, crème brûlée, coffee beans, dark chocolate, butter, and even a subtle hint of smokiness. In general, I prefer a darker syrup for baking and lighter syrup for pancakes, but that is a personal preference — and I am most likely to use whatever jar is open and in the fridge.

When the sap is flowing, collect it daily. If you can't boil the sap immediately, or if you collect more than will fit in your boiling pan, keep the sap cold, preferably below 38°F (3°C), and use within 7 days of collection. If there is still snow on the ground, you can keep the storage containers outside, in the shade, packed in snow. You can also store the sap in your refrigerator, or for longer-term storage in your freezer (but who has room?). Some folks discard any ice that forms on the sap in storage, figuring it is mostly water (but taste it for sweetness before discarding).

Making Maple Syrup

The well-known statistic is that it takes 40 gallons of maple sap to make 1 gallon of syrup. In fact, the ratio is anywhere from 20:1 to 40:1. Some years all the trees yield sweeter sap than other years, and there is always variation from tree to tree. If you drink sap, which many people do, you can often taste

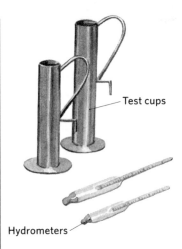

Test cups

Hydrometers

the variation in sweetness. (Some homebrewers make beer with the maple sap.)

The most challenging part of the process is figuring out when the syrup is done. Syrup that is too thin may ferment in storage, or it may change the baking time or texture of any baked goods you make with it. If the syrup is too dense, it may form sugar crystals during storage. You can judge when the syrup is ready by visual cues (risky but cheap), by using a thermometer (you should have one anyway for judging when meat is done and for cheesemaking), or by using a hydrometer. Hydrometers are also used for making wine and beer, but using a different scale; some are calibrated for different uses, some are single use. Hydrometers are highly accurate and can be found for under $25, but you'll need to use one with a special test cup, and that can run another $25 to $35.

How to Make Maple Syrup

Cleanliness will prevent off-flavors from developing in your syrup, so start with buckets and storage containers that are thoroughly cleaned using a mixture of 1 part unscented household bleach to 20 parts clean water. Scrub the containers and triple-rinse with hot water.

Once you've brought home the sap you collected from your tapped maple trees, you're ready for the boil, which will take hours and hours, depending on how large a surface area you are working with. Outdoor evaporators typically are long rectangular pans that offer the maximum amount of surface area. On a stovetop, you are limited by the size of your pan. You can interrupt the boiling process — if you can chill your partially boiled sap — and resume the process the next day. If you are going to use a thermometer to gauge whether your syrup is done boiling, you need to figure out the boiling temperature of water on that particular day. The boiling temperature of water is generally 212°F (100°C), but it will go up or down based on your elevation and on the atmospheric pressure of the day.

EQUIPMENT

Strainer

Coffee filters

5-gallon stockpot

Smaller heavy saucepan for finishing

Hydrometer (with hydrometer cup; found wherever sugaring supplies are sold), thermometer, or chilled plate (set in the freezer), for determining syrup point

Funnel (optional)

Felted wool filters for finishing (optional; found where sugaring supplies are sold)

Sterilized canning jars and lids

① **Begin the boil.** Line a strainer with a coffee filter, and pour the sap through the filter into a 5-gallon stockpot until it is about three-quarters full. The coffee filter will catch any insects, bark, or other debris that has fallen into the sap bucket. Place the pot over your largest burner, bring to a boil, and maintain the boil. Alternatively, boil outdoors in a

Boil the filtered sap in the largest pot you own if you are boiling indoors. This is where a 5-gallon pot comes in handy.

large pot, an evaporator, or a turkey fryer over a propane burner or wood fire. When the sap has reduced by about half, add more sap, but try to maintain the boil. Skim off any foam that collects on top of the boiling sap.

(2) **Transfer to the finishing pot.** When all of the sap has been added to the large pot and the sap is reduced to just a few inches of boiling sap, begin monitoring the sap more closely. When the sap begins to take on a golden color, transfer it into a smaller pot. (People who boil outdoors in a makeshift setup may transfer the sap at this point and finish on the stovetop, too.)

(3) **Boil until the sap reaches the syrup point.** With the sap in a smaller pot, continue to boil the sap until it has reached the consistency of syrup. As it boils, the syrup may suddenly boil up and threaten to boil over. You can calm the boil with a drop of fat — butter or cream is traditional, but vegetable oil can be used. Do this sparingly, since it can contribute an off-taste. As the sap comes close to the syrup point, you will begin to get larger, open bubbles. It is syrup when any or all of the following occur:

Don't fill the finishing pot too full; leave room for the sap to boil up without spilling over.

- The temperature is 7°F (4°C) above the boiling point of water on a candy or instant-read thermometer. At sea level, this is usually 219°F (104°C).

- It has reached a density of 36.0 Baumé or 66.9 Brix, depending on how your hydrometer is calibrated.

- A spoonful dropped on a chilled plate will allow you to leave a trail if you run your finger through it.

- The syrup "aprons" off a spoon in a sheet, rather than forming individual drips.

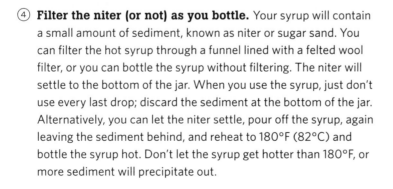

The sap has become syrup when it reaches 219°F (104°C) and will drop off a spoon in sheets rather than single drips.

(4) **Filter the niter (or not) as you bottle.** Your syrup will contain a small amount of sediment, known as niter or sugar sand. You can filter the hot syrup through a funnel lined with a felted wool filter, or you can bottle the syrup without filtering. The niter will settle to the bottom of the jar. When you use the syrup, just don't use every last drop; discard the sediment at the bottom of the jar. Alternatively, you can let the niter settle, pour off the syrup, again leaving the sediment behind, and reheat to 180°F (82°C) and bottle the syrup hot. Don't let the syrup get hotter than 180°F, or more sediment will precipitate out.

Pour the hot syrup into hot, sterilized canning jars, filling the jars to within ¼ inch of the top. Seal with the lids. Let cool on the counter.

Pour the hot syrup into the jars and seal.

⑤ **Store.** Store the syrup in the refrigerator or freezer. (If you have an unheated room, you can store the syrup without refrigeration.)

Fancy, maple leaf–shaped bottles and traditional jugs are available wherever sugaring supplies are sold. The advantage of canning jars is that they are inexpensive, you always have them around, and they can be used for other purposes.

Pairing Cheese and Honey (and Maple Syrup)

For the absolute easiest and most wonderful dessert you could possibly serve, consider the classic pairing of cheese and honey. The combination of sweet and salty and sharp and creamy will dance in your mouth.

Arrange an assortment of three cheeses on a plate with a sliced baguette or crackers with a small ramekin of honey or a plate of comb honey. The idea is to place a slice of cheese on a piece of bread and drizzle a little bit of honey on top — not too much, though, or it becomes too messy to eat and the honey overwhelms a delicate cheese. Or smear a little comb honey on a cracker or slice of bread and top with cheese.

What cheeses? Well, whatever is homemade is always most wonderful, but there are some classic combinations. Generally, people like to put together a cheese board showcasing a hard, a soft, and a blue cheese. It turns out that honey goes particularly well with aged cheeses, such as Parmesan, cheddar, and Gruyère. And it works deliciously with fresh, creamy cheeses like ricotta, chèvre, and feta. Blue cheeses also pair exceptionally well with honey; the sweetness of the honey cuts the sharpness and saltiness.

There's another combination that works really, really well: chèvre and maple syrup. Actually, maple syrup is terrific combined with any fresh, creamy cheese.

Boiled Cider and Cider Syrup

An old New England tradition that is just barely still alive is to boil down fresh apple cider to make boiled apple cider (also called apple molasses) or, with the addition of sugar, apple cider syrup or cider jelly.

Boiled Apple Cider

If you make your own cider, chances are you have a large supply of apples, enough to justify renting, borrowing, or owning a cider press. And if you do have that large quantity, you are probably freezing the cider to keep it fresh, which takes up a lot of freezer space. Both boiled cider and cider syrup are space-saving alternatives — and you can even add water to boiled cider to make cider again (but it won't taste the same as your fresh cider did). It is fine, however, as mulled cider: diluted with water and heated with spices, such as a cinnamon stick, slices of ginger, or whole cloves.

To make boiled apple cider, boil the cider on top of the stove until it is concentrated down to about one-seventh of its original volume. At that point it will be thick, dark, sweet, and somewhat sharp-tasting, like sugarcane molasses. And like sugarcane molasses, it is a fine addition to baked beans and certain baked goods, such as gingerbread and ginger cookies. Use it instead of molasses in your recipes.

Apple Cider Syrup

Apple cider syrup is also boiled-down cider, but it has sugar added to make it sweet enough to pour on pancakes and be used interchangeably with maple syrup in baked goods. Because of the added sugar, it reaches the syrup point (7°F/4°C above the temperature at which water boils) sooner than with boiled cider. You take it off the heat at an earlier point, when it is reduced to about one-quarter of its original volume.

I make cider syrup, and I like to put it on pancakes and use it to flavor granola and home-cured bacon. It makes a lovely drizzle for pound cake and ice cream and is excellent as a sweetener for oatmeal and tea. It does wonders for winter squash and roasted root vegetables. It can be used interchangeably with maple syrup. It is easy to make; it just takes time.

Ark of Taste

Slow Food USA has named boiled apple cider and apple cider jelly two traditional regional foods of New England that deserve to be preserved. I agree.

What about Sorghum Syrup?

Sorghum syrup is another old-fashioned sweetener that has been made on the homestead scale throughout the South since as far back as the early 1600s, when sorghum, a grass, was introduced from Africa, where it is grown in areas too hot and dry for sugarcane. Sorghum syrup is made by crushing sorghum canes to extract the juice, then evaporating the juice until a sweet, molasses-like syrup is produced. Special milling equipment is needed to extract the juice from the crushed stalks, so it is made outdoors, with the evaporating pans fired over wood. Sometimes the syrup is finished indoors, as with maple syrup.

STEP-BY-STEP How to Make Apple Cider Syrup

Here's how to make cider syrup. If you want, you can multiply this recipe by a factor of four (to still fit in a 5-gallon stock pot and make about 8 pints, or a boiling-water-bath canner load), but the time to reduce the syrup will also increase significantly. I make mine 1 gallon at a time and store it in the fridge, without bothering with the boiling-water bath. My timing for the boiling-water bath is the same as the USDA canning time for apple butter.

Sweetened apple cider will reach the syrup point at about 7°F (4°C) above the boiling point of water at your elevation, or 219°F (104°C) on a thermometer (at sea level). But note that the jelling point to make jelly is just 8°F (4.5°C) above the boiling point of water at sea level. So when boiling apple cider, it is easy to cross the line from making syrup to making jelly (though other factors come into play as well). My point is this: pay attention at the end of the process.

As with maple syrup, if you are going to use a thermometer to gauge whether your syrup has reached the syrup stage, you need to figure out the boiling temperature of water on that particular day (see page 8) and adjust accordingly.

Finally, another caveat: even with pasteurized cider, you are likely to make a syrup that appears hazy, caused by the pectin and particulate matter in the original cider. This is an aesthetic issue, not a taste issue. The particulate matter will settle as the syrup cools, forming a layer on the bottom of the jar. Skimming the foam that rises to the top of the pot as the cider heats will reduce but not eliminate the residue.

EQUIPMENT

2-gallon heavy stockpot
Smaller heavy saucepan for finishing
Funnel
Thermometer or chilled plate (set in the freezer), for determining syrup point
Boiling-water-bath canner (optional)
2 sterilized pint canning jars and lids

① **Boil.** Pour 1 gallon of fresh or frozen and thawed apple cider into a heavy stockpot. For a clearer syrup, avoid any sediment that has settled to the bottom of the jug. Add 1½ cups sugar. Then bring to a boil.

② **Judge doneness.** Continue boiling until the syrup reaches the syrup point, which is 7°F (4°C) above the boiling point of water at your elevation, or until a spoonful dropped on the chilled plate will allow you to leave a trail if you run your finger through it. For 1 gallon of cider, it will take 2 to 3 hours to reach the syrup point, depending on the heat of the burner, the sugar content of the cider, and how well the pot conducts heat.

③ **Bottle and store.** Pour the hot syrup into the hot canning jars (using a canning funnel to avoid making a mess), leaving about ¼ inch of headspace, and seal with canning lids. Either cool and store in the refrigerator or freezer or process in a boiling-water bath (see chapter 11) for 5 minutes. Store in a cool, dark place.

Using Natural Syrups in Place of Sugar

White sugar has been the dominant sweetener in American baking for quite a while, so many of our most cherished sweets are made with it. It is possible to substitute liquid sweeteners, but success varies. The following tips apply to honey and maple syrup. I don't have enough experience baking with other sweeteners to be sure of their accuracy, but I encourage you to experiment.

Sugar, honey, and maple syrup are all hygroscopic, meaning they attract water. Honey and maple syrup are more hygroscopic than sugar, so products baked with them stay moist longer. However, this means it is hard — or impossible — to make crisp cookies with honey or maple syrup. Also, moist baked goods are more likely to become moldy, so baked goods made with honey or maple syrup in place of sugar should be stored in the refrigerator.

Whenever a recipe calls for creaming the butter and sugar together, as in traditional butter cakes, the crystalline structure of sugar is key for trapping air in the mixture. If you swap in honey, maple syrup, or apple cider syrup for all of the sugar, the cake will end up flat and dense. The best you can do is substitute half the sugar with a liquid sweetener, and even then results will be mixed.

Both honey and maple syrup are sweeter than sugar, which makes sense only if you consider that 1 cup of sugar weighs 200 grams, while 1 cup of honey weighs in at 340 grams and 1 cup of maple syrup weighs in at 320 grams. So when swapping out sugar for honey and maple syrup in a recipe, you may want to reduce the volume of sweetener you use. It is my personal opinion that honey is an aggressive flavor, so I prefer to use it sparingly. Furthermore:

› When substituting honey, maple syrup, or apple cider syrup in recipes calling for 1 or more cups of sugar, reduce the other liquids in the recipe by ¼ cup for every 1 cup of other sweetener.

› In cookie doughs and in recipes that use eggs as the main liquid, when there is no liquid that can be reduced, increase the flour by 2 tablespoons for each cup of honey, maple syrup, or apple cider syrup.

› Because natural sweeteners are higher in acid than sugar, add ½ teaspoon baking soda for every 1 cup of honey, maple syrup, or apple cider syrup used.

› To avoid overbrowning, reduce the oven temperature by 25°F (15°C).

› In this book, recipes that give you a choice of sweeteners usually list the maple syrup first. That's because it is the sweetener I make in abundance and the one I prefer; you should use the sweetener that you prefer.

CHAPTER 6

Eggs, Birds, and Rabbits

Chickens are the gateway animal to food self-sufficiency. So more likely than not, if you are reading this book, you have chickens or you've thought about having them, probably for their eggs. But why stop there?

Poultry suited to backyard homesteaders includes broiler chickens, guinea fowl, turkeys, ducks, and geese. Guinea fowl, by the way, are known for their prodigious appetite for feasting on ticks and other insect pests — and their prodigious ability to make noise. They are also good to eat, although better braised than roasted because the meat is tougher. Ducks are cute and are wonderfully rich eating; geese are fierce guard animals . . . oh, there's more, but these are the most likely candidates for a backyard homesteader.

Along those same lines, rabbits are an excellent source of protein and are easy to raise. Also, as it turns out, skinless chicken and rabbit recipes are fairly interchangeable.

Although with larger animals you are likely to use a local slaughterhouse for slaughtering and butchering, with poultry and rabbits that job will likely fall to you. If you're accustomed to purchasing your meat in shrink-wrapped packages of nice, neat cuts, you might think that working with a whole animal will be a challenge. With the right tools and know-how, it doesn't have to be.

Chicken Eggs

The average chicken lays 5 or 6 eggs a week. Multiply that by a flock of a dozen hens, and you are looking at 6 dozen eggs a week during the peak warm spring weather. Production does slow when the chickens are getting less than 15 hours of light, or when temperatures fall below 45°F (7°C) or rise above 80°F (27°C). Still, if you raise chickens for their eggs, you will inevitably have an overabundance. How are you going to deal with this incredible bounty?

Storing Chicken Eggs

If your chicken yard isn't muddy, and if the nests are kept clean and lined with fresh litter, and if the eggs are collected regularly, the eggs that come into the kitchen should be pretty clean. Eggs that are slightly dirty can be brushed or rubbed with a dry nylon scrub brush.

Why not just wash the eggs? When freshly laid, an egg is coated with a gelatinous outer layer that quickly dries, sealing pores on the shell to help block bacterial infections. This protective "bloom" extends the shelf life of the egg; you don't want to lose that coating if you can help it. If an egg is really dirty, you can wash it with water that is at least 20°F (11°C) warmer than the egg itself. The water temperature is important because cooler water can allow bacteria to be drawn into the shell. Use a washed egg as soon as possible.

You can leave fresh eggs in a wire basket on the counter, lending your house a "country kitchen" charm. But charm only goes so far. According to an experiment conducted by the editors of *Mother Earth News* in 1977, unrefrigerated, fertilized eggs will keep for upward of 8 weeks, and unfertilized eggs a little less long. But those kept in the refrigerator will last for 7 to 8 months, a huge difference. (Those *Mother Earth News* editors also tested out packing eggs in sand, submerging them in a sodium silicate solution, and submerging them in a lime solution. You can find a description of the whole experiment by searching for "How to Store Fresh Eggs" on the *Mother Earth News* website.) The best way to extend the life of whole fresh eggs is to place unwashed eggs in a carton, pointed side down (to keep the yolks centered and the air pocket up, thus keeping bacteria away from the yolk), then place the carton in the refrigerator.

Separated egg whites and yolks can be stored in the refrigerator in airtight containers for a few days.

If your hens are laying eggs beyond your capacity to store them in the refrigerator,

Accidentally Frozen Eggs

In the winter, it is not unusual to find eggs already frozen in the chicken coop. What then? According to the USDA, if the eggshell breaks or cracks during freezing, the egg should be discarded. If not, let it thaw in the refrigerator; it is fine to use. Do be aware, though, that your cakes may not have the same rise with previously frozen eggs as they would with fresh eggs.

you may want to consider freezing them out of the shell — as whole eggs or with the yolks and whites separated. It would be great if you could freeze them in the shell, but the contents of the egg will expand when frozen and crack the shell. See page 167 for tips on freezing eggs.

Fresh versus Older Eggs

Fresh eggs generally taste better than older eggs, but there are two instances where older eggs are more desirable than fresh eggs:

> When you are beating egg whites separately — to make meringues and mousses, for example, or to lighten a batter — the whites will achieve a greater volume if they are slightly older.

> When you are hard-boiling eggs, older eggs will release their shells and peel more readily than fresher eggs. However, given that the fresher eggs taste better, it is a bit of a trade-off. Losing hunks of hard-boiled white

doesn't matter so much with eggs destined for egg salad, but it does matter when you're making deviled eggs. (If sticking shells are a problem for your hard-boiled eggs, check out the easy-peel method on page 86.)

When is an egg too old? The classic trick of seeing whether an egg floats is still a good way to check for freshness: Fill a bowl with cold salted water. Add an egg. If it sinks, it is fresh; if it floats, throw it out.

Fertilized versus Unfertilized Eggs

If your flock includes roosters, some of the eggs will come into the kitchen fertilized. I was raised to believe that a blood spot on the yolk indicates fertilization, but I have since learned that that's not true. Instead, a fertile egg has a small white bull's-eye on the yolk, which can easily go unnoticed. A fertile egg must be kept at a temperature of at least 85°F (29°C) for several hours in order for that spot to begin developing into an embryo. When that happens, you may be able to see some spidery red lines developing on the yolk. But use the egg anyway because it will taste the same and cook the same as an unfertilized egg. Some people think that fertilized eggs are more nutritious than unfertilized eggs, but there is no science I know of to back that claim.

Egg Sizes

I have several hundred cookbooks in my house, and every single one assumes I will be cooking and baking with large eggs. Good thing chickens can't read, because the young ones, which tend to lay smaller eggs, not to mention certain breeds of hens, would be most offended. The eggs you collect from your flock may not be uniform in size: some may be pullet size, and others small, medium, or large.

It turns out that 1 large egg measures about ¼ cup (4 tablespoons), which makes the math pretty simple. Crack the eggs into a measuring cup until you have the equivalent of whatever the recipe calls for. If a recipe calls for 1 large egg, the equivalent is ¼ cup eggs. If a recipe calls for 2 eggs, the equivalent is ½ cup, and so on. Don't sweat it if the eggs measure out to a little more or a little less. Exact measures are not necessary in home baking and cooking.

Cooking with Eggs

Somehow, Americans have pigeonholed eggs as breakfast food. This is an unfortunate turn of events, since an egg, that perfect protein source, transforms a meal of vegetables into a completely satisfying, stick-to-your-ribs feast. And if those veggies are topped with a sunny-side-up or poached egg, the liquid yolk turns into a luxurious sauce. Additionally, there are egg-based sauces that are transformative for all manner of vegetables (mayonnaise, page 33; aioli, page 33; hollandaise, page 34) and fruit (custard sauce, page 318).

The following methods are for the simple egg dishes that every self-sufficient human being should be able to prepare (look for more recipes in part 3). Figure one to three eggs per serving; timings are based on large eggs.

Hard-Boiled Eggs: The Easy-Peel Method

This is not the standard method found in most cookbooks because the standard method (put the eggs in a pot of cold water, bring to a boil, turn off the heat, leave for 10 minutes, then cool down quickly) doesn't work as well with very fresh eggs, which are notoriously hard to peel.

1. Bring a few inches of water to boil in a large pot. Put the eggs in a steamer basket.

2. Set the eggs in the basket over the boiling water, cover, and steam for 15 minutes.

3. Transfer the eggs to a bowl of ice water and let cool, then crack and peel.

Soft-Boiled Eggs

There are some who say that a soft-boiled egg must be served in an eggcup, a ceramic or china cup that is specially designed to hold just one egg. When you serve a soft-boiled egg in an eggcup, you can neatly tap the top of the shell with a butter knife, lift off the top shell, then scoop out the egg and eat daintily with a small spoon. Since my homestead is nothing like Downton Abbey, I feel fine putting torn toast bits in a bowl, topping with a scooped-out soft-boiled egg, and having at it.

1. Bring a saucepan of water to a gentle boil.

2. With a pin, poke a hole in the broad end of the egg. Lower the egg into the water on a spoon or ladle and carefully release it to the water.

3. For large eggs, cook for 3 minutes for runny yolks and the white not quite set, 4 minutes for the whites to be completely set, and 5 minutes for set whites and set but moist yolks. (Adjust the time for smaller or larger eggs.)

4. Lift each egg out of the water and place in an egg-cup to serve. Alternatively, run the egg briefly under cold water so you can hold it, then crack the shell and scoop out the egg into a bowl.

Poached Eggs

Temperature, temperature, temperature! There are dozens of tips on the Internet for egg poaching, but it is really all about the water temperature. The water must be barely simmering, about 180°F (82°C). Anything much higher and the rising bubbles in the water will shred the egg white. Oh, and no matter what, there will be wisps and tails of eggs. The show-offs and restaurant chefs trim and waste them; the rest of us live with them.

1. Start heating a couple of inches of salted water to a boil in a skillet or wide saucepan. Add 1 teaspoon of vinegar for firm whites, if you want (I don't). The water is ready when it reaches 180°F (82°C). If

you are reaching for perfection, figure out how to maintain the water at that temperature.

2. Working with no more than two eggs at a time, crack each egg into a separate shallow dish or ramekin. Slide each egg into the water (i.e., don't dump them), and use a silicone spatula to coax the egg white over the yolk. Slide the spatula under the egg to make sure it isn't sticking to the bottom, and keep gently pushing hot water over the yolk and encouraging the white to stick close to the yolk. The egg will take 3 to 4 minutes to poach, depending on the size of the eggs and whether you're using them straight from the fridge. The goal is firm, fully cooked whites but still-runny yolks.

3. Lift the eggs out of the water with a slotted spoon and set them on a paper towel to drain; trim away the white feathers and tails, if you must. Then set the eggs on your toast, asparagus, hash, or whatever you are serving them on. If you aren't serving immediately, you can hold the eggs for up to an hour and reheat in hot water for 1 minute before serving.

For poached eggs, the water temperature should be 180°F (82°C) when you gently slide the egg into the water.

Fried Eggs

Any animal fat can be used to fry an egg. Butter and bacon grease are the classics here, but chicken, duck, or goose fat adds a luxurious flavor.

1. Heat a nonstick skillet over medium heat. Add 1 to 3 teaspoons butter or fat to the pan and let it melt.

2. Crack the eggs into the skillet. As soon as the whites begin to set, turn the heat to low, season with salt and pepper, and cover.

3. Cook for 1 to 2 minutes longer, until the whites are completely set. At this point, the eggs are sunny-side up and ready to serve.

4. If you prefer your eggs over easy, flip them over, count to 10, and then serve. If you want them over hard, turn them over and cook for 1 more minute.

Scrambled Eggs

If you like your eggs soft and creamy, add 1 tablespoon milk, cream, or water for every two eggs. If you want them more flavorful, add about a tablespoon of chopped scallions, chopped fresh herbs, chopped cooked meat, sautéed and squeezed spinach, salsa, or anything else that you want. Whatever you do, don't forget salt and pepper. You can make scrambled eggs in as big a batch as your skillet will hold; increase the butter or fat proportionately, and expect a longer cook time.

1. Crack the eggs into a bowl and beat well, adding in milk, cream, or water for softer eggs. Season with salt and pepper and any other flavorings you may desire.

2. Place a skillet over medium heat and add 2 to 3 teaspoons of butter or other animal fat for every 2 eggs.

3. Add the eggs and wait until they begin to set. Then stir and cook until the eggs are as soft or firm and wet or dry as you like.

Baked Eggs

Baking eggs is a great way to prepare eggs for a crowd, if you have enough ramekins. You can add all sorts of flourishes to the basic baked eggs: sprinkle grated cheese, chopped herbs, chopped cooked bacon, and/or chopped fresh tomatoes over the cream, or replace the cream with creamed spinach or other creamed veggies.

1. Preheat the oven to 375°F (190°C). Butter as many small ramekins or custard cups as you have eggs to cook and place them on a baking sheet.

2. Spoon a couple of tablespoons of cream into each cup. If you're cooking the eggs with any other ingredients, such as chopped vegetables, distribute them among the cups. Break an egg on top of each cup. Season with salt and pepper, and cover with a sprinkling of fresh or dried bread crumbs.

3. Bake for 10 to 15 minutes, just until the whites have solidified. (They will continue to cook in the ramekins if you hold them for any period of time.) Serve.

Omelets

Nonstick skillets are helpful here, but a well-seasoned cast-iron pan works just as well. Don't skimp on the butter and don't use too much filling; the egg is the star here. An omelet should make no more than two servings. If you are serving a crowd, make multiple omelets, one at a time.

1. Prepare the filling; see the box at right for suggestions.

2. Beat together 4 or 5 eggs with 2 tablespoons milk, cream, or water until light and fluffy.

3. Melt 2 tablespoons butter in a medium to large skillet over medium-high heat. Pour in the eggs and let set on the bottom, about 30 seconds. With a silicone spatula, push the edges of the eggs toward the center, tipping the pan to allow the still-liquid egg to flow to the edges. Continue the pushing and tipping until the top of the eggs appears wet but not runny, 2 to 3 minutes more.

4. Sprinkle the filling on half the omelet.

5. Fold the unfilled half over. Slide out of the pan and serve.

Yolks and Whites

Some recipes call for only egg whites, others only yolks. Some tips:

➤ Eggs separate easiest when cold (but for highest volume, beat egg whites at room temperature).

➤ When separating whites and yolks, use three bowls: one to catch the white as you separate each egg, one to collect all the yolks, and one to collect all the separated whites. Crack an egg over the first bowl and let the white drop into it. Dump the yolk into the second bowl, and empty the white from the first bowl into the third bowl. This way, if you should break the yolk as you separate an egg, it will affect only the egg you are working with and not the whole batch of whites. (The egg isn't ruined; put it aside and use it for another recipe that calls for whole eggs.)

➤ Egg whites are most often used separately to lighten a batter or to make a meringue.

➤ Beat egg whites in a perfectly clean, grease-free ceramic or metal bowl.

Cleaning Up a Dropped Egg

Cooking with kids is fun, and they particularly enjoy breaking eggs. But, inevitably, one gets dropped. Just sprinkle it with a generous layer of salt, wait a couple of minutes (during which time the salt will absorb the egg), then scoop the whole mess up with paper towels.

Omelet Fillings

Here are a few suggestions. There are really no limits and no rules.

- **Herbs:** Sprinkle a handful of mixed chopped fresh herbs over the egg mixture just before folding.

- **Cheese:** Sprinkle a handful of grated cheese over the egg mixture just before folding.

- **Veggies:** Use any vegetables or any combination of vegetables you like; leftovers are great here. The individual pieces should be pretty small. Briefly sauté in butter and/or oil, about 5 minutes for raw vegetables, 1 to 2 minutes for already cooked vegetables.

- **Mushrooms:** Sauté a handful of chopped mushrooms in butter, any animal fat, or oil over medium-high heat until the mushrooms give up their liquid, about 5 minutes.

- Egg whites beat best at room temperature and in the presence of a little acid. Acid will leach naturally from a copper bowl or can be provided by the addition of $1/8$ teaspoon cream of tartar or lemon juice for every 2 egg whites as they begin to be frothy.
- When folding in beaten egg whites, stir in about one-third of the whites first to lighten the batter. Then fold in the remaining whites. Use a large silicone spatula and bring the batter up from the bottom of the bowl over the whites, rotating the bowl with each folding motion.
- Egg yolks are used alone to add richness to a batter or to bind a mixture such as a custard (page 318) or mayonnaise (see page 33).
- When adding egg yolks to a hot mixture, always temper the yolks by adding a small amount of the hot mixture into the yolks to warm them. Then add the heated yolk mixture to the hot mixture.
- Egg yolks blended with oil make mayonnaise (page 33), plus garlic makes aioli (page 33). Egg yolks blended with butter and lemon juice make hollandaise sauce (page 34). Egg yolks blended with hot milk and sugar make a soft custard sauce (page 318) to use as a dessert sauce or the basis of ice cream or rice pudding (page 328).

Duck, Geese, and Turkey Eggs

When it comes to eggs, Americans tend to be chicken-centric. But if you are raising poultry for meat (or coaxing wild birds to migrate via your pond by leaving out grain), you may be able to collect fresh eggs from other birds, particularly in the spring. You may also be able to find these eggs in a farmers' market, but not with any consistency.

Whereas chickens have been bred to be egg-laying machines, geese and turkeys lay most of their eggs in the spring, when they are most likely to be able to hatch and raise them. Turkey farmers rarely have extra eggs to sell because the eggs are their breeding stock. Duck eggs are more readily available, and there are some breeds that really excel at year-round egg production (such as Khaki Campbells and Runners).

The shells of waterfowl eggs (duck and goose) are more porous than those of chicken eggs, so bacteria can more easily enter the eggs. If the eggs are at all dirty, they should be rinsed off, again in water that is at least 20°F (11°C) warmer than the eggs. Then store in the refrigerator, not on your kitchen counter, and use promptly.

Egg Comparisons

The eggs of turkeys, geese, and ducks are larger, have larger yolks, and have a larger percentage of yolk than chicken eggs. Their shells are much stronger than chicken eggs; it is most noticeable with goose eggs, which require a good knock to break. Size aside, you can use other poultry eggs just like chicken eggs in most *stove-top* recipes. Scrambled eggs, omelets, and the like will be noticeably richer in flavor and darker in color when made with nonchicken eggs. Goose eggs are particularly prized for making pasta. And, obviously, a scrambled goose egg yields more than a scrambled chicken egg.

When it comes to baking, the greater proportion of yolk to white in nonchicken eggs makes a big difference. I made two pound cakes, one with duck eggs and one with chicken eggs. To compensate for the size difference I used two duck eggs to the three chicken eggs. The duck egg cake, while edible, was noticeably denser and greasier (which isn't quite the same as richer); it clearly needed less butter and probably other adjustments as well.

Our desserts have been developed over hundreds of years with millions of bakers working with chicken eggs. In modern cookbooks, recipes are standardized to use large chicken eggs. It takes experimentation to standardize a cake recipe to another size egg, and experimenting with other types of eggs is harder still. On the Internet I've found swapping formulas (one goose egg for every two large chicken eggs, and other such formulas). But if you raise chickens, you know that the size of the egg varies by the age of the chicken and the breed. The same is true for other fowl, so don't count on these formulas. At right are some weights of different eggs by type, based on eggs I have bought (or was given) and USDA standards. Unfortunately, I wasn't always able to learn the breed of the egg-laying bird or its age.

Meat Birds

Although poultry stock catalogs distinguish between layers and meat birds, on a homestead any bird that you cook, including layers you have culled and mean ol' roosters, are meat birds.

Different types of poultry have striking similarities and striking differences. They all have relatively tender meat under an edible skin. They are

Chicken Egg Sizes (per USDA)

Size	Weight per Egg
Jumbo	Greater than 2.25 oz
Large	Greater than 2 oz
Medium	Greater than 1.75 oz
Small	Greater than 1.5 oz
Peewee	Greater than 1.25 oz

Notice that there is a 1-ounce difference between pullet eggs (peewee eggs) and jumbo eggs. Bantam chicken eggs weigh about 1.5 ounces.

Other Poultry Eggs (in My Own Experience)

Type of Egg	Weight per Egg
Goose	4.4 to 5.6 oz
Turkey	3.1 to 3.7 oz
Duck	2.7 to 3.5 oz
Guinea fowl	1.5 to 1.6 oz

Notice the huge range in sizes. If you are adjusting a recipe to accommodate other poultry eggs, you can try to adjust the egg amount by weight; this will yield slightly more accurate results than just replacing the egg by volume (remembering that 1 large chicken egg equals ¼ cup). You may also want to reduce the amount of butter or fat you use.

Goose egg

Duck egg

Chicken egg

all readily adaptable to most cooking methods: poaching, stewing, roasting, grilling, broiling. How to handle the differences depends, at least in part, on whether your bird is a land fowl (chicken, turkey, guinea fowl) or a waterfowl (geese and ducks). And keep in mind that a "meat" bird offers much more than just the flesh under its skin; the fat is a valuable cooking medium, the livers make delicious pâtés, and the giblets make good eating.

Land Fowl

Among land fowl, chickens are the most common in the backyard, and Cornish Cross is the most common breed because the birds gain weight so quickly and efficiently. They are designed to be slaughtered at no later than 8 weeks of age because they get so fat they have difficulty moving around. The meat is exceptionally tender and will dress out at 4 to 5 pounds. You can cook these birds any way you like, with excellent results, and they make the best roasts.

Slower-growing breeds, such as the European rouge or red types, will take 12 weeks to fully mature and dress out at about 3½ to 4 pounds. It seems to me that their meat is leaner, they have proportionately less breast meat, and the carcass is noticeably longer and narrower. Many people say this meat is more flavorful, but I'm guessing they wouldn't be able to tell the difference if both types of birds were poached and they tasted them blind. I think these leaner birds are best for poaching, braising, stewing, and red cooking (see page 299).

Guinea fowl, which dress out at 2¼ to 3 pounds, are also leaner, with less breast meat and a longer and narrower carcass. Guinea hen meat is darker and richer tasting than chicken (some say it tastes like pheasant), and it contains less fat and fewer calories. Guinea fowl are also smaller-boned than chickens, and some breeds have heavier breasts. The average guinea fowl dresses out to 75 percent of its live weight, compared to the average broiler chicken's 70 percent.

Young guinea fowl is much more tender than older birds. The giant guinea is a breed of guinea fowl that was developed for the meat market. It reaches about 4 pounds in 12 weeks, while other guinea fowl can be expected to weigh about 2 pounds in 12 weeks.

Butcher and dress a guinea fowl as you would a chicken. Succulent young guinea fowl can be broiled, roasted, or fried. The traditional way to roast an older guinea fowl is to wrap it in bacon and roast it uncovered at 350°F (180°C) for about 45 minutes, until the meat is tender. Then remove the bacon and run the bird under the broiler to crisp the skin. I think older guinea fowl are best braised, stewed, or red-cooked.

Turkeys are big. Commercial varieties have been bred to have large breasts, while the heritage

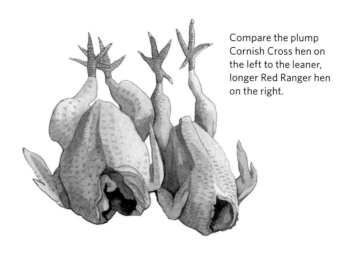

Compare the plump Cornish Cross hen on the left to the leaner, longer Red Ranger hen on the right.

varieties generally yield 50 percent white meat and 50 percent dark meat. Pastured turkeys tend to be juicier than commercial turkeys (lots of gravy!). They tend to cook faster than commercial turkeys.

Waterfowl

Waterfowl are fatty, and that's what makes them so wonderful, if prepared properly. A goose will weigh 9 to 14 pounds and will provide about 1 pound of fat, which will render into close to 2 quarts of cooking fat. The goose's liver will weigh 3 to 4 ounces, which is considerably larger than a chicken liver, which generally weighs in at ¾ ounce (though the goose liver can get even larger if the bird is fed a high-calorie diet with the goal of creating a 1¼-pound liver). The goose doesn't pack much meat on its bones, and an 11-pound goose will just serve five to six people. Ducks weigh in at 5 to 6 pounds, with 2½-ounce livers, and will feed 3 to 4 people.

Bringing the Bird into the Kitchen

If you are raising your own birds for meat, chances are you do the butchering all at once, and most likely the birds are brought into the kitchen once they have been bled out, eviscerated, and plucked. A word about plucking: it is worth doing it right. Dry plucking is likely to tear the skin. Scalding the bird makes it easier to pluck, but the water can't be too hot or the skin will cook. Use a 5-gallon stockpot so that you can immerse the entire bird at once. Heat the water to 145°F to 150°F (63°C to 66°C), and immerse the bird for 1 minute. You can add a drop of dish soap to help the scalding water penetrate the feathers better. You want the skin in good shape to keep the flesh from drying out as it cooks, even if you don't eat the skin. And, hopefully, you can do this outside because it is a messy job.

The birds that come through the door should be accompanied by a container of fat and a container of edible organs (gizzards, hearts, and livers); the necks, fat, and feet may or may not be attached to the carcass. In the step-by-step sequences that follow, you'll find instructions for processing the birds from head (well, neck) to feet, including how to cut them up, what to do with the innards, and how to render the fat. You don't have to do everything all at once. The feet, for example, can be frozen without cleaning and then cleaned before cooking. But do make sure that everything is chilled promptly.

Whenever you're handling raw birds, it's a good idea to sanitize your work area first. You don't have to steam-clean everything, but empty out the sink and clear away anything that might get splashed. Wash everything that will come in contact with the birds with hot, soapy water, then sanitize (page 13). Finally, be sure to thoroughly wash your hands both before and after handling the raw meat.

For all of the processing described below, you'll want to have ready a lot of paper towels, freezer bags (and a vacuum sealer, if you have one) or special poultry shrink bags for the freezer (pages 168–69), and freezer paper and tape. You'll also need a large cutting board, a sharp knife, and, especially if you're going to remove the backbone (spatchcock), sturdy poultry shears. A cleaver will come in handy, especially if the bird is older (not a spring chicken, so to speak), with bigger bones.

How to Handle Freshly Slaughtered Birds

Before you start butchering, you should be clear about how the job ends. You may be thinking of roast chicken for dinner tonight, but I have to tell you that an aged bird will be much more tender than a freshly processed bird. The meat should go through rigor mortis and then relax. Broilers that are 6 to 8 weeks old should age in the fridge for 24 to 36 hours. Age older birds for a full 48 hours. (That said, if you are processing young broilers, they will probably be tender enough to eat, though not as tender as they could be.)

Some people think their job is done when the bird is completely cleaned and left whole. I highly recommend spatchcocking (or butterflying) the bird for a number of reasons: it will cool faster, it will freeze faster, it will take up less space in the freezer, and it will roast faster and more evenly. Some people will want to cut their chickens into parts. Instructions for spatchcocking follows on page 96. You'll find instructions for cutting a bird into parts in the section on cooking poultry (pages 102–3).

① **Examine and rinse the birds.** Rinse each bird under cool running water with the neck end up (to flush out any remaining gunk). Blood left on the carcass will make the bird taste gamy. As you rinse, pull off any fat that you can grab. Just pull it out of the bird and collect it in a container. You'll want to render the fat and use it for cooking (see page 99).

Rinse under cool running water, neck end up.

② **Remove the oil gland (if needed).** If the oil gland, located on the tail end (pygostyle) of the bird, hasn't already been removed, you will need to do it now. It's the bump that is found at the top of the tail end and looks a bit like a pimple. Cut around and under it to remove it without getting the oil onto the carcass. As you cut around it, you will see the gland is yellow, unlike the surrounding pink flesh.

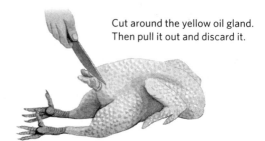

Cut around the yellow oil gland. Then pull it out and discard it.

③ **Remove the feet.** The feet of land fowl make excellent stock and are well worth saving, so please don't throw them out. (I have eaten duck feet at a Chinese restaurant, so I know that they are edible, but I've never cooked any or had any desire to really explore the subject. The texture of the duck webbing is exactly what you'd expect.)

Place the bird on a large cutting board. Locate the joint where the lower leg and drumstick meet. Cut through the skin and the stringy ligaments holding the joint together. You should not have to cut through bone or cartilage. It helps to bend the joint. The feet take some prep work, so set them aside until later. (See page 98 for tips on working with the feet.)

The feet will take some prep work to clean, but they make excellent soup stock. Don't throw them out!

④ **Remove the neck if it is still attached.** Begin by grasping the neck with one hand and use your other hand to pull the skin around the neck down. If you are very, very good with a cleaver, you can whack the neck off. If you don't trust your aim, push the sharp point of a boning knife into the base of the neck where it joins the back until you meet the resistance of bone. Make the same cut two or three more times until the neck is loosened from the body. Now twist the neck

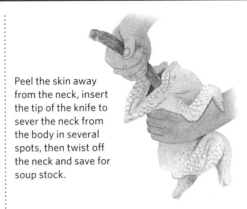

Peel the skin away from the neck, insert the tip of the knife to sever the neck from the body in several spots, then twist off the neck and save for soup stock.

off and set it aside for soup stock. Cut off the extra skin around the neck area and add it to the fat you've collected.

⑤ **Final rinse and chill.** Give the bird a final rinse and remove any remaining feathers. At this point, it is necessary to chill the bird. Most people chill their freshly slaughtered birds in a bath of ice water. The goal is to chill the bird to 40°F (4°C) (as measured in the breast with a temperature probe) within 4 hours for a 4-pound bird, 6 hours for a 4- to 8-pound bird, and 8 hours for a larger bird. Make sure ice and water fill the body cavity and that the chicken is completely submerged. After all that work, take a minute to do whatever cleanup is necessary. Get the gizzards, livers, and feet in the fridge. You can deal with them later — even a day or so later. After chilling, the birds are ready for the refrigerator. Pat dry with towels and seal in airtight plastic bags. Even if you plan to spatchcock your bird, give it a rest in the refrigerator until rigor mortis has passed.

Chill in an ice bath. An insulated cooler is shown here, but any tub or basin can be used.

How to Spatchcock a Bird

To spatchcock a bird (chicken, turkeys, guinea fowl, ducks, geese, and so on) means to remove the backbone and flatten the bird. You can use the word *butterfly* instead. The reason for doing this is to enable the bird to be cooked more evenly. In fact, a spatchcocked bird cooks faster and with crisper skin that is always on top and not sticking to the pan. It takes up less space in an oven and less space in the freezer because the bird ends up in a flatter package. If you package the spatchcocked bird in a ziplock freezer bag, the bird can be quickly defrosted with a soak in cold water (see page 170), whereas a whole bird frozen in a poultry shrink bag must be thawed in the refrigerator because the poultry shrink bag is not waterproof. Before and after cooking, a spatchcocked bird is much easier to cut into parts or carve. And finally, it gives you a lovely backbone for making stock.

You can spatchcock a bird at any point before it goes into the oven. Chickens are easy to spatchcock, as are ducks. Geese take a bit of muscle, and turkeys take a lot of muscle.

① **Cut along one side of the backbone.** Start with the bird breast-side down. Use a sharp knife to cut along the spine, beginning at the neck end. If you hit a tough spot, try cutting with just the tip of the knife. Sometimes you need a cleaver; with a goose or turkey, you will also need a soft mallet to push the cleaver through the bone.

② **Cut out the backbone.** Use poultry shears or a cleaver to cut through all of the small bones and along the other side of the backbone. Remove the backbone and set aside.

The first cut is along one side of the backbone, from neck to tail. The second cut is on the other side of the backbone. Save the backbone for soup stock.

③ **Flatten the breastbone.** Take hold of both newly cut edges and open the bird. With a turkey, you will literally be breaking bones. With a young chicken, this really isn't necessary. Remove any large pieces of fat. Turn the bird breast-side up. Place your hand on one side of the breast, close to the breastbone, and push down firmly until you hear a crack. Repeat on the other side. (For better leverage as you work on a turkey, you may want to stand on a stepstool.)

Open the bird like you are breaking the spine of a book.

Place a hand on each side of the breast and press firmly to flatten the bird.

④ **Chill, refrigerate.** If you don't intend to eat the bird right away, wrap or bag it, seal, and freeze. The flattened birds will be easier to stack in the freezer.

You can use the backbones for making stock (page 107). If you don't intend to do so right away, package up the backbones together and throw them in the freezer.

What goes into the freezer is a flat, stackable package.

How to Handle the Edible Innards

Why save the giblets, livers, necks, and hearts? Because they are edible, even delicious, and you already paid for them.

① **Clean the gizzards.** If the gizzards have not yet been cleaned, you need to slice them open and clean them. Slice each one from hole to hole, and open it up. Inside will be grit and possibly some food. Dump this out, peel off the skin, and rinse the gizzards under cold running water. Drain on paper towels. (The gizzards can be used in soup stock as they are. But if you are planning on cooking them in a dish, you will want to remove the silverskin that connects the two lobes. This is fussy work and should be reserved until you are ready to cook.)

② **Clean the hearts.** If necessary, place the hearts in a bowl and run cold water over them until the water runs clear. Cut away any veins or membranes. Poke the tip of the knife into the holes where the veins were and remove any blood clots. Drain on paper towels with the gizzards.

③ **Clean the livers.** The gall bladder should have been removed already, but if not, remove it carefully so that the bile does not leak out. (It is an unmistakable-looking green sac.) Rinse the livers. If necessary, place in a bowl and run cold water over them until the water runs clear. Cut away any membranes, fat, or stringy bits. Remove any black or greenish spots. Drain on paper towels.

④ **Package and freeze.** Pack up in 1-pound packages. Package the gizzards and hearts together because they are usually cooked together. Package the liver separately. If you're not going to use the innards right away, freeze them.

Cleaned gizzard

Split open gizzard contains stones and grass.

Uncleaned gizzard

Meticulous cleaning, including removing any yellow membrane and silverskin, will make the gizzard more tender.

Heart

The heart has blood vessels poking out of the top end. Just cut them off.

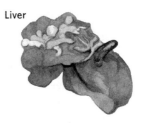

Liver

Cut away any fat, membranes, or greenish areas from the livers.

How to Clean Chicken Feet

Those chicken feet (and the feet of other land fowl) that you removed from your birds are dirty! The chickens have been walking around outside, without shoes on, so who knows what's on them? And let's face it: those talons pretty much define unappetizing. But the stock the feet will make (see page 107) is worth the trouble. Here's how to clean those dirty, scaly feet.

① **Set up for blanching and prep the feet.** Bring a large pot of water to a very low boil. Set out a large metal steaming basket that will allow you to immerse the feet and then lift them all out at once. While you're waiting for the water to heat, set a bowl of ice water near the pot. Set up a cutting board, poultry shears or chef's knife, and a bowl to hold the cleaned feet. Put the feet in a big bowl and rub with a generous sprinkling of kosher or coarse salt. (This is optional, but I think it makes the skin easier to peel.)

Rub the feet with coarse salt to make peeling easier.

② **Blanch the feet.** You will blanch the feet for only 3 to 5 seconds. Too little time, and the skin won't peel; too long, and the feet start cooking and the skin won't peel. It is a good idea to blanch the feet one at a time, until you decide on the perfect blanching time for the feet you are working with and the water temperature. Then you can work in bigger batches, as big as your steaming basket will allow. Put the feet in the steamer basket, dip into the water for the allotted time, and then pull them out and immediately plunge them into the ice water. Let them sit for 5 minutes (or more) to fully cool off.

Blanch briefly in boiling water, then cool in ice water.

③ **Peel.** Peel the skin off the feet; it should come off easily. The only tricky part is the pad of the feet. You can use a scrub brush under running water to get any bits that are hard to peel off.

The skin should easily peel off.

④ **Remove the talons.** Sometimes you can pull off the talons when you are peeling the feet. Those that don't come off easily can be clipped off with poultry shears or chopped off with a sharp knife.

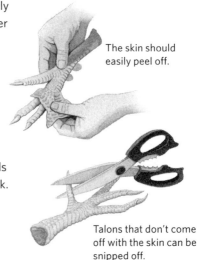

⑤ **Bag for the freezer or cook.** Figure that 1 pound of feet equals about 10 feet, and that 1 pound will make about 2 quarts of stock. If you're not going to use the cleaned feet to make stock right away, bag them up, seal, and freeze.

Talons that don't come off with the skin can be snipped off.

How to Render Poultry Fat

You can easily render the fat from chickens, geese, and ducks for use in cooking. (Turkeys, on the other hand, are rather lean and won't produce much fat.) Poultry fat, and especially goose and duck fat, has fabulous flavor, especially when used for roasting potatoes and root vegetables. It is also more challenging — but not impossible — to use it in baking. In the Jewish cooking traditions of northern Europe, chicken fat was often rendered with onions for flavor. In the French cooking tradition, goose fat and duck fat are more common and are generally not flavored. Either way, savory foods are delicious cooked in poultry fat.

Poultry fat is higher in polyunsaturated fatty acids than either lard or beef suet, which is why it is softer at room temperature. It is stable at high heat, and the rendered fat will keep for at least 2 months in the refrigerator or for 1 year in the freezer. After about 2 months in the fridge, though, the fat becomes rancid and has an off-odor that will be transmitted as an off-flavor to any dish it is cooked in.

Even if you are buying your birds from a farmers' market or a supermarket, you should be able to collect enough fat to make it practical to render it. I recommend collecting chicken fat in the freezer until you have a few cups. You can do the same with ducks and geese, though chances are that you roast them more infrequently. One commercial duck will still yield ⅓ to ½ cup rendered fat, while one commercial goose will yield about 2 quarts.

① **Cut the fat into small pieces.** Some of the fat, especially from geese, is in large pieces. Cut the fat into small pieces to reduce the time it takes to render and to reduce the chance of the fat scorching.

Cut the fat into pieces that are 1 inch or smaller.

② **Combine the fat with water and apply heat.** Place the fat and any skin scraps or the ends of backbones in a heavy, nonreactive pot, along with a diced onion, if you like. Add enough water to just cover the fat. Cook over very low heat, stirring occasionally, until the scraps render most of their fat, about 2 hours. Watch carefully during the last 30 minutes or so because the water will boil off, which could allow the fat to burn, which you do not want.

A little water at the start of the process keeps the fat from burning; it will eventually evaporate away.

③ **Strain and store.** When the fat has lique-
fied, turn off the heat and let cool for a few
minutes. Strain through several layers of
cheesecloth, a single layer of butter muslin,
or a double layer of paper coffee filters into a
clean canning jar or freezer container. Cover
tightly and store in the refrigerator for up to
2 months or in the freezer for up to 1 year.

Strain the liquid
fat through butter
muslin or a coffee
filter to remove
all the solids, or
cracklings.

④ **Fry the cracklings.** There will be bits of
skin (and onion, if you used it) remaining
after the fat is drained off. This is called
gribenes in Yiddish; there is no real English
equivalent. Like pork cracklings, gribenes are
unbelievably tasty, especially if there is onion
in the mix. Fry them over medium heat until
crisp, then drain on paper towels. Try not to
eat all of the gribenes; you can sprinkle them
over salads and other dishes as you would
sprinkle bacon. Store in the fridge and refry
as needed to make crisp again.

Fry the cracklings over medium
heat until crisp and sprinkle on
salads or whatever pleases you.

Schmaltz and Other Poultry Fats

My ancestors came from Poland and Russia
and kept kosher. Chicken fat was used for
cooking all meat dishes; butter was used
for cooking all dairy dishes. Cooking oils
weren't readily available in eastern Europe
in the late nineteenth and twentieth centuries. Outside of the Jewish enclaves, people
cooked with lard. Only in southern Europe
and the Middle East was olive oil a popular
cooking medium.

Today chicken fat, goose fat, and duck
fat are enjoying a minor revival — as well
they should. It is easy to render the fat to
make it possible to use it for cooking. It will
keep for 2 months in the refrigerator and
even longer in the freezer. As for its reputa-
tion as being very unhealthy for you, see the
sidebar on page 137; goose fat and duck fat,
in particular, are possibly better for you than
butter, in terms of amount of saturated fat.

Chicken fat is sometimes referred to as
schmaltz, which is Yiddish for chicken fat; it
has also come to mean "excessively senti-
mental or corny." Jewish schmaltz is often
flavored with onions, but the onion is not at
all necessary.

Because poultry fat has a medium-high
smoke point (higher than butter but lower
than peanut oil), it can be used for browning
meats and sautéing vegetables. It can be
used instead of other fats in most pâtés.
Goose fat and duck fat make the best
roasted potatoes and roasted root vegetables, and chicken fat is used in both traditional matzo balls and chopped liver. I have
done only limited baking with chicken fat,
enough to learn that it does not create flaky
pastries as lard does, and cakes made with
chicken fat tend to be dense and greasy.

Cooking Poultry

Birds that spend most of their time walking around and scratching in the dirt — chickens and turkeys — have well-developed leg muscles, which become dark meat. Wings and breasts, which don't get much use by these landed birds, tend to be primarily white meat, which is softer and less dense.

In some breeds the breasts are quite large, something nature wouldn't bother to develop. Today's commercial turkey varieties, inevitably the intensively bred Broad Breasted White, both male and female, usually have about 70 percent white meat and 30 percent dark meat. Selective breeding has eliminated white meat/dark meat gender differences, though toms still grow larger than hens. Heritage breeds of turkey and chicken and birds that haven't been as intensely bred for commercial characteristics, like guinea fowl, tend to have a 50:50 split between dark meat and white meat.

White meat typically has a milder flavor than dark meat and is lower in fat. That makes it easy to overcook, which results in dry meat. Darker cuts have more fat and take longer to cook, so they tend to be juicier, but they also have a more pronounced taste that some people find "gamy."

Ducks and geese are all dark meat, as are quail, guinea fowl, pheasants, and pigeon (squab).

There are almost infinite ways to cook poultry. To begin, there's roasting. Roasting is simple, but it is important to distinguish between roasting relatively lean birds (chickens, guinea fowl, turkeys), a process that includes making gravy, and roasting fatty birds (ducks and geese), whose juices you will not want to turn into gravy. Lean or fatty, I think birds roast most successfully when spatchcocked. Roasting does little to tenderize older hens and roosters, though; with them you might try making stock (page 107) or braising (page 335). Poultry can also be fried, sautéed, stir-fried, poached, broiled, and barbecued.

Judging Doneness

The USDA says to cook all types of poultry to 165°F (74°C). In fact, breast meat is fully cooked at 150°F (66°C), when it is still juicy. Cooking beyond that point causes the muscle fibers to contract and allow the juices to run out. Leg meat, on the other hand, should be cooked to 165°F (74°C), or the juices will still be pink or red, and the meat won't be as tender as it should be. When you spatchcock a bird, you'll see that the breast meat sits taller and has more mass. The legs are splayed out with better air circulation around them, allowing them to cook more than the breasts. In this way, spatchcocking encourages the bird to cook more evenly, with breasts and legs more likely to reach doneness at the same time.

USDA cautions aside, duck breast is usually served medium-rare (150°F/66°C) in restaurants.

Test for doneness with an instant-read thermometer, taking care that the probe is not touching a bone. Test a few spots to be sure the entire breast or leg has reached the desired temperature. Also, when you withdraw the probe, the juices should run clear, not pink or red. Although duck breast meat will be tender served medium-rare, the leg meat should be cooked to the full 165°F (74°C); otherwise it will be stringy, tough, and bloody.

The USDA says to cook all types of poultry to 165°F (74°C). In fact, breast meat is fully cooked at 150°F (66°C), when it is still juicy. Leg meat, on the other hand, should be cooked to 165°F (74°C).

How to Cut a Bird into Parts

There are plenty of reasons to cut birds into parts, not the least of which is that a turkey is too big for most family meals. Although ducks and geese are all dark meat, the breasts cook in less time than the legs, so if you are harvesting these birds in batches, you may want to package breasts and legs separately. The process of cutting a bird into parts is the same for all poultry. The instructions below assume you are starting from a spatchcocked bird. If not, do that first (see page 96).

① **Cut off the leg quarters.** Place the bird on a cutting board, breast up. Grasp the chicken's left leg. Pull it away from the body so you can see where the leg and hip bones connect. With a sharp knife cut through the skin to expose where the leg and breast meet. Pull the leg out as far as you can to allow the joint where the thigh bone connects to the carcass to pop out and cut through. Repeat these steps on the other leg.

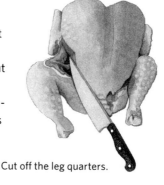

Cut off the leg quarters.

② **Divide the thighs and drumsticks.** Place the leg quarter skin-side down on the cutting board. The drumstick is the smaller part of the leg; the thigh is the larger, meatier part. Grab the thigh in one hand, the drumstick in the other, and bend the drumstick backward to expose the joint between the drumstick and thigh, which is the easiest place to cut, and cut through to separate the drumstick and thigh. Repeat these steps on the other leg.

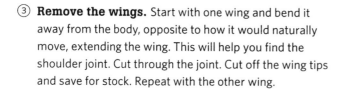

Separate the thighs and drumsticks.

③ **Remove the wings.** Start with one wing and bend it away from the body, opposite to how it would naturally move, extending the wing. This will help you find the shoulder joint. Cut through the joint. Cut off the wing tips and save for stock. Repeat with the other wing.

Remove the wings.

④ **Divide the breast.** Turning the breast bone-side up, find the center of the breastbone (called the keel or sternum) and slice down firmly. This should slice the breast fairly evenly in half. The bone in a young chicken will give little resistance, but a turkey may require a cleaver and some muscle (or a mallet). Continue cutting until you have two distinct halves. If you like, cut each breast half in half again to equalize the size of the pieces. Repeat with the other breast half. The bird is now ready for cooking.

Divide the breast.

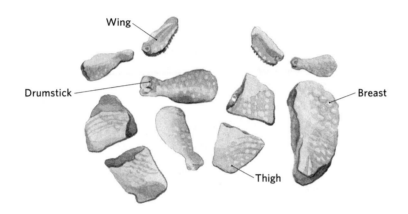

Wing

Drumstick

Breast

Thigh

STEP-BY-STEP **How to Roast a Chicken or Guinea Fowl**

You can find lots of information in cookbooks about roasting birds, whether or not to stuff, whether or not you need a rack in the roasting pan, whether or not to truss. I'm going to keep it simple: try roasting spatchcocked birds to save time, to keep the skin crisp, to ensure the breast meat doesn't overcook, and to make the carving easy.

① **Preheat the oven and prepare the bird.** Preheat the oven to 450°F (230°C). If you haven't done so already, spatchcock the bird (page 96). Rub the bird on all surfaces with 1 tablespoon oil or butter. Season generously with salt and freshly ground black pepper. If you like, sprinkle with 2 teaspoons chopped fresh or 1 teaspoon dried thyme, sage, oregano, and/or rosemary. If you plan to make gravy, you can also add chopped aromatic vegetables (onions, celery, carrots, garlic) to the pan to enhance the flavor of the gravy.

② **Roast.** Position the bird on a rimmed baking sheet or in a shallow roasting pan so that the breasts are aligned with the center of the pan and the legs are close to the edge. A roasting rack is not necessary. Roast until the thickest part of the breast close to the bone registers 150°F (66°C) on an instant-read thermometer and the joint between the thighs and body registers at least 165°F (74°C), 45 to 60 minutes for an average-size (3- to 5-pound) bird, but start checking with an instant-read thermometer after 30 minutes. (If you're using a probe thermometer, remember to test a few different spots to be sure the desired temperatures have been reached throughout.)

The bird sits flat in the roasting pan for even cooking.

③ **Rest, then carve.** Transfer the bird from the roasting pan to a cutting board, tent loosely with foil, and allow to rest for at least 10 minutes before carving. Resting is critical to allow the meat to reabsorb the juices.

To carve, remove the legs (this will be obvious) and cut through the joint to separate the drumstick and thigh. Slice off the wings. Carve the breasts into slices.

Variation: Roasting a Turkey

The same method outlined for spatchcocked chickens (above) can be adapted for a whole turkey. Plan to cook the turkey at 425°F (220°C) for 20 minutes, then reduce the heat to 350°F (180°C) and roast for a total of 1½ to 2 hours. Roast until the breast meat reaches 150°F (66°C) and the thighs read 165°F (74°C). If the breast reaches that temperature before the thighs, remove the bird from the oven, remove the breast, and return the thighs to the oven. The thermometer is a more important gauge than the timing.

How to Carve a Spatchcocked Roasted Turkey

A spatchcocked turkey requires a slightly different carving technique than a bird cooked the traditional way, but the basic approach remains the same: remove the legs and wings, and then slice the breast meat. The same method applies to other birds, but generally speaking, you will just cut smaller birds into individual parts.

① **Cut the legs from the breast.** With a sharp chef's knife, remove each leg by cutting through the turkey where the thigh connects to the breast.

Cut off the leg quarters.

② **Separate the drumsticks and thighs.** At the joint of each leg, cut the drumstick from the thigh. Transfer the thighs and drumsticks to a warm platter. Tent with foil.

Slice the thigh meat off the bone, if you like.

③ **Cut off the wings and breast meat.** On one side, find the joint connecting the wing and breast, and cut through it. Repeat to cut off the other wing. Cut the breast meat into two pieces, slicing with your knife along either side of the breastbone.

④ **Slice the breast meat.** Slice the breast meat across the grain. Arrange on the platter with the dark meat, and add the wings.

Slice the entire breast off the bone.

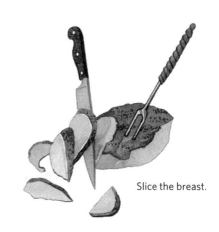

Slice the breast.

How to Make Gravy

A free-range bird makes fabulous, flavorful gravy, and it isn't difficult to prepare. If you don't have poultry stock on hand, be sure to prepare some as the bird roasts. If the bird arrived with the neck and giblets, put them in a saucepan with a chopped onion, a couple of ribs of celery, and a bay leaf or garlic clove. Cover with water and simmer for about 1 hour, then strain. Although chicken stock does not taste exactly like turkey stock or guinea fowl or duck stock, they can all be used interchangeably.

① **Pour out the pan drippings.** Transfer the bird from the roasting pan to a rimmed baking sheet, cover loosely with aluminum foil, and set aside to rest. Pour the pan drippings (through a strainer if necessary) into a tall measuring cup or 1-quart fat separator. The fat will rise to the top and the drippings will settle. How many cups of drippings you have will depend on the type and size of the bird. Some free-range turkeys are incredibly juicy, others less so.

— Fat separator

② **Remove the fat.** If you have a fat separator, you can pour off the drippings to a large measuring cup, leaving the fat in the separator. Otherwise, you can let the fat rise to the top of your tall measuring cup and then skim it

Fat rises to the top

off. Do not discard this fat; you will need it in step 5!

③ **Deglaze the pan.** Set the roasting pan over medium-high heat on the stovetop, spanning two burners, if necessary. Pour in 1 cup stock or water, and then scrape up all the bits from the bottom of the pan with a silicone spatula. Add to the drippings.

④ **Do the math.** Sorry, but a little math now is unavoidable. To calculate how many cups of gravy you need, figure ½ cup per serving. (Some people would say that ¼ cup or ⅓ cup gravy per person is sufficient, but I like to be generous.) Dilute the pan drippings as needed with stock to equal the total amount of gravy you need. Leftover gravy can be frozen and served with any roasted bird, or used to enrich a soup or pot pie.

⑤ **Make a roux.** For every 1 cup of drippings and stock, you will need 2 tablespoons flour and 2 tablespoons fat. The flavor of the gravy is really enhanced by using the fat you separated from the drippings in step 1; you can also use butter or a combination of the two.

Add the fat to a saucepan and heat over medium-high heat. When the fat is hot, whisk in the flour to form a thin paste. Cook for a few minutes, whisking constantly, until bubbly and deeply golden brown.

⑥ **Add the diluted pan drippings.** Pour the pan drippings into the roux, whisking to combine. Bring to a boil.

Add the drippings plus stock to the roux.

⑦ **Finish the gravy.** If the gravy is too thin, cook to reduce, stirring occasionally. If it is too thick, whisk in some stock until you have the desired thickness. Taste, and add salt and pepper as needed. Serve warm.

STEP-BY-STEP **How to Make Poultry Stock**

The first time I made soup stock from an older stewing hen, it was a complete revelation. I threw the bird in a pot with a couple of onions and a bunch of parsley. I forgot my usual celery and carrots. That stock was so flavorful, it was tasty even without salt. It was probably about ten times tastier than both my normal all-dark-meat soup stock, in which I had taken such pride over the years, and my backbone-and-spare-parts stock.

The bird was an 18-month-old egg layer that had been culled from a flock. It astounds me that stewing hens don't show up in supermarkets. Why isn't there a huge demand for this outstanding product? It is worth raising chickens just to have a supply of old birds for soup stock.

For those of you who have never made soup stock, the process is easy and you don't need to fuss over it while it simmers on the back of the stove for 4 to 6 hours. For the best-tasting chicken stock, use an old bird — a laying hen or rooster. Or save the parts you don't normally eat, such as wings, backs, necks, and feet, for making stock. The greater the proportion of bones to meat (as when using all backs or feet), the more gelatin will be released to thicken the stock. When chilled, a stock rich in gelatin will be semisolid, like Jell-O. Writers in the *Nourishing Traditions* school of thought and followers of the Paleo diet suggest that a "bone broth" is richer in minerals and will even add vinegar to a stockpot to make the minerals more likely to leach from the bones. I don't know about that; all I know is that a gelatinized stock is a rich and good-tasting stock — whether you call it bone broth or chicken stock (or any other type of stock). Gizzards can also be thrown in (or see page 109 for alternative ideas for the gizzards). When buying chicken specifically to make stock, choose dark meat if you don't have access to feet or backs. It is less expensive than white meat and more flavorful. The quantities for making stock are easily doubled. You can also save the bones of a roasted bird and use those for a somewhat less robust stock. Ducks, geese, guinea fowl, and turkeys all make good stock.

① **Combine the ingredients.** In a 2-gallon stockpot, combine 3 to 4 pounds of a stewing bird or bird parts or chicken feet, or a roasted bird carcass, with 1 large onion (quartered), 4 ribs celery, 4 garlic cloves, and 1 bunch parsley. Add enough water to cover (about 4 quarts).

② **Cook.** Cover and bring just to a boil. Immediately reduce the heat and simmer gently for 4 to 6 hours, with the lid partially on. Do not allow the stock to boil (to keep the stock clear), if possible.

③ **Strain.** Strain and discard the vegetables. Remove the meat from the bones if you started with fresh bones and meat (not roasted), and save it for another use, such as chicken salad or pot pie. (Some people think the meat is too dry and stringy at this point; they may discard it or use it for pet food.)

④ **Chill and skim off the fat.** Chill the stock for several hours. Skim off the fat that rises to the top and hardens. You can use the fat for cooking or discard.

⑤ **Use or store.** To finish the stock, season to taste with salt. Or leave unsalted and use as a base for soups and grain dishes. Use immediately or pressure-can (see chapter 11); process pints for 20 minutes and quarts for 25 minutes. Or cool, then refrigerate. It will keep for about 3 days in the refrigerator or 4 to 6 months in the freezer.

Canning Poultry Stock

Stock, with or without meat, can be canned in a pressure canner (see chapter 11). Do not consider using a boiling-water-bath canner. I have read bloggers on the Internet who don't like to fuss with the pressure canner, so they just increase the boiling-water-bath canning time. This is not a safe practice! No matter how long the contents of the jar are processed, the internal temperature will never rise above 212°F (100°C) unless pressure is applied, and botulism spores can survive that temperature. You need to bring the contents above 240°F (116°C), which can only be done under pressure. That's science.

Stock vs. Broth

Is there a difference between stock and broth? It depends on whom you ask. In this cookbook, stock is the strained liquid that results from cooking meat, fish, or their bones and/or vegetables in water. A brown stock is made by roasting the bones and vegetables first. Depending on the cook, stock may or may not be seasoned with salt. I don't salt stock because I want to be able to use it with salty ingredients and not worry about adding too much salt to a dish. Broth is seasoned stock, ready for serving. You can use the words *broth* and *stock* interchangeably. Whatever you call it, just be aware of whether the liquid has been salted or not.

Tips for Cooking Roosters and Older Birds

Roosters and older birds, such as unproductive laying hens, don't take well to roasting. Dry heat makes the meat almost too tough to chew. But take your time with them, and they will make exceptional fare. Roosters differ from older hens in that they have sturdier bones (harder to cut), more cartilage, and denser muscles. Also the breasts are much smaller, and there is a greater proportion of dark meat. But the cooking rules remain the same.

➤ Let the bird age in the refrigerator for 2 to 4 days. You can keep it in a container of water or just wrapped in plastic (after washing and drying well).

➤ Marinate for at least 12 and up to 48 hours, if you are planning to eat the meat. This isn't necessary if you are simply making stock. Any marinade will do; coq au vin (see page 296) is traditionally made with an old rooster (the *coq*) and marinated in red wine (the *vin*).

➤ Cook long and slow. In a Dutch oven with a lid, cook at 200°F/95°C for at least 6 hours, or until the meat is falling off the bone. The manual for my slow cooker says *high* equals 212°F/100°C, *low* equals 200°F/95°C, *simmer* equals 185°F/85°C, and *keep warm* equals 165°F/74°C. If you are going to use a slow cooker, it is worth checking to make sure that *low* is the proper temperature; many run higher than that.

➤ Old birds vary! This is not a standardized piece of meat. Do not plan to serve the day you are cooking the bird, unless you plan to start very, very early in the morning. Far safer is to cook the bird a day in advance and give it as much time as it requires to become tender. Then skim off the fat, reheat, and serve.

A lean old bird

The Edible Tidbits

The edible tidbits of poultry include the neck, liver, gizzard, and heart. There are numerous ways to cook each.

Neck. Necks are mostly bone with meat clinging to it. They can be thrown into any stew or braise if you don't mind eating with your hands and putting a lot of effort into getting a little bit of meat. I think they are best suited for stock. Save them up in a bag in the freezer until you have a few pounds, and then make stock (see page 107).

Liver. Either you love it or you hate it. If you don't know where you stand on liver in general, start by sampling poultry liver. To prepare poultry liver for cooking, remove any greenish or black spots and any fat or membrane. Rinse well under running water to remove all traces of blood. If necessary, put the livers in a bowl and run cold water over them until the water runs clear. Then pat dry. Pan-fry livers in butter over medium heat until they are seared on the outside but still pink inside. That's it. Or dress it up with a little onion, garlic, and/or fresh thyme. This is the basis of some incredible pâtés (see page 295) and, of course, Jewish chopped liver, which is a rustic pâté by another name. You can also turn the liver into a pasta sauce, sautéed with onions or bacon or both.

Gizzard and heart. No matter how you prepare these mild-tasting morsels, they are going to be chewy. Those who don't like gizzard or heart generally have an issue with the texture, not the flavor. If you are among the texture protesters, use them in soup stock and then discard. However, they can be cut into small pieces and stewed or braised; I like them red-cooked (see page 299). They can be poached in water or stock until cooked through; then thinly sliced, battered, and deep-fried, or they can be thinly sliced, marinated in buttermilk, then coated with crumbs and deep-fried. Or after poaching, you can chop finely and add to poultry stuffings or gravy. Before cooking, remove any membranes, fat, or darkened spots and rinse well.

How to Roast a Duck or Goose

When it comes to cooking them, ducks and geese provide unique challenges because they are so fatty. Of course, this is a good thing. An 11-pound goose may yield as much as 3 cups of delicious fat. The trick when roasting a duck or goose is to render out all the fat so that the meat is tender but not greasy and the skin is crispy.

Another challenge is that the breast meat is tender when it reaches 150°F (66°C), but the legs are tender at 165°F (74°C) or higher. You'd think the breast meat would therefore be white, as with chickens and turkeys. But no, all the meat from these birds is dark and quite rich. You can get around this problem by removing the breasts from the oven before the legs.

Low-temperature roasting works best with these fatty birds. Roasting at a high temperature causes the fat to smoke and set off smoke alarms. Be aware, however, that roasted ducks and geese are never as tender as chicken and turkey.

Fruity sauces (including cranberry sauce) make the best accompaniments because they help cut the richness.

① **Prep the bird.** Preheat the oven to 325°F (165°C). If you haven't done so already, spatchcock the bird (page 96). Remove the wing tips and save for stock. Remove and save excess fat from the body cavity and neck. Remove and save any excess skin around the neck area. Score the skin (do not slice into the meat) and prick the skin all over with a needle or the tip of a sharp knife.

Place the bird skin-side up on a rack in a roasting pan and pour boiling water over the bird to tighten the skin. Leave the water in the pan (to prevent the fat from smoking), but pat the bird dry. Rub all over with salt and pepper.

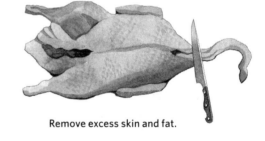

Remove excess skin and fat.

Boiling water tightens the skin.

Remove wing tips.

2. **Roast.** Roast the bird for about 45 minutes (small ducks) to 60 to 75 minutes (larger ducks and geese). Test the temperature of the breast meat with an instant-read thermometer. When the breast temperature reads 150°F (66°C), remove the breasts. Place the breasts under a tent of foil and return the legs to the oven to continue to roast for about 15 minutes more, until the meat in the thickest part of the thigh reads 165°F to 170°F (74°C to 77°C). The temperature is more important than the timing, so put your trust in the thermometer and allow yourself extra time. (If you're using a probe thermometer, remember to test a few different spots to be sure the desired temperatures have been reached throughout.)

3. **Rest.** Rest the thighs under a tent of foil for at least 15 minutes. The fat in the roasting pan can be strained and saved in the refrigerator; it is already rendered.

4. **Crisp the skin.** Meanwhile, if needed, run the breasts under the broiler for a few minutes to make the skin crisp.

5. **Carve.** Slice the breast meat and separate the legs and thighs. Most of the meat will be in the breasts.

The carved bird can be laid out attractively on a serving platter.

Rabbits

I wanted to call this chapter "Eggs, Birds, and Bunnies." But we don't like to think about eating bunnies, do we? In fact, if the bunny connection is very strong, rabbit will be a tough sell at the dinner table.

Rabbit is easily compared to chicken, more because of size than flavor. It is also like chicken in that you probably will have to slaughter and butcher the rabbit yourself, in which case it won't arrive in your kitchen all neatly vacuum-bagged and ready for the freezer.

You can compare the flavor of rabbit to that of dark-meat chicken, but it is actually closer in flavor to squirrel. Unless you happen to have a hunter in your house, this comparison will be meaningless, so let's stick with the chicken metaphor. Because rabbit is leaner and less meaty than the chicken, the meat is more likely to be tougher, bonier, and drier. Some pieces are meatier than others and will cook more slowly. All the meat is dark.

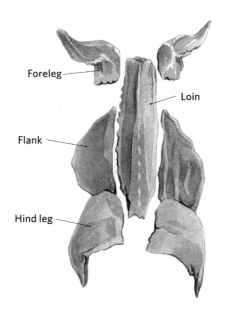

Foreleg

Loin

Flank

Hind leg

If you are raising rabbits yourself, you might want to harvest the animals in batches and freeze all the hind legs together (the meatiest parts), and everything else together (a lot of bony parts). This gives you the opportunity to cook a batch of rabbit parts to the same degree of tenderness and doneness. Even if you are freezing single animals, you may still want to cut them into pieces before you cook them. Some people save only the hind legs and discard the rest. You also want to be sure to harvest your rabbits young, certainly before they are 6 months old. The older the rabbit, the tougher the meat.

Cooking Rabbit

As with all other animals, make sure the rabbit rests in the refrigerator for at least 24 hours after slaughter. Cook rabbit like skinless chicken. It does best in stews and braises. It can also be soaked in buttermilk, coated with crumbs, and deep-fried. If you want to roast it, wrap it in bacon first.

Anytime you are handling raw meat, it is a good idea to sanitize your work area and equipment with a sanitizing solution (see page 13). Rinse the animal under running water in the sink and pat dry. Remove the head, if it is still attached, and any membranes, silverskin, and clotted blood. Then gather your tools and you are good to go (if your cutting tools are sharp; if not see page 12).

Woodchuck: Tastes Like Rabbit

If you garden anywhere from eastern Alaska, through much of Canada, into the eastern United States and south to northern Georgia, you have probably had a problem with woodchucks. One solution is to shoot and eat them. Every gardener in the area will thank you. (You could just kill the woodchucks, but most hunters feel pretty strongly that whatever you kill, you must eat.) I would rather eat a woodchuck than share my garden with one, so if my son is willing to shoot a woodchuck that trespasses on my garden, I will cook it.

Woodchucks, for all their mass, don't yield much meat. They average around 2 pounds after the fur and organs are discarded. A 2-foot critter is mostly just voracious appetite and fur. It should be noted that woodchucks, as well as most other small food animals such as squirrels, have scent glands that should be cut out as soon as possible to avoid tainting the meat. When dressing woodchucks, look for and carefully remove without damaging any small gray or reddish-brown kernels of fat located under the forelegs, on top of the shoulder blades, along the spine in the small of the back, and around the anus.

Woodchuck can be cooked like rabbit, which is why I mention it here. Any way you would cook a rabbit, you can cook a woodchuck. You can also adapt your favorite beef stew or chicken gumbo recipe. I understand Southern-fried woodchuck is perfectly fine, but I prefer my woodchuck cooked until it is no longer recognizable. But that's just me.

1. **Remove the forelegs.** Place the rabbit on its side so that one foreleg is up. Pull the front leg away from the body to identify the natural seam where the leg is attached (by flesh, not by bone). Cut through the seam, keeping the blade of your knife against the ribs and pulling the foreleg away from the body. Repeat on the other side.

2. **Remove the flank.** Turn the rabbit over onto its back. Identify the flank, or belly meat, which is a thin muscle that is attached to the hind legs and runs up along the sides. With a boning knife, cut the flank away from the body and slice along the line where the saddle (or loin) starts; then run the knife along that edge to the ribs. When you get to the rib cage, you can cut the meat off the ribs, as far as you can go, which is usually where the front leg used to be.

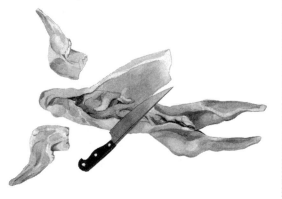

3. **Slice off the hind legs.** With the rabbit still on its back, cut into the flesh along the pelvic bones until you get to the ball-and-socket joint. When you do, grasp either end firmly and bend it back to pop the joint. Then slice around the back leg with your knife to free it from the carcass.

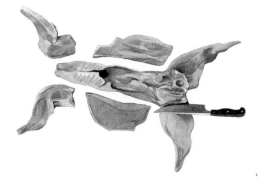

4. **Divide the loin.** The loin is left. Remove as much silverskin as you can. Chop the loin into serving pieces with a cleaver, smashing through the spine.

CHAPTER 7

Fresh Milk

It is a happy homestead that can provide itself with plenty of fresh milk. You'll enjoy drinking it, of course, and pouring it over your morning granola, but one thing is certain: when there are dairy animals in the barn, there is a surplus of milk in the kitchen. Whether you're milking a cow or a few dairy goats, you'll have extra milk, and you'll have to find a way to preserve it. This creates a wonderful opportunity to make butter, cheese, yogurt, and, of course, ice cream. These preservation methods are covered in later chapters, but for now the focus is on how to handle all that fresh, raw milk in the kitchen.

Cow versus Goat

On a backyard homestead you are more likely to raise goats than dairy cows because of space constraints. A single cow requires about an acre of grass, while a quarter of an acre of pasture will support a couple of goats.

Even if you don't raise dairy animals, raw organic milk, from both cows and goats, is available for sale in many states. Even if your state does not allow the retail sale of raw milk, it may allow farm sales, or it may be possible to buy a "share" in a dairy animal, which will give you access to the milk.

American dairy culture is exceedingly cow-centric, so most people are surprised at their first taste of (chilled) goat's milk, which is noticeably richer than cow's milk. Cow's milk contains an average of 3.8 to 3.9 percent butterfat, while goat's milk contains about 6 percent fat, about as much as the buffalo milk that's used to make the best mozzarella cheese. It is also completely lacking in off-flavors or odors, contrary to some people's expectations. As long as the milk has been collected in a sanitary fashion and the buck is kept away from the doe, there is no "goaty" aroma or aftertaste.

Raw cow's milk is generally nonhomogenized, which means that the fat globules rise to the top and form a layer of cream. You can ladle off all or some of the cream for making whipped cream or cultured cream products (see chapter 15). Shaking the jar before pouring will ensure a good blend of milk and the remaining cream.

In goat's milk the fat globules are smaller and disperse more readily, making the milk naturally homogenized. Since the cream will not separate on its own, if you want to make goat's-milk butter, you'll need to acquire a cream separator. Another difference you may notice is that goat's milk (and sheep's milk, too) appears whiter than cow's milk because the milk does not contain any beta-carotene.

In case you were wondering, relative to cows and even goats, sheep produce far less milk — about 1 quart a day, compared to 3 to 6 quarts a day from a goat and 2 to 4 gallons a day from a dairy cow. Sheep's milk is much higher in proteins and butterfat (milk solids), so a gallon of sheep's milk will yield more cheese than a gallon of cow or goat's milk. It is considered to have higher nutritional value and to be easier for humans to digest than cow or goat's milk.

From Barn to Kitchen

Sanitation and rapid chilling are the keys to producing milk that tastes good, makes cheese without any off-flavors, and remains fresh for drinking for 7 to 10 days.

Good sanitation in the barn means that all milking equipment is washed in hot, soapy water, rinsed in hot water, and allowed to air-dry. The dishwasher is good for this, but you can also wash by hand. Everything that comes in contact with the milk — bucket, milk tote, strainer, funnel, storage jars — should be sanitized before using.

If you are milking more than one cow, doe, or ewe, you will probably milk into a bucket and then transfer the milk to a milk tote. However you do it, you should start cooling the milk as soon as possible. A milk tote, for example, can be set in a larger container that is packed with ice or ice water to start the cooling.

Next, strain the milk. You can use a proper milk strainer, which is a funnel fitted with a mesh screen, or improvise a strainer with a reusable coffee strainer and funnel or a funnel plus strainer plus butter muslin. Strain the milk into 2-quart or smaller mason jars.

The best milk strainers are made from stainless steel and include a funnel that fits both regular and wide-mouth canning jars.

A sink basin that can be drained and refilled with more ice water easily will quickly and efficiently cool down milk.

Don't use gallon jars because the milk in a gallon jar cools too slowly. Top each jar with a plastic canning lid and label the date and time of milking (noting A.M. or P.M.).

Unless you are making cheese right away, immediately chill the milk. The goal is to take the temperature of the milk from about 100°F (38°C) to about 38°F (3°C) within an hour. You can put the milk in a freezer, in a cooler filled with ice, or in a container of ice water in the refrigerator. The circulating air of a refrigerator is not sufficient on its own for rapidly cooling the milk, unless the milk is in very small containers.

Keep the milk chilled at 38°F to 40°F (3°C to 4°C). Do not add warm milk to previously chilled milk; adding the warm milk to the older milk will encourage bacteria in the older milk to grow. The naturally occurring bacteria in milk, lactobacilli, will thrive in warm temperatures, making lactic acid, which gives soured milk its characteristically tangy taste and reduces its shelf life.

Immediately after setting the milk to chill, rinse your collection containers and filter to remove most of the milk. Wash everything in very hot, soapy water, rinse well, and air-dry. If you used a filtering cloth, boil it for a minute or two, and hang to dry.

Pasteurizing Milk

Many people choose to pasteurize their fresh milk. Pasteurization is the process of heating milk to a high enough temperature for a long enough time to kill any bacteria in the milk. Passion runs high on both sides of the pasteurization question. Proponents of pasteurization say that it prevents illness and prolongs shelf life; opponents say that it destroys beneficial enzymes and negatively affects the nutritional value and flavor of the milk. You must make your own decision on the risks and benefits of raw milk. I think the flavor of raw milk (and cheeses made with it) is superior. I will go out of my way to buy raw milk directly from a farm, and I'll buy local pasteurized milk over ultra-pasteurized milk, which involves higher-than-normal pasteurization temperatures and is done to further extend shelf life, even if the latter is organic (it doesn't taste good to me).

STEP-BY-STEP **How to Pasteurize Raw Milk**

If you choose to pasteurize your milk, there's another choice to be made: high-temperature pasteurization (bringing the milk to 165°F/74°C for only 15 seconds) or low-temperature pasteurization (bringing the milk to 145°F/63°C and holding it there for 30 minutes). Most tasters prefer the low-temperature process, which is less damaging to the enzymes and protein structure of the milk, but obviously the high-temperature process is easier and quicker.

In either case, you will need to set up a double boiler (to avoid overheating the milk) and a kitchen thermometer.

① **Set up a double boiler.** Pour the raw milk into a stainless steel pot and set the pot inside a larger pot with a few inches of water at the bottom.

② **Slowly heat the milk.** Over medium heat, slowly bring the temperature of the milk to 145°F (63°C) or 165°F (74°C), stirring occasionally.

A double boiler will prevent the milk from scorching, but keep an eye on the thermometer.

③ **Hold the milk at the proper temperature for the proper amount of time.** Hold the temperature of the milk at 145°F (63°C) for exactly 30 minutes. Do not let the temperature of the milk dip below 145°F (63°C), or you will have to start over. Or hold the milk at 165°F (74°C) for just 15 seconds. You may need to increase and decrease the heat under the double boiler to keep the temperature constant.

④ **Cool.** Remove the pot of milk from the heat and place it in a sink or large bowl filled with ice water. Stir constantly until the temperature drops to 40°F (4°C) or less.

⑤ **Store.** Transfer the milk to sterilized or sanitized canning jars, and store in the refrigerator.

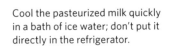

Cool the pasteurized milk quickly in a bath of ice water; don't put it directly in the refrigerator.

Sterilizing Storage Jars

High in protein and sugars, and low in acidity, milk is the perfect medium for bacteria — both the lactobacilli that we use to convert milk into cheese and the spoilage bacteria. So sanitation is key to everything you do in the kitchen when you are handling milk.

To sterilize canning jars for filling with milk, submerge the jars in a large pot of water, such as a boiling-water-bath canner, and boil for 10 minutes. Or use the sterilizing cycle on your dishwasher. If you prefer, you can use a sanitizing solution (see page 13), like the solution beer brewers and winemakers use, to sanitize your storage jars.

Storing Milk

Keeping milk chilled is critical to keeping it fresh. Whether you are storing raw milk or pasteurized milk, you should always keep it in the refrigerator. It should never sit out at room temperature. If all you plan to do with your milk is drink it, then store it in clean glass jars, 2-quart size or smaller. Every time a jar is opened and exposed to air, there is the possibility of contamination. If you can divide your milk into 1-quart jars, even better. Kept well chilled, milk should stay fresh for 7 to 10 days.

Using Milk and Cream in the Kitchen

Depending on the size of your household, the number of animals you are milking, and the time of year, you may be faced with more milk than you need for drinking, eating with cereal, and using in cooking. In this case you can culture excess milk and cream to make butter, yogurt, or cheese; see chapter 15. Excess milk can also be frozen; see chapter 10. When all else fails, use up the extra milk in custards, puddings, and ice cream; see chapter 20.

Making Whipped Cream

Making whipped cream from raw milk takes a little bit of planning. First you must separate the cream from the milk by allowing the milk to stand in the refrigerator for several hours, or overnight. At the same time, you should be chilling your bowl and beaters in the freezer. Skim off the cream. If you have the time, let the cream sit in the refrigerator for a few more hours; you may end up with a layer of milk in the bottom of your jar. Either skim off the cream again or use a turkey baster to siphon the milk from the cream. Then whip the cream with a whisk, an immersion blender, or the whisk attachment of your stand beater.

If you have trouble getting the cream to whip, you probably have too much milk in with it. The thicker the cream, the more easily it will whip. You want the cream to form soft peaks: when you lift the whisk or beaters, a peak forms but then drops to the side and does not hold its shape. If you beat for too long, the cream will start to get grainy and eventually separate out into homemade butter and whey, which is not what you are going for.

Fresh whipped cream from raw cream doesn't need to have anything added to it, particularly if you are planning to use it to top a sweet dessert. However, a little maple syrup, honey, or sugar for sweetening and a little vanilla extract or fruit liqueur (page 53) for flavoring can be a nice touch.

CHAPTER 8

MEAT
Goat, Lamb, Pork, and Beef

If your meat arrives in the kitchen in 25-pound boxes, all packaged as vacuum-sealed cuts and frozen without any input from your point of view as the cook, then you have missed out on opportunities to work with the best meat possible. This may be meat you raised yourself, or it may be meat that you purchased from a farmer as a whole animal or as a side.

If your homestead includes animals you raise for meat, the first place where your voice as the cook should be heard is in the choice of animal, both the type and the breed. For example, some breeds of pigs have been developed to be quite lean. Does the breed you are raising produce enough lard?

Some factors that will affect your meat may be beyond your control. For example, a pastured lamb may dress out at 25 to 35 pounds, while a grain-fed lamb will be larger. You may prefer pastured lamb, but if you don't have enough land to provide that pasture, then of course your livestock will be grain-fed. And if you're buying your meat from local farmers, you'll have to live with the choices they make about the breeds of animals and how they raise them. At the very least, you should be well informed about the livestock choices your suppliers are making.

If you are raising your own meat, your next important job is choosing a slaughterhouse and butcher (they may or may not be one and the same). If you buy from a farmer, that choice will be made for you. In many areas of the country, small independent slaughterhouses are overwhelmed by demand, so you will have to book your time with the slaughterhouse early, and maybe your animal will be smaller or larger than you would have liked by the time your processing date, which you made months earlier, rolls around. So be it.

Whether you're raising your own meat or buying from a farmer, you should be able to fill out a "cut sheet" to direct the butcher to break down the animal in the ways that you want it. (For an example, see page 121.) The cut sheet will look pretty straightforward and easy to fill out. It is only when you compare cut sheets from different butchers that you begin to realize that maybe one butcher isn't offering you everything you may want. Some cut sheets, for example, do not make it clear that if you want certain roasts, you won't get certain chops — because it is an either/or choice. When I bought my first lamb, there was no mention of the breast. Where did it go? I had a choice of "riblets" or ground meat instead. I didn't know riblets existed as a cut. (There is very little meat on a riblet, and the meat is tough; I throw them in with stews.)

Furthermore, the language of butchering is not consistent. One butcher may call the belly of the lamb the brisket. Another many call it the breast. A tenderloin is the same from animal to animal, but a standing rib roast (beef) is equivalent to a rack (lamb), which is equivalent to a crown roast (pork). Beef short ribs are pretty much equivalent to pork spareribs, but much meatier. Pork has hams, lamb has legs, and beef has rounds.

Primals are the basic ways in which an animal is divided. The primals are then divided into retail cuts. It would be terrific if the cut sheets were organized by the primals, but they rarely are. The primals of the animals are shown on the chart to the right.

The primals are only very roughly equivalent. The shoulder of the pork and lamb are very roughly equivalent to the chuck plus foreshank and brisket in beef. The pork belly is roughly equivalent to the plate plus flank in beef and the breast in lamb. The round in beef is very roughly equivalent to the leg in the lamb and the ham in the pork.

If you don't have a good understanding of anatomy, you may end up with cuts you

Primal Cuts

Beef	Pork	Lamb/Goat
Chuck	Shoulder	Shoulder
Foreshank and brisket	(included in shoulder)	(included in shoulder)
Rib	(included in loin)	Rack
Short Loin	Loin	Loin
Sirloin	(included in loin)	(included in leg)
Plate	Belly	Breast/foreshank
Flank	(included in belly)	(included in breast/foreshank)
Round	Leg (ham)	Leg

don't know how to cook or more ground meat than you want to deal with. Unless you specifically ask for it, you may not get the lard and organ meats you were expecting. You may not get all the trimmings, which you can grind for sausage yourself. You may not get bones for soup and for your dog. Don't assume anything; ask for what you want, and ask about anything you don't see on the cut sheet.

When you have the choice of butcher, find out whether the butcher is flexible about the cuts and willing to adapt to your specifications. Can the butcher provide both fresh sausages (usually breakfast, sweet Italian, and hot Italian, and sometimes chorizo) and smoked meats (usually bacon and ham)? Will the beef be

aged properly — that is, hung for 14 to 24 days in a chilled locker where the temperature is maintained between 32°F and 38°F (0°C to 3°C)? Some of the best butchers will also age lamb.

Understanding anatomy can also be helpful in figuring out which retail cuts you want, and how you should cook them. At the very least, be aware that the closer a cut is to the head or feet of an animal, the harder working that muscle will be and the tougher the meat. Shanks, for example, are legs, but don't mistake a leg of lamb (the back leg, which is delicious roasted rare), for a shank (the front leg, which should be braised to falling-off-the-bone tenderness). Both are delicious, but they require different cooking methods to bring out the best flavor and texture.

Tough cuts are often the most flavorful; they just need long, slow cooking — braising or stewing or barbecuing (but not grilling) — until fork-tender or well done. Another way to tenderize tough meat is to grind it, and a lot of tough cuts will be turned into ground meat unless you request otherwise. Tough cuts can also be cut into stew meat (with or without the bone) or sliced into matchsticks for stir-frying (you will have to do this yourself), so don't have it all ground up. Braises and stews can be exquisitely flavorful. In general, I ask for most cuts to be on the bone, even the ones I plan to stew or braise, because the bones make the dish more flavorful.

Tender cuts, such as steaks from the loin or ribs, can be cooked by dry-heat methods — roasting, grilling, broiling, pan-searing, and pan-frying. (See the appendix for an explanation of these cooking methods if you need a refresher.) Again, these will be more flavorful on the bone, where appropriate.

Meat from any part of any meat animal can be ground; the ground meat is suitable for cooking in all the ways that ground beef is suitable for cooking: as burgers, in stir-fries, in meat sauces for pasta, in sausage, in casseroles. Most hunters I know grind most of their venison, moose, and bear meat because it is easiest to cook. Likewise, goat meat can be stewed or braised, but is easier to cook when ground.

Chops and steaks are cut from a few different areas, both somewhat tough and tender. Most can be grilled, broiled, pan-fried, or pan-seared. All can be thinly sliced and stir-fried. Some chops are excellent braised, which is a moist-heat method. Tender roasts should be roasted at high heat; less tender roasts should be braised or roasted low and slow. Meat labeled "kabob meat" can be cut from anywhere and should be tender enough for broiling, grilling, sautéing, or pan-frying. Meat labeled "stew meat" may or may not contain bones and should always be stewed or braised.

About those bones: all meat bones can be used to make stock. Lamb stock can be used for lamb gravy for lamb roasts and for hearty soups (it does have a distinctive flavor). Pork stock is used extensively in Asia and eastern Europe; it plays a role in giving Asian soups their distinctive flavor. Pork stock is easily used anywhere you might use beef or chicken stock. Beef stock, of course, can be used for gravies, sauces, and soups.

A stock made from any type of bones that are first roasted is a brown stock (page 142). Be sure to ask your butcher for your bones.

Most cut sheets allow you to specify the size of each package, by weight or by the number of chops or steaks per package. You should be allowed to specify the thickness of the chops and steaks. In general, you are less likely to overcook a thick chop or steak than a thin one. On the one hand, many cut sheets include sausage and smokehouse options; on the other hand, you may want to control this aspect yourself. You can't give a butcher a recipe to execute; the recipes for sausage used by the butcher have to be tested and approved by the USDA.

Cut sheets for pork usually give you the opportunity to declare your interest in getting the lard. With beef, you usually have to ask if you want the suet; a 1,000-pound steer will yield somewhere between 15 and 30 pounds, depending on the steer itself and the butcher. Even if you don't want to cook with tallow, you may want to make candles from it. Although ethnic communities that eat a lot of lamb and goat do make use of the fat, most Americans find it too strongly flavored. However, you can still make surprisingly odor-free candles from the tallow.

Lamb Cut Sheet

Side 1 (Choose one option under each section)

Side 2 (Choose one option under each section)

☐ Use the same preferences as Side 1

NECK
☐ Boneless
☐ Bone-in Slices
☐ Stew
☐ Grind

SHOULDER
☐ Blade & Arm Chops *Thickness:*_____ *(at least 1" recommended)*
☐ Boneless Arm Roast & Boneless Shoulder Roll
☐ Boneless Shoulder
☐ Stew Meat

RACK
☐ Rib Chops *Thickness:* _____ *(at least 1" recommended)*
☐ Bone-in Rib Roast *Frenched?*_____ *Fat cap?*_____
☐ Boneless Rib Roast *Fat cap?* _____

LOIN
☐ Loin Chops *Thickness:* _____ *(at least 1" recommended)*
☐ Boneless Loin Roast *Fat cap?* _____

BREAST
☐ Bone-in
☐ Boneless
☐ Grind

RIBS
☐ Denver Ribs
☐ Riblets
☐ Grind

SIRLOIN
☐ Sirloin Chops
☐ Boneless Roast

SHANKS
☐ Bone-in *Crosscut?*_____
☐ Grind

LEG
☐ Bone-in & Whole *With Sirloin?* _____
☐ Leg Steaks *Thickness* _____ *(at least 1.25" recommended)*
☐ Boneless *Butterflied?* _____
☐ Small Roasts
☐ Kabobs

NECK
☐ Boneless
☐ Bone-in Slices
☐ Stew
☐ Grind

SHOULDER
☐ Blade & Arm Chops *Thickness:*_____*(at least 1" recommended)*
☐ Boneless Arm Roast & Boneless Shoulder Roll
☐ Boneless Shoulder
☐ Stew Meat

RACK
☐ Rib Chops *Thickness:* _____ *(at least 1" recommended)*
☐ Bone-in Rib Roast *Frenched?* _____ *Fat cap?* _____
☐ Boneless Rib Roast *Fat cap?* _____

LOIN
☐ Loin Chops *Thickness:* _____ *(at least 1" recommended)*
☐ Boneless Loin Roast *Fat cap?* _____

BREAST
☐ Bone-in
☐ Boneless
☐ Grind

RIBS
☐ Denver Ribs
☐ Riblets
☐ Grind

SIRLOIN
☐ Sirloin Chops
☐ Boneless Roast

SHANKS
☐ Bone-in *Crosscut?*_____
☐ Grind

LEG
☐ Bone-In & Whole *With Sirloin?*_____
☐ Leg Steaks *Thickness* _____ *(at least 1.25" recommended)*
☐ Boneless *Butterflied?*_____
☐ Small Roasts
☐ Kabobs

VARIETY MEATS
☐ Brains
☐ Heart
☐ Lungs (Lights)
☐ Sweetbreads
☐ Caul Fat
☐ Kidney
☐ Spleen
☐ Tail (Oxtail)
☐ Cheeks
☐ Liver
☐ Stomach
☐ Tongue

BONES
☐ Marrow Bones *Thickness* _____
☐ Stock Bones
☐ And All the Rest!

SAUSAGES

Lamb Sausage: *A traditional tasting sausage with garlic, fennel, and other spices* Qty.: _____ lbs. Linked: _____ or Loose: _____

Merguez: *A spicy sausage with red pepper, garlic, cumin, and other spices* Qty.: _____ lbs. Linked: _____ or Loose: _____

Lamb with Parmesan and Mint: *A moderately spicy sausage with bright flavors* Qty.: _____ lbs. Linked: _____ or Loose: _____

Goat

If you are raising goats for milk, you are probably breeding them annually to keep them in milk production. Male goats can be raised for meat, while the females usually are kept for building and renewing the milking herd. There are also some breeds of goat that are raised specifically for meat. Goat meat from a young animal may be called *cabrito; chevron* is meat from an adult animal.

Anatomically, goats and lambs are quite similar. In fact, the goat cut sheet is often a dual-purpose one, to be used with either goat or lamb. However, goats are much more active than lambs; they burn up their calories rather than put on fat. Goat meat is therefore quite lean, and lean often means tough.

Unless you are butchering your goat young (for an outdoor barbecue or to roast whole), most of the meat should be cut into stew meat (with or without the bones) or ground. The ground meat can be used for sausage, burgers, and the usual ground meat dishes. Even the most tender cuts, such as rib chops, are tougher than the equivalent lamb chops, though tasty enough. But my advice comes from my perspective as an American from a non-goat-eating tradition. I have read of people who prefer eating goat over lamb, and certainly within certain ethnic communities — Latino, Arabic, and Caribbean, to name a few — goat meat is sought after. In some parts of the country, there is a greater demand for goat meat than butcher shops can supply, so even if you don't like goat meat yourself, you may be able to find a buyer for it.

My experience is with tough, lean goat meat, best suited to braising and cooking until falling-off-the-bone fork-tender. Any lamb stew or braise recipe can be made with goat. The farmer I have bought my goat meat from advises simply using my usual beef stew recipe.

Goat Primals

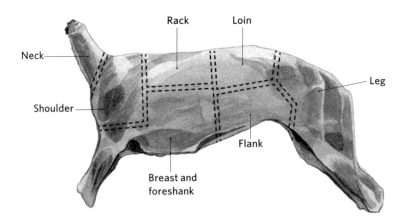

The rack and loin are the most tender, so if you are looking for kabobs or any meat to grill, this is where you'd want it cut from. Often, all the meat is cut into either stew meat or ground meat.

Lamb

Lamb isn't as popular as beef and pork, but the reason may simply be that the flavor is less familiar than that of other meats. In pre–World War II days, an awful lot of mutton (meat from adult sheep) was eaten, and not happily. In those days, sheep were raised for their wool, and mutton was culled from the herd and eaten when the animal was no longer productive. Few farmers were raising tender lambs just for their meat. Therefore, many of us were deprived of eating lamb because our parents or grandparents ate too much strongly flavored mutton that was "lamb" in name only.

Today, lamb may be less popular because it is more expensive than pork or beef. If it is pasture-raised and American, it is particularly pricey; it is somewhat less expensive but has a high carbon footprint if it is imported from Australia. In any case, lamb is distinctively flavored, and it can be fatty, though pastured lambs tend to be less fatty than grain-fed lambs.

A whole dressed pastured lamb will weigh only 25 to 35 pounds and will fit into two large cartons or about three paper grocery bags. A grain-fed lamb is usually older and larger, with a dressed weight of about 65 to 75 pounds, more than double the amount of meat.

A lamb is butchered into five primal cuts: shoulder, rack (or rib), breast, loin, and leg. The primals are then broken down into subprimal and retail cuts. From a 36-pound lamb, you may get:

> 1 shoulder roast (5 pounds) and 12 shoulder chops (½ pound each)
> 2 rib racks (2 pounds each)
> 2 riblet racks (¾ pound each)
> 2 bone-in leg roasts (4 to 5 pounds each)
> 2 shanks (1½ pounds each)
> Ground lamb (3 pounds)
> Tongue (less than ¼ pound), heart (about ¼ pound), kidneys (just less than ¼ pound)

Shoulder

The shoulder is basically the front part of a lamb. The shoulder may include the neck, shoulder blade, upper rib portion, and upper front leg. This area gets a lot exercise, so the meat is well suited to slow, moist-heat cooking, like braising, to tenderize the muscle and connective tissue; it is tough but flavorful. Any cut from this primal that you don't specifically ask your butcher for is likely to be turned into ground meat.

Neck. Makes a delicious meat for stew meat, usually with the bone in. The classic Irish stew is made from the neck.

Shoulder roasts or chops. Cut from the back of the shoulder, roasts should be braised. You can ask for the roast to be bone-in or boneless. Alternatively, this part of the animal can be sliced into chops, called blade chops, shoulder chops, or arm chops. The meat next to the rib bone is somewhat more tender than the meat around the blade (shoulder) bone. Shoulder chops can be grilled, broiled, pan-seared, or braised. A shoulder roast can be treated like a pork shoulder: grilled over low heat or roasted at low heat in an oven. Shoulders can also be cut into stew meat.

Forelegs. These are also called lamb shanks, and they are delicious braised.

Rack

Next to the shoulder, along the back of the animal, is the rib section of the lamb, known as the rack. It is located on either side of the backbone between the shoulder and loin. It is tender and delicately flavored. A rack of lamb roast consists of seven or eight ribs and can either be cut into individual chops or left whole as a rib roast. Rib chops are very tender and flavorful with a thin layer of fat. They are best grilled, broiled, or pan-seared; the rib roast should be roasted. Meat from this section is best cooked to rare or medium-rare.

Breast

Next to the shoulder and under the rack, along the underside of the animal, is the breast. It is a relatively small portion, roughly equivalent to the belly on a pig. Like a pork belly, it is a fatty cut. It is sometimes called the brisket. Generally, you have to ask specially for the breast to be left whole, in which case it can be stuffed and slow roasted or barbecued. The choice

Lamb Primals and Retail Cuts

There are the specific cuts you may want to ask for, but there are a lot of either/or choices. For example, if you go for the rack of lamb, you won't get lamb rib chops. If you want the breast, you have to ask for it specifically. The top part of the leg is the sirloin.

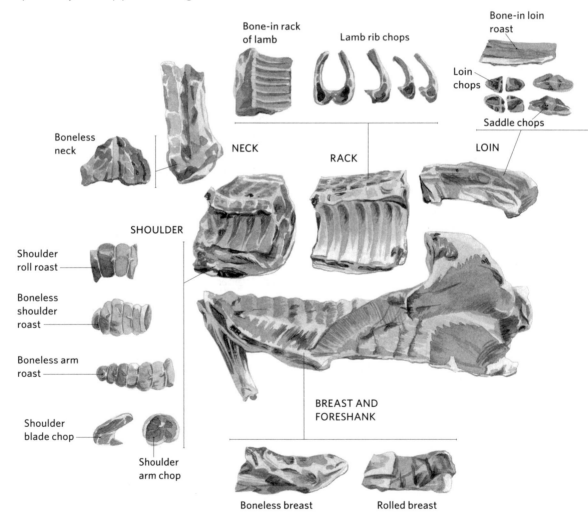

Bone-in rack of lamb

Lamb rib chops

Bone-in loin roast

Loin chops

Saddle chops

Boneless neck

NECK

RACK

LOIN

SHOULDER

Shoulder roll roast

Boneless shoulder roast

Boneless arm roast

Shoulder blade chop

Shoulder arm chop

BREAST AND FORESHANK

Boneless breast

Rolled breast

on many cut sheets is either riblets or ground meat. The riblets look like tiny rib chops, but the tiny amount of meat is tough and fatty. You can broil or grill these (watch out for the dripping fat), or roast or braise them.

Loin

The loin section runs along the lamb's back from the 13th rib and extends to the hips. It is a very tender area, from which you can get two loin roasts or a single saddle, which is a double loin roast from both sides of the backbone. Alternatively, the loin can be cut into loin chops. You can ask for the tenderloin, which runs along the backbone and is rather small. The loin yields relatively lean meat for lamb, and it should be roasted, grilled, broiled, or pan-seared and cooked only until rare or medium-rare. It is the perfect cut for kabobs, though cut sheets frequently don't offer it; ask for it or cut your own kabobs from a loin roast or thick-cut chops.

Leg

Only the lamb's rear legs are sold as leg of lamb. The legs are usually offered whole (weighing between 5 and 9 pounds) or in halves, boned and tied or butterflied. It is more flavorful cooked on the bone, but tricky to carve neatly. If you want the leg broken down further, you can have the sirloin, which is the top portion of the leg and is sold bone-in or boneless. It is meatier and more tender than the shank half of the leg and is best roasted. The shank halves can be braised like the foreshanks. Chops are also cut from the sirloin, and the meat is good for cutting into kabobs.

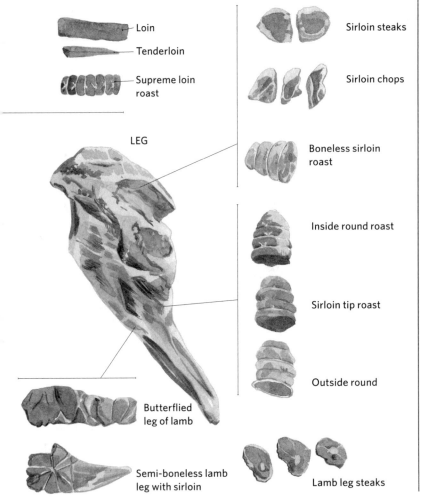

Loin

Tenderloin

Supreme loin roast

LEG

Butterflied leg of lamb

Semi-boneless lamb leg with sirloin

Sirloin steaks

Sirloin chops

Boneless sirloin roast

Inside round roast

Sirloin tip roast

Outside round

Lamb leg steaks

Pork

asture-raised pork is often a revelation to folks used to supermarket pork. Pastured pork is dark, well marbled with fat, and generally flavorful. Raising your own swine or buying a side of pork from a farmer gives you the opportunity to make bacon and sausage, bake with lard (which is lower in saturated fat than butter and makes excellent pastries), and have chops cut to your preferred thickness (go for thick ones).

The primal cuts of pork include the shoulder, loin, belly, and leg (or ham). But wait, there's more: the

Pork Primals and Retail Cuts

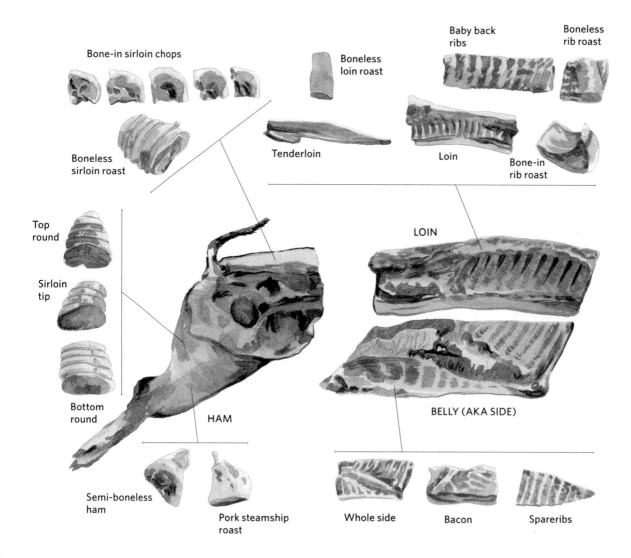

Bone-in sirloin chops

Boneless loin roast

Baby back ribs

Boneless rib roast

Boneless sirloin roast

Tenderloin

Loin

Bone-in rib roast

Top round

Sirloin tip

Bottom round

LOIN

HAM

BELLY (AKA SIDE)

Semi-boneless ham

Pork steamship roast

Whole side

Bacon

Spareribs

additional parts of the hog don't break down into retail cuts. That includes the fatback, leaf lard, tail, neck or whole head, which includes jowls (to be cured for guanciale or enjoyed braised), ears, and snout. Organ meats include the heart, tongue, and liver.

Generally, a hog is ready for slaughter at 250 to 260 pounds. It will produce a 200-pound carcass, which will yield about 150 pounds of pork and pork products or more, depending on whether you opt for the head, the organ meats, and the fat. That's actually quite a lot of meat. This is what you may

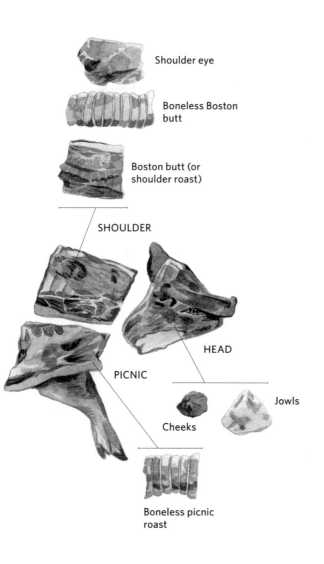

Shoulder eye

Boneless Boston butt

Boston butt (or shoulder roast)

SHOULDER

HEAD

PICNIC

Cheeks

Jowls

Boneless picnic roast

Edible Tidbits of Pork

You must ask for these if they aren't included on the cut sheet.

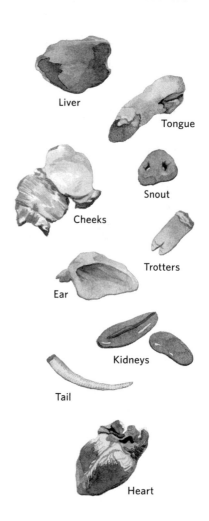

Liver

Tongue

Snout

Cheeks

Trotters

Ear

Kidneys

Tail

Heart

be bringing home from the slaughterhouse:

> 1 shoulder, broken down into 1 pork butt roast and 1 pork shoulder roast (6 to 8 pounds each)
> 1 pork loin, broken down into 16 pork chops, cut 1½ inches thick
> 1 rack of spareribs (3 to 3½ pounds)
> 1 pork belly (12 to 14 pounds) or 8 pounds bacon, sliced and wrapped in 1-pound packages
> 1 ham, smoked or fresh (20 pounds)
> 2 hocks, fresh or smoked
> 6 pounds sausage (breakfast, Italian, and/or chorizo)
> About 20 pounds pork suet (of which only 2 pounds is leaf suet, the rest fatback)
> Organ meats and odd bits, including heart, liver, tongue, kidney, jowls (also called cheeks), ears, tail, snout, trotters.

There probably will be additional smokehouse charges. On at least one cut sheet I've seen, there was a statement (requiring the customer's signature) noting that "the pork products from my hog/s may be commingled with meat from other hog/s that are processed the same day during mixing, grinding and/or stuffing operations." Unless you feel confident about all the animals raised in your community, you might want to consider that a reason to make your own sausage.

Shoulder

You can choose to have the shoulder left whole. A whole shoulder usually weighs 25 to 30 pounds. This is something you might choose to do if you were planning a big barbecue. Alternatively, the shoulder can be cut into two pieces, making the Boston butt and the picnic, both of which are also good for barbecue. This primal also yields two ham hocks and trotters, smoked or not. The shoulder is a well-used part of the hog; the meat will be tough unless plenty of time is allowed for low-temperature roasting, barbecueing, or braising. Then it is truly flavorful.

Boston Butt

I know, an odd name for a part from the front, but the butt is from the upper part of the pork shoulder, from the shoulder socket up to the spine. It has the least amount of bone of the two shoulder roasts. A well-exercised weave of muscles, fat, sinew, connective tissue, and bone, butts can weigh from 4 to 14 pounds. "Boneless butts" often are tied with string because they fall apart easily. Alternative names are the Boston roast, pork butt, shoulder butt, shoulder roast, country roast, and shoulder blade roast. This is the cut that is best for pulled pork, but it can also be cut into shoulder chops, blade steaks, country-style ribs, or stew meat, or ground for patties and sausage.

Beyond pulled pork, butts are delicious roasted at a low temperature or slowly braised in the oven or in a slow cooker.

Picnic

This is the bonier, lower part of the shoulder and may or may not include the hock. You

Headcheese

Headcheese is a loaf of meat that is typically made by simmering the whole head (with the brains and eyes removed) and sometimes the trotters in water, vinegar, herbs, spices, and onion, then removing the meat, chopping it, mixing it with the cooking liquid, and pouring it into a loaf pan, where the gelatin from the broth turns it into a jelled loaf with bits of meat within. It is typically sliced and served with bread. Making it is a big project — not for everyone. I have never made it.

can have this cut bone-in or boned, rolled, and tied. It is great on the barbecue. On the other hand, if barbecue isn't your thing, you can oven-roast or braise the picnic. The picnic is often used for sausage and ground meat.

Loin

In the midsection of the hog is the loin, the most tender of the primals. It is further divided into three subprimals: the tenderloin, the rib end, and the sirloin.

Tenderloin

The tenderloin comes from the strips of muscle that lie on either side of the backbone. The loin can be left whole and boned, cured, and smoked to make Canadian bacon. Or you can opt for the two tenderloins, with the rest of the loin cut into chops or roasts and ribs. If you opt for all pork loin chops, you get the pork equivalent to a beef T-bone, containing both the rib and a piece of the tenderloin, making it a superior cut. When you see a pork chop on the menu of a high-end restaurant, this is often the cut.

Rib End

It should come as no surprise that this subprimal, adjacent to the Boston butt, contains ribs. This is where you get either a crown roast (using two racks) or baby back ribs (also called back ribs, baby backs, loin back ribs, and loin ribs). These ribs are connected to the backbone and nestled beneath the loin muscle.

The most tender and leanest ribs are baby backs. They are called "baby" because they are shorter than spareribs. A typical full slab has 11 to 13 bones and tapers from 3-inch-long ribs on one end to 6-inch long ribs on the other end. There isn't a lot of meat here, only enough for one or two people, but everyone enjoys ribs whether they are grilled, barbecued, or braised.

Pork rib chops are the pork chop standard in America, containing a rib bone and a nice round section of fine muscle fibers for grilling, broiling, pan-searing, and braising.

Sirloin

The section nearest the ham, the sirloin makes a delicious oven roast, or it can be sliced into steaks or cutlets. The central loin is usually cut into chops; opt for chops at least 1 inch thick to avoid overcooking; 1½ inches is even better. These chops, called end chops, are similar to rib chops, but may have slightly more connective tissue. It is the pork equivalent of a sirloin beef steak.

Belly (or Side)

The belly lies beneath the loin and contains the spareribs. Once the ribs are removed, you are left with the pork belly or fresh bacon, which is most often cured to make bacon (see page 253); bacon is most often smoked as well. The last 6 to 8 inches is the cut most often cured to make salt pork (see page 254).

It's well known that everything tastes better with bacon; you'll find it enlivening salads and sandwiches; lifting up potatoes, vegetables, and casseroles; and even embellishing chocolates, cupcakes, and popcorn. It makes liver palatable to some (more on liver on page 135). What isn't quite as commonly known is that pork belly is delicious fresh (on the cut sheet it may be called fresh side pork). Try braising it until tender, then running it briefly under the broiler to make it crisp. Red-cooked pork belly (see page 299) is perhaps the most delicious pork that has ever crossed my lips.

Leg (or Ham)

The leg is the rear end of the pig, and often this is sent whole to the smokehouse for a whole smoked ham, which includes the shank. A full ham can weigh 15 to 20 pounds, which is fine if you are planning a big gathering and have a really big oven. Alternatively, you can opt to have the ham divided into two roasts: the shank end and the butt end (sometimes labeled the sirloin end). The shank end tends to be fattier and, with one straight bone, is easier to carve, while the butt end is leaner and has the tricky aitchbone to work around. The ham can also be cut to yield ham steaks and ham hocks.

If you opt for all fresh ham, it can be cut into roasts and shanks. The shanks are quite tasty and can be braised like lamb shanks; one pork shank will feed three people.

Cooking Pasture-Raised Pork

Everyone fears trichinosis, although the incidence in farmed animals is quite low. The trichinae bacteria are killed at 137°F (58°C), so pork that is cooked to 145°F (63°C), which is medium-rare and still pink, is fine (and sanctioned by the USDA). Since the meat will continue to cook in the interior after the chop (or roast) is removed from the heat, pork is ready to be removed from the oven, tented with foil, and rested at 140°F (60°C). The resting for chops, steaks, and roasts is important; it allows juices to be reabsorbed and guarantees the meat will be juicy and succulent. The residual heat in the meat will continue to cook the meat to 145°F (63°C) or higher. The rest period should be for a minimum of 5 minutes or up to 30 minutes for large roasts.

The USDA recommends that ground pork and sausages be cooked to 160°F (71°C) because *E. coli* is killed at 155°F (68°C), and the bacteria can be introduced as the meat is ground or mixed. (*E. coli* is unlikely to be found in the interior of a roast or steak and would be killed if on the surface, where the heat is more intense.)

Chops

There are a lot of chops in one butchered hog, so mastering the cooking of pork chops is really key to enjoying your meat.

> Whether thick or thin, try dry brining them before cooking (see page 140), and definitely do not overcook.
> Grill, broil, or pan-sear them fast and hot to 140°F (60°C), then let them rest under foil for 10 minutes.
> Sear, then braise in the oven for about 1 hour, or until tender.
> Oven-roast at 200°F (95°C) for about 30 minutes, until the chop reaches 120°F (49°C), then pan-sear. This is a counterintuitive cooking method, but it yields an unbelievably good result. (For a recipe that includes a 24-hour dry brine, see page 141.)

Pork Roasts

How to cook a pork roast depends on where on the animal it originated. A bone-in roast will cook faster than a boneless one because the bone will conduct heat faster than the meat.

> **Loin and rib roasts:** Roast uncovered at 375°F to 450°F (190°C to 230°C), until medium-rare. Start with a preheated oven. Trim off much of the exterior fat. Season with salt, pepper, and herbs. Place the roast on a rack in a shallow roasting pan. Roast to an internal temperature of 140°F (60°C) for medium doneness. Rest for 15 to 30 minutes before slicing.

Nose-to-Tail Pleasure

There are cookbooks devoted to nose-to-tail eating and even cookbooks devoted to just the "odd bits." If you want to dip your feet into cooking these parts, some of the best recipes I have come upon are posted at serioussats.com. Also, when in doubt, try braising in a soy sauce, a method known as "red cooking" (see page 299).

> **Shoulder roast:** Cook low and slow in the slow cooker or for 2 to 3 hours in the oven at 325°F (165°C), or barbecue over indirect heat until fork-tender.

Ham

> **Fully cooked ham:** Roast for 10 minutes per pound at 325°F (165°C).

> **Partly cooked ham:** Roast for 12 minutes per pound at 325°F (165°C).

Beef

One steer yields a lot of meat. Here's what the math looks like: a 1,000-pound steer will lose about 39 percent of its weight during slaughter and dressing (when the blood, hide, hooves, viscera, heart, and lungs are removed). Generally, the price of the meat is based on the weight of the dressed animal, known as its "hanging weight." During butchering, about 18 percent of the animal is lost to trimmings, bone discarding, and normal shrinkage. So in the end, about 430 pounds of meat is boxed up and returned to you.

Beef comes from eight primals: the round, the sirloin, the loin, the flank, the rib, the plate, the chuck, and the brisket/foreshank. Your cut sheet probably won't make the various primal areas clear, but it probably will make clear that you can get either steaks or roasts (or half and half) from the tender primals (rib, loin, sirloin). It may or may not make clear that if you want, say, the T-bone and porterhouse steaks, you won't get the tenderloin. The cut sheet may or may not give you a choice of brisket or ground beef or stew meat. On some cut sheets, most of your choice is devoted to ground meat in 1- or 2-pound bags and shaped into patties or left in bulk. Knowing more about beef anatomy may help you get more from your beef. How much ground beef do you really want?

Even if you don't see it on the cut sheet (and you probably won't), you can ask for the suet (which renders into tallow and is perfectly fine for cooking and frying). Oxtail and beef cheeks aren't always on the cut sheet, but you can ask for them; both are good for stewing and braising. Liver may be on the cut sheet (ask for it sliced into 1-pound packages); a beef liver can weigh 10 to 12 pounds. Tongue is often available on a cut sheet and can weigh anywhere from 1½ to 3 pounds. If you ask for and utilize these "extras," you will see a significant improvement on your investment. You can and should ask that all trimmings be ground and that all bones be saved (for making stock).

The Round

The round is big and is usually divided into top round, bottom round, eye of round, and knuckle or round tip. The eye of round is typically left as one large, whole roast. It is lean and flavorful and should be cooked to rare or medium-rare and thinly sliced (this is the cut used for deli roast beef). It particularly benefits from a low-temperature roasting. The top round can be cut into roasts or steaks and London broil. The bottom round can be cut into roasts for pot roasts or ground into hamburger. The knuckle or round tip can be slow-roasted to rare or medium-rare and served thinly sliced.

The Sirloin

Adjacent to the short loin lies the sirloin, a very flavorful area. The top sirloin is usually the most tender. It makes a great roast and delicious steaks. Some people like to have some or all of the sirloin ground into hamburger because it adds great flavor.

The Loin

The loin consists of the short loin and tenderloin, which are generally thought of as the best beef cuts. From the loin you can get T-bone steak, porterhouse, strip steak, and filet mignon. If you want the tenderloin cut into filet mignon, it will automatically provide you with strip steaks. It is not possible to request filet mignon along with T-bone and porterhouse steak. The T-bone and porterhouse have a piece of tenderloin on one side of the bone (like a filet mignon) and the strip on the other.

The Flank

Beneath the sirloin and short loin lies the flank, source of the flank steak and flap meat, which is retailed as sirloin tips. These cuts are both excellent marinated and grilled, but I haven't ever seen either mentioned on a cut sheet. Ask for them; if you don't, they will be ground automatically.

The Rib

The rib area lies behind the chuck and yields an excellent quality meat with good marbling. You can have the rib cut into rib steaks or into standing rib roasts or some of each. These cuts are perfect for high-heat, uncovered roasting in the oven, under the broiler, or on the grill.

Beef Primals

Here's how a side of beef is broken down, including some retail cuts I've never seen or heard of. The retail cuts probably won't be listed on your cut sheet. Most cut sheets, however, will allow you to make notes of the cuts you especially want. Also, when breaking down a side of beef for home use, most butchers will not necessarily note the cut on the label. It will mostly likely be labeled simply "steak" or "roast" from whatever subprimal it was cut. So it helps to be able to recognize the cut, to know, for example, that flat iron steaks are from the chuck, but are great for grilling. And you

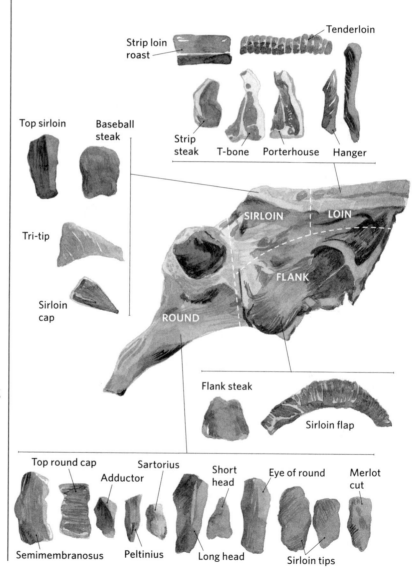

have to ask for the flat iron steaks specifically, or that cut may end up ground or as part of a larger roast. The hind quarter gets less exercise than the front quarter, so the meat is more tender there. The round is the source of roasts that benefit from low and slow roasting. The meat is exceptionally flavorful, so don't have it all ground. The sirloin yields steaks or roasts. From the short loin, you have a choice of steaks (strip steak, T-bone, porterhouse, hanger) or roasts (strip loin roast and tenderloin). From the rib, you can get roasts (bone-in rib roast or eye of rib-eye roast) or rib steaks or beef back ribs. From the chuck comes roasts and steaks suitable for pot roasting. From the brisket (or arm) comes the brisket and crosscut beef shanks (for osso buco). Be sure to ask for the skirt steaks for the plate, the traditional cut for fajitas. The flank yields sirloin flap, good for the grill, and flank steaks, also suitable for grilling.

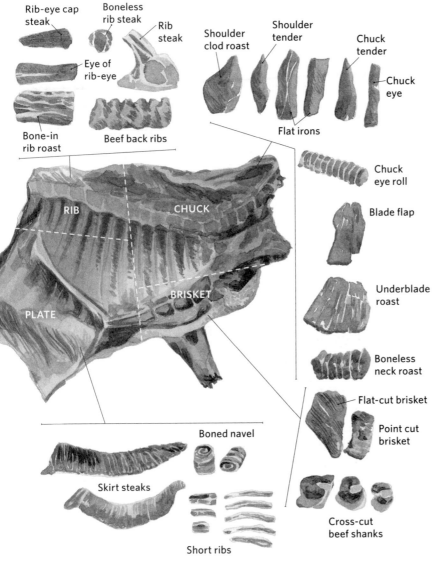

Rib-eye cap steak

Boneless rib steak

Rib steak

Eye of rib-eye

Bone-in rib roast

Beef back ribs

Shoulder clod roast

Shoulder tender

Chuck tender

Chuck eye

Flat irons

Chuck eye roll

Blade flap

Underblade roast

Boneless neck roast

Flat-cut brisket

Point cut brisket

Cross-cut beef shanks

Boned navel

Skirt steaks

Short ribs

RIB

CHUCK

BRISKET

PLATE

Beef Breakdown

This chart shows how the Oklahoma Department of Agriculture breaks down a 1,000-pound steer. Your steer may be much smaller, but the distribution of cuts will be similar, with the chuck and the round, both hardworking (and thus tougher) areas, accounting for much of the meat.

Primal or Subprimal	Retail Cuts	Total Weight
Round	Round steak, rump roast, sirloin tip steak, Pikes Peak roast (or heel or round roast), cubed steaks, stew beef, ground beef	103.2 pounds
Sirloin	Sirloin steak, stew beef, ground beef	38.7 pounds
Loin	Porterhouse steak, T-bone steak, stew beef, ground beef	34.4 pounds
Flank	Flank steak, short ribs, ground beef	17.2 pounds
Rib	Rib-eye steak, rib steaks, back ribs, stew beef, ground beef	38.7 pounds
Short plate	Skirt steak, short ribs, ground beef	30.1 pounds
Chuck	Chuck roast or steak, arm roast or steak, short ribs, stew beef, ground beef	107.5 pounds
Brisket or foreleg	Brisket	25.8 pounds
Shank	Shank soup bone, stew beef, ground beef	17.2 pounds
Suet		17.2 pounds

The Plate

The plate is the source of skirt steaks and short ribs. Skirt steaks, which are often used in fajitas, can be tricky to cook since they are so thin. Basically, you want to sear the steak over a very, very hot flame quickly enough so the outside is cooked but the inside is still medium-rare. If you are cooking it inside, use a cast-iron skillet that is preheated to get the good sear. Short ribs should be braised, but boneless short ribs can also be grilled to medium-rare and paired with kimchi for Korean tacos, a food truck favorite.

The Chuck

A lot of chuck in this country is ground into hamburger. And if you want 100 pounds of hamburger in your freezer, then go for it. The chuck also yields delicious pot roasts and flat-iron steaks, so I'd suggest making sure you include some on your cut sheet. There will still be plenty of ground meat for you.

The Brisket/Foreshank

Beneath the chuck lies the brisket and the foreshank. Make sure you get the brisket; it is perfect for Texas-style barbecues, for Jewish pot roasts, and for corned beef. The foreshank (like the hindshank) can be crosscut for osso buco or used for any low, slow braise. It would be a shame to have any of this meat turned into hamburger.

The Other Edible Bits

Liver, heart, kidneys, tongue, tripe, sweetbreads — they are all edible, and many people find them delicious. You can call them variety meats, organ meats, or offal. Vermont butcher Cole Ward, author of *The Gourmet Butcher's Guide to Meat*, says that the term *offal* comes from "off-fall" — the parts that fall off the animal carcass. They are certainly worth exploring; you may even love them.

The flavor of tongue is rich, quite unlike any other meat, and the texture is unique: soft but firm, almost like bologna. Tongue can be cured, in which case it is called pickled tongue. Cured or fresh, the usual way to prepare it is to boil it for 2 to 3 hours with aromatic spices and vegetables, then peel off the skin and slice the meat (see the recipe on page 316). If you find you like tongue, then I recommend you explore how it is cooked in Mexico. Indeed, you can judge the authenticity of a taqueria, or so I am told, by whether it serves *tacos de lengua*, beef tongue tacos. For those tacos, the tongue is boiled until tender, then diced and braised with garlic and onions and served with salsa verde. I don't mind tongue, but I don't love it either. I'm glad animals have only one.

I would be hard-pressed to distinguish the flavors of pork,

A Side of Beef

If you have trouble envisioning what a side of beef will mean for your meal planning, it might be something like this:

- 8 chuck steaks, each 1 inch thick
- 2 chuck roasts, 3 to 4 pounds each
- 4 shoulder London broil roasts
- 2 briskets, 3 to 4 pounds each
- 16 rib steaks or 4 rib roasts
- 4 packages short ribs
- 1 flank steak
- 8 to 10 porterhouse steaks, each 1 inch thick
- 7 to 8 sirloin steaks
- 2 top round roasts, 4 pounds each

- 4 top round London broils
- 2 top sirloin roasts, 5 pounds each
- 3 bottom round roasts, 4 to 5 pounds each
- 1 eye of round roast, 5 to 6 pounds
- 10 to 15 pounds stew beef
- 70 to 80 pounds ground beef
- Soup bones
- 10 to 15 pounds suet
- 1 beef liver, 10 to 12 pounds

lamb, or beef liver in a blind taste test, and the same probably holds true for the other organ meats. If the meat is at all bloody, put it in a bowl and run cold water over it until the water runs clear, not bloody. Then pat dry. Liver is classically cooked with bacon or onions, or both. It should be cooked rare, still pink inside. I think it makes a fine pâté (see page 295), best enjoyed in small doses.

When in doubt, thinly slice these variety meats (but not tripe), dip in buttermilk and then crumbs, and pan-fry. You might really, really like them. This is certainly a good way to cook heart and liver. I don't have much experience with the other organ meats.

Lard and Tallow

Rendering and using animal fats is pretty much a lost kitchen skill, but one that should be reclaimed. These fats are lower in saturated fat than butter, have high smoke points, and make food taste good. Where I live in Vermont, some folks are experimenting with growing sunflowers for the oil, and there is a lot of butter that can be made. But throwing out the fat from the animals we eat rather than rendering and cooking with it makes

no sense at all. Plus it is easy to do.

My butcher, Jim Blais at Green Pasture Meats in New Haven, Vermont, refers to unrendered fat from beef and pork as *suet*. Once rendered, beef suet and pork suet become tallow and lard, respectively.

There's a lot of suet on a 1,000-pound steer, something like 20 to 30 pounds, so if you raise beef, you will never run out of tallow to cook with and should consider taking up candle making. It is an excellent fat for deep-frying many foods, especially French fries, and has a high smoke point (400°F/200°C). (By comparison, peanut and corn oil have

the highest smoke points at 450°F/230°C.)

A 250-pound pig yields a lot less lard. Since World War II, the most popular breeds of pigs are the ones that produce leaner meat; these include the Berkshire, Duroc, Hampshire, Poland China, and Yorkshire. The less popular lard breeds have not been preserved, and only three breeds of traditional lard type remain today: the Choctaw, Guinea Hog, and Mulefoot. Unless you are raising one of these lard-type pigs, you will probably be able to harvest only 4 to 8 pounds of lard. You've probably heard that leaf lard is the best lard for pastry, and it probably is. But your fat may not come

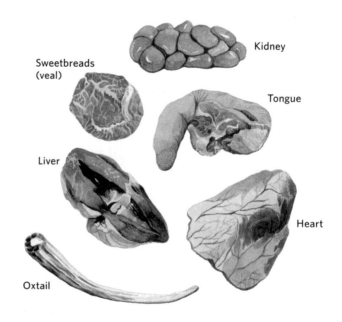

Sweetbreads (veal)

Kidney

Tongue

Liver

Heart

Oxtail

The Homestead Diet, Animal Fats, and Health

I often get strange looks when I tell someone that I cook with lard or chicken fat on a regular basis. Even though recent studies have called into question the link between saturated fat and heart disease, most people, especially older folks, are still fairly fat averse. And of course there is still a link between obesity and all sorts of health risks, and lowering dietary fat is one of the paths to maintaining a healthy body weight.

As far as saturated fat goes, any fat that is solid at room temperature contains some saturated fat. Animal fats are solid at room temperature, but they don't all contain the same proportion of saturated fats. A definition may help: whether or not a fat molecule holds as many hydrogen atoms as it can determines whether it is saturated or not. It turns out that animal fats are not totally saturated; rather, they are a mixture of saturated and unsaturated fats. Butter and beef suet contain 50 percent saturated fat, lard is 39 percent saturated fat, duck fat is 33 percent saturated fat, and chicken fat is 30 percent saturated fat. (For comparison purposes, fish fats range from 15 to 30 percent saturated fat, and even though olive oil is mostly monounsaturated fat, about 13 percent of it is saturated fat.)

Some fat is necessary in most cooking and baking processes. Fats keep our meats succulent, juicy, and flavorful; they keep our vegetables and eggs from sticking to the pan. They add flavor and slow down digestion, so you feel satisfied longer.

Animal fats are readily available in many homestead kitchens. Eating the animal fats is part of a nose-to-tail eating ethic, it lowers the carbon footprint of a kitchen, and it reduces waste.

If you are going to make a pie, why not use lard rather than butter? Lard is lower in saturated fat than butter and produces a flakier crust. And, it turns out, Crisco and other solid vegetable shortenings are made with hydrogenated vegetable oils, and consuming these hydrogenated oils, or trans fats, has indeed been linked to heart disease.

So the question of whether saturated fat is good or bad is not the right question to ask. The question is, what is the alternative? Are duck-fat-slicked, oven-fried organic potatoes better for your health than frozen potato fries from the supermarket? The answer seems obvious, especially when you factor in the knowledge that you didn't have to drive to the store for the duck fat, that the potatoes have no carbon footprint because you grew them yourself, and that there are no preservatives in your homemade fries, nor did any chemical fertilizers nuture those potato plants. Oh, and the homemade duck-fat potatoes are unbelievably tasty.

In his 2009 book *Food Rules*, Michael Pollan distilled recent dietary studies into 64 principles. Three of these in particular could just as easily be described as a manifesto for a homesteader's diet: eat whole foods, mostly plants, and cook them yourself. That's what this book is all about — cooking from scratch with real food you raised yourself.

separated into leaf lard and fatback or back fat, and I think you will be happy with the rendered lard nonetheless, for both baking and cooking. It is a good fat for frying and has a smoke point of 370°F (188°C).

Pure lard actually has a pretty favorable nutritional profile. It has no trans fat (unlike the shelf-stable hydrogenated lard you can find in supermarkets, which you should never buy), and the saturated fat it contains is high in stearic acid, which is possibly good for lowering cholesterol. Lard is also high in oleic acid, which is a monounsaturated oil, making it compare favorably to olive oil.

The goal when rendering animal fat is to end up with an odorless, snow-white lard or tallow. To accomplish this, you need to keep the temperature of the fat as low as possible and to spoon off the fat as it melts so that it isn't sitting on the cracklings and absorbing their odor and flavor. The oil you spoon off will have a golden cast, but it will become white when it hardens. You should get a pint of lard or tallow for each pound of fat you render.

STEP-BY-STEP How to Render Lard and Tallow

Have you ever walked down the midway at a fair where all the food trucks are parked and end up feeling and smelling like a vat of French fries? That's how you and your house will smell when the fat is rendering. The odor will linger for a few days. Keep your windows open, turn up the ventilation fans, or set the slow cooker outside on the porch.

EQUIPMENT

Cutting board and knife, or meat grinder
A large heavy pot, Dutch oven, or slow cooker
Ladle
Strainer lined with paper coffee filter
Glass canning jars and lids

① **Prepare the fat.** Freeze the fat to make it easier to work with, and chill your chopping or grinding equipment. Then chop or grind the fat into the smallest pieces possible. If the pieces are big, the process will take longer, you and your house will absorb more odor, and the fat will absorb more porky or beefy flavor. You will also run the risk of scorching the fat, which will give it a bitter flavor.

Cut the frozen fat into the smallest pieces possible, by hand or in a meat grinder. If the fat is well frozen, you can chop by hand, then grind in a food processor.

② **Melt.** Add the fat to the pot or slow cooker along with about ½ cup water. Place over medium-low heat or set the slow cooker on low. (The water will prevent the fat from burning before the fat starts to melt. It will end up evaporating out.) Let the fat melt, stirring occasionally. When the mixture starts making popping sounds, after about 1 hour, stir more often.

Melt over very low heat.

③ **Strain.** When the cracklings sink to the bottom of the pot, the lard or tallow has been rendered. Ladle off the liquid fat and pour it, through a strainer lined with a paper coffee filter, into the glass canning jars. Save the cracklings left behind in the pot. (They will still be soft at this point and will still be sitting in fat.)

Save the solids you strain out. These are the cracklings.

④ **Store.** Let the lard or tallow cool on the counter, then put on the lids and refrigerate. The fat will solidify and turn white. It will keep in the refrigerator for about 3 months and in the freezer for up to 1 year.

⑤ **Finish the cracklings.** Pork cracklings, which are delicious morsels, can be further cooked down until crisp and browned. The fat that melts off them can be strained and used in cooking. It will not be white and will taste rather meaty. Use this savory fat for cooking savory dishes (it's very good with refried beans). Snack on the cracklings, use them to garnish salads, or sensibly feed them to the chickens.

The melted fat was golden, but it is white — and odorless — when chilled.

Cooking Grass-Fed and Pastured Meat

Grass-fed beef is famously lean, and pastured pork is famously succulent. (Pastured lamb is supposed to be lean as well, but that hasn't been my experience.) Theoretically, pastured cattle and sheep eat what comes natural to them — grasses, not grain — and get more exercise as they munch, hence the leaner meat. With pastured pork, usually the breeds are chosen to produce more fat and, strangely, less lean meat. While pasture-raised pork and sheep do not present any big challenges, beef is tougher — metaphorically and actually. For the most part, it is over-cooking that toughens grass-feed beef.

Here are some principles to keep in mind:

> Use a thermometer to judge doneness, and cook to rare or medium-rare temperatures (see the list at right).

> Marinating is a good idea for lean cuts, such as the strip and sirloin steaks.

> Grass-fed beef usually requires less cooking time than supermarket meats.

> Let the cooked meat sit covered in a warm place for 5 to 30 minutes after removing from the heat to let the juices redistribute.

> Always preheat your oven, pan, or grill before cooking grass-fed meat to reduce cooking time.

> When cutting meat, whether cooked or raw, cut against the grain. This will prevent the muscle from shrinking and becoming tough.

Doneness Temperatures

Doneness temperatures are a little controversial because there are recommended USDA doneness temperatures and then there are doneness temperatures recommended by chefs. The USDA recommends cooking beef, lamb, goat, and pork to 145°F (63°C), but ground beef should be cooked to 160°F (71°C). If you stray from the USDA recommendations, it should be because you are confident that your meat has been properly raised and handled.

Beef, lamb, and goat:

Rare: 125°–135°F (52°–57°C)

Medium-rare: 130°–140°F (54°–60°C)

Medium-well: 150°–160°F (66°–71°C)

USDA recommended: 145°F (63°C)

Pork:

Chops: 140°–145°F (60°–63°C)

Roasts: 140°–145°F (60°–63°C)

Ground meat: 160°F (71°C)

USDA recommended: 145°F (63°C)

Better Steaks and Chops: Dry Brining and Reverse Searing

There are thousands of reasons for raising your own meat, starting with turning your homestead into a sustainable system where the animal inputs (manure) enable the best diversified crops of fruits and vegetables. But ultimately, the reward for raising (or buying sides of) meat is being able to affordably cook high-quality steaks and chops.

Begin by asking on the cut sheet that the steaks and chops be cut 1 to 1½ inches thick. Then there are two techniques that can help guarantee success: dry brining and reverse searing.

Dry Brining

Quite simply, dry brining is the salting of meat at least a few hours before cooking. It works pretty much like a dry rub that is used in barbecuing, but stripped down to its barest essential: salt. The technique was popularized by the late chef Judy Rodgers of

San Francisco's famous Zuni Café and has been adapted by many chefs, bloggers, and home cooks — and it's probably not something your mother taught you.

The salt alters the structure of the proteins in the meat to allow the meat to retain more juice as it cooks. At first, the salt draws moisture from the meat, but over time most of the moisture is reabsorbed, along with the salt, and the meat retains that moisture even when heat is applied. Although the salt doesn't penetrate more than a fraction of an inch into the meat, it is absorbed into the tissues on the surface that will be most affected by heat.

Although you can find writers willing to set down firm rules and guidelines, there really are none. How much salt to use depends on your flavor preferences, and how far in advance to apply the salt depends on what is convenient for you. The dry brine is not rinsed off before cooking, unless you are feeding salt-averse diners. Here's what you do:

1. Start by rinsing the meat so that any surface juices are washed away. Pat dry with paper towels.

2. Apply kosher salt by sprinkling it on all the surfaces of the meat. Folks use anywhere from 1 teaspoon to 1 tablespoon of kosher salt for each pound of meat. If you want to ramp up the flavor, also sprinkle on brown sugar, minced garlic or garlic powder, and your choice of herbs or spices.

3. Place the meat on a rack on a rimmed baking sheet, and refrigerate. The rack is necessary to keep the surface of the meat dry. A dry surface will brown better once heat is applied.

4. Dry-brine roasts and thickly cut chops and steaks (at least 1½ inches thick) for 4 to 24 hours, and thinner cut steaks and chops for 1 to 24 hours.

5. When you are ready to cook, you can rinse and pat as dry as possible, but I don't.

Reverse Searing

I was taught to sear meat in a hot pan or over a hot fire in the grill, then move the meat to a warm oven or to the cooler part of the grill to finish cooking. With pork chops, that was almost always a recipe for dry meat. Then I learned about the technique of reverse searing, which calls for cooking the meat on a wire rack over a baking sheet in a low oven (250°–275°F/120°–135°C) until very barely rare, then searing it quickly on a hot grill or cast-iron pan. *Cook's Illustrated* first touted this method in 2007; since then it has slowly trickled across the Internet. I learned about this method from the very good website Serious Eats.

The advantage of reverse searing is that the first phase of cooking at a low temperature thoroughly dries the surface of the meat, which allows it to sear very well when it hits the hot pan. According to *Cook's Illustrated*, there is also some enzyme action happening that tenderizes the meat.

It turns out that this technique is pretty forgiving, but it does require a thermometer with a probe and an alarm to let you know that the meat has reached the right temperature (90°F/32°C for beef; 110°–120°F/43°–49°C for pork). As the meat approaches the right temperature, begin heating a cast-iron skillet on top of the stove (and turn on the ventilation). Add a little oil to the pan for lean cuts, but not for fatty cuts. Pull the temperature probe out of the meat. Then, using tongs to turn the meat, sear the meat quickly (1 to 2 minutes per side), on all sides, especially those edges that are covered with a layer of fat. The salt or dry rub forms a delicious, slightly crisp crust. Let the meat rest for 5 to 10 minutes (and prepare a pan sauce if you wish). For true decadence, baste the meat with melted butter as it sears.

When reverse searing is coupled with dry brining, the result is often "Wow! I'd be happy to pay money for this at a restaurant."

Accompaniments: Gravy and Pan Sauces

A well-prepared roast or pan-seared steak or chop doesn't necessarily need gravy, and the mashed potatoes that accompany it don't need the gravy either, but everyone you serve will be happy to dollop it on. And gravy and sauces make reheating leftovers easy, so why not make everyone happy?

Gravies

You can make beef or pork gravy from the drippings of a roast just as you would make roast chicken gravy (the instructions are on page 106). Use brown stock instead of chicken stock.

Pan Sauces

While pan-searing a piece of meat will not create enough drippings to make a tradi-tional gravy, you can still make use of what remains in the pan to make a delicious sauce for the meat.

Brown Stock

Makes 4 to 6 quarts

Brown stock can be made with any bones — including poultry — but is most often made with beef or pork bones. Lamb bones can certainly be used, but not everyone appreciates the resulting flavor. Of all the classic soups of the world, only Scotch broth, a hearty barley and vegetable soup, is traditionally made with lamb (but it is more often made with beef in this country). Pork broths are typically used in many Chinese soups, while beef broth is the foundation of many classic soups, including French onion soup. Whatever bones you use, and whatever dish you plan to make, the method is the same: the bones are first roasted and then boiled. You'll need a couple of large rimmed sheet pans or roasting pans and a large stockpot. The vegetables are a suggestion only; use what you have on hand but avoid cabbage-family vegetables.

INGREDIENTS

8 pounds cracked beef marrow, shin, and/or shank bones, with meat on them

8 quarts water, plus more as needed

2 large onions, chopped

2 carrots, chopped

2 celery roots, chopped, or the top half of a bunch of celery

2 leeks, or the tops of several leeks saved for just this purpose, chopped

4 bay leaves

3 tablespoons peppercorns

Salt

1. Preheat the oven to 425°F (220°C).

2. Put the bones in a single layer in a large roasting pan or two. Roast for about 45 minutes, turning the bones occasionally, until well browned.

3. Drain the fat from the roasting pan and discard. Transfer the bones to a large stockpot and set aside. Place the roasting pan over two burners on top of the stove and

add 2 cups of the water. Bring to a boil, stirring to scrape up all the browned bits on the bottom of the pan. Repeat with the additional pans as needed.

4. Pour this browned water into the stockpot. Add the remaining 7½ quarts water, the bones, onions, carrots, celery roots, leeks, bay leaves, and peppercorns. Bring to a boil, then reduce to a simmer. Skim the surface of foam until no more appears. Partially cover and simmer on a very low heat for 4 to 5 hours, adding more water if the bones become exposed.

5. Strain the stock and discard all the bones, meat, vegetables, and peppercorns. Now pour the stock through a strainer lined with cheesecloth into another bowl or pot. Season with salt and pepper, or leave unsalted to use as a base for soup and grain dishes.

6. Refrigerate the stock for several hours, until a hardened layer of fat congeals on the top and can be lifted off. Refrigerate and use within 4 days or freeze for up to 6 months.

How to Make a Pan Sauce

Pan-seared meat has to rest and reabsorb its juices before you serve it, so you might as well make a pan sauce — that is, a sauce made in the pan the meat cooked in.

① **Remove the meat.** Remove the pan-seared meat from the skillet and keep warm under a tent of aluminum foil. Leave 1 to 2 tablespoons of drippings in the pan and pour off the rest (if there is any) and reserve. If necessary — if there isn't an adequate amount of drippings — add 1 to 2 tablespoons of butter to the pan.

What's left in the pan is the basis of a delicious sauce.

② **Add aromatics and sauté.** Over medium-high heat, add minced shallots or garlic, chopped mushrooms, if you like, and sprigs of finely chopped fresh herbs (thyme,

Herbs, garlic, shallots, mushrooms — all add flavor.

rosemary, oregano, and sage play nicely with meat) or a sprinkling of dried herbs. Sauté until fragrant, about 1 minute.

③ **Deglaze the pan.** Measure out 1½ cups of brown stock (page 142) or chicken stock (page 107), or a mixture of half stock and half wine (whatever you are drinking with dinner). Pour the stock into the pan and bring to a boil, scraping up the browned bits on the bottom and sides of the pan with a wooden spoon.

Stock and wine give volume to the pan sauce.

④ **Reduce the sauce.** Boil until the sauce has reduced to about 1 cup; this should take about 3 minutes, depending on the size of the pan. Tilt the pan occasionally to estimate the amount of liquid remaining in the bottom.

⑤ **Thicken the sauce (optional).** If you'd like the sauce to be thicker, make a slurry of 1½ teaspoons cornstarch and 2 tablespoons cool water in a small bowl and stir to blend. Whisk it into the simmering sauce, then bring to a boil just until the sauce thickens; this should take 1 minute or less.

If you want, thicken the sauce with a cornstarch slurry. Alternatively, just reduce it by boiling.

⑥ **Finish the sauce with butter (optional, but recommended).** For a professional touch, remove the pan from the heat. Cut 1 tablespoon of butter into small cubes. While whisking constantly, drop in the butter cubes, 1 or 2 at a time. The sauce will thicken slightly and develop a lovely sheen. Season to taste with salt and pepper.

If you haven't used the cornstarch, finish the sauce with a little butter.

How Do I Cook It?

You pull a piece of meat out of the freezer. Do you know how to cook it? Here's a quick guide.

Moist Heat

Whether beef, pork, lamb, or goat, tough cuts are best suited for cooking with liquid: braising (as in pot roasts) and stewing. Any of the cuts listed below can be cut into chunks for stewing. Note that some of the cuts listed below can also be stir-fried, barbecued, or cooked with dry heat.

- Chuck roasts and steaks (beef)
- Shoulder roasts and steaks (Boston butt for pork; lamb and goat)
- Shanks, whole and cut (beef, pork, lamb, goat)
- Short ribs (beef)
- Brisket (beef) and breast (lamb)
- Belly (pork)
- Round roasts and steaks (beef) or leg roasts and steaks (pork)
- Neck (lamb, beef)
- Sirloin roasts and steaks (lamb)
- Chops (pork)

Searing Dry Heat

Tender cuts can be cooked with searing dry heat — as in grilling, broiling, pan-frying, pan-searing, and roasting. The goal here is to achieve a good sear on the outside and rare to medium-rare meat within.

- Short loin steaks and roasts (beef), loin steaks and chops (pork)
- Sirloin roasts, steaks, and chops (beef, pork, lamb)
- Rib roasts and steaks (beef), rib roasts and chops (lamb)
- Boneless short ribs (beef)
- Skirt steaks (beef)
- Flank steaks (beef)
- Tenderloins (beef, pork, lamb)

Low and Slow Oven Roasting

Particularly lean cuts of meat, such as round roasts, do well with low and slow cooking in the oven. After bringing the meat to just barely rare, you can then sear the outside in a searing hot cast-iron pan, if you like.

- Round roasts (beef)
- Ham
- Chops (thick-cut pork chops)

Low and Slow Barbecuing

Low and slow cooking also makes great barbecue. The meat is put over a drip pan and the fire is on the other side of the covered grill or barbecue. In the case of barbecue, you want the meat to be well done.

- Shoulder cuts (Boston butt for pork, lamb)
- Brisket (beef)
- Spareribs (pork), baby back ribs (beef, pork), short ribs (beef)

Stir-Frying

Any cut can be used in a stir-fry, but there is no point in using your most tender cuts. You do the tenderizing by cutting the meat into thin strips, so any boneless steak or chop will work.

PART 2

Food Preservation

One of the hallmarks of a typical homestead kitchen is that much effort is placed on preserving the foods that you raised yourself. Much depends on time, space, and equipment on hand. You can't freeze without a freezer; you can't store veggies in a root cellar you don't have. There is also a learning curve involved for each of these methods, though none are particularly difficult. Some methods take more active time (canning); some take more waiting time (curing). Some of these methods are well suited for working in small batches, which is particularly useful for those who are time-challenged and those with smaller harvests to deal with.

Generally speaking, freezing yields a better product, closer to fresh, than canning. Freezing vegetables blanched but unseasoned yields the most versatile product, while freezing vegetables in a finished dish (eggplant Parmesan, for example) yields the most convenient and often the highest-quality product. Of course, root vegetables, cabbages, potatoes, winter squash, and onions can be kept in cold storage with little effort, and then prepared just as you would if they were freshly harvested. Apples, pears, and citrus fruits can be kept in cold storage for at least a month or two, or they can be frozen or canned in a boiling-water bath. Pressure canning is not needed for fruits because they are high in acids and sugars. Many people find pressure-canned vegetables unpalatable; but it yields an acceptable product for meats and poultry.

One thing I am quite clear about: you should concentrate your efforts on the foods people want. There's no point to putting up quarts of dilly beans if your family will eat only frozen beans slipped into a soup or stew. There's no point putting up quarts of spaghetti sauce if you don't eat pasta or pizza that often.

Sometimes it makes the most sense to preserve basic ingredients, like tomatoes. Sometimes it makes more sense to freeze or pressure-can finished soups or stews. What works best? That's a question you'll have to work out for yourself, based on what you and your family like to cook and eat.

When it comes to making pickles and jams, mastering the necessary skills is only the first part of the process. Finding or developing recipes that everyone will enjoy can be a multiyear endeavor. And then there is making cheese and curing meats, both of which can turn into lifelong searches for perfection.

Let's get started.

CHAPTER 9

Cold Storage

Refrigerators are fine for short-term storage of fruits and vegetables, but for long-term storage, a refrigerator is too limited in space. The alternative is a root cellar, which provides ideal moist cold storage for potatoes, root vegetables, cabbages, and apples. If you don't have a root cellar, there are other options for moist cold storage, including unheated basements, underground mounds, and clamps (heaped root vegetables insulated against the cold with straw and soil). For dry cold storage, which is preferable for vegetables like garlic and onions, unheated attics, closets, and garages may work well. There are many excellent guides to building and using root cellars and cold storage spaces; see the resources (page 339) for some suggestions.

The name *root cellar* is something of a misnomer, because more than root vegetables are stored in a root cellar. You may, for example, store cabbages, Brussels sprouts, and leeks in a root cellar, and also citrus fruits, apples, and pears.

Some root crops (carrots, parsnips, salsify), rather than being stored in a root cellar, can be left in the ground through the winter if mulched heavily. This means covering these root crops before the ground freezes with 1 to 2 feet of a mulch such as hay, leaves, or straw. In a really cold, snowy climate, it becomes quite a chore to go out once a week and dig up a week's worth of vegetables, so I consider this an option of last resort. Those same root vegetables can also be left in the ground until spring and then harvested and consumed quickly, before they break dormancy — but that option doesn't feed you through the winter.

Most root vegetables in storage will keep best at temperatures between 32°F and 40°F (0°C and 4°C) with 90 to 95 percent humidity; potatoes do best at the same temperature, but slightly lower humidity. But don't worry about achieving the perfect environment for your cold storage. As long as the temperature where you store your harvest is above freezing, cold storage is better than warm kitchen storage. True, if you can keep the stored crops only moderately cool, or only moderately damp, they won't last as long, but you still will have extended your garden-vegetable-eating season.

Fall is a busy time, but don't forget to clean your storage areas before bringing in the new harvest. Sweep out all debris, and scrub all containers with hot, soapy water.

Curing before Storage

Some vegetables need to be cured after harvest. This involves exposing the produce to warm, dry air so that the outer skin hardens (in the case of winter squash) or dries (in the case of onions).

> **Garlic:** Wash to achieve white skins, then let dry in the sun for 2 weeks.

> **Onions and shallots:** Harvest on a sunny day and leave to dry in the garden for 2 to 3 days. Brush off dirt gently and cure in a dry, airy place for 2 weeks.

> **Potatoes, sweet:** Cure for 10 days under moist

conditions (such as under a tarp) at 80°F to 85°F (27°C to 29°C).

> **Potatoes, white:** After the vines die back, allow the potatoes to cure in the ground for another week or two to harden the skins. Harvest, then cure in darkness at 50°F to 60°F (10°C to 16°C) for 14 days.

> **Winter squash and pumpkins:** Wash with a mild bleach solution and dry well. Cure in a warm (70°–80°F/21°–27°C), well-ventilated area (perhaps near a woodstove) until skins harden before storing; this should take 10 to 14 days.

any fruits and vegetables with signs of rot, bruising, mold, or fungus; they will not improve in cold storage and may in fact contaminate all the fruits and vegetables around them.

In most cases you'll store the fruits and vegetables in bins or crates layered with hay, straw, sawdust, dry leaves, or sand. (In older books, this list might have included peat moss, but peat moss is no longer considered a sustainable choice.) Sort vegetables for size and arrange them so that you can use the smallest ones first, because

the large ones store longer. The exception to this rule is apples; small ones hold their quality better than larger ones.

When removing vegetables from storage, check for signs of mold and fungus, and remove any contaminated produce as needed. Mold and fungus may be an indication of inadequate air circulation in your storage area.

Note that apples and pears release ethylene gas as they ripen and should be stored away from vegetables, particularly potatoes, if possible.

Cold Storage Basics

Not all produce is well suited to cold storage. The table on pages 150–51 lists those fruits and vegetables that generally do best. Among those types of fruits and vegetables, choose varieties that have been developed to store well. In general, late-ripening varieties are more likely to store well than early-ripening ones. With the exception of winter squashes, which require washing with a mild bleach solution to prevent mold growth, you don't generally have to wash any produce destined for cold storage. Just gently brush off any lingering soil. Pull out

Cooking from the Root Cellar

The only problem with a well-stocked root cellar is remembering to cook from it and to make the dishes fresh and interesting all winter long, even as the supermarket tempts you with fresh veggies from around the world. A few years ago, I responded to this dilemma with a book titled *Recipes from the Root Cellar*, which contains my favorite recipes using the veggies stored in the cellar — root vegetables, potatoes, onion-family veggies, and cabbages. I have more than a dozen cabbage salad recipes (the secret there is to finely shred the cabbage on a mandoline and vary the dressings nightly (go beyond mayo). And I have lots and lots of recipes for root veggies. The secret there? Use root veggies in place of summer vegetables in all your favorite dishes (mac and cheese, minestrone, chicken pot pie). And when in doubt: roast! But roast them properly: diced (not big chunks!), slicked with olive oil, spread out on a sheet pan (not crowded in a baking dish!), and cooked in a hot oven (450°F/230°C).

Storing Specific Fruits and Vegetables

An unheated attic may provide the ideal cool, dry conditions, while an unheated bedroom may be perfect if the need is for warm and dry conditions.

Definitions

Cold: 32°–40°F (0°–4°C)
Cool: 35°–40°F (2°–4°C)
Warm: 50°–60°F (10°–16°C)

Very damp: 90–95 percent humidity
Damp: 80–90 percent humidity
Dry: 60–70 percent humidity

Fruit or Vegetable	Best Storage Conditions	Length of Storage	Comments
Apples	Cold, damp	3–4 months	Store in open bins or baskets in shallow layers. Keep away from other vegetables; some varieties keep better than others.
Beets	Cold, very damp	4–5 months	Trim off greens and long taproots; pack in sand, straw, sawdust, etc.
Brussels sprouts	Cold, damp	3–5 weeks	Hang whole plants from rafters upside down and strip off sprouts as needed.
Cabbage, Chinese and Napa	Cold, very damp	1–2 months	Remove outer leaves. Replant heads in boxes of soil.
Cabbage, green and red	Cold, damp	3–4 months	Wrap individual heads in newspaper and place on open shelves, root-end up.
Carrots	Cold, damp	4–6 months	Trim off greens and long taproots; pack in sand, straw, sawdust, etc.
Celery	Cold, very damp	1–2 months	Plant in boxes of damp sand.
Celery root	Cold, very damp	4–5 months	Trim off greens and roots; pack in sand, straw, sawdust, etc.
Citrus fruits	Cold, damp	1–2 months	Wrap individual fruits in newspaper and store in shallow layers
Endive	Cold, damp	1–2 months	Replant in soil in buckets or crates.
Garlic	Cool, dry	4–6 months	Good air circulation is critical.

Fruit or Vegetable	Best Storage Conditions	Length of Storage	Comments
Jerusalem artichokes	Cold, very damp	1–2 months	Pack in damp sand.
Kohlrabi	Cold, very damp	2–3 months	Trim off leaves and long taproots; pack in sand, straw, sawdust, etc. Does not last as long as other roots.
Leeks	Cold, very damp	1–2 months	Can be replanted in soil in buckets or crates for longer storage.
Onions	Cool, dry	4–6 months	Store in mesh bags or slatted crates.
Parsnips	Cold, very damp	1–2 months	Trim off greens and long taproots; pack in sand, straw, sawdust, etc.
Pears	Cold, damp	1–3 months	Wrap fruit individually in newspaper. Store in shallow layers; very prone to bruising.
Potatoes, sweet	Warm, damp	1–2 months	Wrap individual sweet potatoes in newspaper and store in shallow layers. Very sensitive to bruising and imperfect storage conditions.
Potatoes, white	Cold, damp	4–6 months	Keep in dark.
Pumpkins	Warm, dry	5–6 months	Store on open shelves.
Rutabagas	Cold, very damp	2–4 months	Trim off leaves and long taproots; pack in sand, straw, sawdust, etc.
Salsify	Cold, very damp	4–6 months	Trim off leaves and long taproots; pack in sand, straw, sawdust, etc.
Squash, winter	Warm, dry	4–6 months	Store on open shelves
Tomatoes, green	Warm, dry	1–2 months	Wrap individually in newspaper; bring to room temperature to ripen as needed.
Turnips	Cold, very damp	4–6 months	Trim off leaves and long taproots; pack in sand, straw, sawdust, etc.

How to Prepare Root Vegetables for Cold Storage

To ready root vegetables (beets, carrots, celery root, parsnips, rutabagas, salsify, and turnips) for the root cellar, it is best to harvest on a cool, sunny, or at least not rainy day. Potatoes and sweet potatoes are technically tubers, not root vegetables. For guidelines on how to prepare them for storage, see the chart on pages 150–51.

① **Trim.** Remove the green, leafy tops from the root vegetables, leaving just a short stub. Trim off the long roots as well.

② **Save the greens.** Although all the tops of root vegetables are "edible," the most enjoyable ones are the beet, rutabaga, and turnip tops. Carrot tops are quite bitter (and I haven't tasted the others). Bring those tasty greens inside, wash and dry, wrap in paper towels inside plastic bags, refrigerate, and use within a few days.

Snip off the tops and tap roots from all root veggies.

③ **Wash or brush off the dirt.** Spread the roots out on the grass or in the open air. If you can spread them out somewhere that won't turn to mud (grass, wooden deck), you can spray-wash on all sides with the garden hose, and allow to dry for an hour or two. Alternatively, just brush off the dirt; letting them stay out in the air for an hour or two makes the brushing off easy. Don't scrub or otherwise handle roughly, and keep the veggies cool.

④ **Dry** Allow to dry in the open air for a few hours.

Wrap the greens in paper towels, then put in plastic bags.

⑤ **Pack.** Pack the vegetables in separate containers (sturdy cardboard boxes, barrels, large plastic bins or buckets, wooden boxes or crates), layering them with sand, hay, straw, dry leaves, or sawdust.

For long-term keeping in good quality, pack the root veggies in sand, straw, sawdust, etc. Without the extra packing materials, they will still keep for 6 to 8 weeks at least.

At the End of the Season

Even if you have provided the best possible environment for your root cellar vegetables in terms of temperature and humidity, before the next growing season even begins, the vegetables become less than pristine. They start sprouting, grow root hairs, and otherwise indicate that they are ready to go back in the ground to produce seeds (root veggies are biennials). Those that don't sprout often become limp or shriveled. Garlic and onions may sprout, mold, or dry out and often become much less flavorful. Cabbages become significantly drier, and if you use them to make sauerkraut, they need additional brine. These veggies are all still fine to use, however, particularly in soups and stews where the soft texture won't be noticed.

Take note of which vegetables and fruits keep well in your particular storage space, and which do poorly. Also evaluate your consumption. Did you store too much of some vegetables and not enough of others? Over the years I have learned that I *can* definitely have too many beets, but I have never had enough onions, shallots, or garlic. I am still trying to figure out the best carrot varieties and planting dates for storage. There can be (have been) buckets of carrots in the root cellar, but when they don't remain crisp and sweet, I'm not inclined to use them.

Before you order seeds for next season, take stock of the durability and quality of the past season's harvest, and consider whether you want to continue with the same types of vegetables and varieties you have been growing or whether some changes are in order.

A well-stocked root cellar can be a source of pride. But check frequently and make adjustments as needed. Is the space free from critters (mice)? Are the apples set away from the vegetables? Can you reach everything?

CHAPTER 10

Freezing

When it comes to preserving food, nothing beats the freezer. Without freezers, we'd be pickling or canning all the homegrown fruits and veggies we can't store (canned peas, anyone?) and salting or smoking all our meats. Besides producing a high-quality preserved food, freezing is easy. And it can be done in small batches, which means you can keep up with the harvest with a spare hour here or there. The freezer can also accommodate a large amount of butchered meat.

Drawbacks? Electricity and plastic — the environmental costs of the modern world. Even if your household is off the grid, energy hogs such as freezers are usually fueled by propane, so you are looking at increased energy costs. Also, the best containers for freezing, including vacuum-sealed bags, are made of plastic. Many plastic containers are made with bisphenol A (BPA), a widely used chemical that was banned by the FDA for use in baby bottles in 2012 (though the EPA continued to rule that BPA presented no health risks). Though you can use only BPA-free plastic containers, a question remains: what health risks might the BPA-free plastics pose? After all, BPA-free plastics by necessity contain numerous other chemical compounds, and we can't know whether any of them pose health risks. BPA itself was in widespread use for more than 60 years before any concerns were raised about it. Yes, you can freeze in glass, but glass breaks easily, and frigid glass breaks more easily still. Regular freezing and thawing of foods in glass does seem to age the jars, making them more prone to breakage.

Nevertheless, freezing is, without question, the easiest and quickest way to preserve foods. However, packaging must be chosen with some thought, and there is some processing involved for fruits and vegetables.

Freezer Containers and Wrappers

Freezer air is the enemy of frozen foods, so you'll need to stock up on freezer containers and wrappers that are moisture- and vapor-proof to maintain the best quality. Your choices range from freezer paper to rigid plastic containers to plastic bags made especially for freezing. Thin plastic sandwich bags or recycled bread wrappers won't do the job.

Label all freezer containers and wrappers, or you may lose track of what you have. Seriously: labeling significantly cuts down on waste because you're unlikely to defrost and use that which you can't identify. Freezer tape is available in some supermarkets and hardware stores; I substitute blue painters' tape when I can't find freezer tape. A permanent marker or China pencil works for writing on grease-free surfaces.

Your choices for packaging include the following:

> **Plastic freezer bags.** Use bags that are designated for freezing, which are made of thicker material than regular plastic bags and are more resistant to moisture and oxygen. For the best results, use a vacuum sealer (see page 9). Alternatively, you can remove much of the extra air with a drinking straw: insert the straw into the ziplock bag, close the zipper as far as possible, suck out the air, withdraw the straw, and quickly zip the bag shut. Plastic bags can tear in the freezer or develop tiny pinholes from rough handling; if you are freezing odd-shaped packages, such as meat, or if you know the food will remain in the freezer for a while, consider wrapping your plastic bags in freezer paper for extra protection.

> **Rigid plastic containers.** Use sealable, rigid containers designed for freezing. You can find a few different brands that are BPA-free. Use correctly sized containers so that you aren't enclosing a lot of extra air.

> **Mason jars.** Use only wide-mouth glass jars; they are less likely than narrow-mouth jars to crack as the contents expand. To allow for food expansion, allow at least 2 inches of headspace. Never put glass jars filled with hot foods directly into the freezer (the jars may break!); cool for 12 hours in the refrigerator first. Freezing does age jars and make them more prone to breakage.

> **Freezer paper.** This heavy-weight paper has a waxy coating on one side that provides a moisture-vapor barrier. It is particularly useful for wrapping odd shapes, especially meat, fish, and poultry. Freezer paper alone doesn't provide enough protection from the drying air of the freezer; freezer paper plus a plastic freezer bag or plastic wrap is effective.

> **Plastic wrap.** You can use thick plastic wrap in conjunction with another wrapper, either plastic bags or freezer paper. Used alone, it isn't very effective.

> **Aluminum foil.** Heavy-duty aluminum foil is somewhat more moisture-resistant than plastic wrap, but again, it is best used in conjunction with another wrapper.

> **Aluminum foil pans.** These inexpensive pans are a good choice for freezing already prepared dishes that will go directly into the oven, such as eggplant Parmesan. Cover the pan with foil, then slip the entire pan into a plastic freezer bag or wrap in freezer paper.

Vacuum Sealing for the Freezer

Vacuum sealing is the gold standard for packaging fresh meat. This is how butchers package meat, but there are also vacuum sealers designed for homeowners; they can be used for freezing not just meats but also fruits and vegetables, soups and stews, purées, and more.

With most foods destined for the freezer, using a vacuum sealer is straightforward (see page 9 for step-by-step instructions). But with liquid and soft foods, there are a couple of tricks:

> When sealing a liquid or semiliquid substance, like a soup or stew, there is always the potential of the vacuum pulling the liquid into the upper reaches of the bag and preventing a good seal — or any seal at all. To prevent this, fill the bags, place in the door of the freezer, and allow the contents to freeze. When the contents are frozen, then vacuum-seal.

> When sealing soft fruit, such as strawberries or raspberries, or blanched peas, tray-freeze first (see page 159), and then transfer to the plastic bags and vacuum-seal. Otherwise the force of the vacuum may turn your soft produce into mush.

Stacking Plastic Bags

Plastic bags do create a stacking problem. You can get around this by freezing your plastic bags on flat trays, then stacking them when they have achieved a rigid flat shape. Removing as much air as possible helps make a bag lie flat. If you don't have a vacuum sealer, you can do a pretty good job of removing air by sucking it out with a drinking straw. Alternatively, you can buy and use reusable cardboard boxes that force the bags into a square shape.

Wrapping Food for the Freezer

There are two time-tested methods for wrapping foods for the freezer. Why one is called the drugstore wrap and one the butcher's wrap, I can't tell you, but the butcher's wrap has a slight advantage over the drugstore wrap for irregularly shaped foods (like a whole bird).

The Drugstore Wrap

1. Cut a piece of freezer paper large enough to wrap all the way around the food, plus a couple of inches extra, and place it shiny-side up. Place the food in the center of the paper.

2. Bring the two opposite edges together and roll them down until the rolled edge is snug against the food; flatten the rolled edges, and tape down securely with freezer tape.

3. Flatten the extra wrap at one end, and fold in the corners to make a point. Fold that end up snugly over the taped seam, and tape. Flatten the remaining loose end and repeat, squeezing out as much air as possible as you go. Secure with freezer tape. For anything you plan to keep longer than a few weeks, repeat with a second sheet of freezer paper. Be sure to label the package before putting it in the freezer.

The Butcher's Wrap

1. Cut a piece of freezer paper large enough to wrap all the way around the food several times over and place it shiny-side up, with the length of the paper parallel to you. Place the food near one of the lower corners of the paper.

2. Fold this corner over the food and tuck the end under the food. Flatten the sides of the paper and crease tightly, expelling the inside air.

3. Fold the two near ends of the wrap over the food, and roll the package over and over until all wrap has been used, squeezing out as much air as possible as you go. Seal the edges with freezer tape, and label.

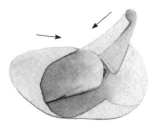

Freezer Burn

When a package of food in the freezer develops a leak, the dry air of the freezer will pull moisture from the frozen food, resulting in freezer burn, which appears as grayish-brown leathery or dried-out spots. Foods that show signs of freezer burn are perfectly fine to eat, but there will be a loss of texture and nutrients. Sometimes there will also be an unpleasant taste created when the exposed food absorbs flavors from the air in the freezer. Whether to throw out such foods or use them entirely depends on how you feel about waste, but certainly there has been a loss of quality.

Freezing Fresh Vegetables

For the best-quality frozen vegetables, you must first blanch the veggies in boiling water or in steam to set the color and destroy the enzymes and bacteria that eventually turn the vegetables into compost. Microwave blanching isn't recommended because microwaves cook unevenly.

Having a ready supply of vegetables in the freezer is convenient, but the very best frozen vegetables, in my opinion, are actually vegetables frozen in a finished dish — as in spaghetti sauce, ratatouille, stewed zucchini and tomatoes, eggplant Parmesan, and vegetable soup.

How to Blanch and Freeze Vegetables

Work with small batches (about 1 pound of vegetables) at a time; otherwise the blanching water will cool down too much when you add the vegetables, and the vegetables won't blanch evenly. You can use the same blanching water two or three times. Change the water if it becomes cloudy, and top up as needed with boiling water from a kettle.

Rapidly cool the blanched vegetables by dumping them into ice water to stop the cooking process, then drain and dry them before packaging them. The drier the vegetables before you freeze them, the better the quality. I spread bath towels out on all my table and counter surfaces and let the veggies dry for as long as possible before bagging them up.

① **Prep the vegetables and ready the equipment.** Wash the vegetables and drain. Then slice, dice, or trim. Fill a large bowl or basin with ice and water; set aside. Bring about 4 quarts of water to a rolling boil for blanching 1 pound of vegetables at a time (leafy greens need 8 quarts water per pound). For steam blanching, bring a few inches of water to a boil.

② **Blanch.** Put the vegetables into a wire basket and submerge the basket in the boiling water or in the steam above the water. Cover the pot and begin counting the blanching time according to the table on page 160. You do *not* have to wait until the water returns to a boil to begin the count. (However, if you are blanching more than one batch of vegetables, you need to start each batch in rapidly boiling water.)

Prep and blanch. Trim the pieces so they are all the same size for even cooking. Blanch only 1 pound at a time.

③ **Chill.** Lift the basket out of the water or steam, and immediately dump the vegetables into the basin of ice water. When the vegetables are cold, drain them thoroughly.

④ **Dry.** Spread the vegetables out on towels on the kitchen counter and let dry. Or spin-dry in a salad spinner, working with small quantities at a time. Some people use handheld hair dryers or fans to help with the drying.

Chill in ice water. The colder the water, the faster the veggies chill, the higher the quality.

⑤ **Package and freeze.** Pack the vegetables into freezer containers, remove as much air as possible, seal, label, and freeze. Alternatively, you can tray-freeze the blanched vegetables, then pack them in plastic bags to make it easier to remove small quantities at a time. However, if the vegetables go into the freezer containers fairly dry, tray freezing should not be necessary.

The blanched veggies should be as dry as possible before they are put in the freezer. Sometimes this means letting them dry overnight and finishing the job in the morning. Don't rush it.

How to Tray-Freeze without Blanching

Life is short and the harvest season is long. Sometimes it is better to get the veggies frozen quickly rather than following the best practice of blanching first. Try this method with peppers, herbs, celery, corn in husks, cabbage, sugar snap peas, grated summer squash, chopped young tender broccoli, and green beans. You can also tray-freeze onions this way, though onions do well in cold storage.

These vegetables will be fine for at least a couple of months, after which they should be cooked in soups, stews, or sauces or used in pickle relishes for the best results. By that, I mean that the veggies will have lost color and the texture will be soft, so they are best served in well-cooked dishes where you won't be bothered by their unfresh taste and appearance.

① **Prep the veggies.** Wash the vegetables, and peel or chop as needed. Spread the veggies out on towels to dry, or spin-dry in a salad spinner. Make sure they are as dry as possible.

② **Freeze.** Spread the prepared vegetables out in a single layer on a baking sheet lined with parchment paper, and freeze.

③ **Package.** When the vegetables are frozen, transfer to plastic bags, remove the air, seal, label, and return to the freezer.

Blanching Times

Vegetable	Boiling-Water Blanching Time*	Comments
Artichoke (hearts)	7 minutes	Freeze hearts only
Asparagus	2-4 minutes	Depending on thickness
Beans, shell	2-4 minutes	Depending on size
Beets	Variable	Cook fully before freezing (boil for 30-50 minutes), rather than just blanching
Broccoli	3 minutes	1½-inch florets plus sliced stems
Brussels sprouts	3-5 minutes	Depending on size
Carrots	2-5 minutes	Diced, sliced, or cut into strips
Cauliflower	3 minutes	1-inch florets
Corn, kernels	4 minutes	Remove from cob after blanching
Corn, on the cob	7-11 minutes	Depending on size
Edamame (green soybeans)	5 minutes	Still in pods
Greens, hearty	2 minutes	Includes kale and cabbages. Add 1 minute for collards
Greens, tender	30 seconds	Includes spinach and beet greens
Okra	3-4 minutes	Depending on size
Peas, green	1½ minutes	Shell first
Peas, snap and snow	1½-3 minutes	Remove blossom ends and any strings
Pepper, bell	2 minutes	Strips or rings
Squash, summer	3 minutes	Sliced
Squash, winter	Variable	Cook fully before freezing, rather than just blanching
Tomatoes	30 seconds	Peel after blanching

*Multiply boiling-water blanching times by 1.5 for steam blanching.

Using Frozen Vegetables

Freezing vegetables is relatively easy. Using the frozen vegetables is more challenging, especially when you are tempted by the fresh, from-the-other-corner-of-the-globe produce at your supermarket. The sad truth is that supermarket frozen veggies are flash-frozen and may retain more texture and color than your home-frozen bounty.

If you froze your vegetables in casseroles, soups, and stews, then using frozen vegetables is a simple matter of pulling dinner out of the freezer and reheating. If your veggies are blanched and sitting in freezer bags and containers, casseroles, soups, and stews are still where they will do best.

The Best Freezer Shortcut for Tomatoes

Keep a jumbo resealable plastic bag in the freezer and add the tomatoes you aren't going to eat or have time to properly deal with. You can include every kind of tomato: paste, slicing, salad, and cherry. Just wash them first, dry, and then throw them in the bag. Keep adding to the bag as the harvest mounts up. When you have the time (and the kitchen has cooled off), make purée or sauce by throwing the frozen tomatoes in a large pot. Let them thaw or just add a little water to keep them from burning. When the tomatoes are fully thawed and broken down, run through a food mill to separate out the seeds and skins. Then can, freeze, or use immediately.

Tips for Using Frozen Vegetables

> Frozen vegetables do not have to be thawed before they are cooked.
> Use blanched frozen veggies within 6 months for best quality.
> Use unblanched tray-frozen vegetables within 2 months for best quality.
> When adapting a recipe to use frozen vegetables, consider tossing the vegetables with a tablespoon or two of cornstarch or flour if you are afraid the frozen vegetables will add too much liquid (as in a quiche).

Recipes Using Frozen Vegetables

Most soups, stews, braises, and casseroles that call for fresh vegetables can be adapted to frozen vegetables. Recipes in this book that will do particularly well with frozen vegetables include the following:
> Cream of Any Vegetable Soup (page 38), with a full-flavored, preferably homemade stock
> Tomato-Vegetable Soup (page 274)
> Vegetable Gratin (page 277)
> Shakshuka (page 269)
> Eggs Florentine (page 270)
> Saag Paneer (page 281)
> Bird and Biscuits (page 298)

Summer Vegetable Stew for the Freezer

Makes about 4 quarts

This stew is dinner on the day it is made; the intentional leftovers are packaged up and frozen, to be served as a vegetable side dish, a topping for rice or pasta, or a hearty stew when combined with cooked fresh or leftover chicken or other meat. It can also be combined with an equal quantity of stock to make a lovely vegetable soup, in which case the addition of cooked dried or canned beans makes it a meal. The 6 cups of chopped vegetables the recipe calls for can be whatever vegetables you want to preserve in the freezer (zucchini, corn, peppers, green beans, leeks) without the fuss of blanching. The eggplant gives the recipe a meaty quality (and my family loves eggplant), but mushrooms would work just as well.

INGREDIENTS

- 12 cups chopped tomatoes (about 6 pounds)
- ½ cup extra-virgin olive oil
- 1 large onion, diced
- 1 bulb garlic, minced
- 6 cups chopped eggplant
- 6 cups chopped mixed vegetables
- Handful of fresh herbs (basil, mint, parsley, sage, thyme)
- Salt and pepper

1. Put the tomatoes in a heavy saucepan and cook over medium heat, stirring occasionally, until the tomatoes are very soft, 30 to 45 minutes. Strain through a food mill to remove the seeds and skins. Return to the saucepan and boil down until you have reduced the volume by about half. Reduce the heat to low.

2. In large skillet, heat ¼ cup of the oil over medium-high heat. Add the onion and garlic, and sauté until softened, about 3 minutes. Transfer to the tomato sauce with a slotted spoon.

3. Add the remaining ¼ cup oil to the skillet and heat over medium-high heat. Add the eggplant and cook until tender and cooked through, about 10 minutes, stirring frequently.

4. Transfer the eggplant to the tomato mixture along with the chopped vegetables and herbs. Season with salt and pepper. Simmer for about 30 minutes, until all the vegetables are tender. Taste and add more salt and pepper if needed.

5. Serve. Package the leftovers in airtight containers and freeze. Defrost overnight in the refrigerator before reheating and serving.

Freezing Fresh Fruit

Freezing fruit is somewhat easier than freezing vegetables. The fruits are generally peeled, hulled, or sliced as needed, then packed dry or with a sprinkling of sugar. The sugar helps the fruit retain color, flavor, and texture, but dry frozen fruit is fine in baked goods.

With fruit, you have a few choices: tray freezing (the quickest method, but the lowest-quality product), freezing with a dusting of sugar (sugar pack), or freezing in a sugar syrup (syrup pack). Or you could go ahead and convert the fruit into pie filling and freeze that (great if you make a lot of pies).

Preventing Discoloration

Some fruits, like peaches, will discolor when peeled and exposed to air. To prevent this, treat the fruit with lemon juice, ascorbic acid, or a commercial mixture such as Ball's Fruit-Fresh. If all you have are vitamin C tablets, you can crush them: 1,500 mg of vitamin C is equivalent to ½ teaspoon crystalline or powdered ascorbic acid.

> **Tray freezing:** If you are tray-freezing fruits, make a solution of 1 teaspoon crystalline or powdered ascorbic acid or ¼ cup lemon juice per 2 cups water in a bowl. Add the peeled and sliced or diced fruit to the solution. Let stand for 10 minutes. Then lift out of the solution and spread out on towels to dry thoroughly before freezing.

> **Sugar pack:** Add ascorbic acid or a commercial mixture directly to the sugar. Follow the label directions for the commercial mixture (1 tablespoon of the mixture mixed into 1 cup of sugar is generally recommended). Use 1 teaspoon of crystalline or powdered ascorbic acid for every 2 cups of sugar.

> **Syrup pack:** Use ½ teaspoon crystalline or powdered ascorbic acid for each quart of syrup (for pears in syrup, use 1 teaspoon). Dissolve the ascorbic acid in a little cold water before adding to the syrup.

Freezing Herbs

You can freeze herbs by plucking the leaves, sealing them in bags, and freezing them. The leaves will discolor but can still be added to soups and stews.

Alternatively, chop the herbs and put them into ice cube trays. Pour in water to cover, and freeze. Once the cubes are solid, pop them out and transfer them to freezer bags. Add them directly to simmering soups and sauces and stews as needed.

You can also make a pesto by puréeing herbs in a food processor with olive oil, then freezing the pesto in ice cube trays or serving-size containers. Including nuts (pine nuts, walnuts, almonds, pecans, sunflower seeds) and grated cheese (traditionally Parmesan) is optional. (You may have read elsewhere that you should freeze the pesto without the cheese and add it later, before serving. I haven't found that it makes a difference in flavor or texture. I freeze the pesto with the cheese — then it is ready for an instant meal, without the worry of whether I have the Parmesan on hand.)

How to Tray-Freeze Fruit

Any fruit can be tray-frozen, but the quality of the frozen fruit will vary. I think this method is particularly well suited to blueberries. More delicate berries, such as strawberries and raspberries, do not hold up as well. Peaches, cherries, and other fruits are okay tray-frozen, but not great.

① **Prepare the fruit.** Wash the fruit and dry well. Stem, peel, pit, and/or slice as needed. If the fruit is light-colored, treat with an ascorbic acid solution (see page 163) to prevent discoloration.

② **Freeze.** Spread out in a single layer on baking sheets and freeze. Don't crowd the fruit.

③ **Package.** When frozen firm (fruit may not become entirely solid when frozen), transfer to freezer containers, removing as much air as possible. (Use a vacuum sealer if you have one.) Label and return to the freezer.

How to Freeze Fruit in a Sugar Pack

The rule of thumb is to add about 1 cup sugar to 4 to 5 cups of fruit, but you can use more or less, depending on the fruit and your preferences. Is the fruit particularly sweet or tart? Do you prefer to cut back on the sugar you use?

① **Prepare the fruit.** Wash the fruit and dry well. Stem, peel, pit, and/or slice as needed. If the fruit is light-colored, treat with ascorbic acid by mixing ascorbic acid into the sugar (see page 163).

② **Mix with sugar.** Sprinkle the sugar over the fruit, and toss gently with a silicone or rubber spatula to mix. Let stand for 10 to 15 minutes, until the sugar has formed a syrup with the fruit juices.

③ **Package and freeze.** Pack in freezer containers, remove as much air as possible, seal, label, and freeze. (If you want to use a vacuum sealer, freeze the bag standing open and upright, then vacuum-seal when the contents are fully frozen.)

STEP-BY-STEP How to Freeze Fruit in a Sugar Syrup

The same syrups that are used for canning fruit are used for freezing fruit. Alternatively, you can use fruit juice, such as apple or white grape juice. Generally a medium syrup (see the table on page 166) works best for frozen fruit. Heavy syrups overwhelm the delicate flavor of most fruits; likewise, syrups made with honey or maple syrup can also overwhelm the fruit, though they are perfectly safe to use.

① **Make the syrup.** Make the sugar solution according to the proportions given in the table on page 166, and let cool to room temperature. Generally, you will need about 1½ cups of syrup for every 4 cups of fruit. If the fruit is light-colored, mix ascorbic acid (see page 163) into the sugar syrup.

② **Prepare the fruit.** Wash the fruit and drain. Stem, peel, pit, and/or slice as needed.

③ **Combine and pack.** Combine the fruit and sugar syrup. Make sure the fruit is covered with syrup. Pack in freezer containers, remove as much air as possible, seal, label, and freeze. (If you want to use a vacuum sealer, freeze the bag standing open and upright, then vacuum-seal when the contents are fully frozen.)

Freezing **165**

Sugar Syrups for Freezing and Canning Fruit

Suspending fruit in a solution of sugar and water helps fruit maintain its color, flavor, and texture when frozen or canned. If you are averse to sugar, you can use a fruit juice instead, but the results will be less pleasing. A syrup of maple syrup, honey, agave, or other sweetener can be used, but I think sugar syrups yield the best results.

Type of Syrup	Granulated Sugar	Water	Yield
Light	2 cups	4 cups	5 cups
Medium	3 cups	4 cups	5½ cups
Heavy	4¾ cups	4 cups	6½ cups

Thawing and Using Frozen Fruit

Thaw fruit in its original package at room temperature or overnight in the refrigerator. To speed up the thawing process, submerge the package in cool water. The fruit doesn't need to be fully defrosted if you are using it in smoothies or on top of ice cream.

Frozen fruit will inevitably be softer than fresh fruit, and as it thaws it will melt into a puddle of fruit juices. This isn't a problem if you are serving the previously frozen fruit in smoothies or as a topping for pancakes or ice cream or other desserts. But it does create a problem for using in pies and other baked goods.

If your thawed fruit is going to be too juicy to use in a baked item, you can drain it, but don't discard the juice. Instead, cook it down to reduce it and then add it back to the fruit. This builds flavor. Drain the fruit in a colander set over a saucepan. Put the saucepan with the collected juice over medium heat and boil until the juices are reduced to a thick syrup. This will take more or less time, depending on whether or not the fruit was frozen with added sugar. Let the juices cool, then combine with the thawed fruit. This is the technique I use for making pies from frozen berries (see page 321).

Freezing Dairy

If you are milking a goat or a cow and have a fairly small household, it is easy to become overwhelmed with milk and dairy products. Culturing milk to make cheeses and yogurts greatly enhances the refrigerated shelf life of dairy foods. Is the freezer an alternative way to store these foods? The answer is a qualified *yes*, meaning yes it is safe, but you will sacrifice both texture and flavor (as you do with fruits and vegetables). Here's a rundown on freezing dairy.

> **Raw milk** loses some flavor, some beneficial bacteria, and some nutrition when frozen. The cream is likely to separate out and will not readily combine with the fluid milk again. People report that blending the milk both before and after thawing helps keep the fat in solution. Some people say that quickly thawing the milk in a basin of warm water results in milk that tastes better than milk thawed slowly in the refrigerator.

> **Pasteurized milk** loses some flavor and some nutrition. Stirring, shaking, or blending may help restore the texture.

> **Cream** can be frozen on its own. The higher the fat content, the better it freezes. Previously frozen cream will not whip to the same

volume as never-frozen cream. Sweetened whipped cream can be tray-frozen in individual mounds, then bagged and served when semifrozen.

> **Butter** freezes well but easily picks up off-odors. It should be triple wrapped in plastic, then wrapped in freezer paper. Cultured butter and well-salted butter freeze better than fresh, unsalted butter.

> **Cultured sour cream, yogurt, and buttermilk** can be frozen but will develop a grainy texture and more sour flavor. They are fine to use in cooked dishes.

> **Hard and semihard cheeses** become drier and crumbly when frozen, and they definitely lose flavor. I think such cheeses freeze best in grated form and are fine used to sprinkle as a topping on pizza and casseroles. A nuanced, artisan cheese (the kind that is sold for $20 a pound) should never be frozen.

> **Cream cheese** becomes drier and crumbly when frozen, but it can be used in baking and for frostings.

> **Ricotta and cottage cheese** can be frozen for up to 1 month but tend to separate and become less creamy.

Freezing Eggs

Legally, an egg can be laid as many as 30 days before it must be packaged. Its sell-by date is another 30 days after that. The egg is still considered fresh for another 3 to 5 weeks after that, so there's no real hurry for getting eggs into the freezer. Indeed, based on experiments done by the editors of *Mother Earth News*, eggs have a surprisingly long shelf life in the refrigerator (see page 85). However, there is such a thing as too many eggs in the finite space of a refrigerator. In that case, freezing is a good option.

Eggs should be removed from their shells for freezing. They can be kept frozen for up to a year, and they should be thawed in the refrigerator the day before you intend to use them. There are textural changes: the yolks get rather gummy, and it is noticeable in omelets and scrambled eggs. They should be used only in dishes that will be completely cooked and combined with other ingredients, such as in custards and baked goods such as cookies and cakes. Cakes will not rise quite as high with frozen and thawed eggs, but the difference may not be that dramatic.

> **Whole eggs:** To freeze whole eggs, crack the eggs into a bowl and gently stir to break up the yolk, but do not beat them; you want to avoid incorporating air into the eggs. Egg yolks gelatinize when frozen, becoming so thick and solid they are impossible to use. To prevent this and maintain the best texture, stir in ½ teaspoon salt per cup of eggs. Label the container with the date and the number of eggs (and a reminder of the salt, if you need it).

> **Egg yolks:** The problem with egg yolks gelatinizing when freezing is even greater when you freeze yolks alone. To prevent this as much as possible, stir in either ⅛ teaspoon salt or 1½ teaspoons sugar per ¼ cup of egg yolks (about 4 yolks). Label the container with the date and the number of egg yolks and whether salt or sugar was added.

> **Egg whites:** Raw egg whites do not gelatinize when frozen, so no added salt or sugar is needed. Label the container with the date and the number of egg whites. Once thawed, whites will beat to a better volume if allowed to sit at room temperature for about 30 minutes.

Frozen Egg Math

You'll want to freeze eggs in convenient sizes for defrosting relatively small amounts at a time. Some people like to use ice cube trays for freezing the eggs, then transfer the eggs into freezer bags. (If you use plastic ice cube trays, be scrupulous about removing any egg residue before reusing the ice cube trays for ice.)

1 whole egg = 2 cubes

2 egg yolks = 1 cube

1 egg white = 1 cube

2 cubes = ¼ cup

4 cubes = ½ cup

6 cubes = ¾ cup

8 cubes = 1 cup

1 tablespoon thawed egg yolk = 1 large fresh egg yolk

2 tablespoons thawed egg white = 1 large fresh egg white

3 tablespoons thawed whole egg = 1 large fresh egg

Freezing Poultry

On page 96, I give reasons why I think spatchcocked birds are best for freezing, not the least of which is because a flattened bird will fit into a vacuum sealer bag. A nice round, whole bird isn't ideal for the vacuum sealers and may be too big for some home units. That's when people turn to shrink-wrapping. Special bags are required, and some are sized perfectly for all types of fowl, including chickens, turkeys, and ducks. The bags come with special zip ties and are thick enough to withstand the rigors of being piled up in freezers; many brands of bags are BPA-free. Immersing the bagged bird in hot water causes the bag to shrink, expelling air through a tiny hole (which you'll seal later). You can use these bags for parts as well as for whole birds. First, of course, you must butcher and chill the birds (see page 94).

STEP-BY-STEP **How to Use Poultry Shrink Bags**

To shrink-wrap a whole bird, you will need a pot large enough to submerge the entire bird. (This process also works for small animals, such as rabbits, but for the sake of simplicity, let's just talk poultry here.) A 5-gallon stockpot will do the job for most chickens, but turkeys will require a turkey fryer — filled with water, not oil. You will also need a knife for poking a hole in the bag, a marker to mark it, and a label to cover the hole. A clean pair of insulated rubber gloves will help protect your hands from the bubbling water that results from the air in the bag being expelled. A pair of scissors for trimming the bag is handy.

① **Prepare the bird and bath.** Bring the water in a large pot to 180°F (82°C), or to the temperature the manufacturer of your bags recommends (usually between 180°F and 200°F/82°C and 95°C). Put the bird neck-end first into the bag.

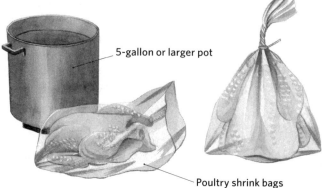

5-gallon or larger pot

Poultry shrink bags

② **Close the bag.** Hold the bag at the top, twist the top several times, expelling as much air as possible, and then close with a zip tie.

③ **Pierce the bag with a vent hole.** Use a knife to make a small slash, about ⅜ inch long, in the bag, right over the bird's breast. Use a marker to mark the hole, which may be hard to find later.

Pierce a small vent hole.

④ **Dip the bag in hot water.** Holding the bag at the top, slowly lower the bagged bird down into the hot water until the bird is submerged just below the zip tie; allow it to go no farther. You do not want to let water in through the top. Keep the bird submerged for two or three seconds, while the air bubbles out and the bag shrinks, then take it out.

⑤ **Trim the bag and seal bag with label.** Dry off the bag and affix a label over the air hole to seal it. With a pair of scissors, trim off the excess bag at the top and the excess tail of the zip tie. Now the bird is ready for the freezer.

Heat will cause the bag to shrink instantly.

Make sure the label is placed so it seals the vent hole.

Freezing Meat

If you can arrange it, it is best to have your butcher cut, wrap, and freeze your meat, because adding a whole lot of unfrozen meat at once to a home freezer will result in a lengthy freezing time. The slow freezing can cause large ice crystals to form in the meat; the results may include freezer burn and the loss of meat juices during thawing.

At least one butcher I know prefers to wrap meat in freezer paper; he thinks the sealed plastic is at risk for developing tiny pinholes that allow air in the packages. However, most customers demand Cryovac sealing, the type of plastic sealing that has become the industry standard.

At home, however, you can take the precaution of adding a wrapping of freezer paper to the cuts your butcher has prepared. If you do this, be sure to label in big letters. Your own labeling on freezer paper is generally more readable than the computer-generated labels from the printer, saving you time and money in front of the opened freezer as you search for a particular cut of meat.

Safe Thawing of Meat

According to the USDA, which researches the question, there are three safe ways to thaw meat: in the refrigerator, in cold water (in an airtight or leakproof bag), and in the microwave. Never thaw meat by leaving it out at room temperature.

It's best to plan ahead for slow, safe thawing in the refrigerator. After being thawed, the raw meat will keep in the refrigerator for 3 to 5 days. During this time, if you decide not to use the meat, you can safely refreeze it without cooking it first.

The cold-water method of defrosting should not be used with poultry frozen in the poultry shrink bags. The air hole you created to allow air out was sealed with a freezer label, which is not waterproof.

When microwave-defrosting meat, plan to cook it immediately after thawing because some areas of the food may become warm and begin to cook during microwaving. Foods defrosted in the microwave or by the cold-water method should be cooked before being refrozen because some parts of the meat may have been held at temperatures above 40°F (4°C), which allows the growth of bacteria.

It is safe to cook frozen meat in the oven, on the stove, or on the grill without defrosting it first; just be aware that the cooking time may be about 50 percent longer than for unfrozen meat. Use a meat thermometer to check for doneness. Do not cook frozen meat in a slow cooker.

USDA Recommended Storage Times for Frozen Meat

These times represent limits on the food maintaining best quality. Food that is frozen longer will lose quality but remain safe to eat.

Meat	Storage in Freezer
Bacon and sausage	1–2 months
Meat-based casseroles, soups, stews	2–3 months
Game, uncooked	8–12 months
Ground meat	3–4 months
Ham	1–2 months
Poultry, uncooked parts	9 months
Poultry, uncooked whole	12 months
Roasts, uncooked	4–12 months
Steaks and chops, uncooked	4–12 months

CHAPTER 11

CANNING
Boiling-Water-Bath and Pressure Canning

Of all the preserving methods, canning provides the most convenient product. Open a jar of home-canned fruit, and you have an instant dessert. Open a jar of jam, spread it on toast, and you have breakfast. Open a jar of bread-and-butter pickles, and a tuna sandwich is genius. Open a jar of chicken and stock, and you are halfway to a chicken pot pie.

Are you scared of canning? A lot of people are. Certainly there is no reason to be scared of boiling-water-bath canning. You are only going to use the boiling-water canner to seal jars of high-sugar or high-acid foods, like jams or pickles. If those foods go bad, you'll know it because you will see the mold or taste the off-flavors, but even if you eat them, it is unlikely they will make you or anyone else sick.

Pressure canning is different. Because you are sealing jars of low-acid foods, if the time in the canner isn't long enough or the pressure in the canner isn't sufficient to bring the foods to 240°F (116°C), to kill off any bacteria or bacteria spores (specifically, the spores of *Clostridium botulinum*, which cause botulism), your home-canned foods could make people sick. What's the solution? Follow the rules, don't take shortcuts, and all will be well.

How big is the risk of botulism? According to the website of the U.S. Centers for Disease Control (CDC), "Home-canned vegetables are the most common cause of botulism outbreaks in the United States. From 1996 to 2008, there were 116 outbreaks of foodborne botulism reported to CDC. Of the 48 outbreaks that were caused by home-prepared foods, 18 outbreaks, or 38 percent, were from home-canned vegetables. These outbreaks often occur because home canners did not follow canning instructions, did not use pressure canners, ignored signs of food spoilage, and were unaware of the risk of botulism from improperly preserving vegetables."

Read between the lines, and it is likely that most of those issues developed from not using a pressure canner when it should have been used. So, if you use a boiling water bath canner for your high-acid or high-sugar foods and a pressure canner for everything else, you should be fine.

Oh yeah, one small thing: wash your vegetables. The soil in which the veggies grew harbors botulism spores. But you were going to do that anyway, weren't you?

Foods to Seal in a Boiling-Water-Bath Canner

> Fresh-pack pickles, such as dilly beans and bread-and-butter cucumber pickles
> Jams
> Jellies
> Fruit
> Fruit pie fillings
> Applesauce
> Tomatoes and high-acid tomato products, like ketchup

Foods to Seal in a Pressure Canner

> Vegetables packed in water
> Soups
> Soup stocks and broths
> Meats, chicken, and fish and anything containing them
> Tomato sauces with lots of veggies and/or meat

Canning Equipment and Supplies

Beyond the basic kitchen equipment you already have, most everything you will need for canning is readily available at supermarkets and hardware stores.

Boiling-Water-Bath Canner

For processing fruits, pickles, and high-acid vegetables only. The canner is basically a large pot that comes with a lid and a wire rack to hold the canning jars off the bottom of the pot. A large one will hold nine quart jars; a smaller one will hold seven.

Yes, you can jury-rig a large pot to function as a boiling-water-bath canner as long as you can insert a rack to hold the jars off the bottom and can cover the tops of the jars with at least 2 inches of water, without the pot boiling over. I will warn you that a vigorously boiling bath can knock the jars into each other, and that is how breakage occurs. So a wire cake rack placed in the pot only does half the job, holding the jars above the bottom of the pot, but not preventing the jars from dancing around as the water vigorously boils.

Pressure Canner

For processing low-acid vegetables and meats. The canner is a specially made heavy pot with a lid that can be tightly closed to prevent steam from escaping. The lid is fitted with a petcock, which is a vent that can open and close to allow air and steam to escape from the canner. It also has either a dial or a weighted gauge to register the pressure inside the canner. Smaller pressure canners can hold one layer of quart or smaller jars, while larger ones can hold two layers of pint or smaller jars. A pressure canner can double as

Botulism

The big fear among home canners is botulism. Botulism is a rare but serious illness caused by the bacterium *Clostridium botulinum,* commonly found in soil. *C. botulinum* is anaerobic, meaning it can survive, grow, and produce toxins without oxygen, such as in a sealed jar of food. This toxin can affect your nerves, paralyze you, or even kill you.

The facts are pretty simple:

- *C. botulinum* bacteria are killed when subjected to boiling water for 10 minutes, *but the spores will survive* unless the contents of the jar are brought to 240°F (116°C) for 3 minutes, which can only happen under pressure.

- *C. botulinum* will not thrive in an acid environment. Therefore, the boiling-water-bath canner is safe to use only with fruits and vegetable pickles, which have high acid levels.

a boiling-water-bath canner, but a boiling-water-bath canner cannot double as a pressure canner.

Canning Jars

Made from tempered glass in 2-quart, 1-quart, 1-pint, 1½-pint, and ½-pint sizes, all of which are designed to be reusable. The USDA advises that you do not use jars in which you bought commercially prepared sauce or jam because the glass may not be strong enough to withstand home-canning temperatures and pressures. The rims of commercially used jars are sometimes thinner than those of regular mason jars, resulting in a high rate of sealing failure. If the jars seal properly and the glass doesn't break, however, food canned in such jars is perfectly fine.

There are two major brands of canning jars in the United States: Kerr and Ball. Both brands are now owned by the same company — Jarden Corporation — and are more or less the same. European canning jars are available that seal with gaskets and metal clips. They are definitely more expensive than the usual mason jar and not terribly convenient; if you need a new gasket, you will have to order more online. I don't have experience with that type of jar, and the USDA does not recommend them.

Two-Piece Lids

The typical canning jar uses a flat disk called a dome lid that sits on top of the jar and a screw ring to hold it in place. The lid cannot be reused, but undamaged screw rings can be used again and again. In years past the dome lids contained BPA, but more and more manufacturers are now producing BPA-free and phthalate-free versions. Please note that the lids do not require preheating in simmering water as they once did.

There are now one-piece lids on the market, with a very visible button that depresses when the jar is sealed. The word from the USDA is that the lids are tricky to use properly and aren't recommended.

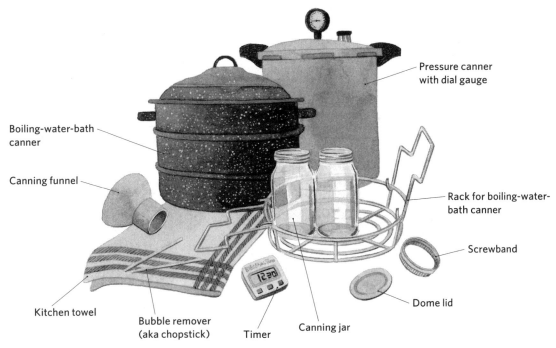

Pressure canner with dial gauge

Boiling-water-bath canner

Canning funnel

Rack for boiling-water-bath canner

Screwband

Dome lid

Kitchen towel

Bubble remover (aka chopstick)

Timer

Canning jar

Utensils and Other Tools

Canners, jars, lids — those are necessary. The following tools and utensils are not absolutely necessary but make canning much easier.

Jar lifter. For easy removal of hot jars from a canner. Remember that in a boiling-water bath the jars will be covered with water too hot for bare hands, though the sort of insulated rubber gloves used for cheesemaking could be worn.

Wide-mouth funnel. To help in packing canning jars cleanly. (I use my canning funnel for other tasks as well — for example, when adding flour and water to my sourdough starter and when putting away leftovers.)

Plastic knife, spatula, or chopstick. For removing air bubbles from the jars.

Clean cloths. For wiping jar rims and general cleanup.

Timer. To keep track of the processing time.

A number of other home-canning accessories such as corn cutters, apple slicers, decorative labels, and special canning spoons are available. These items may simplify the process but generally are not essential.

Hot versus Raw Pack

Foods can be packed into canning jars for both the boiling-water-bath and the pressure canner cooked or uncooked. Cooked food goes into the jars hot (hot pack), and uncooked (raw) food goes into the jars unheated (raw pack). The USDA recommends that the liquid that goes into raw-pack foods be heated to boiling before it goes into the jar.

Most hot-packed foods are cooked in juice, water, syrup, or stock or broth (in the case of pressure-canned meats). Tomatoes and some juicy fruits are often cooked in their own juices. Raw-packed foods are packed in a sugar syrup, fruit juice, or vinegar brine. The advantage of raw-packed foods is that the process is quicker. The advantages of hot-packed foods are that the foods are less likely to shrink and float in the cooking liquid, more food can be packed in each jar, and the food looks better. With raw packing, the canned food, especially fruit, will float in the jars. The entrapped air in and around the food may cause discoloration within 2 to 3 months of storage. Raw packing is more suitable for vegetables processed in a pressure canner.

Hot-packed foods don't have to be cooked to death before they go into the jars. The USDA recommends heating the freshly prepared food to boiling, then simmering it for 2 to 5 minutes, before filling the jars loosely with the boiled food. This little bit of cooking shrinks the food, which allows you to pack more in, which helps keep the food from floating in the jars (there still will be some floating).

Headspace

Recipes for canning in a boiling-water-bath canner or in a pressure canner will include instructions for leaving a specific amount of headspace in the jar. Headspace is the unfilled space above the food in a jar and below its lid. Typically ¼ inch of headspace is needed for jams and jellies, ½ inch for fruits and tomatoes to be processed in a boiling-water bath, and 1 to 1¼ inches for low-acid foods processed in a pressure canner.

Regular canning jar   Wide-mouth jar

The wide-mouth jar is easier to pack, easier to use for fermented pickles, and safer to use in the freezer.

As a jar is heated in the canner, the contents expand and steam is formed, forcing air out of the jar. As the contents of the jar cool, a vacuum is formed, and the rubber compound seals to the rim of the jar. If the vacuum isn't formed, the jar won't seal; and leaving too much or too little headspace is the number one reason jars fail to seal. If you do not leave sufficient headspace, liquid will be forced out along with the air, gumming up the rubber seals. If you leave too much headspace, there will not be enough processing time to drive all the air out of the jar. And if a vacuum is formed but there is still a bigger headspace than required, the food at the top is likely to discolor. The discolored food is still safe to eat, but nutritional content may be decreased.

Boiling-Water-Bath Canning

Boiling-water-bath canning is a safe way to preserve high-acid foods such as jams, jellies, fruit in juice or syrup, pickles, and tomatoes. The boiling-water bath heats the contents of the jar sufficiently to kill bacteria, molds, and other spoilage organisms. During processing, air is forced out of the jars, creating a vacuum. The lid is then vacuum-sealed to the lip of the jar. As long as the jars remain airtight, the vacuum protects the food inside from harmful organisms.

STEP-BY-STEP How to Can Using a Boiling-Water Bath

Canning takes time, so do yourself a favor and undertake canning when you have a few hours with no other demands. Get yourself all set up before you begin, and the whole process becomes much easier. How much heat your stove burners put out greatly affects your time in the kitchen; a gas stove with a power burner makes a big difference.

In the instructions below, I start with prepping the food because that is often the most time-consuming step; jam, for example, may take more than an hour to cook down. On the other hand, if I am simply making pickles, for which the most time-consuming food-prep step is slicing the cucumbers, then I will start by filling my canner and getting the water hot. It's no big deal, however, if the food is ready before the canning water is hot, or vice versa.

① **Prepare the food.** Follow your recipe instructions for preparing the food. For jams and jellies, this means cooking down the fruit or fruit juice. For fruit, it usually means peeling, coring, and cutting into halves or slices. For fresh-pack pickles, it means trimming or slicing the vegetables and assembling (and cooking, if needed) the pickle brine. Tomatoes that will be canned whole are peeled; tomatoes that will be canned as sauce or purée are cooked down and then run through a food mill to remove skins and seeds.

To peel tomatoes for canning, cut an X through the skin on the blossom end. Dip in boiling water for 30 to 60 seconds (depending on size), then immediately chill in an ice bath. The skins should slip off easily.

② **Prepare the jars and set out the lids and screwbands.** Wash the jars, and sterilize them if you will be processing for less than 10 minutes (see the box below).

In the past, people were instructed to submerge the canner lids in hot water in preparation for processing. That isn't necessary anymore; just make sure your lids are new and unused, and that you have enough screwbands on hand.

③ **Prepare the canner.** Fill the boiling-water-bath canner half full with water and preheat to about 180°F (82°C), the temperature at which water simmers. Bring a kettle of water to a boil.

The boiling water in the kettle will be used to top off canning jars if needed for raw pack or to top off the canner if the jars aren't covered with 1 inch of boiling water.

④ **Fill the jars.** For raw pack, you'll fill jars with uncooked food and pour in boiling water, juice, syrup, or pickling brine. For hot pack, fill the jars with the hot, cooked food and, if needed, cover with the boiling cooking liquid. In either case, leave the proper amount of headspace, which is ¼ inch for most jams and jellies, ½ inch for most pickles and fruits.

The canning funnel keeps the rims clean.

⑤ **Cover the jars.** Wipe away any drips on the rims of the jars. Run a clean spatula or chopstick inside the jar to release any air bubbles you may have trapped in the jars as you filled them. Do not stir, which could create more bubbles. Place the lids on top of the jars and

A magnet on a stick comes with canning sets to make setting the lids on the jars easier. It was more useful in the past, when the lids were held in hot water.

Sterilizing Canning Jars

You do not have to sterilize jars used for food that will be processed for at least 10 minutes. Simply wash them in soapy water or in a dishwasher, then rinse thoroughly to remove all traces of soap.

If you are processing for less than 10 minutes, you'll have to sterilize the clean jars: Submerge them in a canner filled with hot (not boiling) water, making sure the water rises 1 inch above the jar tops. Bring to a boil and boil for 10 minutes (or longer if you live at higher elevations; add 1 minute for every 1,000 feet above sea level). Alternatively, many dishwashers have a sterilizing cycle you can use.

secure with screwbands. Tighten the screwband so it just grips. Do not exert undue pressure or make it extremely tight.

⑥ **Process.** Load the jars into the wire rack. Lift the rack by its handles and set it in the canner. Add more boiling water from the kettle, if necessary, to bring the water level to 1 inch above the jars. Turn the heat as high as possible and wait until the water is boiling vigorously. Cover the canner with the lid. Reduce the heat to maintain a moderate boil. As soon as you have covered the canner, set a timer for the recommended processing time (see the table on pages 178–79). If you live at a high elevation, increase the processing time as necessary (see the box below).

⑦ **Cool and store.** When the jars have been in boiling water for the recommended time, turn off the heat, remove the canner lid, and let the jars stand in the canner for 5 minutes. Then remove the jars from the canner using a jar lifter or lift the entire rack of jars by its handles. Set the jars on towels, placing them at least 1 inch apart. Let the jars cool for 12 to 24 hours, then test to establish that the jars have a good seal (see page 187).

Store the jars in a cool, dry place, with or without the screwbands. Do use the screwbands if you plan to give the jars as gifts. They are also convenient if you are going to use only some of the food in a jar and will store what's left in the refrigerator. Do note, however, that the screwband can rust on, making the jar nearly impossible to open again; this is most likely to happen if you store your canning jars in a damp basement. Your choice.

The handles of the jar rack fold over the jars to allow the pot lid to be placed on the canner.

Let the jars cool undisturbed; resist the temptation to test the seal until the jar is completely cool. If you are lucky, you will hear the distinctive "ping" of the seal happening.

Adjusting Boiling-Water-Bath Canning Times for Altitudes

At sea level, water boils at 212°F (100°C). At higher elevations, it boils at lower temperatures and therefore foods must be processed for longer times to ensure that harmful organisms are destroyed. Add 1 minute for every 1,000 feet above sea level when processing foods that require less than 20 minutes in the boiling-water bath. Add 2 minutes for every 1,000 feet for foods that must be processed for more than 20 minutes.

Boiling-Water-Bath Processing Times

Unless noted otherwise, the headspace for all these preparations is ½ inch.

Food	Style of Pack	Jar Size	Processing Time in Minutes
FRUITS			
Apple butter	Hot pack	Half-pint or pint	10
Apple juice	Hot pack	Pint or quart	10
Apples	Hot pack	Pint or quart	25
Applesauce	Hot pack	Pint	20
	Hot pack	Quart	25
Spiced apple rings	Hot pack	Half-pint or pint	15
Spiced crab apples	Hot pack	Pint	25
Apricots, halved or sliced	Raw pack	Pint	30
	Raw pack	Quart	35
Berries	Hot pack	Pint or quart	20
Berries	Raw pack	Pint	20
	Raw pack	Quart	25
Berry or fruit syrup	Hot pack	Half-pint or pint	15
Cherries	Hot pack	Pint	20
	Hot pack	Quart	25
Cherries	Raw pack	Pint or quart	30
Fruit purée	Hot pack*	Pint or quart	20
Grape juice	Hot pack*	Pint or quart	10
Peaches	Hot pack	Pint	25
	Hot pack	Quart	30
Peaches	Raw pack	Pint	30
	Raw pack	Quart	35
Pears, halved	Hot pack	Pint	25
	Hot pack	Quart	30

Food	Style of Pack	Jar Size	Processing Time in Minutes
Plums, halved or whole	Raw or hot pack	Pint	25
	Raw or hot pack	Quart	30
Rhubarb, stewed	Hot pack	Pint or quart	20
Tomatoes, firmly packed, no added liquid**	Raw pack	Pint or quart	90
Tomato juice**	Hot pack	Pint	40
	Hot pack	Quart	45
PICKLES			
Dilled green or yellow beans	Raw pack	Pint	10
Pickled beets	Hot pack	Pint or quart	35
Piccalilli or chow chow	Hot pack	Half-pint or pint	10
Corn relish	Hot pack	Half-pint or pint	20
Cucumber pickles (whole)	Raw pack	Pint	15
	Raw pack	Quart	20
Cucumber pickles (slices)	Hot pack	Pint or quart	10
Pickle relish	Hot pack	Half-pint or pint	15
Pickled mixed vegetables	Hot pack	Quart	15

*Leave ¼ inch of headspace.

**Add 1 tablespoon lemon juice, ¼ teaspoon citric acid, or 2 tablespoons vinegar per pint; add 2 tablespoons lemon juice, ½ teaspoon citric acid, or 4 tablespoons vinegar per quart.

Storage for Home-Canned Foods

Home-canned foods will maintain the best color and texture when stored in a dark, dry area where the temperature is above freezing and below 70°F (21°C). This means keeping the jars out of direct sunlight and away from hot pipes, heat ducts, gas or electric ranges, and woodstoves.

Freezing can damage the seal on a jar, resulting in spoilage. Even without damaging the seal, repeated freezing and thawing will soften the food or make it mushy. If you have no choice but to store the canned goods in an unheated area, consider insulating the jars with blankets, a very heavy layer of newspaper, or a Mylar blanket.

Canned food should never be stored in a damp area, because the dampness may corrode the metal jar lids and compromise the seals.

Tips for Canning Tomatoes

Of all the vegetables we grow, tomatoes are the most likely candidate for canning — because they can be canned in a boiling-water bath and because the end result is so useful in the kitchen, adding flavor or serving as the base for countless soups, sauces, stews, and casseroles. Most households can easily go through a quart of tomatoes and a quart of tomato sauce every week, or 104 quarts of tomato products each year, and that's not even considering tomato ketchup and salsa. Here are some tips to make tomato canning easier.

- For each quart of **canned tomatoes**, you will need 2½ to 3½ pounds of fresh tomatoes. Paste varieties yield better than salad tomatoes — more flesh, less liquid.

- To be sure your tomatoes are **acidic** enough to be safely processed in a boiling water bath, add ½ teaspoon citric acid (available wherever canning supplies are sold), 2 tablespoons of bottled lemon juice, or 4 tablespoons of vinegar per quart. (Add a little sugar when cooking with these tomatoes, if needed.)

- **Raw-pack tomatoes** are more likely to separate and float in the jar. The floating tomatoes aren't pretty, but there's nothing wrong with them. Use the surplus liquid at the bottom of the jar or not, depending on how thick you want the final product when cooking.

- To **raw-pack tomatoes**, fill the quart jars with 5 or 6 whole peeled tomatoes, pushing down to squeeze in as many tomatoes as possible. If you can completely fill the jar with the whole and crushed tomatoes, you don't need to top off the jar with boiling water. If you don't want to crush those tomatoes, fill with boiling water. Then process.

- To make an **unseasoned tomato sauce or purée**, chop whole tomatoes (don't bother seeding or peeling). Add to a saucepan with a little water to prevent scorching and boil until the tomatoes are easily crushed, 5 to 10 minutes or more, depending on the size of your batch. Run the tomatoes through a food mill to get rid of the seeds and skins. Return to the pot, bring to a boil, and either process in quart jars or continue cooking until you have a desired thickness, stirring frequently to prevent scorching. Then process.

- **Peeling and seeding** tomatoes or running the tomatoes through a food mill isn't necessary for safety; it is an aesthetic choice.

- **Tomato sauces and salsas** with lots of added onions and peppers should be pressure-canned.

- When you are pressed for time, **freeze tomatoes** for processing in jars later in the fall.

Pressure Canning

Committing to pressure canning seems to be the hardest step to take in a self-sufficient homestead kitchen. The reluctance to learn how to preserve with a pressure canner seems to be related to fear of food poisoning (you are working with low-acid ingredients), expense (a pressure canner will cost at least $80 but can go upward to $300, compared to $20 for a boiling-water-bath canner), or just plain lack of experience.

There is another reason to avoid pressure canning, and that is a lack of experience with eating pressure-canned foods. Most of us were raised to appreciate that frozen vegetables are superior in color, taste, and texture to canned vegetables; this is true whether the vegetables are in a tin can or a glass mason jar. Furthermore, most of us were raised to have access to fresh and frozen meat, whenever we want it. Pressure canning was a necessity in the days when, in order to preserve meat, you had to either cure and smoke it or pressure-can it. Not only are there relatively few people who pressure-can today, but many books on canning and preserving don't even mention it.

Adjusting Pressure for Higher Altitudes

Home canning recipes assume that you're working at sea level, or close to it. When you're pressure-canning at a high altitude, the processing time remains unchanged, but the pressure is adjusted.

This leads to the question, is pressure canning a necessary skill today? I think it depends on your homesteading setup and lifestyle. Pressure canning is best for safely preserving foods that are ready to eat — the homesteaders' MREs — in the form of soups, stews, meats in broth, cooked dried beans, cooked potatoes, and so on. The pressure canner is also useful wherever electricity for a freezer is unavailable or unreliable. Since extreme weather hits all parts of the country, pressure-canned foods can provide a necessary backup to frozen foods.

Modern pressure canners are safer and easier to use than older canners. Some have turn-on lids fitted with gaskets (the gaskets need replacing every 5 to 10 years); some have machined lids that fit together and seal with wing

Altitude Adjustments for Pressure Canning

Processing times are usually given for canning at altitudes of sea level to 1,000 feet. If you are canning at a higher altitude, the times remain the same, but the pressure is adjusted.

Dial Gauge Pressure Canner

Altitude	1,000–2,000 Feet	2,001–4,000 Feet	4,001–6,000 Feet	6,001–8,000 Feet
POUNDS OF PRESSURE (PSI)	11	12	13	14

Weighted Gauge Pressure Canner

Altitude	1,000–2,000 Feet	2,001–4,000 Feet	4,001–6,000 Feet	6,001–8,000 Feet
POUNDS OF PRESSURE (PSI)	15	15	15	15

nuts. They all have removable racks, an automatic vent/cover lock, a petcock (also called a vent port or steam vent), and a safety release. The pressure canner may have a dial gauge for indicating the pressure or a weighted gauge for indicating and regulating the pressure, or both. Reading your manufacturer's directions and practicing how to properly assemble your canner and how to monitor your gauge will go far in alleviating your fears.

Be aware that the gaskets in some models of pressure canners (and the dial in others) need to be checked from time to time. This was once a service provided by the local county extension office. Such offices are few and far between; if you can't locate an extension agent to check on the safety of your pressure canner, you will have to write to the manufacturer for assistance. Or buy a new one.

STEP-BY-STEP **How to Pressure-Can**

Although the pressure canner relies on steam rather than water, it may take longer to bring the pressure canner up to processing temperature than you expect. For safe processing, the canner needs a "venting" period, during which air and steam escape at full blast for at least 10 minutes before you start the actual processing. Don't set your timer for the 10-minute venting period until you see a large plume of steam venting (as opposed to a small wisp of steam).

Some foods are processed at a higher pressure than others, so check the chart on pages 184–85 to know how to set the counterweight on the valve or how much pressure to maintain. The first couple of times you use your canner, you may have to fiddle with the heat a bit to maintain the proper pressure.

Before you start canning, be sure your pressure canner is in good shape. Don't worry about discoloration on the inside of the canner; that is normal. If your lid has a rubber gasket, make sure it fits properly and is not cracked. This rubber seal usually comes prelubricated, but if it feels a bit dry you can apply a light coating of cooking oil around the ring. Also check that the black overpressure plug on the cover is not cracked or deformed.

1. **Prepare the food in the jars.** Follow your recipe instructions for preparing the food. For raw pack, you'll fill jars with uncooked food and pour in boiling water, broth or stock, juice, or syrup. For hot pack, pack in the hot food and cover with the boiling cooking liquid. In either case, leave the proper amount of headspace, which is 1 inch for most foods.

2. **Prepare the canner.** Fill the pressure canner with 2 to 3 inches of water. For raw-packed foods, bring the water to 140°F (60°C). For hot-packed foods, bring the water to 180°F (82°C), but be careful not to boil the water or heat it long enough that the water level decreases.

Once the jar is filled, remove any air bubbles by running a chopstick or bubble tool (comes with canning kits) around the inside edge of each jar. Wipe the rims clean before placing on the lid and screwband. *Lightly* tighten the screwband.

③ **Put the jars in the canner.** Place the filled jars, fitted with lids and screwbands, on the jar rack in the canner, using a jar lifter. Fasten the canner lid securely. Leave the weight off the vent port or open the petcock (vent).

④ **Vent the air.** Turn the heat under the canner to high. Heat until the water boils and steam flows freely in a steady stream from the open vent port or petcock. While maintaining the high heat setting, let the steam exhaust continuously for 10 minutes.

⑤ **Pressurize the canner, then start timing.** Place the counterweight or weighted gauge on the vent port, or close the petcock (vent). The canner will pressurize in the next 3 to 10 minutes. Start timing when the pressure reading on the dial gauge indicates that the recommended pressure has been reached, or, for canners without dial gauges, when the weighted gauge begins to jiggle or rock as the manufacturer describes. (If you live at a high elevation, you'll need to increase the pressure accordingly; see the box, page 181.) Regulate the heat under the canner to maintain a steady pressure at, or slightly above, the correct gauge pressure. If at any time the pressure goes below the recommended amount, bring the canner back to pressure and begin timing the process over, from the beginning (using the total original process time).

⑥ **Depressurize.** When the proper amount of time has elapsed, turn off the heat and let the canner cool down naturally. While it is cooling, it is also depressurizing.

⑦ **Remove the jars.** When the canner is completely depressurized, remove the weight from the vent port or open the petcock (vent). Wait 10 minutes; then unfasten the lid and remove it carefully. Lift the lid with the underside away from you so that the steam coming out of the canner does not burn your face. Using a jar lifter, remove the jars one at a time, and place on a towel, leaving at least 1 inch of space between the jars during cooling.

⑧ **Cool.** Let the jars sit undisturbed while they cool, from 12 to 24 hours; then test to make sure the jars have a good seal (see page 187).

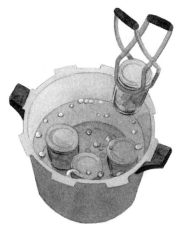

The pressure canner comes with a rack to hold the jars above the bottom of the pot. They will sit in a few inches of water. Use the jar lifter to safely move the jars into place.

Once the water in the pressure canner begins to boil, vent the air for a full 10 minutes.

Start timing only when the proper pressure has been reached. Keep an eye on the dial gauge to be sure you are maintaining the proper temperature.

Pressure Processing Times

Processing times do not vary according to altitude, but pressure does. This table is for foods being processed at an altitude of no more than 1,000 feet above sea level. At that altitude, process at 11 pounds per square inch (psi) in a canner with a dial gauge or 15 psi in a canner with a weighted gauge. Headspace is 1 inch unless indicated otherwise.

Food	Style of Pack	Jar Size	Processing Time in Minutes
Asparagus	Hot or raw pack	Pint	30
		Quart	40
Beans, green, wax	Hot or raw pack	Pint	20
		Quart	25
Beans, lima (fresh)	Hot or raw pack	Pint	40
		Quart*	50
Beets	Hot pack	Pint	30
		Quart	35
Carrots	Hot or raw pack	Pint	25
		Quart	30
Corn, cream style	Hot pack	Pint	85
Corn, whole kernels	Hot or raw pack	Pint	55
		Quart	85
Peas, fresh green	Hot or raw pack	Pint or quart	40
Potatoes, cubed or whole	Hot pack	Pint	35
		Quart	40
Pumpkin or winter squash, cubed	Hot pack	Pint	55
		Quart	90
Spinach or other greens	Hot pack	Pint	70
		Quart	90
Soups (vegetable, meat, poultry)	Hot pack	Pint	60
		Quart	75

Food	Style of Pack	Jar Size	Processing Time in Minutes
Meat or poultry stock	Hot pack	Pint	20
		Quart	25
Meat, ground or chopped	Hot pack	Pint	75
		Quart	90
Meat, in strips, cubes, or chunks	Hot or raw pack	Pint	75
		Quart	90
Poultry, boneless	Hot or raw pack**	Pint	75
		Quart	90
Poultry, with bones	Hot or raw pack**	Pint	65
		Quart	75

*Leave 1½ inches of headspace for lima beans packed raw in quart jars.

**Leave 1¼ inches of headspace for canned poultry.

Is Your Stovetop Made of Glass or Ceramic?

The warranties on some stovetops made of glass or ceramic are voided if the stovetop breaks or cracks when you use a canner on it. On other stoves, there is a sensor that prevents breakage but therefore does not allow the burner to maintain an even temperature high enough for canning — that is, high enough to kill all the bacteria that may be present in the food being canned.

For safety, you need a flat-bottomed canner no bigger than the diameter of your burner. The website PickYourOwn.org has good information regarding the safety of canning on glass and ceramic stovetops, including specific makes and models of stoves and what you can or cannot do on them without voiding their warranties.

Old-Fashioned Canning Methods to Avoid

In almost every workshop I teach, someone offers that his or her mother or grandmother has been reusing canning lids since forever. There is also a lot of chatter on the Internet about old-fashioned methods of canning that worked for Grandma. Will they work today?

- **Open-kettle canning.** This is the sealing method in which you pour hot jam, jelly, or other preserves into a hot jar, quickly wipe the rim, apply the lids and screwbands, and allow to cool. As the food cools, it creates a vacuum and the lid seals. According to the USDA, this vacuum seal is weaker than the ones created with water-bath canning, so you run the risk of losing the seal. Also, you run a higher risk of developing mold or other bacteria in your preserves from the air left in the headspace of the jar. (I do use this method for sealing jars of maple syrup, knowing that the high sugar content protects the syrup.)

- **Paraffin wax seals.** Pour hot jam, jelly, or other preserves into a hot jar, and then pour a thin layer of melted wax over it. Continue to add wax until you have built up a layer about ½ inch thick. When I first started making jam, I had about a 50 percent failure rate with paraffin, with furry blue, green, and white molds growing on top of the jars. Definitely not worth it.

- **Upside-down sealing.** Fill hot, sterilized jars with hot preserves, wipe rims, and apply lids and rings. Turn the jars upside down and cover with a kitchen towel until they're cool. As with open-kettle canning, the seal is weak and you run a higher risk of developing mold or other bacteria in your preserves.

- **Reusing canning lids for canning.** Lids are made these days with a very thin layer of the rubber that forms the seal. In previous times, that rubber ring was thicker and probably could stand up to multiple uses. Today's lids simply aren't made as well. Even if a seal forms, it is likely to let go at some point. By the way, reusing lids for storing foods in the refrigerator, for mixing up salad dressings in a canning jar, and for storing dry foods in a cupboard are all fine — anything but canning.

Pressure-Canning Meat

I don't run into a lot of people who can meat. Those folks who come from a meat-canning tradition are usually hunters, which makes sense if you think about it. Homesteaders who raise animals often get their meat butchered and frozen at a slaughterhouse, or they raise chickens in batches that fit their freezer's capacity. Hunters come home with large animals that have to be dealt with immediately — and packing a home freezer with a huge load of fresh meat is unsafe. But there's no limit to how much meat you can can.

One reason given for canning meat is that it is convenient to have already-cooked meat in the pantry. Yes, it is convenient, but canned meat should always be cooked at a boiling temperature for 15 to 20 minutes before it's consumed, according to the USDA. That makes the idea of, say, making chicken salad from a jar of canned chicken a lot less convenient. The most compelling reason to can meat is that canned meat won't be ruined in the event of a power failure. The reason not to can meat? You end up with a boiled meat product that is a challenge to use. I'm all for canning meat that will be "boiled" (simmered) in tomato sauce — as meatballs or as chili, for example. And I'm all for boiling canned chicken in broth. Beyond that, my imagination fails me.

It should go without saying that the only way to safely can meat is in a pressure canner, according to the times established by the National Center for Home Food Preservation, a division of the USDA. And it is necessary to follow all the steps listed on pages 182–83 for safe pressure canning.

Tips for Canning Meat

I am not an expert on canning meat. The following are tips I have gleaned from the instructions with my Presto pressure canner and from the National Center for Home Food.

> You can use either the hot-pack or the raw-pack method to can meat. Raw-packed meat shrinks significantly in the jar and generally looks less appealing than hot-packed meat.
> To hot-pack cooked meat, the meat may be poached, pan-fried, roasted, or baked. It should be packed in broth, or the meat's cooking juice, but not with flour-thickened gravy.
> Pack hot meat loosely in mason jars, leaving 1 inch of headspace.
> Meats can be processed with or without salt. Recommended amounts are ½ teaspoon fine-grain sea salt, pickling salt, or canning salt per pint or 1 teaspoon per quart, but you can adjust to taste.

> Prepare enough meat for one canner load at a time; in the meantime, keep the remaining meat refrigerated.
> Cut slabs of meat about 1 inch thick, slicing across the grain; then cut with the grain until you have small uniform pieces.
> Make certain that you trim away gristle, bruised spots, and fat. Too much fat may give the meat a strong flavor and may also interfere with the seal.
> Meat can be canned on the bone (if it fits in the jar) or boneless.

Testing for a Good Seal

After a jar has been processed in a boiling-water-bath or pressure canner, it should be sealed. If the seal is faulty, the food inside the jar is not spoiled, but it won't keep long. Store unsealed jars in the refrigerator and use within a week.

To test for a seal:
> Look at the middle of the lid; it should be slightly concave.

Unsealed

Sealed

You may have even heard it seal with a distinctive "ping."
> Press the center hard with your thumb; if it does not "give" (move downward), it is sealed.

The lid should not "give" or move.

> Remove the screwband and hold the jar by the lid; it should not release the jar.

Hold by the lid only.

CHAPTER 12

Drying

Drying is one of the oldest methods of preserving food. It is relatively easy to do, and though it takes time, your attention is not required continuously. Drying preserves much of the vitamins and minerals that would be lost by canning. In warm climates, you can use the drying power of the sun directly or in solar dryers; in more humid climates, there are indoor ovens and electric food dehydrators. Because drying removes moisture, the food shrinks in volume and becomes lighter in weight, reducing the amount of space you need for storage.

Drying as a food preservation technique has undergone different waves of popularity as people learn of new ways to make enhanced dried food snacks. Fruit leathers probably date back to the sixteenth century, but they have become popular as a homemade snack only since the advent of electric home dehydrators. In recent years, dried veggie chips as snacks have boosted the popularity of food drying. The veggie chips on the market tend to be extremely expensive, so making your own makes sense whether you

are dealing with garden surpluses or just want to provide healthful snacks.

Drying preserves food because bacteria, yeast, and molds can't grow in a dry environment. Drying also slows down the action of the enzymes that spoil food (these naturally occurring substances also cause foods to ripen). When you want to use dried foods, you can either snack on them directly (dried fruit and beef jerky) or reconstitute them (add back the water) and cook as you would fresh food. Stored in a cool, dark, dry spot, dried food should keep its quality for anywhere from several months to 2 years.

There is a bit more to drying than you might think, if you are going for quality. Most vegetables should blanched before they are dried. Light-colored fruits should be treated with ascorbic acid to preserve their color. Finally, some fruits and vegetables should be pasteurized (heated or frozen) to make sure all the spoilage organisms are destroyed.

I live in the Northeast, where fall weather is likely to be rainy, so outdoor drying is

pretty much out of the question. I get the most use out of my dehydrator when my son goes foraging for wild mushrooms; in fact, I think drying is the ideal preservation method for mushrooms. I love seasoned dried kale chips (page 194) and sweet potato chips (page 195), but they take forever to dry and the dried chips are eaten faster than I can reasonably produce them. I do dry tomatoes on occasion, and I make beef jerky. I have dried all sorts of vegetables, just to experiment with them, but I prefer the convenience of freezing to just about every other preserving method. Many fruits and vegetables require a quick blanching in boiling water to preserve their color and texture. Once I've done that, I lean toward freezing just so I can wrap things up and move on.

If you are serious about dehydrating, my advice is to build or buy as large a dehydrator as possible. Otherwise, the process is very, very slow, and you have to focus on keeping your vegetables in good quality before you can dry them.

Methods of Drying

You can dry food in the open air, in a conventional oven, or in an electric or solar food dehydrator. There are pros and cons to each method.

Open Air

A hot, breezy climate with a minimum daytime temperature of 86°F (30°C) is ideal for drying fruit outdoors in the sun. But if the temperature is too low or the humidity too high, the food may spoil before it is fully dried. The USDA doesn't recommend drying meat and vegetables outdoors because these foods are too prone to spoilage.

Woven baskets have been used for outdoor drying for centuries, but a screened tray is probably more efficient, if less attractive. Avoid galvanized metal, aluminum, or copper screens, which can impart off-flavors or even potentially toxic salts to the food. Top-quality food-drying screens are made from food-safe plastic screening and are available online. Cover the fruits and vegetables on the trays with cheesecloth or nylon netting to help protect them from birds and insects. Direct sunlight destroys some of the more fragile vitamins and enzymes and causes the color of the food to fade, so you will have better results if you can shade the foods with a dark sheet of cloth or metal. Indoors, it is easy to use screened trays placed on chairs or sawhorses. No further equipment is needed.

If you want to go really low-tech, and you have the climate to make it possible, dry food by draping it over branches or spreading it on wide shallow baskets on a roof. Or thread pieces of food on a cord or a stick and hang it over a fire or woodstove, or from the rafters. Bundle herbs and suspend them from doorknobs or nails in rooms with good ventilation. You can also place screen doors across chairs for use as drying screens, or make shallow baskets of sheets hung between clotheslines outside, or in the attic or an upstairs room with screened windows wide open.

Cover foods drying outdoors with nylon netting to protect from insects and birds.

Pasteurizing Fruits and Vegetables Dried Outdoors

Anything that was dried outdoors — in the sun or on the vine — may be harboring some insects and their eggs. Pasteurizing the dried food will help you avoid having those insects eating your dried food. To pasteurize in the freezer, seal the dried food in freezer-type plastic bags. Place the bags in a freezer set at 0°F (-18°C) or below and leave them for at least 48 hours. Alternatively, you can arrange the dried food on trays in a single layer. Place the trays in an oven preheated to 160°F (70°C) and leave for 30 minutes. After either of these treatments, the dried food is ready to be conditioned and stored.

Solar Dehydrators

Highly effective, solar dryers yield results on par with electric dehydrators, without the expense and carbon footprint associated with using electricity. Solar dryers don't require a low-humidity climate, though they do require sunshine and high temperatures. The only downside is the requirement that you assemble or build your own dryer. There are plenty of kits and designs available online. In rainy climates, look for a dehydrator that can be brought indoors and used with electricity to finish the job.

A solar dryer has three basic parts: a solar collector (such as an old storm window), a box to hold the food, and a stand. The collector captures the heat of the sun to warm air that will circulate around the food. The box is usually made from plywood and holds food trays, which are made from screening to allow greatest air circulation. The most sophisticated solar designs include adjustable vents and thermostats.

Conventional Ovens

You can use the oven in your kitchen to dry foods, but there are several drawbacks: air circulation in a conventional oven tends to be poor, even with the oven door propped open and a fan placed nearby to improve ventilation, so results can be uneven. Also, the process ties up the oven for a long time and is not particularly energy efficient. However, this method requires no new equipment and can be done in any climate. It is the equipment of choice for making beef jerky, which requires a slightly higher temperature than other dried foods. It does a reasonably good job on tomatoes. I would think that convection ovens (which have fans to circulate the air) would do a slightly better, faster job than nonconvection ovens, but I can't use my convection feature for temperatures under 300°F (150°C).

To use an oven to dehydrate food, you must be able to set the oven for 140°F to 170°F (60°C to 80°C). At higher temperatures, the food cooks rather than dries. Your drying racks should be 3 to 4 inches shorter than the oven from front to back. Wire

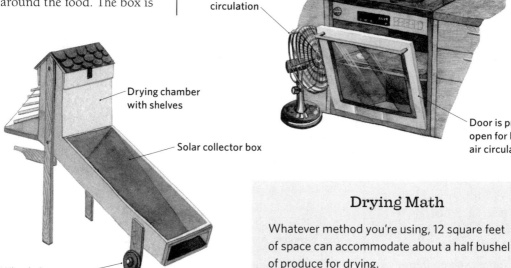

Fan improves air circulation

Drying chamber with shelves

Solar collector box

Door is propped open for better air circulation

Wheels for easy repositioning

Drying Math

Whatever method you're using, 12 square feet of space can accommodate about a half bushel of produce for drying.

cooling racks placed on top of cookie sheets work well for some foods. Set the oven racks that hold the trays 2 to 3 inches apart for good air circulation.

Electric Dehydrators

Electric dehydrators give excellent and consistent results. The only downsides are the cost of buying and running the appliance, the limited amount of food that can be dried at one time in most home models, and the storage space the appliance requires when not in use. If you want to do a lot of drying, buy as large a unit as you can afford; the smaller units can be frustrating to use.

A food dehydrator has an electric element for heat and a fan and vents for air circulation.

Dehydrators are efficiently designed to dry foods quickly at 140°F (60°C). They are widely available in stores and online. Costs vary widely, depending on the features of each model. The most expensive and efficient ones have stackable trays, horizontal air flow, and thermostats.

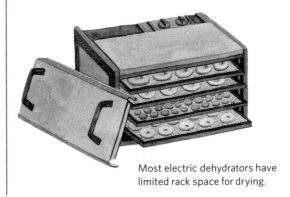

Most electric dehydrators have limited rack space for drying.

STEP-BY-STEP **How to Dry Most Vegetables**

Not all vegetables can be treated the same, so be sure to check the drying chart on page 193 for specific times and whether step 2 (blanching) is even necessary. Beans can be left to dry on the vine (see page 194), though they may need to be finished off in a dehydrator and should be pasteurized (see page 189).

① **Wash, peel, slice.** Wash the vegetables in cool water. Trim, peel, cut, slice, or shred them as desired. Veggie chips should be sliced thinly with a mandoline. Celery, onions, bell peppers, and other vegetables that are headed for a soup or stew pot can be diced. Remove any fibrous or woody portions, as well as any decayed or bruised areas. Keep pieces uniform in size so that they will dry at the same rate.

A mandoline does the best job of slicing vegetables thinly for even drying.

② **Blanch (optional).** For boiling-water blanching, bring 4 quarts of water to a rolling boil for each pound of vegetables (leafy greens need 8 quarts water per pound). For steam blanching, bring a few inches of water to a boil. Immerse a wire basket or mesh bag containing vegetables directly in the boiling water or in the steam above. Cover the pot and begin counting the blanching time as soon as the vegetables are placed in the water or steam. For times for specific vegetables, see page 160.

Blanching sets the color and texture of some vegetables.

③ **Cool.** Lift the basket out of the water or steam and immediately dump the vegetables into a basin of ice water. Dry on kitchen towels. The better job you do of drying, the faster the vegetables will dry in the dehydrator.

Adding oil to veggie chips will help seasonings adhere.

④ **Season (optional).** If you are making chips or other seasoned snacks, toss the veggies with a little olive oil or other vegetable oil and salt and pepper. You might also add some seasoning in the form of onion powder, garlic powder, dried rosemary, dried dill, or dried oregano. Grated Parmesan also works with some veggies. Experiment with flavors, but I recommend avoiding any spices that have bitter nuances, such as curry powder.

⑤ **Dry.** When the vegetables are cooled, patted dry, and seasoned, arrange them on the drying trays. See the drying times on the chart at right.

Pieces on drying trays can start out touching; shrinkage is considerable.

⑥ **Cool and store.** Allow the vegetables to cool to room temperature. Package in airtight containers or vacuum-sealed plastic bags and store in a cool spot.

Drying Cucumbers for Pickles

A surplus of cucumbers and a shortage of time are both fairly standard problems for vegetable gardeners. Here's a tip from Kathy Harrison, author of *Just in Case, Another Place at the Table,* and *One Small Boat.* She slices her cucumbers ¼ inch thick, then dries the slices until crisp. When she wants pickles, she makes up a small batch of hot brine (you could reuse brine, if you want to), adds the dried cucumbers, transfers it all to a jar and tucks it in the refrigerator. The next day, she has a jar of pickles ready to eat, crisp ones at that.

Drying Vegetables

Although all vegetables can be dried, not all vegetables are appealing once dried. For example, Brussels sprouts have a strong flavor once dried; dried cabbage absorbs moisture from the air and is prone to mold; and lettuce, summer squash, and cucumbers are too high in water content to be dried. So the following chart includes only vegetables that are reasonably appealing when dried. Drying times may vary. Experiment with slicking the vegetables in oil and seasoning before drying.

Vegetable	Preparation	Steam Blanching Time	Water Blanching Time	Drying Time
Asparagus	Halve vertically if thick	4–5 minutes	3½–4½ minutes	4–6 hours
Beans, green	Cut in pieces or strips	2½ minutes	2 minutes	8–14 hours
Beets	Cook fully, peel, cut in strips			10–12 hours
Carrots	Trim, peel, cut in slices or strips	3–3½ minutes	3½ minutes	10–12 hours
Chiles and peppers	Seed, dice			8–12 hours
Corn	Cut kernels from cobs after blanching	4 minutes	6 minutes	6–8 hours
Garlic	Peel and mince			6–8 hours
Kale	Strip from stalks, cut into ribbons	2–2½ minutes	1½ minutes	8–10 hours
Okra	Trim, slice into ⅛- to ¼-inch disks			8–10 hours
Onions	Peel, dice			3–9 hours
Parsley	Remove stems			1–2 hours
Peas, green	Shell	3 minutes	2 minutes	8–10 hours
Potatoes	Peel, cut into strips or slices ⅛ inch thick	6–8 minutes	5–6 minutes	8–12 hours
Tomatoes	Halve or quarter			10–18 hours

Drying Vegetables

In the proper climate, it is possible to dry all vegetables without any preparation whatsoever, but the quality is really improved by blanching, which stops the enzyme action that could cause loss of color and flavor during drying and storage. It also shortens the drying and rehydration time by relaxing the tissue walls so that moisture can escape and later reenter more rapidly. Cutting the vegetables into small, thin pieces improves quality by reducing the drying times.

Vine-Drying Beans

To dry beans (navy, kidney, butter, black, great Northern, lima, soybeans, and so on), leave the bean pods on the vine in the garden until the beans inside rattle. When the vines and pods are dry and shriveled, pick the beans and shell them. No pretreatment is necessary. If the beans are still moist, the drying process is not complete and the beans will mold if not more thoroughly dried. If needed, drying can be completed in the sun, in an oven, or in a dehydrator. Dried beans should be pasteurized (see page 189) before being stored.

Making Seasoned Dried Veggie Chips

Like dried fruit, seasoned dried veggie chips are as much about snacking as they are about preserving. But while the sweetness and the chewiness of fruit slow down the snacking, the saltiness and crispiness of veggie chips invite you to eat them as fast as you can make them. Still,

Seasoned Kale Chips

Makes about 8 cups

Any type of kale can be used, but I have a slight preference for lacinato kale because it is flatter and fits better in the narrow space between trays in the dehydrator. Don't overdo the salt; the kale doesn't require a lot. Although not quite as wonderful as freshly roasted kale, these dried ribbons of kale are tasty and compelling. The kale should be washed and well dried before you start.

INGREDIENTS

1	bunch kale, stemmed, leaves chopped (about 8 cups packed)
2	tablespoons extra-virgin olive oil
¼–½	teaspoon salt
¼	teaspoon garlic powder
¼	teaspoon onion powder

1. Toss the kale with the oil until well coated. Sprinkle the salt, garlic powder, and onion powder over the kale; toss to distribute.

2. Spread the leaves on the dehydrator trays or oiled baking sheets in single layers. Do not crowd the leaves or they will not dry evenly. The pieces can touch, but they shouldn't overlap too much.

3. Dry the kale until crispy at 125°F (50°C) in a dehydrator for 3 to 4 hours, or at the lowest temperature setting in your oven for 1½ to 2 hours. When completely cool, transfer to an airtight container to store.

they are a nutritious alternative to fried potato chips and corn chips, and well worth making.

Seasoned chips can be made in the oven or in a dehydrator. Depending on how low a temperature an oven can be set to, chips in the oven take about half as long as chips in a dehydrator.

The vegetable needs to be sliced as thinly and evenly as possible, which makes this a job for a mandoline. You can use a food processor if you have a thin-slice disk. The pieces should be no more than $\frac{1}{8}$ inch thick. Whether or not to blanch the veggies first is up to you; I prefer fully cooking beets and blanching green beans. Sweet potatoes should be raw. Slick the vegetables with any vegetable oil and season with salt, garlic powder, onion powder, or dried green herbs, such as rosemary or oregano. Cinnamon or a cinnamon-sugar mix can also be used. I stay away from spices that have bitter notes, such as curry.

Arrange the veggie chips on lightly oiled baking sheets or dehydrator sheets and dehydrate until crisp. Timing varies, depending on the vegetable.

Rosemary Sweet Potato Chips

Makes about 6 cups

You don't have to peel the sweet potatoes first, though you can if you want.

INGREDIENTS

2 large sweet potatoes, thinly sliced on a mandoline (about 8 cups)

6 tablespoons olive oil or other vegetable oil

1 teaspoon minced dried rosemary

1 teaspoon salt

½ teaspoon black pepper

1. Toss the sweet potatoes with the oil until well coated; use your hands and make sure each chip is oiled. Sprinkle the rosemary, salt, and pepper over the sweet potatoes; toss to distribute.

2. Spread the chips on the dehydrator trays or on oiled baking sheets in single layers. Do not crowd the pieces or they will not dry evenly. The pieces can touch, but they shouldn't overlap too much.

3. Dry the sweet potatoes until crispy and dry at 140°F (60°C) in a dehydrator for about 8 hours, or at the lowest temperature setting in your oven for about 4 hours. When completely cool, transfer to an airtight container to store.

Drying Fruits

Dealing with a surplus of fruits by drying is a no-brainer. Dried fruits are the original snack foods, and we all love to snack. While dried vegetables require seasoning to shine as snacks, fruits are so inherently flavorful that no additions are really needed. However, fruits that darken when exposed to air will benefit from a dip in an ascorbic acid solution, and some fruits also benefit from being blanched in a sugar syrup (see the box on page 197).

Check the drying chart on the right for specific drying times for each type of fruit. Many light-colored fruits, such as apples, peaches, and bananas, darken rapidly when cut and exposed to air, but you can dip the fruit in an ascorbic acid (vitamin C) solution to prevent browning. Ascorbic acid is available in powdered or tablet form from drugstores or grocery stores. Because of the high concentration of sugar in dried fruit, fruit is more prone to mold than vegetables. Before storing dried fruit, condition the fruit (step 4) to equalize the moisture among the pieces and check to see if additional drying is necessary.

① **Wash, peel, slice.** Wash and peel the fruit. Cut in half and core, if needed. Slice if desired. Thin, uniform, peeled slices dry the fastest. Apples can be cored and sliced in rings, wedges, or chips. Bananas can be sliced in coins, chips, or sticks. Whole fruits take the longest to dry.

② **Treat to prevent browning (optional).** Mix 1 teaspoon powdered ascorbic acid (or 3,000 mg ascorbic acid tablets, crushed) in 2 cups water. Put the light-colored fruit in the solution for 3 to 5 minutes. Remove the fruit and drain well.

③ **Dry.** Spray the dryer trays with nonstick cooking spray to prevent sticking, and place the fruit in a single layer on the trays. The pieces should not touch or overlap. See the chart at right for specific times.

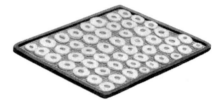

④ **Condition the fruit and store.** Condition the fruit to equalize the moisture among the pieces and reduce the risk of mold growth. To condition the fruit, loosely pack the dried fruit in plastic or glass jars. Seal the containers and let them stand for 7 to 10 days, shaking the jars daily to separate the pieces and check for moisture condensation. If condensation develops in the jar, return the fruit to the dehydrator for more drying. After conditioning, package and store the fruit.

Syrup Blanching: An Optional Step

Syrup blanching sweetens the fruit (obviously), fixes the color, and makes tart dried fruit more palatable. It also takes time and adds sugar and calories, which undermines some of the health benefits of the fruit. Syrup blanching works best with apples, apricots, figs, nectarines, peaches, pears, pie cherries, plums, and rhubarb.

To make the syrup, combine 1½ cups sugar and 2½ cups water in a pot. Bring to a boil, stirring until the sugar dissolves. Add 1 pound prepared fruit and simmer for 10 minutes. Remove from the heat and let the fruit steep in the syrup for 30 minutes. Then lift the fruit out of the syrup and rinse lightly in cold water if desired (rinsing makes the fruit less sticky). Drain on paper towels before drying.

Drying Fruits

Drying times vary a lot depending on the efficiency of the dehydrator, the juiciness of the fruit, and the size of the pieces. Syrup-blanched fruits take longer to dry than fruit that hasn't been blanched.

Fruit	Preparation	Drying Time
Apples	Peel, core, and slice ⅛ inch thick	8–12 hours
Apricots	Pit, then halve or slice	12–14 hours
Bananas	Peel and slice ¼ inch thick	8–10 hours
Berries	Hull	8–10 hours
Cherries	Stem, pit, and halve or leave whole	12–14 hours
Figs	Halve or leave whole	10–12 hours
Grapes	Pit if needed; leave whole or halve	10–12 hours
Kiwi	Peel and slice ¼ inch thick	8–10 hours
Nectarines	Peel, pit, and slice ¼ inch thick	10–14 hours
Peaches	Peel, pit, and slice ¼ inch thick	10–14 hours
Pears	Peel, core, and slice ¼ inch thick	8–10 hours
Persimmons	Peel and slice ¼ inch thick	10–14 hours
Pineapple	Peel, core, and slice ½ inch thick	10–12 hours
Prune plums	Halve	12–16 hours
Rhubarb	Slice ½ inch thick	6–8 hours
Strawberries	Leave whole, halve, or slice ¼–½ inch thick	7–9 hours

How to Make Fruit Leather

Fruit leather is a tasty, chewy way to enjoy fruit. It's made by pouring puréed fruit onto a flat surface for drying. The fruit you purée can start as fresh, canned, or frozen. When dried, the fruit is usually rolled up. It gets the name "leather" because it has the texture of leather.

① **Prepare the fruit.** Wash fresh fruit or berries in cool water. Remove peel, seeds, and stem.

② **Purée.** Cut the fruit into chunks. Use 2 cups of fruit for each 13- by 15-inch fruit leather. Purée the fruit in a food processor or blender until smooth.

③ **Treat to prevent darkening (optional).** Add 2 teaspoons of lemon juice or ⅛ teaspoon ascorbic acid (375 mg) for every 2 cups of light-colored fruit to prevent darkening.

④ **Sweeten (optional).** Sweeten to taste with honey, maple syrup, or sugar.

⑤ **Dehydrate.** Line cookie sheets with plastic wrap. In a dehydrator, use plastic wrap or the specially designed plastic sheets that come with the dehydrator. Pour the purée onto the lined cookie sheets or dehydrator trays. Spread it evenly to a thickness of ⅛ inch. Dry at 140°F (60°C) until no indentation is left when you touch the center with your finger. This takes 6 to 8 hours in a dehydrator, up to 18 hours in the oven, and 1 to 2 days in the sun.

⑥ **Store.** While still warm, peel from the plastic wrap. Cool, rewrap in plastic, and store.

Checking Fruits and Vegetables for Dryness

Is it dry yet? That is the money question. If the dehydrated food harbors moisture, it is prone to going moldy. In general, it is better to overdry than underdry, but if you allow the food to become too dry, it will crumble to dust. Drying times are given as a range. After you hit the minimum time, begin testing. Let a few pieces cool to room temperature for a few minutes, then bite into them. Here's how to tell if they're dry enough:

▸ **Vegetables** should be dried until they are brittle and will snap when bent. At this stage, they should contain about 10 percent moisture (not that you can test it without special instruments).

▸ Dry most **fruit** until it is leather-hard but not sticky or tacky. Cut several cooled pieces in half. There should be no visible moisture, and you should not be able to squeeze any moisture from the fruit.

▸ **Berries** should be dried until they rattle when shaken. After drying, let them cool for 30 to 60 minutes. Then condition the berries (see step 4 on page 196) before packing them away.

Making Jerky

People have been drying meat into jerky in the open air and in dehydrators for years, centuries really. But there are risks with both methods because the meat is never brought to 160°F (71°C), the temperature you need to destroy all the harmful bacteria (the maximum temperature of most dehydrators is 145°F/63°C). The USDA currently recommends cooking the meat first to 160°F (71°C), then drying. The method I use, which I describe below, is neither traditional nor officially sanctioned by the USDA. Instead, I slowly cook/dry the meat at 225°F (107°C), resulting in jerky that I know is safe in just 3 to 4 hours.

Choosing the Meat

When we think about jerky, we usually think of beef jerky, but any very low-fat meat can be made into jerky, including venison and white-meat turkey. The beef cuts most often turned into jerky come from the round. A whole beef round consists of three major muscles: top round, eye of round, and bottom round — all of which are excellent jerky choices. The top round is often cut into round steaks 1 to 1½ inches thick to make London broil, which is the cut recommended by many for making jerky. Flank steaks are also good to use. Whatever meat you use should be as lean as possible. It takes about 4 pounds of fresh, raw meat to make 1 pound of dry jerky.

STEP-BY-STEP **How to Make Jerky**

For a recipe for spicy jerky, see page 201. But really, the seasonings are up to you. Be aware that flavors, particularly salt, will concentrate as the meat dries, so don't go overboard. Using curing salts will enable you to safely store the meat at room temperature, but they aren't necessary if you refrigerate the jerky.

① **Trim the fat.** With a sharp knife, trim away as much fat as you can; the fat becomes rancid and gives the jerky an unpleasant taste. If there is any membrane or silverskin on the meat, trim it away. All you want is the muscle meat.

Trim off as much fat as you can.

② **Slice thinly.** Put the meat in the freezer for 1 to 2 hours to firm it up and make slicing easier. I recommend slicing the meat with the grain; this is opposite most instructions for cutting meat. Slicing with the grain results in a chewier jerky. Some people slice the meat against the grain, which results in a more tender jerky that is likely to crumble. Aim for consistent slices, ⅛ to ¼ inch thick. (Some people use deli meat slicers, but you'd have to make a lot of jerky or cure a lot of meat to justify the purchase.)

Slice with the grain.

③ **Season and marinate.** You can use a wet marinade or dry rub on your jerky; it really doesn't matter. I like a dry rub, converted into a paste with the use of maple syrup, my default sweetener. You'll need about 5 tablespoons of a seasoning mix, including at least 1 tablespoon kosher or coarse salt and 2 tablespoons sweetener for 1 pound of meat. Mix up the rub or marinade, add it to the sliced beef in a glass container or large ziplock bag, massage it into the meat, and refrigerate for as little as 3 and as much as 24 hours.

Marinate for 3 to 24 hours in the refrigerator.

④ **Bake dry.** Line baking sheets with aluminum foil, and set wire racks on the baking sheets. Arrange the meat in a single layer on the wire racks, spacing the meat about ¼ inch apart. Set the oven to 225°F (110°C). Bake the meat for 3 to 4 hours, until the meat is dark and dry and firm to the touch but pliable (not brittle), rotating the trays midway through the baking time.

Drying in the oven at 225°F (110°C) prevents spoilage.

⑤ **Cool and store.** Let cool to room temperature. Pat dry with paper towels. Store in a plastic bag in the refrigerator for 1 to 2 months. For longer storage, keep in the freezer.

Spicy Beef Jerky

Makes about 8 ounces

Y ou can play with the seasoning mix as you like. This version is pretty spicy, so unless I am making it for hotheads, I cut back on the chipotle or the hot paprika, or both. My son calls my less-spicy versions "primitive." He explains himself this way: "When you cut back on the spice, you really taste the meat — and it is really meaty meat . . . what I think the cowboys must have kept in a shirt pocket to eat on the range."

INGREDIENTS

- 1 pound London broil or flank steak
- 4 teaspoons kosher salt or other coarse salt
- 1 teaspoon ground chipotle chile powder
- 1 teaspoon smoked hot paprika
- 1 teaspoon black pepper
- 1 teaspoon garlic powder
- 1 teaspoon onion powder
- 2 tablespoons honey or maple syrup

1. Trim all fat from the meat; this is important because the fat could cause spoilage. Pat the meat dry and freeze for 1 to 2 hours to make it easy to slice thinly.

2. Combine the salt, ground chipotle powder, paprika, black pepper, garlic powder, and onion powder in a large bowl. Stir in the honey or maple syrup.

3. Remove the steak from the freezer. Cut the steak in half with the grain to create two pieces about 4 inches wide. Cut the meat with the grain into strips about ¼ inch thick.

4. Add the meat to the seasonings and mix well. Use your hands to massage the seasonings into the meat. Either cover the bowl or transfer the meat and all of the seasonings to a resealable plastic bag and refrigerate for 8 to 24 hours, turning the meat and giving it a good massage once or twice.

5. Line a large baking sheet with aluminum foil and set wire racks on the baking sheet. Arrange the meat in a single layer on the wire racks, spacing the strips about ¼ inch apart.

6. Set the oven to 225°F (110°C), using the convection function if you have it. Bake the meat for 3 to 4 hours, until it is dark and dry and firm to the touch but pliable (not brittle), rotating the trays midway through the baking time.

7. Let cool to room temperature. Pat dry with paper towels. Store in a plastic bag in the refrigerator for 1 to 2 months.

Storing and Using Dried Foods

Cool dried foods completely before packaging them for storage in clean moisture-resistant containers. Glass jars, metal cans, or freezer containers with tight-fitting lids are good storage containers. Plastic freezer bags are acceptable, but they are not insect- and rodent-proof.

Dried fruits and vegetables should be stored in a cool, dry, dark place. Most dried fruits can be stored for 1 year at 60°F (16°C), or 6 months at 80°F (27°C). Dried vegetables have about half the shelf life of fruits. Fruit leathers should keep for up to 1 month at room temperature. Jerky, as previously noted, should be stored in the fridge and will keep for up to 2 months. To store any dried product longer, keep it in the freezer.

Dried fruits can be eaten as is or reconstituted. Unseasoned dried vegetables usually are reconstituted. Once reconstituted, dried fruits or vegetables are treated as fresh. Seasoned vegetables, fruit leathers, and meat jerky are eaten as snacks, as is.

To reconstitute dried fruits or vegetables, add water to the fruits or vegetables and soak until the desired volume is restored. For soups and stews, add the dehydrated vegetables without rehydrating them; they will rehydrate as the soup or stew cooks. Also, leafy vegetables and tomatoes do not need soaking. Add enough water to cover, and simmer until tender.

Enjoying Dried Tomatoes

Tomatoes are easy to dry — and easy to use. Just soak the dried tomatoes in warm water for 30 minutes and they will become soft and pliable, ready to add to soups, sauces, casseroles, and quiches. (Reserve the soaking liquid to add flavor to stocks and sauces.) Once reconstituted, use dried tomatoes within several days or pack them in olive oil and store in the refrigerator for up to 2 weeks.

To use oil-packed tomatoes, drain the tomatoes from the oil and use. Keep the tomatoes left in the jar completely covered with olive oil, which may mean adding more oil as you use the tomatoes. Add a sprig of basil and a clove of garlic for extra flavor, if you like. Don't toss out that oil when you're done with the tomatoes. It will pick up flavor from the tomatoes and be delicious in salad dressings or used for sautéing.

CHAPTER 13

Pickling

Pickling is another ancient way of preserving food, in this case by immersing the food in an environment too acidic for most spoilage bacteria and yeasts to survive. And along the way, the food is seriously altered in flavor — deliciously so.

There are two basic methods for making pickles: packing in a vinegar (acetic acid) brine (bread-and-butter pickles) or fermenting in a salt brine (kosher dills), which creates lactic acid and acetic acid to preserve the veggies. Salsas, chutneys, and relishes are vinegar-brined pickles; for them, the vinegar is cooked with the vegetables. For long-term storage, vinegar pickles are refrigerated or canned in a boiling-water bath. There are even some recipes for freezer vinegar pickles. Although fermented pickles can be canned in a boiling-water bath, I think it ruins their texture. It also destroys the probiotic bacteria in a ferment. I don't recommend it.

Fermenting vegetables to make pickles is enjoying a major culinary revival these days due to a confluence of interest in preserving and interest in eating foods that enhance digestion through "friendly" probiotic bacteria.

People used to make a lot more pickles than they do today, partly to preserve excess vegetables but also to add zest to a diet that could be monotonous and bland. Today we are more likely to avoid boredom at the table by eating across global influences — Korean one night, Mexican the next, Southern the next. While pickles today are less necessary to stimulate jaded palates, they can perform an alternative service of providing authentic flavors: kimchi with Korean barbecue, salsa with Mexican tacos, bread-and-butter pickles with Southern fried catfish.

As a way to preserve excess vegetables, pickles can be a great alternative to pressure canning or freezing — but only if you start to think of pickles as more than a garnish. If all of your cucumber pickles end up as a trio of chips on a plate next to a burger, then don't bother to put up more than one canner load of sliced dills or sweet bread-and-butters. And if you remember to eat dilly beans only as a late-night snack, then those jars of beans may not all be emptied by the time the next harvest rolls around. I think the best way to think about pickles — which, incidentally, is how they functioned in the past — is as a vegetable serving. Although cucumber pickles may be a lightweight, low-nutrition vegetable, pickled okra, pickled beets, and pickled green beans provide at least as much nutrition as their canned, unpickled counterparts. Another great (and traditional) way to serve pickles is as an hors d'oeuvre with olives and sliced veggies.

Whether you serve them as a garnish or as a featured vegetable, make only those pickles that taste delicious to you. And everyone's taste varies. For example, my son likes a stronger vinegar presence than I do. And both of us agree that most recipes that come from the southern United States are way too sweet. When you are just starting out in pickling, it is a good idea to seek out recipes that make small quantities. When you find the ones you really like, make them in larger quantities by multiplying all the ingredients. (My book *The Pickled Pantry* has a whole chapter on single-jar recipes for that very reason. Who needs to accumulate jars of pickles that are too good to throw out but not good enough to finish quickly?)

Ingredients for Pickling

As with every type of preserving, higher-quality ingredients result in a higher-quality finished product. This is especially true of the fresh vegetables you want to pickle; however, avoid homemade vinegar unless you know its acidic strength.

Vegetables

Slightly immature, small vegetables will have small seeds and crisp flesh and will make a crisper, better pickle than overgrown vegetables, which have large seeds and pulpy centers.

Pickling cucumbers make a crispier pickle than salad cucumbers. Salad cucumbers can be used as long as they are not waxed (most supermarket salad cucumbers are waxed). I'm a big fan of Asian and Middle Eastern varieties of cucumbers for pickling because they tend to grow long, not fat (no soggy centers), and they have tender skins. With all types of cucumbers (and summer squash), cut off about 1/16 inch from the blossom end, which, if left on, releases enzymes that will soften the pickle.

If you are harvesting from your own garden, pick early, avoiding the heat of the day. If you're not going to pickle them right away, store the vegetables, unwashed, in the refrigerator or on ice in insulated coolers. Before pickling, wash all vegetables thoroughly in cool running water and scrub with a soft vegetable brush to remove any dirt.

If the vegetables you are about to pickle are less than prime, consider making a relish instead of a whole or sliced pickle.

Vinegar

Vinegar is the preservative for a fresh-pack pickle. The acidity level of vinegar is measured by "grain strength," which is ten times the acetic acid content. As long as the vinegar has a 40- to 60-grain strength (that is, 4 to 6 percent acetic acid), it can be used safely to make pickles. This includes most commercial vinegars, as well as most homemade herb vinegars made from commercial vinegars.

White distilled vinegar is commonly used in pickle brines because it doesn't compete with the distinctive flavors of the herbs and spices used to make pickles, and because it is inexpensive. Cider vinegar imparts a rich, fruity flavor that is sometimes desirable, particularly with sweet pickles.

Homemade vinegars aren't recommended for pickling because their acetic acid strength is not consistent. I have found information on testing the acidity of homemade vinegar on the Internet, but the tests are either expensive or time-consuming. And, as with all knowledge gained on the Internet, it may or may not be accurate. There's nothing I can vouch for.

Salt

The "pickling salt" or "canning salt" called for in many recipes is simply table salt without the iodine or anticaking agents, additives that can make a pickling liquid cloudy. It is sold in supermarkets. Can you use table salt instead? You can, though your brine may be cloudy and some people claim they can taste the added iodine. Sea salt is fine to use, as long as the fineness of the grind matches the fineness of the pickling salt used to develop a particular recipe.

The salt that you use in vinegar pickles is there for taste only. So you can alter the amount you use — but do so carefully. Salt is really, really important for balancing flavor. A vinegar pickle without salt will taste especially sour, even if balanced with more sugar.

In fermented pickles, salt draws the water out of the cells of the vegetable and starts the pickling process. Then the bacteria kick in. Not everyone follows the recipes exactly, though I recommend that beginning fermenters do. If your ferments taste too salty to you when they're done, just rinse them with water before eating. The rule of thumb with fermenting: the more salt you use, the slower the fermentation process and the longer the food will stay in good quality; the less salt you use, the quicker the fermentation and the quicker the food will soften and become unpleasant.

Sweeteners

Sweeteners balance the harsh flavor of vinegar. White sugar is preferred by many because it doesn't darken the pickle (as brown sugar does) or make the brine cloudy (as honey does), but the choice is yours. Generally speaking, sweeteners aren't needed in fermented pickles because the lactic acid

produced in the fermentation process is pretty mellow. Adding a sweetener to a ferment may cause the bacteria to go into hyperdrive, and the results can be unpleasant. That said, I do add apples, with their natural fruit sugars, to some of my kale ferments to balance the bitterness and speed up the fermentation, and fruit, particularly Asian pear, is not uncommon in kimchi recipes.

Water

The ingredient we take most for granted is a crucial one. Use only nonchlorinated water in fermented pickles. Hard water can cause soft pickles. If you live in an area with hard water, use bottled water in all your pickles, both fermented and vinegar-brined.

Herbs and Spices

To avoid making the brine cloudy, use only whole herbs and spices when pickling. Dill is a commonly used herb. Sprigs of immature dill can be used interchangeably with mature dill heads. Use spices sparingly in long-fermented pickles so that the flavors don't overwhelm the ferment; in sauerkraut, a mere tablespoon of caraway seeds or juniper berries (classic flavorings) for a 5-pound batch is more than sufficient.

Crisping Agents

With vinegar pickles, a crisp pickle is ideal. Older recipes relied on alum (aluminum sulfate) to keep pickles crisp. It definitely worked because its astringent properties cause tissues to shrink. But alum can also irritate the eyes, the skin, and the respiratory tract and is corrosive upon ingestion. Ingestion of 1 ounce (30 grams) has killed adults. Recipes that call for alum require that it be used in a solution and washed off before the pickle is finished. The USDA recommends using food-grade lime instead. But lime has its hazards, too — it neutralizes or removes the acidity that you need to keep bacteria at bay — and you have to rinse the pickles in several changes of water to wash it off.

So it was with great relief that I adopted Pickle Crisp, pelletized calcium chloride from our friends at Ball. Pickle Crisp does what lime and alum used to do, but without the fuss. You just add a rounded 1/8 teaspoon of Pickle Crisp granules to a pint of pickles (a rounded 1/4 teaspoon to a quart) right before sealing the jar and processing in a boiling-water bath. If you make a batch of pickles where one jar has Pickle Crisp added and one does not, the difference in crispness is noticeable.

I especially recommend using it for all pickles made with cucumbers and zucchini, which tend to soften quite a bit, but you can use it for any vinegar-brined, fresh-pack pickle.

Equipment for Pickling

First, a caution: Do not use cookware made from brass, copper, galvanized metal, iron, or aluminum, which will react with the acids and salt and produce off flavors.

For salt-cured pickles, much depends on the size of your batch. For a large batch, you will need a large crock or bowl to get the ferment started. After that, I strongly urge you to work in small batches — and by small batches, I mean 1- or 2-quart canning jars. Let's say you want to turn 10 pounds of cabbage into sauerkraut. You mix it up, then you pack it into a large crock. Every time you open the crock to check on your ferment, you are exposing the sauerkraut to airborne yeasts and molds. Yes, you can spoon off the yeast and mold colonies. But why not pack the ferment into quart-size jars and delegate only one jar for opening to test the pickles' doneness? When one jar is ready, they all are. Put them in the fridge or some other cold place. Eat the first jar you sampled from. Finish it and go on to open the next jar. And so on. The quality of each jar will remain high. The largest batch I ever make is a 1-gallon jar of dill pickles. And as soon as we open the jar, I transfer the pickles to smaller jars. This greatly extends the life of the pickles, even half-sours.

Another problem with ceramic crocks, as I see it, is that over time they develop hairline cracks, not enough to leak but enough to allow spoilage organisms to enter. Another problem is that they are expensive.

You will need a kitchen scale for recipes, such as sauerkraut, that specify ingredients by weight. The weight measures are necessary to ensure correct proportions of salt to vegetable.

If you are going to process your vinegar-packed pickles for long-term storage, you will need a boiling-water-bath canner and the appropriate jars and lids (see chapter 11).

Vinegar Pickles

Vinegar pickles, fresh-pack pickles, quick-process pickles — there are many names for pickles that are packed in a sweet or sour mixture of vinegar and spices, then left to "pickle" without fermenting. These pickles may be kept in the refrigerator or processed in a boiling-water bath for long-term storage. Without the processing, you can expect these pickles to last for a couple of months in the refrigerator.

How to Make Vinegar Pickles

If you are going to process the pickles in a boiling-water bath, your process should begin with preparing the canner and canning jars according to the instructions on pages 175–76. If you don't plan to process the pickles, make room in the refrigerator. Pickles that are never exposed to heat will be crisper than pickles that you process.

① **Organize yourself.** Gather your equipment; then wash the vegetables, and chop or slice as required. With cucumbers and zucchini, don't forget to remove the blossom end. In general, thinly sliced pickle chips are crisper than thickly sliced ones.

② **Give the veggies a salt brine as needed.** Vegetables that are made up of a lot of water, especially cucumbers and zucchini, are often given a bath in a salt brine for 30 minutes to 6 hours to remove some of that water. Do not skip this step. The timing isn't that crucial, but don't skip this step if you want crisp pickles.

Add ice to the salt brine to keep the veggies crisp.

③ **Make the vinegar syrup.** Follow the instructions in your recipe to make the syrup. If the syrup tastes too sour, increase the sweetener. Heat to boiling.

④ **Pack the jars.** Pack the jars with the vegetables; then pour in the syrup to cover them, as specified in your recipe. If you are going to be processing the pickles, leave the proper amount of headspace, again as specified in the recipe (it's generally ½ inch). Add Pickle Crisp granules, if using, for a crisper pickle (highly recommended if you are going to

process the pickles in a boiling-water bath). Gently run a chopstick or knife around the edges of the jar to remove any air bubbles. Wipe the jar rims clean, and then place on the lids and add the screwbands.

Pack the jars as tightly as possible — without squishing the veggies.

⑤ **Process or store in the refrigerator.** If you're not canning, store the jars in the fridge. If you *are* canning, follow the instructions in chapter 11. Process the jars in a boiling-water bath for the length of time your recipe specifies, which is usually 10 minutes for sliced cucumber pickles in pint jars. Begin counting the time when the water returns to a boil. When the processing time is up, turn off the heat, remove the canner lid, and let the jars stand in the canner for 5 minutes. Then remove the jars and place on a folded towel or wooden rack. Allow to cool for 24 hours, then check the seals (see page 187). For best flavor, allow the pickles to mature for 4 to 6 weeks — in the refrigerator or in sealed jars — before opening.

Dill Chips

Makes 1 pint

This recipe makes a single jar. If you like these chips, then make them again, this time multiplying the amounts to make as big a batch as you like.

INGREDIENTS

2¼–2½ cups thinly sliced pickling cucumbers
  ½ small onion, thinly sliced
  1 tablespoon pickling, canning, or fine sea salt
  6 tablespoons distilled white vinegar
  6 tablespoons water
  1 teaspoon sugar
  1 teaspoon dill seeds
  1 tablespoon chopped fresh dill or 1 teaspoon dried
  3 garlic cloves
  ½ teaspoon mustard seeds
  ½ teaspoon black peppercorns
  Pickle Crisp (optional, but recommended)

1. Combine the cucumbers, onion, and salt in a large bowl. Mix well. Cover the vegetables with ice water and let stand for at least 2 hours and up to 6 hours. Drain.

2. Combine the vinegar, water, and sugar in a nonreactive saucepan and bring to a boil, stirring to dissolve the sugar.

3. Pack the dill seeds, fresh dill, garlic cloves, mustard seeds, and peppercorns into a clean, hot pint jar. Pack in the cucumbers, leaving ½ inch of headspace. Pour in the hot vinegar mixture, leaving ½ inch of headspace. Add a rounded ⅛ teaspoon of Pickle Crisp granules (if using). Remove any air bubbles and seal with the lid.

4. Process in a boiling-water bath for 10 minutes, according to the directions for canning on page 179. Let cool undisturbed for 12 hours. Store in a cool, dry place. To allow the flavors to develop, do not open for at least 6 weeks.

Making Salsas, Relishes, and Chutneys

The process of making salsas, relishes, and chutneys is similar to making vinegar pickles. The ingredients are usually cooked together, then either canned in a boiling-water bath or stored in the refrigerator. Again, the vinegar is the preserving agent, so don't reduce the amount called for in a recipe; if you think it tastes too vinegary, add sweetener (or sometimes salt) to balance the flavors.

Fermented Pickles

In contrast to vinegar pickles, fermented pickles don't rely as heavily on exact recipes. For the most part, ferments are simply a mix of vegetables and salt, and it is the action of the naturally occurring lactobacilli that produces the flavor. These naturally occurring bacteria generate lactic acid from sugars stored in the vegetables. In the process of digesting sugars in the vegetables, the bacilli give off carbon dioxide, and you can monitor the process by watching for the gas bubbles in the brine of your fermenting vegetables. The lactic acid that is produced gives the fermented pickles a distinct sharp flavor, mellower than acetic acid, which is in the acid in vinegar. Both the salt and the lactic acid are preservatives.

If all you did was combine 5 pounds of 20 different chopped or shredded vegetables with 3 tablespoons of salt in 20 different containers, you would end up with 20 different-tasting pickles. Add seasonings like the chili paste used in making kimchi, and then the flavors of the ferments really dance.

The Importance of Cleanliness

Bacteria and yeasts are everywhere, and some of these organisms have the potential to ruin a ferment. Obviously it is important to wash your vegetables. The bacteria that cause botulism are naturally found in the soil; they're not likely to survive the fermentation process, but washing makes sure of that. It should also be obvious that if your produce is damaged or moldy, it is already harboring microbes that could destroy your pickles, and you shouldn't use it.

It is also important to wash everything that comes in contact with your ingredients and equipment. You might want to sanitize your equipment. Some dishwashers

Fermenting Basics

There are three basic rules for fermenting vegetables:

1. Make sure all your ingredients, equipment, and containers are clean.
2. Make sure the fermenting vegetables stay submerged in the brine.
3. Minimize contact between the ferment and the air. Pack the ingredients in your ferment tightly to expel as much air as possible. Don't open your fermenting vessel any more than you have to.

have a sterilizing cycle, which makes sterilizing everything pretty easy. If you're using glass canning jars, you can sterilize them by boiling them for 10 minutes (see the box on page 176). Finally, you can use a wine- and beer-making sanitizing solution to sanitize your equipment (follow the manufacturer's directions for use). At the very least, all your equipment should be rinsed with boiling water before use. Be especially thorough when washing crocks and sanitize them inside and out, in case they have developed any cracks that can harbor yeast and bacteria.

Before I start a batch of fermented veggies, I always spray sanitizing solution on my counters, in the sink, just about everywhere. And I rinse my equipment with the solution (I don't have a dishwasher). If I open a jar to taste the ferment, I remove some with a clean utensil (never my

hands!), and I close up the jar as quickly as possible.

I haven't had a batch go skunky on me in a long time. Cleanliness will make a difference!

About the Brine

In some recipes, the brine is a combination of the salt you add to the vegetables and the water that the salt draws from the cell walls. Typically, fresh vegetables are chopped or grated in preparation for fermentation; this creates a lot of surface area for the salt to act upon. The veggies are then salted and left to stand for a while. Through the process of osmosis, the salt pulls water out of the cell walls. Pounding or tamping down on the vegetables breaks down cell walls to allow even more liquid to escape from the cells.

You'll then transfer the grated or chopped veggies and any brine they've released to your fermentation vessel.

Some people use a crock, but I prefer jars. In this case it is okay to get rough with your vegetables — in fact, it is desirable. Use muscle to pack the vegetables tightly in the jars. I use a 1-inch wooden dowel for tamping down the mixture as I pack. You can improvise with a potato masher or your fist. Whatever you use, keep packing and pressing as you go. The vegetables should exude enough liquid to be covered by brine. If the packed vegetables are not well covered in brine, you will need to make up additional brine (by mixing salt into fresh water) and add it to the jar. Freshly harvested cabbage will definitely have enough water, so extra brine isn't needed; but a cabbage that has been stored for several months in a cooler or root cellar may need the extra brine.

In recipes when you are fermenting firm vegetables that you leave whole or in pieces — like cucumbers, green beans, green tomatoes — you'll need to make up a brine of water and salt.

Old-style recipes used a 10 percent salt solution, meaning that 10 percent of the weight of the solution was comprised of salt. With this concentration of salt, spoilage microbes are unlikely to survive. On the other hand, a pickle fermented in such a strong brine must be freshened (rinsed) in several changes of water before it is even edible. Brining in a 10 percent solution is a survival method. With refrigeration available, a weaker brine can be used.

The USDA's standard is 3 tablespoons of canning, pickling, or fine sea salt per 5 pounds of vegetables. More

salt will slow the fermentation process; less will speed it up. The more salt, the longer the pickle will keep without getting too soft or too sour. If you use less salt, your pickles will be vulnerable to spoilage, but there are plenty of picklers who just salt by taste.

Keep the Vegetables Submerged and Air Excluded

The whole purpose of keeping vegetables submerged in brine is to exclude air, which may contain yeasts, bacteria, or mold that will contaminate and ruin your ferment. In recent years, a number of different gadgets have come onto the market, some expensive and some not, that keep air excluded quite handily. But before taking out your wallet, consider my method, developed before all these gadgets became easily available.

I work in small batches and ferment everything in 1- or 2-quart glass canning jars. I fill the jars with the vegetables and brine to the very top, then place the metal lids and screwbands (barely tightened, so gases can escape) on the jars. I set the jars on saucers to catch overflowing brine. And they do overflow once the fermentation starts. But with the lid in place, air cannot flow back in. I top off with additional brine as

Brine Strength

Brine strength is the percentage of salt by weight in a given volume of water.

Water	Salt (Pickling, Canning, or Fine Sea Salt)	Brine Concentration
4 cups	1½ tablespoons	2.7%
4 cups	2 tablespoons	3.5%
4 cups	3 tablespoons	5.4%
4 cups	4 tablespoons	6.9%

Here are three low-cost methods to exclude air: buy a special canning jar lid with airlock, fill a plastic bag with brine (in case it develops a leak) and stuff it in the jar, or fill the jar to the brim and let the brine overflow when fermenting starts.

needed. Since I switched from crock fermenting to jar fermenting, I haven't had any batches of pickles go bad. (I have had one jar explode because the screwband was overly tight. No one has claimed responsibility . . .) I often switch from a dome lid and metal screwband to a white plastic storage lid when putting the jar in the refrigerator, but I prefer to control the amount of brine that can escape with the metal lids.

On occasion, fermenting vegetables may rise up out of their brine. With my simple method, which excludes any air from coming in contact with the vegetables, this is not a problem until you open the jar. At that point you can either eat the exposed vegetables or cover them with brine. Until it is exposed to fresh air, the vegetables in an air-excluded ferment can go dry.

You can also buy plastic canning lids that have an airlock fitted in. These airlocks allow the release of gases without the release of any brine, so the vegetables stay submerged. They come in various styles — some fitted into plastic lids, some fitted into cork lids, some fitted into the standard metal lids with screwbands. And some are sold to fit only the glass jars that come with them. These run around $20 a unit.

If you are fermenting in a crock, or in any other container without an air-excluding lid, you will need to keep the vegetables held under 1 to 2 inches of brine. There are various ways to accomplish this. You can fill it about two-thirds full with the vegetables, then add a generous amount of brine, until the crock is filled to within a couple of inches of the top.

Set a plate on top of the vegetables and weight it down to hold them under the brine; then cover the crock with plastic wrap, or with a lid and an airlock that lets gases escape. (Many places also offer little glass weights that will fit into a mason jar to keep the vegetables submerged.) Alternatively, you can place a food-safe ziplock bag on top of the ferment, then fill it with brine until it completely covers the surface of the ferment, weighting down the vegetables and excluding air.

Check Daily and Taste Frequently

Fermenting vegetables will taste salty at first. As the vegetables ferment, the flavor goes from sharply salty to mildly sour. When the vegetables are more sour than salty, the fermentation has pickled the vegetables. You can slow down further fermentation by refrigerating the pickles, or you can let the fermentation continue. Eventually all the sugars in the vegetables will have been digested, and then fermentation is complete. Over time, the pickles will soften. Fermentation is a natural process; it progresses faster in warmer temperatures and faster with vegetables that contain more sugar. A low-salt, half-sour cucumber pickle will be ready to eat in about 5 days; sauerkraut takes 2 to 4 weeks.

Here are two more reasons to ferment in canning jars: you can do a visual check of the ferment without opening the jars, and you can taste a batch by opening only one jar and not exposing the rest to airborne contaminants. When you do your daily checks, what are you checking for? You want to see bubbles of carbon dioxide rising through the brine (beginning 12 to 36 hours after you start your ferment). Check for a bulging lid; if there is no give to the lid, loosen the screwband. What you don't want to see is any brownish scum (yeast colony) or fuzzy mold growing on top of the brine or clinging to the wall of the crock; if you do, remove it.

Temperature Is Key

Fermentation proceeds at an ideal pace between 65°F and 75°F (18°C and 24°C). In cooler temperatures, fermentation is slow, giving spoilage bacteria a chance to take hold. Overly fast fermentation is equally undesirable and may produce soft, slimy pickles. If you can't produce the ideal temperature, be aware that your ferment may be ready sooner or later than a recipe suggests. In the winter, I generally ferment on my kitchen counter. In the summer, I put my ferments in the cooler basement.

STEP-BY-STEP **How to Make Fermented Krauts and Kimchis**

Here's a step-by-step guide to making ferments with vegetables that will make their own brine. These include cabbages and other hearty greens, broccoli, and most root vegetables. I use the standard ratio of 3 tablespoons salt to 5 pounds vegetables. These pickles are plenty salty; you can use less salt, but spoilage is more likely.

For tips on making kimchi in particular, see page 216.

① **Wash, clean, sanitize.** Start by washing all bowls, crocks, canning jars, knives, and utensils. Wash down all the counters and anything that will come in contact with the ferment. If you have a dishwasher with a sterilizing cycle, use it. If you use a crock, rinse it with water that has just boiled. I also spray everything with a no-rinse sanitizing solution used in winemaking and beer brewing.

② **Wash the vegetables.** Wash the vegetables carefully. Scrub gently with a vegetable brush under running water or in several changes of water. Lift the vegetables out of the water; don't let the dirty water run out of the sink and redeposit dirt on the produce. Drain the produce in a colander.

③ **Weigh the produce and do the math.** The weight of the produce will determine how much salt and seasoning (such as chili paste or ground chiles for kimchi) to use. In general, you'll need 3 tablespoons of pickling salt, canning salt, or fine sea salt for every 5 pounds of vegetables. Measure out the salt and seasonings, and have them at the ready.

④ **Prepare the vegetables.** Most recipes call for slicing or shredding the vegetables. Thin, uniform slices and shreds are ideal for sauerkraut. Kimchi typically is cut into 1-inch slices. Beets are sometimes fermented to make kvass, a fermented liquid. Because beets are so rich in sugar, they should be sliced and not shredded to prevent an overly rapid fermentation. As you slice or grate, transfer the veggies into a large bowl and sprinkle with the measured salt and seasonings (if using). Work the salt and seasonings into the veggies, mixing and pounding with a potato masher or your hands to break down the cell walls.

Handle roughly.

⑤ **Pack the jars or crock.** Layer the vegetables and spices in the jar or crock according to the recipe. Tamp down on the vegetables until they release enough liquid to cover themselves by an inch or two. If they don't release enough liquid, add brine (1 cup water plus 1¼ teaspoons salt). If you are using a crock, leave at least 4 inches of space at the top. If you are using a canning jar, leave about 1 inch of space at the top for the addition of more

Pack tightly.

brine or the release of brine from the veggies themselves.

⑥ **Cover.** If you are using a crock, cover the vegetables with a plate. Weight the plate to hold the vegetables under the brine; a clean rock or a clean glass jar filled with water works well as a weight. Then cover the crock with food wrap or its cover. Alternatively, set a food-grade ziplock bag on the ferment and fill it with brine, with the goal of weighting the vegetables so that they remain submerged.

If you are using a canning jar, fill with brine to the top and cover with the lid, then loosely affix the screwband. Set aside any extra brine; you may need it to top off the jar.

If you have an airlock, insert it into the cover or lid and use as the manufacturer instructs.

⑦ **Allow the pickles to cure.** Set jars on a rimmed baking sheet or saucer to catch the brine that will overflow once fermenting starts. Move the crock or jars to a spot where the temperature will remain between 65°F and 75°F (18°C and 24°C) if you can. Fermentation should begin within a day or two, depending on the temperature. If you gently tap on the crock or jar, you should see gas bubbles rising. Check daily and remove any mold or foam that collects on the top. Loosen the screwband on the canning jar as needed.

⑧ **Taste-test.** Begin tasting after 7 days. Once the pickle is cured to your satisfaction, refrigerate to halt fermentation.

Fermentation is complete when gas bubbles stop rising to the top of the crock or jar. This will happen sometime between the second and fourth weeks. It is perfectly fine to halt — or slow down — the fermentation before the pickle is fully soured.

STEP-BY-STEP **How to Ferment Cucumbers, Green Tomatoes, and Snap Beans**

Here's a step-by-step guide to making ferments with vegetables that will ferment in a brine you make up.

① **Wash, clean, sanitize.** Start by washing all bowls, crocks, canning jars, knives, and utensils. Wash down all the counters and anything that will come in contact with the ferment. If you have a dishwasher with a sterilizing cycle, use it. If you use a crock, rinse it with boiling water. I also spray everything with a no-rinse sanitizing solution used in winemaking and beer brewing.

② **Prepare the vegetables.** Wash the vegetables carefully. Scrub gently with a vegetable brush under running water or in several changes of water. Lift the vegetables out of the water; don't let the dirty water run out of the sink and redeposit dirt on the produce. Drain the produce in a colander. Be sure to slice off the blossom end of cucumbers and summer squash, which contain enzymes that can soften the pickles. Top and tail snap beans.

③ **Make the brine.** The volume of your crock or jars will determine how much brine to make. I don't know of any formula to use for this. Generally, you will need about 4 cups of brine for every 2-quart canning jar, or 8 cups for every gallon your crock will hold. Make more than you think you will need.

To make the brine, combine water and salt in the proportions you need (see the chart on page 210) in a large pot over medium heat. Stir as the water heats; as soon as the salt is completely dissolved, remove from the heat. Cool the brine to room temperature.

④ **Pack the crock or jars.** Add the seasonings (dill, garlic, etc.) to your crock or jar. Fill with the vegetables, packing firmly but not squishing the veggies. Fill a crock about two-thirds full. If you are using a canning jar, leave about 1 inch of space at the top; often you can layer the vegetables horizontally so that the shoulder of the jar keeps the veggies from floating. Fill with the cooled brine, leaving 2 to 3 inches of space above the brine in a crock, or filling to the very top with a canning jar.

⑤ **Cover.** If you are using a crock, cover the vegetables with a plate. Weight the plate to hold the vegetables under the brine; a clean rock or a clean glass jar filled with water works well as a weight. Then cover the crock with food wrap or the lid. Alternatively, set a food-grade ziplock bag on the ferment and fill it with brine, with the goal of weighting the vegetables so that they remain submerged.

If you are using a jar, fill with brine to the top and cover with the lid, then loosely affix the screwband. Set aside any extra brine; you may need it to top off the jar.

If you have an airlock, insert it into the cover or lid and use as the manufacturer instructs.

6. **Allow the pickles to cure.** Set jars on a rimmed baking sheet or saucer to catch the brine that will overflow once fermenting starts. Move the crock or jar to a spot where the temperature will remain between 65°F and 75°F (18°C and 24°C) if you can. Fermentation should begin within a day or two, depending on the temperature. If you gently tap on the crock or jar, you should see gas bubbles rising. Check daily and remove any mold or foam that collects on the top. Loosen the screwband on the canning jar as needed.

7. **Taste-test.** Begin tasting after 3 days with a 2.7 percent brine; wait longer with stronger brines. Once the pickle is cured to your satisfaction, refrigerate to halt — or slow — fermentation.

   Fermentation is complete when gas bubbles stop rising to the top of the crock. This will happen sometime between the second and fourth weeks. It is perfectly fine to halt the fermentation before the pickle is fully soured.

Kale, Carrot, and Apple Ferment

Makes 1 quart

Plain fermented kale makes an interesting seasoning for Chinese stir-fries, but it isn't something I enjoy eating by the forkful (though my son does). This ferment, however, is balanced by the sweetness of carrot and apple, which completely transforms the kale into a lively and delicious ferment. Once you get into fermenting vegetables, you'll find it fun to experiment with different combinations; if you can envision it in a salad, it will probably make a tasty ferment. Pack the ferment in a sterilized or sanitized 1-quart canning jar.

INGREDIENTS

6 cups packed kale, stemmed and cut into thin ribbons

2 carrots, grated

1 apple, cored and grated

4 teaspoons pickling salt, canning salt, or fine sea salt

2 cups water

1. Combine the kale, carrots, apple, and 2 teaspoons of the salt in a large bowl. Toss to mix and set aside for at least 1 hour, up to 6 hours.

2. Meanwhile, gently heat the water with the remaining 2 teaspoons salt until the salt completely dissolves. Set aside to cool to room temperature.

3. Using a potato masher or your fist, pound and press the vegetables until they release their liquid and are quite wet.

4. Firmly pack the vegetables into a sterilized or sanitized 1-quart canning jar, pressing down on the layers as you pack — it should all fit. Add as much of the cooled salt brine as needed to fill the jar to the very top. Place the lid on the jar and just barely tighten the screwband.

5. Place the jar on a saucer and set aside to ferment in a dark spot at room temperature (65°–75°F/18°–24°C) for about 2 weeks. Taste. If pleasantly sour and fermented, keep refrigerated or enjoy.

Salt-Cured Dilly Beans

Makes 1 quart

After tasting these beans, you may never eat a fresh bean again.

INGREDIENTS

- 2¾ cups water
- 1 tablespoon pickling salt, canning salt, or fine sea salt
- 2 tablespoons distilled white vinegar
- 1 dill head or 6 sprigs fresh dill
- 3 garlic cloves
- About 4 cups trimmed (topped and tailed) green beans

1. Heat the water and salt until the salt is fully dissolved. Stir in the white vinegar and let cool to room temperature.

2. Pack the dill and garlic into a clean 1-quart canning jar or crock. Tightly pack with the green beans. Pour the cooled brine over the green beans. The brine should completely cover the beans and fill the jar to the very brim; you will probably have more than you need, but it is important to have the beans completely covered and air excluded from the jar. Set aside any extra brine in a covered jar.

3. Place the jar on a saucer to catch the overflow that will start when fermentation begins. Set the jar where the temperature will remain constant: 65°F to 75°F (18°C to 24°C) is ideal. Let the beans ferment for about a week. Check frequently and top off with more brine as needed. When the beans taste pleasantly pickled, store in the refrigerator. The pickles will keep for at least 3 months in the refrigerator.

Making Kimchi

Kimchi is the highly spiced Korean ferment. There are about 160 basic recipes for kimchi, and then there are many, many more regional variations and traditional family recipes. There are also seasonal variations in kimchi, reflecting available ingredients and ambient temperatures. Summer kimchis are lighter and more quickly made; winter kimchis are slow-fermenting, made to last through the winter. But, like many other ethnic foods that have become popular in the United States, kimchi is in the process of becoming Americanized by people like myself.

Like every other topic in this book, kimchi is a rich topic that could be expanded into a whole book. We'll stick to the basics here, beginning with the following tips:

› Use a Korean chili paste (*gochujang*) or ground dried peppers (*gochugaru*). The Korean chile is bright red, fruity, and medium hot. Substitute another Asian chili paste only if you have to.

› Many recipes call for a rice-flour paste made with 1 cup water to 2 tablespoons sweet rice flour. The rice-flour paste helps the seasoning cling to the vegetables and keeps the ground chiles in suspension, and the starch acts as fuel for the fermentation bacteria. Some Korean chili pastes already contain the rice flour.

› Because of the fuel added by the rice flour, fermentation tends to begin early and continue rapidly. If you are fermenting in a canning jar, keep a careful eye on the lid; if it starts to bulge, loosen the screwband. Begin tasting after 3 days of fermenting.

› Salted dried shrimp, shrimp paste, anchovy paste, and Asian fish sauce all add a distinctive umami quality to a kimchi. The word *umami* translates from the Japanese as "delicious essence" — you know it when you taste it.

› Kimchi, like all other ferments, changes over time. Even after it becomes too sour to eat plain, it makes a delicious addition to soups, stews, and stir-fries.

Mild Kimchi

Makes 1 quart

If you like your kimchi hot, increase the amount of chili paste. Korean chili paste is worth seeking out in Asian food stores or on the Internet, but other Asian chili pastes can be used instead — my son sometimes use sriracha sauce.

INGREDIENTS

8 cups chopped Napa cabbage or green cabbage (20 ounces), cut into 2-inch pieces

2 carrots, sliced

1 (6-inch) piece daikon radish, sliced

4 garlic cloves, minced

2 tablespoons Korean chili paste (*gochujang*)

1 teaspoon minced fresh ginger

2¼ teaspoons pickling salt, canning salt, or fine sea salt

BRINE (OPTIONAL)

1 cup water

1¼ teaspoons pickling salt, canning salt, or fine sea salt

1. Combine all the ingredients in a large bowl. Mix with your hands to evenly distribute the seasonings, rubbing them into the vegetables. Let stand for at least 2 hours, and up to 6 hours, until the vegetables release plenty of liquid.

2. Pack the mixture into a clean 1-quart canning jar. Add enough of the liquid the vegetables released into the bowl to cover the mixture and fill the jar to the top. If the liquid released by the vegetables doesn't cover the vegetables, make the brine: combine the water and salt in a saucepan and heat just enough to dissolve the salt. Let cool to room temperature, then pour enough brine into the jar to top it off. Cover the jar to exclude air, but do not tighten the screwband.

3. Set the jar on a saucer where the temperature will remain constant: 65°F to 75°F (18°C to 24°C) is ideal. Watch for fermentation to begin. Brine will be forced out of the jar, and you will see small bubbles, like carbonation, rising in the jar.

4. Begin tasting after 3 days and refrigerate after 3 to 5 days. The kimchi continues to age and develop flavor. Store in the refrigerator. It will keep for several months.

CHAPTER 14

Making Fruit Preserves

Making fruit preserves is the best way I know to pack the flavors of summer into a jar. With the term *fruit preserves*, I am including all manner of spreadable fruit: jams, jellies, preserves (fruits in a gelled syrup), conserves, marmalades, and butters. The process of making all these types of spreads is pretty much the same.

To turn fresh, juicy fruit into something spreadable on toast, you must cook the fruit. The old-fashioned way is to cook the fruit slowly, slowly, slowly, until most of the liquid is either evaporated out or combined into a gel in the presence of pectin, a naturally occurring substance that is found in many fruits, especially apples. High-pectin fruits, such as blackberries, don't take much time by this method; others, like strawberries, are low in pectin and very slow to gel. But the result is a jam that tastes intensely of fruit, with sugar (or honey) added to taste.

A less labor-intensive method of making jams and jellies is to use commercial pectin. This requires you to measure accurately and time carefully. In the end, you will have a jam or jelly with great consistency, but it may (or may not) have required more sugar than you might have wanted to use. Low-sugar pectins are just as easy to use as the traditional pectins, which require almost equal measures of fruit and sugar. If you follow the directions on the container or package of pectin faithfully, it is a pretty foolproof method.

Sugar, combined with the naturally occurring acid in fruit (sometimes with a boost from lemon juice), is the preservative in jams and jellies. Theoretically, you can store the jams and jellies in the fridge, but the less sugar you use, the more quickly they will spoil from mold. A better way to add shelf life to preserves is to process them in a boiling-water bath (see chapter 11). Alternatively, you can make jams and jellies using pectin specially formulated for freezing. There isn't much cooking involved, so the preserves taste closer to the fresh fruit.

If the idea of making preserves in the heat of the summer lacks appeal, no problem. Just freeze the fruit without any sweetener (see chapter 10) and make the preserves in cooler weather.

Ingredients for Preserves

The three ingredients common to all preserves are fruit, pectin (whether natural or commercial), and sweetener. If you use commercial pectin and many low-acid fruits, you'll also need acid to activate the pectin. Recipes often call for lemon juice.

Fruit

Fruit is the primary ingredient. It doesn't have to be picture perfect, but it must be free from mold or any spoilage. In the case of delicate fruits like strawberries and raspberries, it is necessary to make preserves almost as soon as the fruits are picked. Wash the fruit and cut it up as specified in the recipe. You can use frozen or canned fruit, so if you can't make the preserves in a timely fashion, freeze the fruit for making preserves later.

Pectin

Pectin occurs naturally in fruit; it contributes to the structure of the cell walls. As the fruit ripens, the pectin degrades, which is why under-ripe (hard) fruits have more pectin than overripe (soft) ones. Commercial pectin, which is sold in powdered or liquid form, is extracted from citrus peels and seeds or apples. It first hit the market in the 1920s and 1930s; before that, people added pectin-rich fruits to jams when they wanted a firm set.

Most apples, Concord-type grapes, blackberries, cranberries, and cherries have enough pectin that added pectin isn't necessary to make preserves with them. Other fruits are more easily made into preserves with the addition of pectin. When using commercial pectin, it is important that you follow the recipes from the manufacturer; different commercial brands of pectin are not interchangeable.

The first commercial pectins to hit the market — Sure-Jel and Certo — were formulated to be activated by white sugar and acid. They required almost as much sugar by volume as fruit. Today there are many different brands of pectin formulated to work with no-sugar or low-sugar combinations. Some of the low-sugar formulas will work with alternative sweeteners, such as honey, and some will not, so read the packages carefully. The no-sugar formulas will work with any sweetener, as well as with sugar to taste. (Adding even a small amount of sugar brings out the fruit flavors and firms the texture, so I recommended adding at least some sugar.) For more about pectin, see page 227.

Sweeteners

White sugar is used to sweeten most preserves. Sometimes honey and maple syrup (and other sweeteners such as agave nectar) can be used instead. If you are using a commercial pectin, make sure it works with the sweetener you plan to use (it should say so on the label). Alternative sweeteners will, however, alter the flavor of the preserves and mask some of the fruit flavor.

If you are making a jam or jelly without added pectin, you can sweeten to taste, and that includes using less sugar than a recipe might call for. You will need to include at least some sugar, though, to form a solid gel. Also, sugar is a preservative. One thing to consider: if your main use of fruit preserves is on toast, consider that the sweetness of the jam is the balance for the salty/savory flavor of the bread. Some of my very-low-sugar (albeit healthy) jams have been less than popular with the toast-makers. And when an opened jar of low-sugar jam lingers in the refrigerator, it becomes moldy.

Acid

To activate the pectin and contribute flavor, acid is usually required. It also seems to brighten the color of the preserves. Most recipes call for a small amount of lemon juice; do not omit. Do yourself a favor and buy a bottle of lemon juice to have on hand during the summer/fall preserving season. This is one place where the less-than-fresh flavor of bottled lemon juice does not matter.

Definitions

High: If not overripe, these fruits have enough natural pectin and acid to gel with only added sugar.

Medium: These fruits are low in acid or pectin and may need the addition of either acid or pectin in order to gel.

Low: Always needs added acid or pectin, or both, in order to gel.

Fruit	High	Medium	Low
Apples, green (unripe)	X		
Apples, ripe		X	
Apricots			X
Blackberries, ripe		X	
Blackberries, sour	X		
Blueberries			X
Cherries, sour		X	
Cherries, sweet			X
Crabapples	X		
Cranberries	X		
Currants	X		
Elderberries		X	
Gooseberries	X		
Grapefruit		X	
Grapes, California		X	
Grapes, Concord	X		
Guavas			X
Loganberries	X		
Nectarines			X
Oranges		X	
Peaches			X
Pears			X
Plums, Italian			X
Plums, Japanese	X		
Quince	X		
Raspberries			X
Strawberries			X

Equipment for Making Preserves

You probably already have the equipment you need to make jam. Jelly requires some special equipment, to extract the juice.

Tall heavy saucepan. A heavy-duty 2-gallon stockpot is ideal here because fruit preserves must boil vigorously — without boiling over. A heavy pan will prevent scorching, which is a risk with fruit. Unless made of copper, your grandmother's cookware may have been made with aluminum or another metal that will react with the acids in fruit.

Make sure your pot is stainless steel and heavy.

Thermometer. Although there are tests for judging when the gel point is reached (see the following discussion), a thermometer takes away the guesswork. Here's another place where I prefer the type of thermometer with a long probe. Alternatively, a candy and deep-fry thermometer that has a large dial and clips onto the side of the pot works. What doesn't work is the type of candy thermometer or digital thermometer with a standard 6-inch probe that will steam up as you hold it in the boiling jam or jelly mixture. I'd also avoid the old-fashioned glass tubes with liquid inside; those really steam up and become hard to read.

Steam juicer or jelly bag. Both are used to extract fruit juices to make jelly or just for drinking. The steam juicer is a three-pot unit with a steam compartment, a juice compartment with a rubber tube that channels away the juice (it should come with a clamp), and a colander to hold the fruit. Steam juicers are easy to use, but they take up a lot of storage space. Alternatively, a jelly bag is simply a muslin bag on a stand. You can buy one or make your own. It is perfectly fine to use the same butter muslin you use for cheesemaking and hang it from a cupboard or sink faucet to drain.

Boiling-water-bath canner. Used to process preserves for long-term storage (see chapter 11).

Half-pint canning jars and lids. It is best to can in small jars that can be used up quickly.

Testing for Doneness without a Thermometer

Every homestead kitchen should have a thermometer, for judging doneness of meat, for making maple syrup and cheese, and for testing fruit preserves, among other things. The temperature at which fruit syrups gel is 220°F (104.5°C),

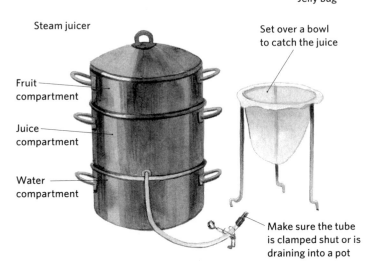

Steam juicer

Fruit compartment

Juice compartment

Water compartment

Jelly bag

Set over a bowl to catch the juice

Make sure the tube is clamped shut or is draining into a pot

The steam juicer works to cook the fruit and separate the fruit from the juice. With a jelly bag, you must cook the fruit on the stove, then pour it into the jelly bag to drain.

or 8°F (4.5°C) above the boiling temperature of water. But thermometers break, malfunction, have dead batteries, and get lost. When that happens, you can test for doneness the old-fashioned way, using the "sheet test" or the "cold plate test."

The Sheet Test

Dip a metal spoon into the boiling fruit mixture and lift the spoon out of the steam so that the mixture runs off the side. When the mixture first starts to boil, the drops will be light and syrupy. As the mixture continues to boil, the drops become heavier and will drop off the spoon two at a time. When the two drops form together and "sheet" off the spoon, the gel point has been reached.

When a single sheet of gelled fruit falls off the spoon, the jam or jelly is done.

The Cold Plate Test

Place a small plate in the freezer to chill. Drop a small amount of the fruit mixture onto the chilled plate and return the plate to the freezer for a few minutes. If the mixture gels when you push it with a finger, it should be

When your finger leaves a distinct trail through the jam or jelly spooned onto a chilled plate, it is done.

done. While you're waiting to see the results of this test, remove the rest of the mixture from the heat to prevent overcooking; you can always put it back on the burner if the gel isn't yet firm enough.

Making Jams, Jellies, and Other Preserves

The big questions when starting out to make any fruit preserve are whether or not to add pectin to help the gelling process, whether or not to add a sweetener (and how much), and whether to add any flavoring.

If you don't have enough of one type of fruit to go to the bother of making a preserve, but the fruit will go by, either freeze the fruit for making preserves later or consider combining it with other fruits. You can't go wrong combining berries or combining stone fruits (cherries, peaches, plums, nectarines).

Some cooks really thrive on making fruit preserves with unusual flavors. You can find recipes for strawberry basil jam, blueberry balsamic jam, or peach lavender jam. Purée fresh herbs with some of the fruit, or make an infusion and add to the fruit. Don't forget that the flavors will intensify, so use a very light hand. I don't go that route myself. I want jams to put in peanut butter sandwiches (for kids young and old) and to have with tea and toast on those busy mornings when finding time for even a few bites is a challenge. To me, those fancy flavors are for tea parties and leisurely Sunday brunches — and I just don't have the time.

The yields for jams and jellies vary tremendously depending on how much sugar you are adding and whether you are cooking it down or adding pectin to gel it.

How to Make Jams, Preserves, and Conserves without Added Pectin

This method works for all preserves except jelly. If you want to make a fruit preserve with commercial pectin, follow the manufacturer's directions.

① **Prepare the equipment.** If you plan to process the jars of preserves in a boiling-water bath for long-term storage, prepare the canner, canning jars, and lids according to the instructions on pages 175–76. Jars should be sterilized if the processing time is less than 10 minutes, which is the case with most fruit preserves (see the box on page 176 for instructions).

② **Prepare the fruit.** Wash the fruit and prepare according to the recipe directions by peeling, pitting, chopping, slicing — to get rid of unwanted skins and pits and to hasten the cooking process. The pieces that go into the pot don't have to be tiny; you can do some crushing once the fruit has begun to cook down.

③ **Cook.** Combine the fruit, sugar, lemon juice, and any other ingredients called for in the recipe in a large heavy saucepan. Cook over low heat until the sugar dissolves; then bring to a boil. Boil, stirring frequently, until the mixture begins to thicken. Adjust the heat as needed to avoid scorching, and stir more frequently. Continue to boil until the mixture reaches 220°F (104.5°C), or 8°F (4.5°C) above boiling on a thermometer (or use one of the tests on page 222).

④ **Pack into jars.** Remove from the heat and skim off any foam that has formed on top. Pour into jars, leaving the amount of headspace specified in the recipe, usually ¼ inch for half-pint jars. Wipe the rims clean, set the lids on the jars, and then lightly tighten the screwbands to close the jars.

⑤ **Refrigerate or process for long-term storage (optional).** If you're not going to process your preserves for long-term storage, refrigerate the jars of preserves.

If you are going to process the preserves, follow the instructions in chapter 11. Process in a boiling-water bath for the length of time the recipe specifies, usually 5 minutes for a half-pint jar. Begin counting the time when the water returns to a boil.

When the processing time is up, turn off the heat, remove the canner lid, and let the jars stand in the canner for 5 minutes. Then remove the jars and place on a folded towel or wooden rack. Allow to cool for 24 hours, then check the seals (see page 187).

Peach Jam

Makes about 10 half-pints

Please note that this recipe will not work if you substitute another type of pectin, or if you add the pectin at the wrong time. Do not multiply this recipe; make a second batch if you want to make more.

INGREDIENTS

- 5 pounds very ripe peaches
- ¼ cup lemon juice
- 2 tablespoons Ball's RealFruit Low or No-Sugar Needed Pectin
- 2½ cups sugar

1. Prepare the boiling-water-bath canner, half-pint jars, and lids according to instructions on pages 175–76. You will need to sterilize the jars (see the box on page 176).

2. Bring a large saucepan of water to a boil. Fill a large bowl with ice water.

3. To peel the peaches, work in batches of 3 or 4 peaches at a time. Lower the peaches into the boiling water for 30 to 60 seconds. Using a slotted spoon, transfer peaches from the boiling water to the bowl of ice water. When the peaches are cool enough to handle, use a knife or your fingers to peel the skin from each peach. Working over a bowl to catch all the juices and using a sharp knife, cut each peeled peach in half around the pit. Gently twist each half to expose the pit. Using the knife, or your fingers, pry the pit out of the peach. When all the peaches are peeled and pitted, chop into small pieces, again trying to save all the juices.

4. Combine the peaches with their juice and the lemon juice in a large saucepan. Gradually stir in the pectin. Bring the mixture to a full rolling boil that cannot be stirred down, over high heat, stirring constantly.

5. Add the sugar. Return the jam to a full rolling boil. Boil hard for 1 minute, stirring constantly. Remove from the heat. Skim off any foam, if necessary.

6. Pack into the prepared canning jars, leaving ¼ inch of headspace. Wipe the rims clean, set the lids on the jars, and then lightly tighten the screwbands to close the jars.

7. Process in a boiling-water bath for 5 minutes. Turn off the heat, remove the canner lid, and let the jars stand in the canner for 5 minutes.

8. Remove the jars and place on a folded towel or wooden rack. Allow to cool for 24 hours, then check the seals (see page 187).

How to Make Jelly

Use at least one part underripe fruit to three parts just-ripe fruit to ensure sufficient naturally occurring pectin to gel. If you want to make a jelly with commercial pectin, follow the manufacturer's directions.

① **Extract the juice.** Wash the fruit. Chop as needed, but do not peel. If you like, add an apple or two for its pectin.

If you have a steam juicer, fill the bottom part of the steam pan with water to about 1 inch from the top. Place the collection pan on top of the water pan. Then place the fruit colander filled with fruit on top of the collection pan. Cover the pan and place over high heat. Make sure the rubber drain tube is unclamped and securely placed inside a collection jar. It will take about 1 to 1½ hours to steam all of the juice out of most fruit if you are working with a full batch.

If you don't have a steam juicer, put the fruit in a heavy saucepan. Add just enough water to prevent scorching. Crush soft fruits to get the juices flowing. Cook for about 30 minutes, until the fruit is completely tender. Pour the fruit mixture into a damp jelly bag or colander lined with a double thickness of cheesecloth set over a bowl, and allow the fruit juice to collect overnight. If you want a clear jelly, do not squeeze the fruit.

② **Prepare the equipment.** If you plan to process jars of jelly in a boiling-water bath for long-term storage, prepare the canner, canning jars, and lids according to the instructions on pages 175–76. The jars should be sterilized (see the box on page 176).

③ **Cook.** Working with up to 4 cups of juice at a time, add ¾ cup sugar for each cup of juice and combine in a tall saucepan. Add lemon juice as specified in the recipe. Cook over low heat until the sugar is dissolved; then bring to a boil. Boil, stirring frequently, until the mixture reaches 220°F (104.5°C), or 8°F (4.5°C) above boiling on a thermometer (or use one of the tests on page 222). Remove from the heat and skim off any foam that has formed on top.

The advantage of the steam juicer is that steam provides a gentle heat to cook the fruit and extract the juice. When cooking on top of the stove, there is the risk of scorching the fruit before the juice is ready to be drained. When cooking the fruit juice, stir frequently to avoid having the juice boil over and to avoid scorching.

Steam juicer

Jelly bag

Skim off foam

④ **Pack in jars.** Pour into jars, leaving the amount of headspace specified in the recipe, usually ¼ inch for half-pint jars. Wipe the rims clean, set the lids on the jars, and then lightly tighten the screwbands to close the jars.

⑤ **Refrigerate or process for long-term storage.** If you're not going to process your jelly for long-term storage, refrigerate the jars.

If you are going to process the jelly, follow the instructions in chapter 11. Process half-pint jars for 5 minutes in a boiling-water bath, counting the time when the water returns to a boil.

When the processing time is up, turn off the heat, remove the canner lid, and let the jars stand in the canner for 5 minutes. Then remove the jars and place on a folded towel or wooden rack. Allow to cool for 24 hours; then check the seals (see page 187).

STEP-BY-STEP How to Make Fruit Butters

A fruit butter is basically a fruit purée cooked down to a spreadable consistency. No pectin is added. You can cook fruits with the skins and pits, and then strain the mixture though a food mill, or you can peel and core first and skip the purée step. You can cook down the fruit on top of the stove (warning: high scorch factor!), in the oven (reduced scorch factor, but don't forget about it), or in a slow cooker (make sure you are providing low heat).

① **Prepare the fruit.** Prepare the fruit according to the recipe. Generally you can simply halve or quarter the fruit; peeling and coring are optional.

② **Begin cooking.** Put the fruit in a heavy saucepan. Add just enough water or complementary fruit juice to prevent scorching. Cook until the fruit is completely tender. Now, if you didn't peel the fruit, pass the mixture through a food mill to remove the skins and pits. Then return to the saucepan.

③ **Continue to cook or bake.** Continue to cook, stirring frequently, until the fruit has cooked down to a spreadable consistency. This process will take several hours. Alternatively, transfer the fruit to a 200°F (95°C) oven and bake, stirring occasionally, for up to 8 hours. Or transfer the fruit to a

The fruit butter is done when a spoon leaves a visible trail when it is drawn through it.

slow cooker and cook over low heat with the lid off, for up to 12 hours. The butter is done when it will hold the trail of a spoon that is drawn through it. It will have darkened in color considerably.

④ **Prepare the equipment.** If you plan to process the jars of fruit butter in a boiling-water bath for long-term storage, as the fruit butter nears the end of its cooking time, prepare the canner, canning jars, and lids according to the instructions on pages 175–76. The jars should be sterilized (see the box on page 176).

⑤ **Sweeten and flavor.** Sweeten to taste with maple syrup, honey, or white or brown sugar. Add spices such as cinnamon, if desired.

⑥ **Pack into jars.** Pack into jars, leaving the amount of headspace specified in the recipe, usually ¼ inch for half-pint jars. Wipe the rims clean, set the lids on the jars, and then lightly tighten the screwbands to close the jars.

⑦ **Process for long-term storage or refrigerate.** If you're not going to process the fruit butter for long-term storage, refrigerate the jars.

If you are going to process the fruit butter, process half-pint jars in a boiling-water bath for 5 minutes, counting the time when the water returns to a boil.

When the processing time is up, turn off the heat, remove the canner lid, and let the jars stand in the canner for 5 minutes. Then remove the jars and place on a folded towel or wooden rack. Allow to cool for 24 hours; then check the seals (see page 187).

Strong Opinions about Pectin

If you visit any online forums regarding jam making, you'll find a lot of opinions about brands of pectin. Generally speaking, people tend to stick to the brands they have had success with, and all the brands will yield successful products if you follow the manufacturer's directions. Crazy people like me will test out different brands and compare results.

Before there were supermarkets and commercial pectins, women made jam by cooking down their fruit — sweetened or not — until it reached the desired consistency: thick enough to spoon onto bread or toast. With fruits that don't contain much natural pectin, such as strawberries, the the fruit was cooked for hours, preferably in a copper kettle. The resulting jam was rich with notes of caramelized fruit.

Then came commercial pectins, like Certo and Sure-Jel. These products, derived from apples or orange peels, made jam making a cinch. You followed the instructions on the package, being sure to add the amount of sugar required. Then you brought the fruit and sugar mix to a boil, added the pectin, returned the mixture to a boil, and voilà: no-fail jam.

Commercial pectins like Certo and Sure-Jel are still popular, and with good reason: they require no judgment on the part of the cook, and they maximize your yield because the fruit is not cooked down very much and enough sugar is added to significantly increase the yield. Another bonus: jams made with tons of sugar keep well (at least 6 months in a covered jar in the refrigerator). But jams made with most commercial pectins are quite sweet and don't have a rich fruit flavor.

Enter Pomona's Universal Pectin, most frequently found in natural food stores and sold online, which allows you to sweeten to taste. Sales took off. And many, many jam makers adopted Pomona's as their go-to brand. Pomona's pectin is activated by calcium (included in the box). It is a little fussy to use in my opinion, but works fine. I think the added calcium solution dilutes the flavor of the fruit, but less so than a ton of sugar does.

Since Pomona's became successful, and since many nutritionists have decried the amount of sugar in the diets of Americans, many other manufacturers have come up with their own no-sugar and low-sugar pectins. If you require precision and consistency in your jams, use any of the commercial pectins and follow the manufacturer's directions. I have a favorite brand: Ball's RealFruit Low or No-Sugar Needed Pectin. It is ridiculously easy to use and gives a nice, soft set. Ball's online store (freshpreserving.com) has a jam and jelly calculator that lets you pick the fruit and the pectin to use and calculates how much of everything to use. It is quite handy. And here's the thing: as much as I prefer to avoid commercial products, using a commercial pectin gets me out of the kitchen much faster than going the old-fashioned route. My yields are high enough that I can count on having jars of jam to give away during the holidays, and my jam making can be fit in between dinner and bedtime, when the kitchen is somewhat cooler.

If, on the other hand, you are willing to experiment, explore, or use a certain amount of judgment in your jams, you can add apples or a homemade liquid pectin solution derived from apples and go from there.

Homemade Pectin

In the past, when I've needed pectin for my jam and I haven't wanted to use (or haven't had available) commercial pectin, my method has been to add apples to my jam. I start my batch of jam by making applesauce with four tart apples (or whatever I have on hand). I quarter the apples, put them in a saucepan with just enough water to keep them from scorching, cover the pan, and cook for about 15 minutes, until the fruit is completely soft. While the apples cook, I prepare my fruit (washing and hulling strawberries, peeling and slicing peaches, etc.). When the apples are soft, I run them through a food mill as though I were making applesauce. I add the applesauce to the jam pot along with the fruit and start cooking. I prefer a lightly sweetened jam, so I add about 1½ to 2 cups sugar to 12 cups of fruit. I also add 1 tablespoon of lemon juice to every 12 cups of fruit. The added sugar acts as a preservative, preventing mold and fermentation, and the added acid activates the pectin. Then I cook the mixture down until it reaches the proper consistency. It is not as long-cooked as the jams made with

---

====== **Names for Fruit Preserves** ======

Butter: Fruit pulp cooked down to a spreading consistency

Conserve: Whole pieces of fruit in a gelled syrup, usually with nuts

Jam: Crushed or puréed fruit in a gelled syrup

Jelly: Clear fruit juices gelled to a firm, spreadable consistency

Marmalade: Clear jellies in which pieces of fruit, usually citrus fruit, are suspended

Preserves: Whole pieces of fruit in a gelled syrup

no pectin, and it is somewhat sweeter, but I think those are positive attributes. And, in a blind tasting, only one person — my husband — in the tasting group detected the presence of apples. My husband is a super-taster, an actual category of people with more than the average number of taste buds. He is an extreme case.

Another way to add pectin is to make a liquid pectin solution from tart green apples such as Granny Smiths or your own homegrown, unripe apples or crabapples. The recipe is at right.

Using Homemade Pectin

Your homemade liquid pectin will vary in gelling ability, just as your fruit will vary in natural pectin, so there is no exact formula to use. As a general guideline, combine ⅔ cup homemade pectin and 1 tablespoon lemon juice with each 4 cups of fruit. (If the fruit is very tart, you can use less lemon juice.) Bring to a boil. After 2 to 3 minutes of boiling, add 2 to 3 cups of sugar and boil rapidly until the gelling stage is reached. Then pour into jars and process in a boiling-water bath (see chapter 11).

Homemade Liquid Pectin

INGREDIENTS

3 pounds tart green apples (like Granny Smith), with peels and cores, chopped

4 cups water

2 tablespoons lemon juice

1. Combine the apples, water, and lemon juice in a heavy saucepan and bring to a boil over high heat. Boil the mixture until it reduces almost in half, 30 to 45 minutes.

2. Strain the mixture through cheesecloth or a jelly bag. Discard the solids and return the liquid to the saucepan. Boil for another 20 minutes. Pour the mixture into clean, sanitized jars, seal, and let cool. Then store in the refrigerator for 3 days or in the freezer for longer. (You can also can in a boiling-water bath for 10 minutes; see chapter 11.)

CHAPTER 15

Culturing Milk and Making Cheese

Culturing milk means introducing friendly bacteria to transform the milk or cream into a soured (but tasty), thickened product such as cultured butter, crème fraîche, or yogurt.

Making cheese also involves culturing milk, but that is just the start. Once the milk is cultured, rennet is added to help form curds, which are then drained, salted, and pressed or molded. Time and temperature, not to mention the type of milk and type of culture, play a huge role in making the various cheeses. As a home cheesemaker, the part that is the most challenging, I think, is maintaining the proper temperatures. That and having the patience to work in the time frame the curds require, not the schedule of your household.

Better Butter and Crème Fraîche

The best thing about making butter is that you can make better butter than the standard American store-bought butter. Better butter starts with cultured cream. Not surprisingly, this was the American standard not so long ago.

Typically, the cream was left out all night to culture, or "clabber." Clabbered milk is milk that has thickened slightly and ripened in flavor. The flavor is pleasantly rich, nutty, and slightly tangy but not at all sour. In France, clabbered cream is known as crème fraîche. A German version is called quark. So, if you want to make crème fraîche, just culture the cream,

Sanitation Measures

Anytime you are dealing with friendly bacteria, as with culturing milk, and anytime you are dealing with a protein (milk) that can go bad, cleanliness is important. Before I set out to make cheese especially, or any other dairy product, I wipe down my counter and then spray it with a "no-rinse" beer-brewer's sanitizing solution (page 13). Next I gather all the pots and utensils I will need for the recipe, spray them with the sanitizing solution, and set them on the sanitized counter. Then I am good to go.

I once bought some butter and cheese from a farm, and I thought it tasted a little off. One day I happened to visit that farm when cheese and butter were being made. I was unimpressed with the sanitation standards, and I think that accounted for the off-flavors. You've been warned.

following the first couple of steps in the butter how-to at right.

Once agriculture was industrialized and refrigeration was introduced, butter making moved off the farm and into creameries. These creameries made "sweet butter" from fresh cream, in part because it speeded up the process. Consumers grew used to its mild, unctuous flavor.

Sweet cream butter became the standard American butter, the butter most of us were raised on. Although salt was once added as a preservative, refrigeration made that unnecessary. Salted and unsalted butter (the latter sometimes called "sweet butter") became the standard. But it is all sweet (in the original meaning of "not cultured") butter.

What was lost in the switch from cultured to sweet butter? Only the flavor. Naturally occurring lactobacilli ripen fresh cream into cultured cream. When the thickened cream is churned into butter, it is rich and flavorful, as opposed to unctuous, smooth, and neutral tasting.

So, unless you are in a hurry or you are making pastry that requires sweet butter, I highly recommend culturing the cream before you make butter.

How to Make Butter (and Crème Fraîche)

The steps couldn't be easier. I make butter in a stand mixer, and the following instructions assume that you'll use one as well. But you can also use a food processor, a blender, or an immersion blender in a mason jar. The churning step can also be done by putting a marble in a mason jar along with the cream and shaking the jar, but I have broken a jar that way and won't try it again. Another alternative is to make the butter in a pint jar using 1 cup heavy cream without the marble, but be prepared to shake for 15 to 20 minutes. Crazy, huh? You can buy both electric and manual butter churns designed for the kitchen.

① **Collect the cream.** If you're starting with raw milk, let it stand overnight in the refrigerator until the cream rises to the top. Skim off the cream or siphon it off with a clean turkey baster.

Depending on the breed of cow, her diet, her lactation cycle, and a few other factors, 2 quarts of milk will yield about 1 cup of cream.

② **Culture the cream.** If you want cultured butter, let the cream stand at room temperature overnight. The flavor will ripen and the cream will thicken slightly. If you are using pasteurized cream, add 2 tablespoons cultured buttermilk to each 2 cups of cream (or use a buttermilk culture) and let stand overnight at room temperature. (See page 232.)

If you're making crème fraîche, stop here; you're done.

③ **Beat the cream.** If the cream is warmer than 60°F (16°C), chill it a little; otherwise the butter will be soft and hard to handle. Pour the cream into the bowl of a stand mixer fitted with a whisk attachment. Beat on medium-low speed until you have whipped cream.

When you first start beating the cream, throw a towel over the mixer so milk isn't flung all over the kitchen.

Continue beating until the cream separates into globules of fat and a milky liquid. Stop beating immediately (don't overbeat). Strain out the butterfat (the milky white solids) over a bowl. You'll want to keep the buttermilk (the milky liquid that drains out) for drinking, making a creamy salad dressing, or using in pancakes or biscuits. Fresh buttermilk is delicious, which shouldn't come as a surprise but always does.

4 **Wash.** Hold the strainer with the butterfat under running water until the rinse water runs clear. Briefly knead the butter with two wooden spoons or your hands to squeeze out any remaining moisture. This step is really important for the flavor of the butter. Any remaining buttermilk will sour and give the butter an off-flavor. Fold in salt, if you like. I prefer to add a flake salt, like Maldon sea salt. Use about ½ teaspoon salt to 2 cups of heavy cream.

Be patient and wash away any remaining buttermilk.

5 **Store.** The yield on 2 cups of cream is about 1 cup of butter. Butter should be stored in a covered dish and will keep, refrigerated, for several weeks. Excess butter can be stored in the freezer for up to 9 months; double-wrap in plastic wrap before bagging or wrapping in freezer paper, or use a vacuum sealer. (Butter picks up off-odors in the freezer.)

Store well wrapped; butter picks up off-odors from the refrigerator and freezer.

Culturing Cream

If you are starting with raw cow's milk, let the milk sit in the refrigerator for 24 hours so that all the cream rises to the top of the jar. (Note: this won't work with goat's milk, which is naturally homogenized.) Siphon or ladle off the cream, and let the cream sit on the counter overnight.

You can make cultured butter from store-bought pasteurized cream, but not from ultra-pasteurized cream. Read the labels carefully. My only source for pasteurized, not ultra-pasteurized, cream is a local dairy. All the national brands are ultra-pasteurized. To culture pasteurized cream, you can use cultured buttermilk (2 tablespoons buttermilk to 2 cups cream). Bring the cream to 68°F to 70°F (20°C to 21°C), add the cultured buttermilk, and keep covered and warm for the next 6 to 12 hours, depending on how strongly cultured you want your cream. Do not let it fall below 68°F (20°C) or rise above 78°F (26°C). Alternatively, you can add a buttermilk culture, which you can purchase from most cheesemaking supply stores (see Resources, page 339).

After ripening, the cream should be noticeably thicker and slightly shiny. It should have a well-developed aroma and taste delicious and just slightly sour, with no after-taste. If the cream is bubbly or smells off, yeasty, or gassy, you have a contamination problem; throw the cream away and start over.

Making Yogurt

I once thought I knew all there was to know about making yogurt. Any milk can be used to make yogurt, whether it's raw or ultra-pasteurized, or cow's or goat's milk. You add some commercial plain yogurt to the milk, keep it warm, and yogurt happens. If it cultures too rapidly or at too high a temperature, it may taste extra tangy. Adding powdered milk makes it taste slightly richer (particularly if you are starting with skim or low-fat milk). Draining it brings it close to Greek-style yogurt.

What I didn't know was that different cultures make differently flavored yogurt. For example, the New England Cheesemaking Supply Company (see Resources, page 339) sells cultures that make a Bulgarian-style yogurt, a creamy yogurt, and a sweet yogurt. The sweet yogurt culture is quite remarkable; it makes a yogurt noticeably lacking in acidity.

Yogurt cultures do age and become less effective. If you are making yogurt by culturing with a spoonful of the previous batch, and it takes longer and longer to culture and produces softer and softer yogurt, it is time to use fresh culture — either from a cheesemaking supply company or from a freshly purchased commercial yogurt. Any cultures you can buy usually have a limited life span; read the labels.

Equipment for Making Yogurt

Despite the proliferation of electric yogurt makers on the market, everything you need to make yogurt is probably already in your kitchen. Yogurt cultures require a warm environment. You can provide that warm environment with an electric yogurt maker or with something improvised, like a slow cooker (but only one with a "warm"

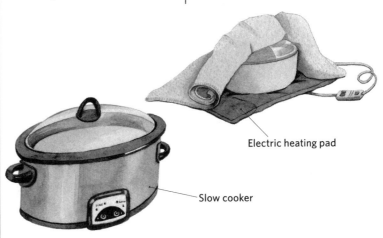

Picnic cooler with hot water bottles and towels

setting) or a picnic cooler lined with an electric heating pad or hot water bottles. Or you can wrap your container in blankets and place it in a warm spot such as a shelf above a woodstove or a radiator. You will also need two or three 1-quart glass containers (canning jars work well), a saucepan, and a kitchen thermometer. If you want to make Greek-style yogurt, you will need a whisk and a colander lined with butter muslin.

Electric heating pad

Slow cooker

Yogurt should culture in 4 to 8 hours. It may be somewhat slower in colder temperatures. Generally speaking, the longer you culture the yogurt, the more sour it will become; it will not get any thicker.

① **Scald the milk.** Heat the milk to 170°F to 180°F (77°C to 82°C) to kill any bacteria that might be present. Let cool to lukewarm, 105°F to 110°F (41°C to 43°C). (This step isn't necessary with ultra-pasteurized milk.)

② **Add the culture.** You will need about 2 teaspoons of active plain yogurt for every quart of milk, or as much yogurt culture as its label specifies. Stir the plain yogurt into a few tablespoons of the scalded milk until smooth and add to the remaining scalded milk, or sprinkle the culture over the milk. Stir to distribute the culture evenly throughout the milk.

③ **Incubate.** Transfer the yogurt mixture into glass canning jars and set in a warm place where the milk can maintain a temperature of 100°F to 112°F (38°C to 44°C). Incubation takes anywhere from 4 to 8 hours, but 6 hours is ideal. If you are using hot water as a heat source, renew the hot water every 2 hours. Also, avoid bumping the cooler; the yogurt needs stillness to firm up.

④ **Test.** Check for doneness after 4 hours (or a bit longer, if the ambient temperature is below 100°F/38°C); the yogurt should be firm. Test by gently turning it to see if it keeps its shape. There will be some slightly milky liquid on the top. This is whey. You can either pour it off or just mix it into the yogurt when you eat it.

⑤ **Optional: make Greek-style yogurt.** If you're happy with your yogurt the way it is, move on to step 6. But to make Greek-style yogurt, transfer the fresh yogurt to a colander lined with butter muslin and drain for 2 hours. Transfer to a bowl and stir briskly with a whisk for the best consistency.

⑥ **Flavor and refrigerate.** If you like, you can flavor the yogurt with honey, maple syrup, sugar, jam, or fresh fruit. You can also use soda and coffee flavoring syrups (like Torani brand) to add a range of really interesting flavors.

Store the yogurt in a covered container in the refrigerator, where it will keep for 2 to 4 weeks.

Making Fresh Cheeses

No one goes into cheese-making without a guide. I took some classes, consulted with farmer friends, read some good books, and visited a few good websites (see Resources, page 339). Becoming an expert cheesemaker is a lifetime pursuit, requiring patience, persistence, and resourcefulness. This chapter contains a few recipes and some basic information to get you started with fresh cheese. Aged cheeses, such as cheddar, require additional equipment (such as a cheese press) and steps (such as aging), and they take more work than the average homesteader — or anyone aspiring to homesteader skills — is up for. If you're interested in taking up cheesemaking as a serious endeavor, find yourself a good guide devoted to cheesemaking (again, see Resources).

Paneer (or panir), an Indian fresh cheese, and queso blanco, found in Mexican and Spanish cuisine, are both the same cheese and very easy to make, requiring only milk and lemon juice or vinegar. If you are doubtful about committing yourself to cheesemaking, this is the cheese to start with. It is so easy to make that you can skip down to the recipe (page 240) before you read all the introductory information.

Equipment for Cheesemaking

The basic equipment you will need for making fresh cheese is a double-boiler arrangement for a 2-gallon pot. What works for me is setting a boiling-water-bath canner on top of a 5-gallon stockpot. My friend Sandy sets her 2-gallon pot inside a large boiling-water-bath canner. Whatever works is fine.

You will also need a thermometer, a long knife for cutting curds, a large metal strainer or colander set in a large bowl for straining the curds, and a slotted spoon or ladle to stir the curds. Everything should be made of stainless steel, not plastic or wood. You will also need butter muslin to line the strainer or colander; cheesecloth is too loosely woven for draining curds when making cheese. Those items that you don't already own can be found online wherever cheesemaking supplies are sold (see Resources, page 339).

More equipment is needed for making hard cheeses, which is another reason to start with soft cheese.

Large pot

Cheese knife

Spider

Slotted ladle

Butter muslin

Thermometer

Butter Muslin

Butter muslin is used for separating curds and whey in cheesemaking and milk fat and buttermilk when making butter. It can be reused until it falls apart. Before you use new butter muslin, machine-wash with an unscented detergent. After each use, rinse it in cold water to remove all particles and machine-wash it with an unscented detergent. (Butter muslin can function as an all-purpose strainer and can be used to make a jelly bag when making jelly.)

Ingredients for Cheesemaking

There aren't a lot of different products that go into making the various cheeses. What produces the tremendous variations in cheese are the effects of time, types of milk and cultures, and amount of rennet or other enzymes you use. With the exception of the milk, all the ingredients needed for making cheese are available from online cheesemaking suppliers (see Resources, page 339).

Milk

You can use either raw or pasteurized milk from a cow, goat, or sheep; do not use ultra-pasteurized milk. Pasteurized milk will, however, yield a softer cheese than raw milk will, because the pasteurization process decreases the amount of calcium in the milk. Therefore, some cheesemakers add calcium chloride to their milk — just as pickle makers add calcium chloride to their pickles in the form of Pickle Crisp granules. All of the recipes in this chapter were tested with raw and pasteurized milk, without the addition of calcium chloride, which is used for making hard cheeses.

In general, 1 gallon of milk will yield 2 pounds of soft cheese or 1 pound of hard cheese. The higher the butterfat content of the milk, the greater the cheese yield.

Acidifier or Starter Culture

You will need either an acidifying ingredient, such as vinegar, lemon juice, or citric acid, or a starter culture, or both, depending on the recipe. Cultured buttermilk, which contains active bacteria, is also used in some recipes. With the starter culture, the bacteria do the work to acidify the milk and develop lactic acid. Acidifying the milk produces curds.

Cultures fall into two basic categories: mesophilic (those that grow in medium temperatures) and thermophilic (those that grow in high temperatures). Mesophilic cultures work on milk that never exceeds 102°F (39°C), and thermophilic cultures work with milk scalded to 104°F to 140°F (40°C to 60°C).

Rennet

A complex of enzymes, rennet speeds the formation of curds and firms the curds. Although the most well-known source of rennet is the stomach lining of calves, rennet from vegetable sources is available.

You can purchase rennet in liquid, tablet, or powdered form. How to choose which form to buy? Powdered rennet is recommended for large batches of cheese that use more than 2 gallons of milk, so I recommend using either liquid or tablet rennet. There are pros and cons to each:

> **Ease of use.** Liquid animal rennet (usually simply called liquid rennet) comes in bottles with a dropper and is always diluted in nonchlorinated water before being added to the milk; once diluted, it must be used within 30 minutes. Liquid vegetable rennet is double-strength; you will always need to use half as

Way Too Much Whey

Milk contains about 87 percent liquid and 13 percent solids. So when making cheese, the yield will be about 87 percent whey and 13 percent cheese. That's a lot of whey.

Because whey is so acidic and unlike the normal liquid waste that a household generates, it is a bad idea to send it into a septic system. So you need to find ways to deal with whey. I give it to my blueberry plants, which thrive in acid soil. Chickens and pigs enjoy drinking it. Some people cook grains with it or use it instead of water when making bread.

¼ teaspoon liquid animal rennet = ¼ rennet tablet =
⅛ teaspoon liquid vegetable rennet

Testing Rennet

Many of us pick up new skills with great enthusiasm, then slowly lose motivation. Maybe the season changes, or our responsibilities change, and suddenly there is no time! No time! This happens to household cheesemakers all the time. Rennet has a shelf life of about 9 months. How do you know if your rennet will still cause the milk to form curds?

This is how I learned to test rennet from the New England Cheesemaking Supply Company: Heat 1 cup whole milk to 90°F (32°C). Dissolve ¼ rennet tablet or ¼ teaspoon liquid rennet in ½ cup cool, nonchlorinated water and stir well. Stir 2 tablespoons of this diluted rennet into the milk, while the milk is still at 90°F (32°C). Stir gently from the bottom to the top for 30 seconds. If the rennet is working, the milk surface will begin to firm or form a slight film after 2 minutes. After 6 minutes, it will have formed a curd that will hold a knife cut. If not, you must buy fresh rennet before you can make cheese again.

much as the recipe calls for (and the rennet's labeling will make this clear), so you need to be mindful of which rennet you are using. It, too, must be diluted in nonchlorinated water before being added to the milk.

➤ Rennet tablets often need to be cut and have score marks to make that easier. They are also dissolved in nonchlorinated water before use.

➤ **Shelf life.** Rennet tablets will last for at least 5 years, if kept frozen. At room temperature, they will last at least 1 year; no one recommends refrigerating them. Liquid rennet should be refrigerated, never frozen. Liquid animal rennet will last for up to 1 year, while liquid vegetable rennet will last for 5 to 6 months. After the suggested shelf life, the strength will gradually decrease and you will get softer and softer curds.

Salt and Enzymes

Most recipes require either salt or cheese salt for flavoring. Cheese salt is a flaky, noniodized salt. Whatever salt you use (cheese salt, canning salt, pickling salt, fine sea salt, or kosher salt), it should be noniodized. The recipes here call for the salt I normally stock: canning, pickling, or fine sea salt. You may have to adjust for the coarser grind if you use kosher salt or cheese salt from a cheesemaking supply company.

Some recipes (particularly if you are using pasteurized milk) will call for lipase powder. Lipase is an enzyme naturally found in varying amounts in milk, but it's destroyed by pasteurization. It provides a distinctive flavor and aroma to certain types of cheese, such as Romano and feta.

Water

Water is used to dilute the rennet. It should be non-chlorinated because chlorine will kill the bacteria you are attempting to grow.

How to Make Soft Fresh Cheese

These instructions will yield a mildly flavored, soft fresh cheese that you can use as a topping for a casserole, a filling for pasta or enchiladas, or as a seasoned spread for bread or crackers. Most cheesemaking follows the same basic steps, though mozzarella has additional steps of cooking and stretching the curds (see the step-by-step instructions on page 243).

① **Warm the milk.** Warm the milk to the temperature required by the recipe, which in turn is controlled by whether you are using a starter culture and which type of culture you are using (mesophilic or thermophilic). Ideally, you will start with milk that is still warm from the animal. If you must use refrigerated milk, warm the milk slowly in a double boiler. (Heating directly on the stove will allow hot spots to develop and kill off the bacteria you are trying to encourage.) Aim for raising the temperature of the milk no more than 2°F (1°C) every 5 minutes. In addition to providing an ideal temperature for the starter culture, this step encourages bacteria present in the milk to begin converting milk sugars into lactic acid, which provides flavor.

Heat the milk slowly.

② **Add the starter culture or acidify the milk.** Add the culture or acid directly to the warmed milk and stir to mix thoroughly. If you are adding acid, the milk will begin to curdle almost immediately, in which case you can skip to step 7. If you are making mozzarella or feta, leave the pot in the double-boiler setup to maintain the milk at the optimal temperature. If you have started with warm milk and haven't set up a double boiler, you can fill a sink with hot water and place the pot in the sink to maintain the warm temperature of the milk. The milk becomes acidified as the bacteria break down the milk sugars (lactose). The recipe will dictate how long the milk needs to acidify or culture; it can take 1 to 15 hours.

③ **Add the rennet.** Rennet is an enzyme that causes curds to bind together to develop a solid, soft curd. If your recipe calls for it, dissolve the rennet in a small amount of water to allow it to distribute more evenly in the milk, and stir it in. Not all soft cheeses require rennet; cheeses without rennet, like ricotta and chèvre, have small curds.

Add the starter culture.

④ **Set the curd.** After stirring the rennet in, keep the milk at a constant warm temperature, as dictated by the recipe, to allow the curd to set. This stage is completed when the curd will break cleanly when a knife is inserted into it. You will see that the curd looks solid, like silken tofu, and whey is collecting on top.

⑤ **Cut the curd.** Cutting the curd encourages the release of whey. With a long, sharp knife, slice the curd all the way through at 1-inch intervals. Turn the pot 90 degrees and cut again all the way through at 1-inch intervals, making a kind of checkerboard pattern. Now, holding the knife at a 45-degree angle, slice through the columns of curds. Turn the pot a quarter turn and slice at an angle again. Repeat twice more. Then let the curds rest for 5 to 10 minutes. As they rest, you will see the whey rising and the curds separating from each other. After the curd has rested, use a large spoon to lift and cut any remaining large pieces into small curds.

⑥ **Cook the curds.** Cooking the curds further encourages them to release whey and firm up; it also increases acidity. It is important to bring the temperature up slowly (unless the recipe states otherwise) to 105°F to 107°F (41°C to 42°C) over 30 to 60 minutes (usually). If you raise the temperature too quickly, the curds will develop a skin and the whey will be held in. Stir the curds regularly and gently to prevent them from matting together or sticking to the bottom of the pot. Let the curds rest again for 5 to 10 minutes.

⑦ **Drain and salt the curds.** Line a colander with butter muslin, and set it in a large bowl. With a slotted spoon or ladle, gently spoon the curds into the colander. Let drain, then add salt, as specified by your recipe. A very soft cheese will be drained, salted, and refrigerated. A firmer cheese will be drained, salted, and molded. The amount of time you drain and mold varies by cheese, as does the amount of salt. The salt is added at the end to prevent further bacterial action, which has continued to acidify the cheese.

⑧ **Finish.** At this point, some cheeses are finished. Some soft cheeses are molded; others are brined. Hard cheeses require additional steps of pressing, drying, and aging. Some are inoculated with mold.

The curd looks like silken tofu.

Cutting the curd

Draining off the whey

Paneer (Queso Blanco)

Makes about 9 ounces

Paneer should be your gateway to making more complex cheeses. What do you do with paneer? It is used as a meat substitute in Indian cooking. Saag (spinach) paneer is a dish frequently found in Indian restaurants and is a good way to enjoy your first harvest of spinach in the spring (see the recipe on page 281). Paneer is an interesting cheese because it does not melt, so you can brown it in oil. Or call it queso blanco and use it in enchiladas or other Mexican dishes. The recipe can be multiplied if you have more milk (and a bigger pot). Before you begin, figure out where you are going to hang the cheese to drain. You may be able to tie it to your sink faucet. I tie mine to a cabinet handle and set a bowl beneath it to catch the dripping whey.

INGREDIENTS

1 gallon whole milk (cow's or goat's milk)

¼ cup white vinegar or bottled lemon juice

1. Line a large colander with butter muslin and set it in a large bowl.

2. Pour the milk into a large, wide pot and heat slowly over medium heat until it is almost ready to boil, about 200°F (95°C). Stir frequently to prevent the milk from scorching on the bottom of the pan.

3. Stir in the vinegar and decrease the heat to low. The milk will immediately begin to separate into curds (white milk solids) and whey (greenish liquid).

4. Remove the pot from the heat and carefully pour the contents into the lined colander set over a bowl. Grab the ends of the muslin and twist the ball of cheese to squeeze out the excess whey. Hang, and allow the whey to drain from the cheese for 5 to 10 minutes.

5. Place the muslin-wrapped cheese on a rimmed plate on the counter and open it up. Using a pastry scraper or the dull side of knife, scrape the curds into a mound and compress them into a block. Tightly fold the muslin over and around the block of curds. Set another plate on top. Weight the second plate down with cans of beans or a heavy pot. Transfer to the refrigerator and let it sit for 20 minutes or longer.

6. If you don't want to eat it or cook with it immediately, wrap the cheese in plastic wrap and refrigerate for up to 3 days.

Ricotta Cheese

Makes 3 to 4 cups

Ricotta is another cheese that is very easy to make, and it doesn't require any ingredients beyond what you can purchase at your local grocery store. There is no better use for ricotta than filling your own pasta. See page 285 for a tortelloni recipe that uses wonton skins instead of homemade pasta; the results are wonderful, and you won't have to spend the whole day in the kitchen. In Italy, ricotta is traditionally made from whey, but I've had mixed results with that method, so I recommend using whole milk instead.

INGREDIENTS

1 gallon whole milk

6 tablespoons bottled lemon juice, or more if needed

2 teaspoons pickling salt, canning salt, or fine sea salt, or to taste

1. Line a large colander with butter muslin and set it in a large bowl.

2. Pour the milk into a large, wide pot and heat slowly over medium heat until it has reached 185°F (85°C). At that temperature the milk will be steaming. Stir frequently to prevent the milk from scorching on the bottom of the pan.

3. Add the lemon juice, remove the pot from the heat, and stir to evenly distribute the lemon juice throughout the milk. Let the pot sit undisturbed for 10 minutes.

4. The curds will settle to the bottom of the pot, with the whey on top. If the pot still contains what looks like milky whey, add another 1 tablespoon of lemon juice and let sit for 2 to 3 minutes. Repeat if necessary, until you see curds and greenish, watery looking whey. Carefully pour the contents into the lined colander and let drain for about 8 minutes. If the ricotta is the consistency you want, transfer it to a bowl. If it still seems soupy, drain for another 5 to 10 minutes.

5. Stir in the salt, cover, and refrigerate for 2 hours. The ricotta is now ready to use. It will keep in the refrigerator in an airtight container for up to 5 days.

Chèvre

Makes 1 to 1¼ pounds

The making of soft, fresh goat cheese is one of the best examples I know of culinary magic. You take a rich-tasting milk that has no traces of goatiness, and with the action of bacteria, heat, and time, you end up with a distinctively flavored cheese that can't be mistaken for anything other than goat.

INGREDIENTS

1 gallon fresh raw goat's milk

1 packet direct-set chèvre culture (it will contain the necessary amount of rennet)

¼ teaspoon pickling salt, canning salt, or fine sea salt, plus more to taste

1. In a double-boiler, slowly heat the milk to 170°F (77°C). While the milk heats, make a bed of ice in the sink. When the milk reaches 170°F (77°C), immediately transfer the top pot to the bed of ice and cool the milk rapidly, replacing the ice as needed to cool the milk to 70°F to 72°F (21°C to 22°C).

2. Move the pot to the counter. Sprinkle the culture powder over the surface of the milk and allow it to rehydrate for about 2 minutes; then stir it in. Cover the pot with a towel and let the cheese sit, undisturbed, for 8 to 15 hours, until the mixture looks like thick yogurt. The longer the curd sets, the more acid will be produced.

3. When a good curd has formed, you will see a thin layer of whey over the curd mass. The curd may show cracks and separation from the sides. Now it's time to check for a "clean break," meaning you can cut the curd into cubes that will hold their shape. Wash your hands thoroughly. Plunge a bent finger into the coagulated milk, and then lift your finger up and out. The cheese should at first look like a pudding trying to stick to your finger; then it should fall away cleanly, leaving a small puddle of whey where your finger once was. If the break isn't clean, let the curd set for another hour or so, and then check it again.

4. Line a colander with butter muslin and set it in a large bowl. Gently transfer the curd to the colander with a spider strainer, ladle, or slotted spoon. Allow the whey to drain for 6 to 8 hours at 68°F to 72°F (20° to 22°C). The longer it drains, the tangier and drier it becomes.

5. Transfer the cheese to a bowl, gently stir in the salt, cover, and refrigerate. The cheese will keep for 7 to 10 days.

Making Mozzarella

Mozzarella is the fresh cheese most everyone wants to make — especially in this pizza culture we live in. (And if you are in the mood to make pizza, do try the sourdough pizza crust on page 283.) Be aware that despite the proliferation of "easy" mozzarella recipes on the Internet, easy isn't always better — or even successful. There are, however, two websites I have found particularly helpful: those of the New England Cheesemaking Supply Company and Fias Co Farm. Although there are many different methods for making mozzarella cheese, this is the one that works for me.

I was somewhat surprised the first time I made mozzarella. Although the flavor is great, I was expecting a softer cheese, more like the buffalo milk mozzarella you find in Italian cheese shops. This mozzarella is firm enough to grate.

How to Make Mozzarella

What makes mozzarella different from other fresh cheeses is that after you have separated the curds and whey, you heat the curds and then stretch them. I highly recommend wearing a pair of rubber gloves to protect your hands. Any clean rubber gloves are better than nothing, but heavy-duty food gloves (sold where cheesemaking supplies are sold) offer better heat protection. The steps that follow are quite detailed because mozzarella is trickier than other fresh cheeses.

INGREDIENTS

2 gallons milk, raw or pasteurized (but not ultrapasteurized)

1½ teaspoons citric acid

¼ teaspoon or 1 packet thermophilic culture DVI "LH" (direct vat inoculated *Lactobacillus helveticus*)

½ teaspoon liquid animal rennet, ¼ teaspoon vegetable rennet, or ½ rennet tablet

½ cup kosher salt

① **Heat the milk.** Combine the milk and citric acid in the top of a double boiler, and heat the milk to 90°F (32°C), stirring occasionally. Set the alarm on your thermometer, if you have one, for 84°F (29°C). If the temperature of the milk continues to rise rapidly, and you are afraid it might go beyond 90°F (29°C), remove the pot with the milk from the double boiler. Alternatively, you can heat the milk in a pot in a sink filled with very warm water.

This step acidifies the milk to make it more hospitable to the thermophilic cheese culture. Also, a certain level of acidity is necessary to create stretchy curds, which is what gives mozzarella its distinct texture. But don't get carried away; more acidity is not better.

② **Culture the milk.** When the milk is at least 90°F (32°C) and no more than 100°F (38°C), add the culture by sprinkling it over the surface of the milk. Allow it to sit on the surface of the milk for about 2 minutes; then stir it in. Let the milk sit and ripen for 60 minutes.

Add the starter culture.

③ **Add the rennet and allow curds to form.**
Dissolve the rennet in ⅓ cup cool water and
stir it in, moving the spoon slowly from top
to bottom for about 30 seconds. Let the milk
sit, covered and undisturbed, for 45 minutes
while the culture works and the rennet helps
form the curd. Keep the milk at 100°F (38°C)
during this period, preferably using a sink of
warm water or a warm double-boiler setup.
The heat should not be on.

④ **Look for a clean break.** When the milk
looks solid and somewhat shiny — like silken
tofu — check for a "clean break," meaning
you can cut the curd into cubes that will hold
their shape. Wash your hands thoroughly,
stick a bent finger or a knife into the curd at
an angle, and then pull it straight up out of
the curd. If the curd breaks cleanly around
your finger or the knife and whey runs into
the crack that you have made, you have a
clean break. If you don't have a clean break,
let the milk continue to set until you do.

Look for a
clean break.

⑤ **Cut the curds.** Using a long, sharp knife
held vertically, cut ½-inch slices in the curd.
Then turn the pot 90 degrees and cut across
in ½-inch slices the other direction, making a
kind of checkerboard pattern. Now, holding
the knife at a 45-degree angle, retrace your
cuts. Turn the pot a quarter turn and cut
again at a 45-degree angle, and repeat two
more times. Give the curds a brief stir. Let

Cutting the curds.

the curds rest for 5 minutes (10 minutes for
goat's milk) to allow them to firm up. Then
stir gently with a slotted spoon or ladle, and
cut any large curds you missed when cutting
the first time.

⑥ **Cook the curds.** Keep the curds at 90°F to
91°F (32°C to 33°C), covered, for an hour or
so, stirring occasionally during the first half
hour. This is called "cooking" the curds, even
though you are just keeping them warm.
To maintain the ideal temperature, return
the pot to the double-boiler setup or sink of
warm water. If the temperature rises above
91°F (33°C), it isn't a catastrophe, but it will
result in a drier cheese. A brief stir every 5 to
10 minutes will keep the curds separate without causing them to release too much whey.

Transfer the curds to a colander
lined with butter muslin.

⑦ **Drain the curds.** Place a large colander
lined with butter muslin over a pot to catch
the whey, and pour the curds into the colander. Or, if the cheese is a solid mass, just pull
it out with a gloved hand or a sturdy spoon
and place it in the lined colander (to avoid

Suspend the bag of curds over a bowl to catch the whey.

making a big splash). Hang it over a bowl and let it drain for about 2 hours.

⑧ **Reheat the curds in salted water.** Bring a pot of clean water to 180°F (82°C). Stir the salt into the hot water. Unwrap the cheese and cut the curd ball/lump in half; you'll work only half of the cheese at a time, so set the other half aside. Cut remaining curd into 1-inch cubes, more or less. Slide the cubed curds into the hot water (avoid splashing yourself). Let the curd cubes heat for a moment, and carefully stir with a slotted flat ladle or a spider. Squeeze the cubes with your gloved fingertips to test. When the cubes feel soft throughout (not solid in the middle), they are ready to be stretched. Err on the side of a little bit "solid" on the inside of the larger pieces. If the curds aren't soft enough, they won't stretch, but you can always return them to the water to heat up more. But once they get too soft and runny, there is no going back.

Cook the curds in salted water to develop mozzarella's uniquely stringy texture.

Variations in Milk Create Variations in Butter and Cheese

Milk varies by season. During the abundant summer, when cows and goats feast on fresh grass, they yield more milk but the butterfat content is lower. In the winter, when the animals are given hay, they give a smaller quantity of milk but the butterfat content is higher. The higher the percentage of butterfat in the butter and cheese, the richer the flavor. Also, butter that is higher in butterfat is better for baking and has a higher smoking point (it doesn't burn as easily).

⑨ **Test the curds for stretch.** Cut off a small piece of the curd and put it in the hot water. Keep feeling it with a gloved hand and see if it begins to melt. Once it starts to melt, take it out and see if you can stretch it. If it stretches with no problem, you can go to the next step. If it breaks when you try to pull it, put it back in the hot water and continue to warm for another 15 to 20 minutes. Repeat the test until you see a good stretch — that is, until you can stretch the sample to about two to three times its original length without breaking it.

Test for stretch.

⑩ **Stretch.** Carefully transfer the hot curds to a large bowl with the slotted ladle. These curds are hot, so be careful. Handle them gently so that the cream does not separate out (you can see this happening), which results in a dry cheese. Gather the curds in your hands and form them together into one mass. Gently fold one side over on the other to get it all to come together. Don't squeeze; keep folding and stretching until the curd will stretch on its own from its own weight. Keep stretching and folding. As you "work" the curds, they will stretch more and more easily. You will be able to pull the curds longer and longer.

Stretch but don't squeeze or the cheese will be dry.

⑪ **Finish.** Return the stretched cheese to the hot water for a few seconds to warm back up. Place the cheese in a bowl or plastic container and let it rest; it will take the shape of whatever container you set it in. Repeat steps 9 and 11 with the remaining curd. Let the cheese cool at room temperature for a couple hours. Place the cheese (in its mold) in the refrigerator for 2 to 3 days or enjoy right away.

CHAPTER 16

Curing Meats and Making Sausage

For many homesteaders, meat comes into the kitchen in vast quantities: a just-butchered animal ready for wrapping and freezing, or a couple of boxes of meat all butchered, wrapped, and frozen from the slaughterhouse. The meat is hastily put into the freezer or refrigerator, and the job is done.

Traditionally, all this slaughtering and butchering was done in the fall and winter, when the weather could provide some refrigeration. Even so, much of the meat was cured, perhaps smoked, and/ or turned into sausage to slow spoilage. Over time, the various methods of curing, brining, and sausage making to preserve and "improve" meat became a culinary art known as charcuterie.

At its simplest, curing is a way to preserve and flavor meat with the addition of salt. It's easy to see how curing came about as a way to keep food from spoiling. When you pack meat in salt, the salt draws water from the flesh through a process of osmosis. In the high-salt environment, mold is prevented from growing and certain bacteria will ferment the meat, completely altering the flavor — in a good way. Curing is often followed by smoking, which adds another layer of flavor and further preserves the meat.

These days, curing with salt is a homesteading skill that is becoming more and more popular and sophisticated. For the first time in recent memory, charcuterie skills are being taught at culinary schools and cooking schools are offering workshops open to everyone. Here in Vermont, where artisan cheesemaking has been changing the face of dairy farming, charcuterie is changing the economics of meat farming.

Much of charcuterie is within the grasp of home cooks and ordinary homesteaders. This chapter is an introduction to some basic ways to cure meat and some basic sausage-making techniques. Just as cheesemaking can become a lifetime pursuit, so can curing meats. To delve deeper into the subject, I highly recommend the book *Charcuterie* by Michael Ruhlman and Brian Polcyn.

What Are the Safety Issues?

Working with meat makes some people nervous. People can — and do — get sick from eating poorly handled meat. Bacteria, which are present everywhere, find fresh meat an attractive medium to grow on. The spoilage bacteria are particularly active at temperatures between 40°F and 140°F (4°C to 60°C). This is the "danger zone," and meat spoils within a few hours at these temperatures. Traditionally, curing was done with salt and saltpeter (potassium nitrate) to prevent the bacteria from spoiling the meat. Now that refrigeration is widely available, we have more options for charcuterie. Nevertheless, safety remains a priority. So let's get the safety issues out of the way first:

> Chill, baby, chill. No matter what you are making, keep all your meat chilled, even partially frozen. This is probably the most important safety precaution you can take.

> When you cure meat under refrigeration and fully cook the cured meat (as with bacon) before eating, salt is sufficient as a preservative and nitrates or nitrites aren't needed.

> If you are curing meat at room temperature and plan to eat the meat uncooked, you must use a curing mixture that contains nitrates or nitrites; otherwise you do risk spoilage and harmful bacteria.

> Curing a whole (boneless) muscle, as in a pork loin or brisket, is relatively safe. Spoilage bacteria can attach only to the surface of the meat. It is when you grind meat, as with sausage, that you can introduce spoilage bacteria to the mix, so you should take extra precautions there.

> Follow the same common-sense hygiene practices you follow whenever you are preserving. Work with a clean kitchen, and spray down all equipment and work surfaces with a sanitizer (see page 13).

> Trust your senses. If the meat is slimy or if it smells bad, don't eat it.

> Cured meats that are meant to be cooked should be cooked until well done (160°F/71°C).

That brings us to the question of whether nitrates and nitrites, commonly used in curing salts, are safe to eat. Nitrates and nitrites are naturally occurring compounds that are present in beets and in green vegetables such as celery. In the quantities in which they are present in cured meats, they are considered safe. That said, even a teaspoon eaten directly will kill you.

The primary concern with nitrates and nitrites in cured foods is that they may cause cancer. When a piece of meat treated with sodium nitrite is exposed to the heat of cooking, proteins in the meat bond with the sodium nitrite to produce nitrosamines. It is also possible for nitrosamines to form from sodium nitrite in highly acidic conditions, like your stomach. Basically, the frying and eating of nitrite-containing bacon presents the perfect scenario for nitrosamines to enter your system. And nitrosames, under certain circumstances, have been shown to be carcinogenic.

Those "nitrate- and nitrite-free" packages of bacon and hot dogs you find in natural food stores boast about cures made with celery juice and beet juice. The actual amount of nitrates and nitrites with these "natural" cures may be even higher than those that use the curing salts regulated by the FDA. Whether the nitrates are "natural" from celery or part of a curing salt mix, those very same nitrosamines will be formed in your stomach.

You can avoid nitrates and nitrites by curing all your foods under refrigeration with regular salt, avoiding the curing salts, and eating the cured foods quickly (an option in several of the recipes in this section). Or you could just eat your cured foods in moderation — like everything else.

Curing

Curing is a transformative process by which raw meat is changed in color, texture, and flavor with the addition of salt and sometimes sugar. Traditionally, the salt was bought in pellets, called corns, so curing is often called corning (think corned beef). Basically there are two types of curing: dry and wet. With dry curing, the salt mixture is applied directly to the meat; with wet curing (also called brining or pickling), the meat is submerged in salt solution.

Ingredients for Curing Meat

Salt by itself is capable of fully curing meat only at very high concentrations. In previous centuries, salt-cured foods would have to be soaked in several changes of water over the course of a day or more before they would be considered palatable; this is still the case with salt cod. About 200 years ago, people found that saltpeter (potassium nitrate) could enhance the color of cured meat while preventing the growth of harmful bacteria and could be used in much lower concentrations than other types of salt could. Later it was shown that nitrates are converted to nitrites by harmless bacteria, and that nitrite was the active ingredient in the curing process. This has led to numerous cure recipes that combine both salt and nitrates and/or nitrites. Sugar is also added to many cures, as are spices.

Meat

Most of the meat that comes into the kitchen will go straight into the freezer. Let's be clear: the curing covered in this chapter is more about adding flavor and less about preservation. You can defrost any meat when it is convenient for you and then cure it. (Yes, the meat has to be fully thawed before you start to cure because the cure cannot penetrate frozen meat.)

Although all meats can be cured, not all are improved by it. Chicken, turkey, fish, and pork generally do benefit from brining or dry curing. The Jewish deli tradition is based on curing beef, both lean and fatty cuts. Both high-fat (salmon) and low-fat (cod) fish are sometimes cured. Duck and goose breasts are often cured to make a prosciutto-like product, though not a particularly traditional product. As far as I can tell, there is no tradition for curing lamb, beyond a few sausages, such as merguez. However, a friend whose grandfather grew up in Ireland told me that his grandfather remembers eating corned mutton, which was the only way mutton could be made palatable. (He finds the whole American tradition of corned beef and cabbage on St. Patrick's Day to be laughable; no one could afford beef in Ireland, he says.)

You don't have to stick with any particular cut of meat. For example, although corned beef is traditionally made with brisket, you can corn a bottom roast, which will give you a less fatty meat that is still delicious on sandwiches (though a little tougher). The same cure used for pork belly to make bacon can be applied to pork jowls to make guanciale; it can also be applied to pork loin to make Canadian bacon. Although guanciale "should" be air-dried and Canadian bacon "should" be smoked, both can be roasted, just as the bacon is roasted.

Kosher Salt

Salt (sodium chloride) inhibits bacterial growth, tenderizes meats, and adds flavor. Most recipes have been formulated to use kosher salt, so that is the salt you should use. Keep in mind that 1 cup of salt may deliver more or less salt depending on the size of the individual grains. For example, 1 cup of Morton's kosher salt contains about 8 ounces of salt, while 1 cup of Diamond Crystal kosher salt, which is much coarser, contains only about 5.5 ounces. (A cup of regular table salt weighs about 10 ounces.) My recipes are based on using Morton's kosher salt.

Any food that will be served cooked, like corned beef, bacon, and salt pork, can be preserved with salt alone (or salt plus spices) in the refrigerator. You can avoid the nitrates, if you prefer. However, without the curing salts (nitrites), the meat will be an unattractive gray color and will taste more pickled than cured.

Never reduce the amount of salt you use in a meat-curing recipe! Reducing the salt concentration can allow harmful bacterial growth. If the cure is too salty for your taste, it is better to reduce the time of salt exposure or to rinse the meat well before cooking.

Curing Salts (Sodium Nitrate and Sodium Nitrite)

Nitrites inhibit bacterial growth (especially *C. botulinum*) and prevent fats from going rancid; they add both color (pink or red) and flavor to meat. In the United States, though not in Europe, saltpeter (potassium nitrate), which is also used in explosives and fertilizers, has been replaced by nitrites for fast cures and nitrates for slow

As Mark Kurlansky has shown in his fascinating book *Salt*, the history of the world can be told through salt, given how salt transformed food supplies and given the wars that were fought over it. Cod, which was salted and then air-dried in cool northern Europe, was a civilization-changing product, because it was an abundant food that allowed for wide travel, which in turn allowed for long-voyage exploration.

cures because saltpeter yields inconsistent results. Although not absolutely essential for cured meats that will be cooked (such as corned beef and bacon), nitrates or nitrites are needed for raw-cured products, such as dry pepperoni, dry salami, sopressata, and dry coppa.

Curing salts are dyed pink so that they are never mistaken for table salt. You will probably need to order curing salts online. Never substitute pink curing salt for any other type of salt. And keep it away from children.

You'll usually find curing salt in one of two types:
> **Pink salt #1.** Also known as InstaCure No. 1 (formerly Prague Powder #1), DQ Curing Salt, and tinted curing mix (TCM). Use pink salt #1 only in products that you will cook before eating, such as corned beef and bacon. This is used for a "fast" cure and contains 93.75 percent table salt blended with 6.25 percent sodium nitrite.

> **Curing salt #2.** Curing salt #2 is a "slow" cure that contains sodium nitrate in addition to sodium nitrite. It may or may not be pink. Curing salt #2 (also called Prague Powder #2) is used only for making raw-cured products that are dry-aged for long periods and will not be smoked, canned, cooked, or refrigerated. Curing salt #2 is not interchangeable with pink salt #1. Never use curing salt #2 in brine or substitute it for any other type of salt. (This chapter does not contain any recipes that use curing salt #2.)

Sweeteners

Sugar is often used in both wet and dry curing to reduce the harshness of salt. It generally results in a softer texture, depending on how much is used. It also helps brown the meat during cooking. The type is not important; feel free to use white sugar, brown sugar, honey, maple syrup, or apple cider syrup (page 82).

Acid

In some cures, an acid is added in the form of ascorbic acid (vitamin C), vinegar, or wine. Acids act as cure accelerators (they accelerate color formation by nitrites); they may also have antibacterial activity. Acids also add flavor.

Herbs and Spices

Herbs and spices add flavoring. They can be varied in a recipe if you prefer. If you are planning to do a lot of meat curing or sausage making, you may want to invest in a spice grinder so that you can buy your spices whole and grind as needed. The spices most commonly used in cured meats are black and white pepper, paprika (plain and smoked), nutmeg, mace, cloves, ginger, cinnamon, cardamom, chiles, coriander, and cumin.

Equipment for Curing

For the curing recipes in this book, the only extra pieces of equipment you might need are large containers to hold the meat being cured or brined. A 5-gallon stockpot is large enough for most large pieces of meat you might be curing or brining. The first time I brined a brisket, I slipped it into a jumbo-size plastic bag, not anticipating that the meat would give off gas as it brined. The bag didn't explode in the fridge, but I think I was really pushing my luck, and I've never used a bag again.

Dry Curing

Dry curing has been performed the same way since the Middle Ages. Meat is covered in a mixture of salt and nitrates or nitrites, and often with spices and sweeteners for flavor. The salt and nitrate cure is rubbed directly onto the surface of the meat or mixed into the meat. The method differs today only by the degree with which we control for temperature. Dry curing is best for all types of sausages, bacon, and hams that will be air-dried. In some cases, after curing, the meat will be cold-smoked, then air-dried; in other cases, as with the recipe for bacon (page 253), it can be either hot-smoked or cooked.

Gravlax (page 252) is dry-cured salmon. Bacon is frequently dry-cured, then smoked, but you can bake it instead. Homemade bacon, even without smoking, is delicious, simple, and well worth trying.

There are a few basic rules for applying a dry cure:

➤ For cures of 14 days or less: use pink salt #1, at the standard limit of 1 teaspoon pink salt for 5 pounds of meat.
➤ For cures longer than 14 days: use pink salt #2, using 2 ounces pink salt, 12 ounces kosher salt, 5 ounces sugar, plus seasonings for 25 pounds of meat.
➤ Cure for 2 days per pound for the small cuts and 3 days per pound for hams and shoulders.

The Best Way to Cook Bacon

If you want to save your bacon grease for cooking, it is important to avoid burning it. The best way to avoid scorching the grease is to bake the bacon. Here are the steps:

1. Line a baking sheet with metal racks.

2. Arrange the bacon slices on the metal racks and place the baking sheet on the center rack of a cold oven. Turn the oven on to 400°F (200°C).

3. The bacon is done when it is golden brown and crisp, after 20 to 35 minutes, depending on the thickness of the bacon slices and how quickly your oven reaches the target temperature.

4. Transfer the bacon to another sheet pan lined with paper towels to absorb any excess fat.

5. Pour the hot bacon grease through a strainer lined with a coffee filter into a glass jar. Keep the bacon fat refrigerated.

Gravlax

Serves 16 to 24

Making gravlax is a great introduction to the world of curing. Once you see how easy it is to transform a slab of raw salmon into gravlax, you may think about curing with less trepidation. Gravlax is a Swedish specialty of cured salmon flavored with dill. It's the perfect homemade alternative to lox for your next bagel brunch. The cure of salt and sugar causes a chemical reaction that "cooks" the fish. It's very, very easy to make and cures for only 24 hours. Start with fresh, high-quality fish.

INGREDIENTS

1 cup Morton's kosher salt

1 cup white or brown sugar

2 tablespoons cracked black peppercorns

2- to 3-pound fresh salmon fillet (preferably a thick center piece, with skin on)

3 bunches fresh dill, stems included, plus more for a garnish

Capers and lemon slices, to serve

1. Mix the salt, sugar, and cracked pepper in a small bowl. Place the salmon in a large glass or ceramic baking dish. (You may need to cut the salmon into large pieces to fit — the larger the better.) Rub a handful of the cure on both sides of the salmon. Turn the salmon skin-side down in the dish, and sprinkle the rest of the mix on top.

2. Spread the dill over the salmon. Cover with plastic wrap placed directly on the flesh of the fish, not stretched over the pan. Set a flat-bottomed "press" — another baking dish or a piece of wood that's smaller than the original dish — over the fish. Place something heavy (several filled cans will do) on top of the press to weight it down so that it presses the fish.

3. Refrigerate for 24 hours.

4. To serve, remove the salmon from the dish and brush off the cure mixture and dill. Place the salmon skin-side down on a clean cutting board. Using the longest, sharpest knife you have, slice it against the grain, into the thinnest possible slices, cutting the salmon off the skin and sliding the knife to remove the fish from the skin. (This is the only part that is hard; a sharp knife is essential.) Taste a slice. If it is too salty, rinse the salmon under cold running water and pat dry before continuing to slice. Arrange the gravlax on a platter and garnish with capers, lemon slices, and fresh dill sprigs.

If you aren't serving all of the gravlax immediately, you can cut the fillet into smaller, more manageable pieces and wrap each piece tightly in plastic wrap. Gravlax keeps up to 6 days in the refrigerator or up to 2 months in the freezer.

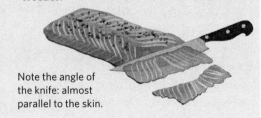

Note the angle of the knife: almost parallel to the skin.

Home-Cured Bacon

Makes about 2¼ pounds

Home-cured bacon is a revelation. Its freshness is what gives it that extra quality, which you won't find even in artisan bacons you might buy. This recipe, which is adapted from Michael Ruhlman and Brian Polcyn's excellent book *Charcuterie*, requires the use of pink salt #1. You can get by with regular salt, but the bacon will look like well-cooked pork (grayish), will taste more like salty pork than like bacon, and will last only a week in the fridge. Instead of roasting the bacon, you can smoke it or hang it to dry in the refrigerator, in which case you will end up with something like Italian-style bacon, or pancetta (but not with the seasonings below). You can easily double this recipe and freeze whatever you won't eat within 2 weeks. But the recipe is so easy, I have no problem working in small batches — and besides, there is so much you can do with a pork belly that it is hard to turn it all into bacon.

INGREDIENTS

- 2 tablespoons Morton's kosher salt
- 1 teaspoon pink salt #1
- 2 tablespoons coarsely ground black pepper
- 1¼ teaspoons Chinese five-spice powder (optional; or substitute other sweet spices, such as cinnamon, coriander, mace, cardamom, allspice)
- 2 tablespoons honey, maple syrup, brown sugar, or apple cider syrup (page 82)
- 3 garlic cloves, minced
- 2½-pound piece pork belly, trimmed to a square or rectangle

1. In a small bowl, mix together the kosher salt, pink salt #1, black pepper, five-spice powder, sweetener, and garlic.

2. Put the pork belly in a gallon-size resealable plastic bag or on a sheet pan or in a plastic container. Rub the salt and spice mixture all over the belly. Close the bag or cover the meat with plastic wrap and refrigerate for 7 days, turning it over and rubbing the spices into the meat midway through the week.

3. Preheat the oven to 200°F (95°C). Remove the bacon from the refrigerator, rinse off all the seasonings under cold water, and pat it dry. Put the meat on a wire rack on a sheet pan.

4. Roast for about 90 minutes, until the meat reaches an internal temperature of 150°F (66°C).

5. Cool to room temperature, then refrigerate it until you're ready to cook it.

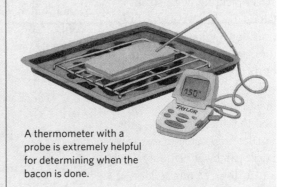

A thermometer with a probe is extremely helpful for determining when the bacon is done.

Salt Pork

Cuisines are shaped by the fats they use in cooking. Think of olive oil in Italy, butter in France, yak butter in Tibet, schmaltz in Jewish cooking. The fat that shaped the cuisine of much of the United States was salt pork; it was especially heavily used in the South, where it was called white bacon or streak of lean.

Salt pork is salted and cured pork fat. Traditionally, it was made from the trimmings after the belly was squared for making bacon and from any back fat and other trimmings. Though you often see salt pork recipes today made with pork belly, I think pork belly is too delicious to waste on salt pork. So ask your butcher for some or all of the trimmings that would normally go into ground pork, and turn those bits and pieces into salt pork instead.

INGREDIENTS

2 tablespoons Morton's kosher salt

1 teaspoon pink salt #1

2½ pounds fatty pork trimmings or fatback

1. In a small bowl, mix together the kosher salt and pink salt #1.

2. Put the pork in a large gallon-size zip-lock bag or in a plastic tub with a lid. Rub the salt mixture all over the pork. Close the bag or cover the meat with the lid and refrigerate for 7 days, turning the fat over and rubbing the salt into it midway through the week.

3. Use immediately or freeze and use within a couple of months. Salt pork picks up freezer odors easily, so make sure each piece is well wrapped.

Wet Curing

Wet curing, sometimes called brining (with salt and water), sweet pickling (with sugar added), or immersion curing, traditionally has been used for larger cuts of meat like butts or hams that were then smoked. With a wet cure, the meat is immersed in a solution that includes water, salt, nitrites, and sometimes sugar. Sugar can be added only if you are curing in a refrigerator; at warm temperatures the sugar may promote fermentation, which will spoil the meat.

Wet curing is tricky with large pieces of meat because there is a danger of meat spoiling from within the center, but it is fine to try with smaller cuts that require only 3 to 14 days of curing at 40°F (4°C). (There are various ways to get around this, but they are beyond our scope here.)

Meats in a wet cure should be turned over daily and weighted down to keep them from floating up to the surface. After curing is complete, the meat should be rinsed in fresh water and placed on wire mesh for draining. The next step is usually smoking, but the meat can be cooked instead, as with the corned beef recipe that follows.

Home-Cured Corned Beef

Serves 8 to 10

Once again, the pink salt is optional but recommended for color and flavor. Although brisket is the traditional cut, other cuts can be used with this brine. If you are using grain-fed beef, the flat-cut or first-cut brisket is preferable, but I find it too lean when it is from grass-feed beef; then I prefer the second, or point, cut. For a recipe for a traditional New England boiled dinner, making good use of the corned beef, see page 315.

INGREDIENTS

- 4 quarts water
- 1½ cups Morton kosher salt
- ½ cup sugar
- 4 teaspoons pink salt #1 (optional)
- 3 garlic cloves, minced
- 4 tablespoons pickling spice
- 1 (5-pound) beef brisket

1. In a container large enough to hold the brisket, combine 2 quarts of the water with the kosher salt, sugar, pink salt #1 (if using), garlic, and pickling spice. Bring to a simmer, stirring until the salt and sugar are dissolved. Remove from the heat. Add the remaining 2 quarts water and let cool to room temperature; then refrigerate until chilled.

2. Put the brisket in the brine, weight it down with a plate to keep it submerged, and cover. Refrigerate for at least 7 days, turning it daily.

3. If you are not ready to cook the corned beef, it can be held in the brine in the refrigerator for another 2 weeks. You can also freeze the corned beef.

A plate keeps the meat submerged in the brine.

Cooking with Cured Meats

In general, meats that have been cured should be rinsed well with fresh cold water before cooking. Brined meats may or not need to be rinsed; follow the recipe directions. If you don't rinse, you should pat dry the surface of the meat with paper towels before cooking.

Making Sausage

The craft of sausage making evolved as a way to utilize all those scraps of meat and fat that remained after butchering an animal — which is another reason to ask for all the trimmings from your butcher. People can spend a lifetime improving their sausage-making skills. On the low end in terms of equipment and skills is fresh sausage, a blend of ground-up meat, fat, and seasonings placed inside a casing or just left loose. On the high end in terms of equipment and skills are dried, cured sausages, what the Italians call *salumi* and the French call *charcuterie*.

Types of Sausage

Sausage can be made from any type of meat, but there are basically four kinds sausage:

> **Fresh sausage.** This category includes any sausage

made with seasoned raw ground meat, from spicy Mexican chorizo (made with pork) to North African merguez (made with lamb). Fresh sausages can be stuffed into casings or left loose. To cook, fresh sausages can be pan-seared, sautéed, or grilled. When cooking fresh sausage, remove the meat from the casings or prick the casings to release moisture to prevent the casings from splitting. Cook until no pink remains; always serve fresh sausage well done (160°F/71°C) because the process of grinding the meat exposes it to airborne bacteria.

> **German-style sausage.** These sausages are often made with cured blended meats (hence the pink color and smooth texture). They are always stuffed into casings. Bologna and hot dogs are examples. Most German sausages are precooked, but pan-searing and grilling boost their flavor.

> **Smoked sausage.** These sausages are either cold-smoked and not fully cooked or hot-smoked and fully cooked by the smoking process. Examples of fully cooked smoked sausage are andouille and kielbasa. Smoked sausage is often cut up and added to dishes as a flavoring.

> **Cured sausage.** Cured sausages are made from fresh meat that is salted (with nitrates) and then air-dried for weeks or months depending on the type. Spanish chorizo, coppa, and Genoa salami are just a few examples of cured sausages. Sometimes the meat is cultured with a specific bacterial culture, which increases the acid content of the meat and allows it to keep without refrigeration. The temperature and humidity at which the sausages are cured need to be controlled.

Ingredients

All sausage contains ground-up meat, fat, and seasonings. The meat can be of any kind, but a high-fat cut such as pork shoulder or butt or picnic ham is desirable. Additional fat, such as back fat, is often needed. In the case of fresh pork sausages, the pork shoulder butt is usually recommended, but this cut is also perfect for barbecue and for slow braises, so you may not want to use it for sausage. An alternative is to have the butcher make 75 to 80 percent lean ground pork from all the trimmings. You can use the ground meat for the sausages and just skip the grinding. By the way, 20 percent fat is much leaner than most commercial sausages.

All sausage recipes will require salt, and some will require curing salt (see page 250). When you get into smoked and air-dried sausage, you will also need powdered protein concentrates (soy or milk), a starter culture of bacteria to ferment the meat, and dextrose (a type of sugar that is ideal for the starter culture bacteria to feed on). Fresh sausages often require vinegar or wine. The acid helps preserve the meat, but it also gives the sausages the pickled flavor that comes from aging. The recipes in this book are for fresh sausages only.

If you want to make links and have the equipment to stuff them, you will also need sausage casings. Casings come in various sizes and from natural sources (animal intestines) or synthetic ones. The natural casings are packed either in dry salt or a salt brine and are sold by diameter and length. Generally, the packaging also includes how many pounds of sausage a particular diameter and length of casing will hold. Stored in the refrigerator, casings will keep for at least a year.

Equipment for Making Sausage

You can get started with sausage making with ground meat from the butcher, in which case all you will need is a mixing bowl and a scale. However, if you want to go further and make stuffed sausage, you will also need the following:

> **Grinder.** This could be a stand mixer with meat-grinding attachment or a stand-alone meat grinder. The advantages of the stand mixer arrangement are that you may already have the mixer and that many grinder attachments also come with sausage stuffers.

Electric grinder

Stuffing attachments

Sausage stuffer

> **Food processor.** If you don't have a grinder or a grinder attachment, you can use a food processor. Before grinding, make sure the food processor bowl and blade are well chilled, that the meat is partially frozen (so the fat doesn't gum up the works), that you work in batches of no more than 1½ cups at a time, and that you use the pulsing action only. It takes me about 30 quick pulses to grind 1 cup of partially frozen meat, a tedious but effective process.

> **Sausage stuffer.** If you want to make links, you will need a stuffer that will extrude the sausage mix into the casings. There are extrusion attachments for stand mixers, stand-alone manual stuffers (about $50 and can often be found used for less), and hydraulic stuffers (very expensive).

Grinder attachment

Stand mixer

Stuffing attachments

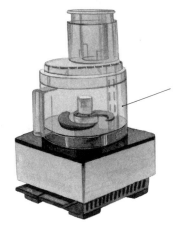

Food processor for grinding

Cleanliness is a priority when making sausage. Make sure you clean and sanitize all of your work surfaces and keep all your ingredients as cold as possible. When you are working with raw meat, you do not want to invite spoilage bacteria to enter into the process.

① **Prepare your equipment.** Line a large sheet pan with freezer paper and place in the freezer. Put the grinder and a couple of large bowls (including, preferably, a stand mixer bowl, with its paddle attachment) in the freezer. You will eventually need a third, larger bowl, big enough to hold one of the now-chilling bowls in ice. Check your ice supply.

Casings need washing.

If you are making links, prepare the sausage casing: Soak the casings for at least 30 minutes in cool water, then flush with cold running water to remove all traces of salt. Leave in a bowl of vinegar solution (1 tablespoon white vinegar to 1 cup water) to soften and render more transparent until you are ready for them.

② **Prepare the meat.** Chop the meat into ½-inch cubes and place in the freezer in one of the large bowls that is already chilling. Chop the fat into ½-inch pieces and add to the meat in the freezer bowl. Both meat and fat should be partially frozen to make cutting easier.

Partially freezing the meat makes it easier to chop and keeps the fat from gumming up the works.

③ **Prepare your seasoning mixture.** Seasonings make the sausage. Use fresh whole spices or chiles if you can; toast in a frying pan on the stove to bring out the flavors. Cool to room temperature; then grind.

④ **Combine the meat, fat, and seasoning.** Add the seasonings to the meat in the freezer bowl and toss to coat. Spread the meat mixture out on the lined sheet pan and return to the freezer until the meat is firm, about 30 minutes.

Keep everything well chilled.

⑤ **Grind and mix — and stop to taste.** Fill a large bowl with ice, and set the second freezer bowl into it. (If you are using a stand mixer bowl, this is the one to use here.) Grind the meat and fat into the bowl. Add the liquid called for in your recipe and mix well. (If you can, mix in the stand mixer with the paddle attachment until the mixture seems sticky.) Form a small amount into a patty and cook it until well browned throughout. Taste, then adjust the flavoring of the meat mixture as needed.

Cook a small patty of the meat mixture and be sure it tastes right before moving on to stuffing.

⑥ **Stuff (optional).** Return the meat to the freezer to chill for 30 minutes while you assemble your stuffer. Lubricate the end of the stuffer with a little oil. Slide one end of a piece of casing over the sausage funnel or over the attachment of the electric grinder. Tie the end of the casing in a knot. Push it along so that the entire piece of casing is on the funnel and the end of the casing is even with the funnel opening.

Remove as much air as possible from the sausage mix by gathering the mix in your hands and slamming it down on the counter. Pack the sausage meat tightly into the chute. Press down to push the meat through the funnel. You'll see the meat start to fill the casings. Pack the meat mixture well, and fully swell the casing. When the casing is filled and the sausage looks to be the length you want, twist the link seven times to start the next link. Fill the next sausage, and, when it's the length you want, twist in the opposite direction seven times. Continue until the casings are filled or the meat has run out. Check for air bubbles and prick the casings with a needle to release the air as needed.

Two people are needed for this: one to feed the meat into the stuffer and one to hold the casing as it fills and twist it into appropriate size lengths.

⑦ **Cook or store.** To cook, poach the links in water, then sauté or grill over very low heat until browned well on the outside and moist in the center. Cook until well done (160°F/71°C). Uncooked fresh sausage links will keep in the refrigerator for 3 days or in the freezer for 3 months.

Making Sausage Patties

An alternative to leaving fresh sausage loose or stuffing the meat into casings is to make patties, something that is particularly useful for breakfast sausage. Place a sheet of freezer paper on the counter, shiny-side up. Put the sausage mixture in the center of the paper and form into a log 4 to 5 inches in diameter. Fold the ends of the paper over the sausage and then roll the sides of the paper as tightly as you can around the log. Tape the package shut and freeze for about 1 hour. Remove the partially frozen log from the freezer, slice into patties, repackage, and freeze.

The Final Frontier: Curing Sausages

Dry-curing sausage is the most tricky and temperamental of the dry-cure preparations. You'll need to use a bacterial starter culture to ensure the meat is sufficiently acidic to keep spoilage at bay and sodium nitrate (curing salt #2) to prevent the specific bacteria that cause botulism. You'll also need to provide a curing environment of 60°F to 65°F (16°C to 18°C) and 70 percent humidity.

Bulk Hot or Sweet Italian Sausage

Makes about 3 pounds

Fennel seeds give this sausage its distinctive flavor. Dried red pepper flakes bring on the heat for the hot version; to make the sweet version, simply omit them. The sausage mix can be used to flavor a tomato sauce for pasta, as a layer in a lasagna, or mixed with ground pork or beef to make seasoned meatballs. You can also top a pizza with sausage; for pizza, package the sausage mix in ¼-pound packages.

INGREDIENTS

3 pounds boneless pork butt with fat (or 3 pounds ground pork containing 20 to 25 percent fat)

1 whole bulb garlic, minced

2 tablespoons pickling salt, canning salt, or fine sea salt

2 tablespoons fennel seeds

2 teaspoons dried oregano

1 teaspoon dried red pepper flakes (optional)

¼ cup dry red wine

1. Chill your equipment as explained in the step-by-step instructions for making fresh sausage (page 258). Line a sheet pan with freezer paper and set in the freezer to chill.

2. Chop the pork and fat into ½-inch cubes and place in a bowl in the freezer.

3. Combine the garlic, salt, fennel seeds, oregano, and pepper flakes (if using) in a small bowl. Add to the meat and toss to coat. Spread the meat mixture out on the lined sheet pan and return to the freezer until the meat is firm, about 35 minutes.

4. Grind the meat mixture into a bowl set over a larger bowl filled with ice. Add the wine and mix well. Form a small amount into a patty and cook it until well browned throughout. Taste and adjust the flavoring as needed.

5. Cook immediately, or divide into portions and refrigerate for up to 3 days or freeze for up to 3 months.

Bulk Fresh Mexican Chorizo Sausage

Makes about 3 pounds

Paprika gives this sausage its distinctive color, while chiles plus vinegar give the sausage its mildly hot and cured flavor. What I always appreciate about making a sausage such as this one is my ability to package it in the quantities I want. A half-pound package, for example, encourages me to use the meat as the flavoring for beans or as part of the sauce in a tortilla casserole.

INGREDIENTS

3 pounds boneless pork butt with fat (or 3 pounds ground pork, containing 20 to 25 percent fat)

3 New Mexico dried chiles

2 onions, quartered

1 whole bulb garlic, cloves separated and peeled

2 tablespoons pickling salt, canning salt, or fine sea salt

2 tablespoons sweet or hot paprika

2 teaspoons dried oregano, preferably Mexican oregano

2 teaspoons ground cumin

1 teaspoon ground cinnamon

½ cup apple cider vinegar

1. Chill your equipment as explained in the step-by-step instructions for making fresh sausage (page 258). Line a sheet pan with freezer paper and set in the freezer to chill.

2. Chop the pork and fat into ½-inch cubes and place in the freezer.

3. Toast the chiles: Heat a dry skillet over medium heat. Stem the chiles, tear into pieces, press against the bottom of the heated pan with a spatula or tongs, and then toast until fragrant and slightly colored, less than 1 minute. Cool to room temperature.

4. Combine the chiles, onions, and garlic in a food processor and chop until very finely minced. Transfer to a small bowl and mix in the salt, paprika, oregano, cumin, and cinnamon.

5. Add the seasoning to the meat in the bowl and toss to coat. Spread the meat mixture out on the lined sheet pan and return to the freezer until the meat is firm, about 30 minutes.

6. Grind the meat mixture into a bowl set over a larger bowl filled with ice. Add the vinegar and mix well. Form a small amount into a patty and cook it until well browned throughout. Taste and adjust the flavoring as needed.

7. Cook immediately, or divide into portions and refrigerate for up to 3 days or freeze for up to 3 months.

PART 3

Homestead Cooking

S ome folks like to follow recipes to the letter, while others prefer to take ideas from recipes and then improvise. The recipes in this section are designed to aid both types of people; they'll yield fine results if followed slavishly, but they also offer opportunities to switch ingredients around. Several of the vegetable and vegetarian dishes are meant to be adapted to whatever is being harvested. Chicken and rabbit can be used interchangeably in any of the recipes that call for either, as can goat and lamb; recipes for tough cuts of meat work equally well with well-exercised portions of beef and pork, and often lamb and goat. Desserts that require frozen fruits can be made with whatever you have in the freezer — peaches, nectarines, plums, or any of the various types of berries.

I do a lot of cooking from the garden, and many of my favorite vegetable recipes can be found in my earlier books (*Serving Up the Harvest* and *Recipes from the Root Cellar*), so the recipes here are an odd mix of this and that. "This and that" includes a few potato recipes that are essential side dishes to meat. You need to be able to make great French fries to accompany your grass-fed steaks, and those fries can be easily made in the oven, with goose or duck fat or beef fat (tallow) if you are so inclined. Mashed potatoes are another essential, as are flatbreads that you can whip up without much effort.

The dessert recipes focus on fruits and dairy foods. If I could grow chocolate beans, I would. But I can't, so I don't consider chocolate to be a true "homestead" flavor, and you'll find only one chocolate dessert here.

A Few Notes about the Recipes

- All eggs are assumed to be chicken eggs.

- If an ingredient has a page number in parentheses after it, it means that you will find directions for making it from scratch elsewhere in this book. If you need to work with store-bought ingredients, that's okay, too.

CHAPTER 17

Breakfast and Egg Dishes

Overnight Steel-Cut Oatmeal

Serves 8

What's important to know about this oatmeal is that you can make it once a week or so and enjoy a bowl whenever you want it (it reheats beautifully on the stovetop or in a microwave), making it the best instant breakfast I know of. We like our oatmeal chewy and pebbly, so I make it with about 3 cups of water for every 1 cup of steel-cut oats. If you want a creamier texture, closer to the texture of oatmeal made with rolled oats, use up to 4 cups of water for every cup of oats and stir while reheating. The flaxseeds contribute heart-healthy omega-3s; they add no flavor. I store them in the freezer and eyeball the amount to pour in; a little more or less won't make a difference. In the winter I add dried fruit, usually raisins, before heating my bowl. In the summer I add berries or diced fresh peaches after the oatmeal has been reheated. When my nieces come to visit, they top the oatmeal with granola for a little crunch.

INGREDIENTS

6–8 cups water

2 cups steel-cut oats

½ cup flaxseeds

2 teaspoons salt

Raisins, berries, or chopped fruit (optional)

Maple syrup, honey, or apple cider syrup (page 82), to serve

Milk, to serve

1. The night before serving, combine the water, oats, flaxseeds, and salt in a heavy saucepan and bring to a boil. Remove from the heat, cover, and let stand overnight.

2. In the morning, reheat in the pot, adding a little more water if needed (not too much — it gets looser as it heats). Or reheat individual servings in the microwave, adding dried fruit if desired. Leftovers can be stored in the refrigerator and reheated to serve.

3. Serve warm, passing chopped fresh fruit, sweetener, and milk on the side.

Vanilla Nut Granola

Makes about 8 cups

This is a crowd-pleasing granola. I add fresh fruit to individual bowls in the summer and raisins or chopped dried apples in the winter. The combination of apples and apple cider syrup makes it taste like I'm eating apple crisp for breakfast.

INGREDIENTS

2 cups uncooked rolled oats (not instant)

1¼ cups uncooked rolled barley or wheat flakes (or substitute more rolled oats)

1¼ cups sliced almonds

½ cup hulled pumpkin seeds

1 teaspoon salt

1 teaspoon ground cinnamon

¾ cup maple syrup, honey, or apple cider syrup (page 82)

½ cup coconut oil, sunflower oil, or canola oil

1 teaspoon vanilla extract

1. Preheat the oven to 300°F (150°C). Lightly oil a half-sheet pan or large shallow roasting pan, or line with parchment paper.

2. Combine the oats, barley, almonds, pumpkin seeds, salt, and cinnamon in a large bowl.

3. Combine the maple syrup with the coconut oil in a small bowl. Heat in the microwave for about 1 minute, or set the bowl in a small saucepan filled with hot water and heat gently for a few minutes. When the mixture is entirely liquid and warm to the touch, add the vanilla. Stir the liquid into the oat mixture. Mix well and spread evenly in the prepared pan.

4. Bake, stirring occasionally, for 40 to 45 minutes, until golden. Do not let the granola become dark. Stir occasionally during the final 15 minutes to avoid scorching at the sides of the pan.

5. Remove from the oven and run a spatula under the mixture so it doesn't stick to the pan, if you haven't used parchment paper. Allow to cool completely. Store in an airtight container.

Sourdough Pancakes

Serves 4

Sourdough makes incredibly light and tasty pancakes. They are so tasty, in fact, you might be tempted to forgo the maple syrup (which I used to think was the whole reason for pancakes). In order to take advantage of the yeast in your sourdough starter, remember to feed it the night before. Then the yeast will be active enough to give you that extra leavening. And, after feeding the starter, take some fruit out of the freezer, allow it to defrost overnight in the refrigerator, and enjoy it with the pancakes. As with all sourdough recipes, a little fiddling with the batter may be necessary to get the right consistency.

INGREDIENTS

SOURDOUGH

Sourdough starter (page 61)

1½ cups all-purpose or bread flour

1½ cups water

PANCAKES

3 eggs

6 tablespoons melted butter or bacon fat

3 tablespoons sugar

¾ teaspoon salt

1½ teaspoons baking soda

2 tablespoons warm water

Butter, for the griddle

All-purpose flour (if needed to thicken the batter)

1. At least 8 hours before you begin making the pancakes, feed the sourdough starter with the flour and water. Leave the sourdough on the counter; do not return it to the refrigerator. (This is one of the reasons your starter should be in a 2-quart jar; if the container is not big enough, you won't have room for the extra flour and water.)

2. When you are ready to make the pancakes, pour 3 cups of the sourdough starter into a large bowl and return the rest to the refrigerator. You do not have to feed it at this time because you already did that. Add the eggs, melted butter, sugar, and salt to the sourdough; mix well and set aside.

3. Dissolve the baking soda in the warm water in a small bowl; set aside.

4. Preheat the oven to 200°F (95°C) and set a plate or baking sheet in the warm oven. Preheat the griddle over medium heat.

5. Fold the baking soda mixture gently into the prepared pancake batter (do not beat). This will cause a gentle foaming and rising action in the batter. Let the mixture bubble and foam a minute or two. The batter should have the consistency of very heavy cream. If it seems thin, add a little flour, a tablespoon at a time. Don't add a lot; you can adjust after making the first pancake.

6. Melt a little butter on the griddle and spread it around. Pour 2 to 3 tablespoons of batter onto the hot griddle for the first pancake. It should spread nicely but not run over the whole griddle. Cook for about 2 minutes, or until bubbles appear on the surface and the edges appear dry. Flip and cook on the other side until done. Transfer to the oven to keep warm.

7. Repeat, adding more flour to the batter if you think it really needs it (the less flour, the lighter the pancakes). Serve warm.

Sourdough Waffles

Serves 4

These waffles can be enjoyed with a variety of toppings, including savory ones. But if you are going savory, don't add the sugar to the batter. Remember to feed the starter the night before — or in the morning if you are going to serve the waffles for dinner, which I frequently do. As with all sourdough recipes, a little fiddling with the batter may be necessary to get the right consistency; in the case of waffles, a thicker batter is better than a thin one. Waffle irons vary considerably in size and in interior coating. If the manufacturer's instructions for using your waffle iron vary from mine, follow the manufacturer's.

INGREDIENTS

SOURDOUGH

Sourdough starter (page 61)

1½ cups all-purpose or bread flour

1½ cups water

WAFFLES

3 eggs

¾ cup melted butter or bacon fat

3 tablespoons sugar

¾ teaspoon salt

1½ teaspoons baking soda

2 tablespoons warm water

All-purpose flour (if needed to thicken the batter)

1. At least 8 hours before you begin making the waffles, feed the sourdough starter with the flour and water. Leave the sourdough on the counter; do not return it to the refrigerator. (This is one of the reasons to keep your starter in a 2-quart jar; if the container is not big enough, you won't have room for the extra flour and water.)

2. When you are ready to make the waffles, pour 3 cups of the sourdough starter into a large bowl and return the rest to the refrigerator. You do not have to feed it at this time because you already did that. Add the eggs, melted butter, sugar, and salt; mix well and set aside.

3. Dissolve the baking soda in the warm water in a small bowl; set aside.

4. Preheat the oven to 200°F (95°C) and set a baking sheet topped with a wire rack in the oven. Preheat the waffle iron.

5. Fold the baking soda mixture gently into the prepared waffle batter (do not beat). This will cause a gentle foaming and rising action in the batter. Let the mixture bubble and foam a minute or two. The batter should have the consistency of very heavy cream. If it seems thin, add a little flour, a tablespoon at a time. Don't add a lot; you can adjust after pouring the first waffle.

6. Lightly spray the grid of your waffle iron with nonstick cooking spray. Pour in enough batter to fill most of the grid of your waffle iron; my standard square waffle iron takes about 1 cup of batter to make four 4-inch waffles. Bake on medium-high to high heat until you no longer see steam escaping from the waffle iron; my waffle iron makes a batch in 4 minutes.

7. Continue making waffles until all the batter is used. Serve at once for best texture, or keep warm in the oven. The waffles will soften in the oven.

Tea Eggs

Makes 12

Ever arrive at a potluck with the third plate of deviled eggs? It happens often in the spring. But it is a rare event that draws these Chinese tea eggs, hard-cooked eggs marbled with a black tea/soy sauce infusion throughout the whites. These are as tasty as they are beautiful. The eggs need to infuse in the soy solution overnight. Although drizzling the peeled eggs with soy sauce and sesame oil makes these too sloppy to eat as finger food, the drizzle is essential for bringing all the flavors together.

INGREDIENTS

12 eggs

4 cups water

2 tablespoons black tea leaves

½ cup dark soy sauce

¼ cup light soy sauce, plus more to serve

1 tablespoon five-spice powder

1 tablespoon honey

Asian sesame oil, to serve

1. Put the eggs in a saucepan and cover with cold water. Bring the water to a boil, remove the pan from the heat, cover, and let the eggs cook in the hot water for 8 minutes. Immediately pour out the water and leave the eggs under cold running water until completely cooled.

2. Meanwhile, combine the water, black tea, dark soy sauce, light soy sauce, five-spice powder, and honey in a saucepan just large enough to hold the eggs in a single layer. Bring to a boil, then remove from the heat.

3. Roll the eggs against a countertop to crack them all over (but do not peel). Add the eggs to the black tea/soy sauce infusion and let cool to room temperature. Then refrigerate overnight, still in the infusion.

4. To serve, remove the shells and cut the eggs into quarters or halves. Drizzle with the soy sauce infusion and sesame oil.

Shakshuka

Serves 4 to 6

Here's an egg dish widespread throughout North Africa and the Middle East. It's claimed by Israel, Lebanon, Morocco, Palestine, Syria, Tunisia, and Turkey, so you can get away with any variation and call it authentic. Me, I like to make it into a supper dish with the addition of whatever vegetables I have on hand. If you prefer, skip the veggies and serve it for breakfast. Whenever you serve it, accompany it with bread to mop up the sauce. Use a skillet large enough for the number of eggs you will be cooking on top of the sauce.

INGREDIENTS

3 tablespoons extra-virgin olive oil

1 teaspoon ground cumin

1 teaspoon pimenton (smoked Spanish paprika)

¼ teaspoon ground cinnamon

¼ teaspoon dried red pepper flakes, or more to taste

1 small onion, diced

1 red or green bell pepper, diced (optional)

3 garlic cloves, minced

3 cups canned or fresh diced tomatoes

2 tablespoons tomato paste

Pinch of sugar (optional)

Salt and freshly ground black pepper

4 cups chopped fresh spinach or Swiss chard, or 2 cups sliced zucchini or mushrooms, or 2 cups frozen vegetables, such as chopped green beans, or 2 cups cooked and drained chickpeas

4–8 eggs

1 tablespoon chopped fresh cilantro

1 tablespoon chopped fresh mint

1 tablespoon chopped fresh parsley

1. Heat the oil in a large skillet over medium heat. Add the cumin, pimenton, cinnamon, and pepper flakes, and sauté until fragrant, about 30 seconds. Add the onion, bell pepper (if using), and garlic, and sauté until softened, about 3 minutes.

2. Stir in the tomatoes and tomato paste. Taste and add sugar, if needed, and salt and pepper. Simmer over medium heat for 20 minutes, until the liquid starts to reduce and thicken.

3. Stir in the vegetables and cook until tender, about 5 minutes.

4. Crack the eggs onto the mixture all around the skillet in a single layer. Cover and simmer for 6 to 8 minutes, until the eggs are done to your liking. Sprinkle with the cilantro, mint, and parsley. Serve immediately.

Eggs Florentine

Serves 4

Many versions of eggs Florentine call for a hollandaise sauce or Mornay sauce (cheese sauce), both of which are quite rich, but this version is lighter and easier. The sauce is nothing more than half-and-half or cream, flavored with Parmesan cheese. Serve with toast and oven-baked fries (page 279) for a fast and easy brunch, lunch, or light supper. Add home-cured bacon (page 253) and you have a feast!

INGREDIENTS

1½ pounds fresh spinach or 1 pound frozen

2 tablespoons extra-virgin olive oil, butter, poultry fat, lard, or tallow

1 shallot, minced

2 garlic cloves, minced

Salt and freshly ground black pepper

½ cup half-and-half or cream

8 eggs

½ cup freshly grated Parmesan cheese

1. If you are using fresh spinach, blanch the spinach in a large pot of salted water until wilted, 1 minute. Drain well. Squeeze to remove any excess water. Coarsely chop. If you are using frozen spinach, thaw and drain well; squeeze to remove any excess water.

2. Heat the oil in a large skillet over medium heat. Add the shallot and garlic and sauté until translucent, about 3 minutes. Stir in the spinach, season with salt and pepper, and cook until the spinach is warmed through, about 3 minutes. Stir in the half-and-half and set aside over low heat.

3. Poach the eggs in barely simmering water for 3 minutes. Remove with a slotted spoon and set on paper towels to drain. (For full details on poaching eggs, see page 87.)

4. Stir the Parmesan into the spinach and taste for seasoning. Spoon the creamed spinach into four individual gratin dishes or pasta bowls, top with the eggs, and serve.

Spaghetti Carbonara

Serves 4 to 6

I'm calling this an egg dish because it is the egg that makes the sauce. This is a rich dish, and simple to make, but it cries out for vegetable side dishes. In fact, without veggies to fill you up, you might be tempted to eat more than your fair share; it is that good. If you have neither salt pork nor pancetta, you can substitute fresh pork belly (or bacon that is less aggressively seasoned than mine on page 253). Timing is everything here: make sure the spaghetti is hot when it is tossed with the eggs because it is the residual heat of the pasta that cooks the eggs and makes the sauce.

INGREDIENTS

4 eggs plus 2 egg yolks

2 cups very finely grated Parmesan cheese

Freshly ground black pepper

8 ounces salt pork (page 254) or pancetta, diced

4 garlic cloves, minced

½ cup dry white wine

1 pound spaghetti

¼ cup chopped fresh parsley (optional)

1. Bring a large pot of salted water to a boil.

2. Beat the eggs and egg yolks in a bowl. Stir in 1 cup of the Parmesan. Season generously with pepper and set aside.

3. While the water heats, heat a very large skillet or Dutch oven over medium heat, add the salt pork, and cook until it renders its fat, about 8 minutes. Add the garlic and continue to sauté until the salt pork is crisp and the garlic is fragrant, 2 minutes more. Do not let the garlic scorch.

4. Pour the wine into the skillet and stir to deglaze the skillet, scraping up browned bits from the bottom with a wooden spoon. Remove the skillet from the heat, but keep it warm.

5. Add the spaghetti to the boiling water and cook until al dente, according to the package directions. When the spaghetti is almost done, return the skillet to low heat.

6. Drain the pasta and add to the skillet. Immediately pour in the egg mixture and toss over low heat until the spaghetti is coated with a thick yellow coating. Sprinkle with parsley (if using) and serve with the remaining cheese on the side.

Mushroom Egg Foo Yong

Serves 3 to 4

No claims to authenticity here; this dish probably has its origin in the 1930s, from a Chinese cook preparing food for Americans. It makes a great supper that can be ready in the time it takes to cook white rice. My version here uses fresh mushrooms, but you could swap finely chopped meat, poultry, or shrimp for the mushrooms, if you prefer. Don't have fresh mushrooms on hand? Substitute 2 ounces dried mushrooms that have been soaked in hot water for 10 minutes (but if you have the time, shiitakes really benefit from a cold-water soak for 2 to 8 hours). Serve with hot rice.

INGREDIENTS

FILLING

- 12 ounces mushrooms (if possible, include some fresh shiitakes), trimmed and chopped
- 4 tablespoons soy sauce
- 2 tablespoons Chinese oyster sauce
- 2 tablespoons Chinese rice wine
- 1 tablespoon Asian sesame oil
- 1 tablespoon sugar
- 2 garlic cloves, minced
- 1 teaspoon minced fresh ginger

SAUCE

- 1 cup poultry stock (page 107), brown stock (page 142), or vegetable stock (page 37)
- 2 tablespoons Chinese oyster sauce
- 1 tablespoon soy sauce
- 1 tablespoon Chinese rice wine
- 2 garlic cloves, minced
- 1 tablespoon cornstarch dissolved in 4 tablespoons water

EGG PANCAKE

- 6 eggs, beaten
- 1 teaspoon soy sauce
- ¼ teaspoon freshly ground black pepper
- 4 scallions, green and white parts separated, thinly sliced on the diagonal
- 1 cup bean sprouts or pea shoots
- 2 tablespoons peanut or other vegetable oil

1. To prepare the filling, combine the mushrooms, soy sauce, oyster sauce, rice wine, sesame oil, sugar, garlic, and ginger. Set aside to marinate.

2. To make the sauce, combine the stock, oyster sauce, soy sauce, rice wine, and garlic in a small saucepan. Bring to a boil, whisk in the cornstarch mixture, and continue to boil until the sauce thickens and clears, about 1 minute. Set aside to keep warm.

3. To prepare the pancake, beat the eggs with a fork until well blended. Add the soy sauce, the black pepper, and the white parts of the scallions (reserving the green parts for a garnish).

4. Heat the oil in a large skillet over medium-high heat. Add the filling mixture and sauté until the mushrooms have given off their liquid, about 5 minutes. Add the egg mixture, then immediately lower the heat to medium. Continue to cook the eggs over medium heat, using the turner to gently lift the edges so the uncooked egg can run under and cook.

Continue to cook for 4 to 5 minutes, or until the eggs start to look firm. Then turn the heat to low, cover, and continue to cook until the eggs are set, 2 to 3 minutes more.

5. When the eggs are cooked, remove the pan from the heat, put a dinner plate over the top of the pan, and invert the pan so that the pancake is centered on the plate. Top with the bean sprouts. Pour the sauce over the pancake, sprinkle with the green parts of the scallions, and serve.

CHAPTER 18

Vegetable, Cheese, and Bean Dishes

Tomato-Vegetable Soup

Serves 4 to 6

This soup is a good one for using up odds and ends of fresh or frozen vegetables. Homemade stock of any kind brings even more flavor and richness to the table, but any canned or boxed broth or stock can be used. This soup can be made in large batches and frozen.

INGREDIENTS

- 3 tablespoons extra-virgin olive oil
- 1 onion, diced
- 1 celery root or 2 ribs celery, diced
- 1 carrot, diced
- 4 garlic cloves, minced
- 6 cups vegetable stock (page 37) or poultry stock (page 107)
- 4 cups canned or frozen crushed tomatoes or tomato purée
- 2 cups mixed chopped or sliced fresh or frozen vegetables (carrots, corn, green beans, parsnips, peas, rutabagas, etc.)
- 1½ cups cooked or canned cannellini beans
- 2 teaspoons dried basil or 1 tablespoon chopped fresh or frozen
- 2 teaspoons dried oregano or 1 tablespoon chopped fresh
- 2 teaspoons dried thyme or 1 tablespoon chopped fresh
- 1 teaspoon fresh or dried rosemary
- 2 cups thinly sliced cabbage, collards, kale, mustard greens, spinach, Swiss chard, turnip greens (remove tough stems from greens before slicing, as needed)
- Salt and freshly ground black pepper

1. Heat the oil in a large soup pot over medium heat. Add the onion, celery root, carrot, and garlic, and sauté for 3 minutes, until the vegetables are slightly tender. Add the stock, tomatoes, chopped vegetables, cannellini beans, basil, oregano, thyme, and rosemary. Bring to a boil, then reduce the heat and simmer for about 30 minutes.

2. Return the soup to boiling. Add the greens and boil gently until the greens are tender, 5 to 15 minutes, depending on the greens. Season with salt and pepper to taste. Serve hot.

Gazpacho

Serves 6

If you haven't whipped up a batch of gazpacho once during the summer, then you haven't done your due diligence as a cook who makes the best of what the garden has to offer. It mystifies me why most gazpacho recipes call for tomato juice without giving the recipe for making the tomato juice in the first place. Why add a commercial juice to your fresh, fresh vegetables? Start this early in the day, or even the day before, so that your homemade tomato juice is icy cold. Then enjoy one of the best dishes of summer vegetables your garden produces.

INGREDIENTS

6 pounds tomatoes, preferably paste tomatoes

Salt

4 garlic cloves

1 large red onion or sweet onion

6 pickling cucumbers or 24 inches of any thin-skinned long (Asian or Middle Eastern) cucumbers

2 red bell peppers, seeded

2 handfuls fresh parsley leaves

½ cup extra-virgin olive oil

½ cup sherry or red wine vinegar

Freshly ground black pepper

1. Set aside 2 tomatoes. Coarsely chop the rest (you should have about 12 cups) and put in a heavy saucepan. Cook over medium heat, stirring occasionally, until the tomatoes are very soft, 30 to 45 minutes. Strain the juice through a food mill to remove the seeds and skins. Season to taste with salt. Pour the juice into a glass jar and refrigerate until cold. You should have about 7 cups of juice.

2. About an hour before serving, finely chop the remaining 2 tomatoes, garlic, onion, cucumbers, bell peppers, and parsley. If you want to make quick work of it, chop each vegetable in a food processor, using the pulsing function, one type of vegetable at a time.

3. Combine all the chopped vegetables in a large bowl. Add the oil and sherry. Season generously with salt and pepper and let stand for about 30 minutes so the flavors can blend.

4. To serve, spoon the vegetables into each bowl and pour the juice over. Alternatively, let your diners make up their own bowls. Leftover vegetables will keep for only 1 or 2 days, but leftover juice will keep for at least a week and can be enjoyed separately.

Tzatziki

Serves 6 to 8

Lamb dishes, especially lamb burgers, beg for tzatziki. But tzatziki works with almost all grilled meats and vegetables, like grilled eggplant. We like it on baked potatoes. Anything you might want to stuff into a pita pocket is enhanced by tzatziki. If your yogurt is thin, drain it for at least 30 minutes in butter muslin or a fine-mesh strainer to achieve a thick consistency. Oh, and you can skip salting the cucumbers and letting them drain only if you plan to serve immediately and not have any leftovers. Over time, the cucumbers will make the tzatziki watery if they aren't drained first.

INGREDIENTS

6 cups quartered and thinly sliced cucumbers (peeled and seeded if necessary)

1 teaspoon salt, or more as needed

2 cups plain yogurt, preferably Greek-style

2 garlic cloves, minced, or more to taste
   Freshly ground black pepper

1. Combine the cucumber and salt in a colander and toss to mix. Let drain for 30 to 60 minutes. Transfer the cucumbers to a clean kitchen towel and pat dry.

2. If you are not using Greek-style yogurt, put the yogurt in a strainer and let drain for about 30 minutes.

3. Combine the cucumbers, yogurt, and garlic in a large bowl. Season generously with pepper and additional salt, if needed.

4. Set aside at room temperature to allow the flavors to develop for at least 30 minutes before serving.

Vegetable Gratin

Serves 4 to 6

Vegetable gratins are generally considered a side dish, but they make a fine main course for a vegetarian meal. A gratin is rather rustic-looking in a 2-quart baking dish. But divided into individual serving-size dishes, it looks all dressed up. Gratins can be assembled several hours in advance and baked at the last minute. This is a good use for frozen vegetables.

INGREDIENTS

4 cups diced, sliced, or chopped vegetables (artichoke hearts, asparagus, Belgian endive, broccoli, broccoli rabe, Brussels sprouts, butternut squash, cauliflower, celery, chard, fennel, leeks, okra, snap beans, spinach)

2½ cups Basic Cheese Sauce (page 34)

1 onion or large shallot, halved and thinly sliced

Salt and freshly ground black pepper

½ cup grated cheese (choose the same cheese that's used in the cheese sauce)

⅓ cup dried bread crumbs

1. Preheat the oven to 425°F (220°C).

2. If using fresh vegetables, blanch them as needed (see the chart on page 160); if using frozen vegetables, thaw them. Set aside.

3. Lightly butter or oil a 2-quart baking dish or 6 individual gratin dishes. Place individual gratin dishes on a large baking sheet. Spread a little cheese sauce in the dish. Layer the vegetables and onion in the dish. Season generously with salt and pepper. Cover with the remaining sauce. Top with the grated cheese and bread crumbs.

4. Bake for 20 to 30 minutes, until heated through and browned on top. Serve hot.

Tempura

Serves 4

Batter-coated, deep-fried vegetables are a treat, especially when you use a variety of vegetables — and maybe some shrimp as well. This recipe also works for squash blossoms.

INGREDIENTS

BATTER

2 cups unbleached all-purpose flour

4 egg yolks

1 cup flat beer

1 cup ice-cold water

1 teaspoon salt

DIPPING SAUCE

6 tablespoons soy sauce

6 tablespoons water

1 tablespoon minced ginger

1 large garlic clove, minced

1½ teaspoons rice vinegar

TEMPURA

Any vegetable oil, for deep-frying

1 cup all-purpose flour

1½–2 pounds firm vegetables, cut into bite-size pieces (bell peppers, broccoli, carrots, cauliflower, eggplant, green beans, summer squash)

1. To make the batter, combine the flour, egg yolks, beer, water, and salt in a blender. Process until smooth. Allow to sit for at least 30 minutes.

2. To make the dipping sauce, combine the soy sauce, water, ginger, garlic, and vinegar in a small bowl. Set aside.

3. Begin heating 3 to 4 inches of oil or fat in a large, deep saucepan over medium-high heat. Set out the flour in a shallow bowl. Pour the batter into another shallow bowl.

4. When the oil reaches a temperature of 365°F (185°C), begin frying. One piece at a time, dip the vegetables into the flour, then into the batter. Then slip just a few pieces at a time into the hot oil. Fry until the pieces are golden, 3 to 4 minutes, turning as needed.

5. Remove from the oil with a spider strainer or slotted spoon and drain on paper towels. Serve immediately, accompanied by the dipping sauce.

Oven-Baked French Fries

Serves 3 to 4

The perfect oven fries are crisp on the outside and tender within. The place to start is with russet, or baking, potatoes. You didn't grow them? Okay, but next year, think about planting them if you want perfect fries (and mashed potatoes!). It is necessary to soak the potatoes to remove the surface starch. You can impart wonderful flavor with goose fat, duck fat, or beef tallow, but olive oil is a fine, if different-tasting, alternative. You'll note the recipe serves only 3 to 4. If you have a convection oven, you can make a larger batch, using two half-sheet pans. Otherwise, you will have to make these fries in smaller batches.

INGREDIENTS

1½–2	pounds russet potatoes (peeling is optional)
3–4	tablespoons melted goose fat, duck fat, tallow, or olive oil
	Fine sea salt
1	handful fresh herbs, such as rosemary, thyme, or sage (optional)
	Coarse salt

1. Cut the potatoes into slices about ⅓ inch thick. Cut the slices into sticks about ⅓ inch wide. Put the potatoes into a large bowl of water as you cut. When all the potatoes are sliced, drain off the water and refill with fresh water. Let sit for 30 to 60 minutes.

2. Preheat the oven to 450°F (230°C). Grease a half-sheet pan with some of the melted fat.

3. Drain the potatoes and lay them out on a thick kitchen towel. Blot them to dry well, using extra towels as needed.

4. Pile the potatoes on the prepared half-sheet pan, pour the rest of the fat over them, and toss to coat. Spread out the potatoes in a single layer. Sprinkle lightly with fine sea salt and the fresh herbs (if using).

5. Roast for 40 to 45 minutes, until the potatoes are golden and crispy, rotating the pan once. Shake the pan or turn the potatoes with a pancake turner a few times to help them cook evenly. Drain briefly on paper towels, sprinkle with coarse salt, and serve hot.

Mashed Potatoes

Serves 4 to 6

I'm not sure anyone needs another recipe for mashed potatoes, but I am sure that every homestead kitchen needs to serve mashed potatoes often, because nothing else goes so well with all the stews and braises you will be making. Whether you are buying your meat by the side or raising it yourself, you will probably find yourself with more tough cuts than you might otherwise have chosen if you were stopping by the market on your way home from work every day. No worries. Mashed potatoes are the best accompaniment, and everyone loves them. Adding garlic to the pot with the potatoes lends a buttery, background flavor that elevates mash to a place of honor at your table.

INGREDIENTS

3 pounds baking potatoes, peeled and cut into chunks

4 garlic cloves, peeled and left whole

¾ cup milk

3 tablespoons butter

Salt and freshly ground black pepper

1. Cover the potatoes and garlic with cold salted water in a medium saucepan. Cover the pot and bring to a boil. Partially remove the lid and boil until the potatoes are tender, about 25 minutes. Meanwhile, heat the milk and butter in a small saucepan or in a microwave until steaming. (If the milk is still warm from the milking, don't bother to heat it.)

2. Drain the potatoes. Mash the potatoes in a mixing bowl or pass through a potato ricer into a mixing bowl. Beat the potatoes as you pour in the heated milk mixture. Season generously with salt and pepper. Serve hot.

Saag Paneer

Serves 4 to 6

Paneer, a type of fresh cheese found in Indian cuisine, is ridiculously easy to make (see page 240), but why make it if you don't know how to enjoy it? This recipe, basically Indian-style creamed spinach, is a delicious way to get acquainted with paneer. The amount of paneer called for here (24 ounces) is about what you'll get from 1 gallon of milk. The amount of spinach used is 1 pound fresh, in season. But after blanching, then tray-freezing, that same 24 cups reduces down to 8 cups.

INGREDIENTS

About 24 packed cups (1 pound) fresh spinach, or 8 cups frozen spinach (14 ounces), thawed

½ cup butter

2 teaspoons curry powder

1 teaspoon ground coriander

1 teaspoon ground cumin

1 teaspoon fenugreek seeds

1 teaspoon dried red pepper flakes, plus more to taste

2 onions, finely chopped

4 garlic cloves, minced

1 (1-inch) piece ginger, minced

2 tomatoes, chopped, or 1½ cups diced canned tomatoes

About 1½ cups cultured buttermilk

Salt

24 ounces paneer (page 240), cubed

Hot cooked rice or flatbreads (page 330), or both, to serve

1. If using fresh spinach, blanch it, in two or more batches, in a large pot of salted boiling water until the spinach is bright green and wilted, 2 to 3 minutes. Drain in a large colander. If using frozen spinach, drain it in a large colander.

2. In a large saucepan, melt ¼ cup of the butter over medium heat. Add the curry powder, coriander, cumin, fenugreek, and pepper flakes, and sauté until fragrant, about 1 minute. Add the onions, garlic, and ginger, and continue to sauté until the onions are transparent, about 5 minutes.

3. Stir in the tomatoes and 1 cup of the buttermilk. Squeeze any remaining moisture from the spinach and add to the pot. Season to taste with salt. Reduce the temperature to low.

4. In a large, heavy, preferably nonstick skillet, melt the remaining ¼ cup butter over medium heat. Add the paneer and spread out in a single layer. Brown on both sides, turning once, about 4 minutes per side. Remove from the skillet with a slotted spoon and stir into the spinach. Taste and adjust the seasoning. Add buttermilk as needed if the mixture is not saucy enough.

5. Serve at once, passing the rice or flatbreads at the table.

Goat Cheese Spread

Makes about 1½ cups

I was exposed to cream cheese and olives for the first time in a seventh-grade home economics class. It was as exotic a dish as I had ever tasted up to that point, and it rocked my world. The combination still inspires me, though this take is more complex and interesting. Serve it on a homemade baguette (page 66) for an appetizer, snack, or lunch.

INGREDIENTS

1 red bell pepper

1 cup (4 ounces) crumbled chèvre (page 242)

1 cup chopped pitted green olives

2 garlic cloves

½ teaspoon lemon juice

Salt and freshly ground black pepper

1. Preheat the broiler. Lightly oil a baking sheet.

2. Place the pepper on the baking sheet. Broil 4 inches from the heat until charred all over, turning several times. This will take 10 to 20 minutes.

3. Place the charred pepper in a covered bowl, plastic bag, or paper bag. Seal and allow the pepper to steam for at least 10 minutes to loosen the skin.

4. Slit the pepper over a medium bowl to catch the juice that runs from it. Scrape or peel the skin and discard. Scrape and discard the seeds and membranes. Throw the pepper into the bowl of a food processor along with the chèvre, olives, garlic, and lemon juice. Process to make a paste. Season to taste with salt and pepper.

5. Pack into a bowl or crock. Allow to rest for at least 30 minutes before serving. Store for up to a week in the refrigerator.

Slow-Rise Sourdough Pizza

Makes two 10- to 14-inch pizzas

The sourdough makes, without a doubt, the very best pizza crust I have ever made. My own homemade pizza crust had been more than adequate for my family for years, but it lacked a certain — I don't know — professionalism? It was good, but not great. This dough has great flavor and great texture, and it isn't any harder to make, just slower to rise. How slow depends on the kitchen temperature and, probably, how active your starter is, so a little judgment is called for. In the summer, the dough can rise in as little as 4 hours; in a cold winter kitchen, it will take more like 6 to 8 hours. You can speed up the rising time by increasing the amount of instant yeast or letting the dough rise in a warm spot; you can slow it down by refrigerating the dough. The sauce and the toppings are up to you.

INGREDIENTS

- 1 cup sourdough starter (page 61)
- ½ cup hot tap water, plus more if needed
- 2½ cups all-purpose or bread flour
- 1 teaspoon salt
- ½ teaspoon instant active dry yeast
- Extra-virgin olive oil (optional)
- Pizza sauce
- Mozzarella (page 243), grated
- Toppings

1. Stir the sourdough starter. Measure out 1 cup and pour into the food processor. Add the hot water, flour, salt, and yeast. Process until the dough forms a ball. If the dough fails to form a ball, add water just 1 teaspoon at a time. Lightly oil your hands and work surface with olive oil and scoop out the dough. Knead the ball of dough on the oiled surface until it is completely smooth.

2. Oil a large bowl, add the dough, and cover with plastic wrap. (The long rise will result in a dry skin on the dough if you use a towel instead.) Set aside to rise until doubled in bulk, 4 to 6 hours.

3. When the dough has doubled, cut it in half. If using pizza pans, oil the pizza pans with olive oil. Place one piece of dough on each pan. Gently press and push the dough toward the edges of the pan. When the dough starts to shrink back, let it rest for 15 minutes, covered, then finish pressing and pushing. Repeat with the second pan and second piece of dough. Cover and let rise for 15 minutes.

   If using a baking stone, sprinkle cornmeal on a piece of parchment paper. Form the dough on the paper, stretching the dough to form a 14-inch round. Cover and let rise for 15 minutes.

4. Meanwhile, preheat the oven to 500°F (260°C), with a baking stone in place if you have one.

5. For each pizza, spread the dough with a light coating of pizza sauce or olive oil. (I highly recommend using the sauce.) If the pizza is on a pan, simply slide it into the oven. If you have preheated a baking stone, slide the pizza, paper and all, onto a rimless baking sheet or peel and from there slide it onto the baking stone, still on the paper. Bake the pizza for 8 minutes, then pull it out of the oven and spread more sauce on top. Top with cheese, veggies, meats, whatever. Return to the oven and bake until the cheese is melting and bubbling, about 8 more minutes.

Cheese Quiche with Vegetables

Serves 4 to 6

Quiche is an incredibly versatile dish, good for breakfast, brunch, lunch, or dinner. The vegetables can be fresh or frozen, and almost any vegetable — or combination of vegetables — works. Any hard cheese will work, though the classics are listed below. If you want something more hearty, you can add ½ cup diced cooked bacon, store-bought or homemade (page 253). For more flavor, add a couple of tablespoons of chopped fresh herbs.

INGREDIENTS

1–1½ cups chopped, sliced, or diced vegetables
(artichoke hearts, asparagus, broccoli,
broccoli rabe, cauliflower, chard, fennel,
leeks, snap beans, spinach)

1 unbaked 9- or 10-inch pie crust (page 333)

¾ cup grated Swiss, Gruyère, Jarlsberg,
cheddar, or other hard cheese

2 tablespoons chopped shallots, onions,
fresh chives, or scallions

3 eggs

Milk or cream

Salt and freshly ground black pepper

1. Preheat the oven to 425°F (220°C).

2. Blanch the vegetables as needed (see the chart on page 160) and set aside.

3. Bake the crust for 5 minutes, until lightly colored. Remove from the oven and let cool. Reduce the oven temperature to 375°F (190°C).

4. Sprinkle ½ cup of the cheese in the pie crust. Spread the vegetables over the cheese. Sprinkle with the shallots.

5. Beat the eggs in a 2-cup glass measuring cup. Add enough milk to make 1½ cups. Season with salt and pepper. Pour over the vegetables. Sprinkle the remaining ¼ cup cheese on top.

6. Bake for 30 to 35 minutes, until puffed and browned. Let stand for at least 10 minutes. Serve warm or at room temperature.

Cheese Tortelloni on a Bed of Greens

Serves 4

Yes, it is cheating to use wonton skins instead of making your own pasta, but the skins do make a delicate case to show off your homemade cheeses. Once the cheese is made (or bought), this is a surprisingly easy dish to make if you get yourself set up properly. Use whatever herbs you have on hand to flavor the cheese filling, but basil is highly recommended. The wonton skins usually come in 12-ounce packages of about 48 skins. Leftover wonton skins can be sliced and cooked as noodles in soup.

INGREDIENTS

- 1 cup ricotta (page 241)
- ½ cup grated mozzarella (page 243)
- ½ cup freshly and finely grated Parmesan cheese, plus extra for sprinkling
- 1 small handful mixed fresh herbs, such as basil, oregano, parsley, sage, and thyme
- Salt
- All-purpose unbleached flour
- About 36 square wonton wrappers
- 4 tablespoons butter
- 2 tablespoons extra-virgin olive oil
- 3 garlic cloves, minced
- ½ cup white wine
- 6 cups stemmed and thinly sliced kale or other greens

1. To make the filling, combine the ricotta, mozzarella, Parmesan, and herbs in a bowl. Taste and add salt if needed (it might not).

2. Dust a large baking sheet with a little flour. Set out a small bowl of water and a pastry brush. Bring a large pot of salted water to a boil.

3. To make the tortelloni, work with a few wonton skins at a time, keeping the others covered with plastic wrap. Lay a wonton wrapper in the palm of your left hand (if you are right-handed) or on a clean cutting board. Place a generous teaspoon of filling in the center of the wrapper.

Moisten the edges of the wrapper with water and a pastry brush or the tip of your finger. Fold the wrapper in half to form a triangle, pressing firmly on the edges to ensure a tight seal. Wet the two side corners of the triangle, gently pull them together, and press firmly to seal. Set on the baking sheet. Continue until all the filling is used.

4. Melt the butter with the oil in a large skillet over medium-high heat. Add the garlic and sauté until fragrant, about 20 seconds. Add the wine and bring to a boil. Boil for 1 minute. Add the kale, stir to coat, then cover and let steam for 4 to 5 minutes.

5. Meanwhile, add the tortelloni to the boiling water and stir to make sure none are sticking. Continue to boil for 3 to 5 minutes, until the tortelloni are tender and floating to the top. Lift the tortelloni from the boiling water with a spider strainer or slotted spoon and transfer to the skillet with the greens. Toss very gently.

6. To serve, divide the kale and tortelloni among four pasta bowls. Top with a sprinkling of the Parmesan.

Berbere Lentils

Serves 6

When it comes to lentils, you can't have enough recipes because, of all the legumes, lentils take the least time to cook and require no presoaking. You may already have a crowd-pleasing lentil soup recipe, but you might like some different flavors for a change. This Ethiopian lentil dish is perfect as both exotic food and homey comfort at the same time. To elevate the humble lentil into a rich vegetarian dish, use plenty of butter or ghee.

There are more than 200 different types of lentils. My preference for this dish is to use red lentils or yellow split peas, but others in my family prefer this dish made with brown lentils.

INGREDIENTS

- 2 cups red or brown lentils or yellow split peas
- 6 cups water
- Salt
- 6 tablespoons butter, plus more if desired
- 2 tablespoons berbere (see the box at right), or to taste
- 3–4 large onions, halved and thinly sliced
- Flatbreads (page 330), injera (Ethiopian flatbreads), or hot cooked rice

1. Combine the lentils, water, and a pinch of salt in a saucepan and bring to a boil. Reduce the heat, partially cover, and simmer until the lentils are tender and most of the water has been absorbed, 20 to 30 minutes. The lentils should be fairly moist but not soupy. If soupy, continue cooking to boil off most of the water.

2. Meanwhile, melt the butter in a large skillet over medium heat. Add the berbere and sauté until fragrant, stirring to prevent scorching, about 30 seconds. Add the onions and sauté until completely soft and well coated with the berbere, about 10 minutes.

3. When the lentils are tender, stir the onions into the pot, scraping the skillet to get all the butter and spice. Stir in and taste. You may need more salt. More butter will make it even more delicious, but you don't absolutely need it. (When do you really need more butter?) Serve with flatbreads or rice.

Berbere

The key to most Ethiopian stews is the spice mixture berbere (sometimes spelled berberi). Berbere is also the name of the chile on which the spice blend is based. Exact ingredients and proportions vary from cook to cook. For convenience you can buy commercial berbere blends, usually in big-city groceries that cater to large immigrant populations, but there is a significant variation in flavor among the different brands.

If you can't find any berbere where you live, you can make your own. This 1-cup recipe is made with ½ cup of ground dried chiles, which means the flavor will vary considerably with the chile you choose. Ground New Mexico chiles are readily available and are a good starting point.

To make 1 cup of berbere, combine the following:

½ cup ground dried chiles	½ teaspoon ground coriander
¼ cup sweet or hot paprika	½ teaspoon fenugreek seeds
1 tablespoon salt	¼ teaspoon freshly grated nutmeg
1 teaspoon garlic powder	⅛ teaspoon ground allspice
1 teaspoon ground ginger	⅛ teaspoon ground cinnamon
1 teaspoon onion powder	⅛ teaspoon ground cloves
½ teaspoon ground cardamom	

Store in an airtight container in a cool, dark place and use within 6 months.

Mujaddara

Serves 4

A Syrian friend taught me how to make this dish of lentils, rice, and sautéed onions. Variations are popular throughout the Middle East, all combining lentils, grain, and onions. This simple dish is wonderfully delicious, whether served hot or at room temperature, meaning leftovers are great for lunch the next day.

INGREDIENTS

1 cup green or brown lentils, rinsed

1 teaspoon salt, plus more to taste

1½ cups uncooked white or brown rice

2¾–3¼ cups water

2 tablespoons butter or extra-virgin olive oil

3 onions, thinly sliced

4 garlic cloves, minced

1¼ cups cultured buttermilk or yogurt

Freshly ground pepper

1. Cover the lentils with water by about 3 inches in a medium saucepan and add ½ teaspoon of the salt. Bring to a boil, then reduce the heat to a gentle boil and cook until the lentils are tender but still hold their shape, about 25 minutes. Drain.

2. Meanwhile, combine the rice, the remaining ½ teaspoon salt, and water (about 2¾ cups for the white rice and about 3¼ cups for brown rice, depending on the variety). Bring to a boil, then reduce the heat to a simmer and cook until the rice is tender and the water is absorbed, 15 to 40 minutes, depending on the type of rice you use.

3. While the rice and lentils cook, heat the butter over medium-low heat in a large saucepan. Add the onions and cook, stirring frequently, until the onions are golden, about 15 minutes. Add the garlic and cook for 3 more minutes.

4. Add the cooked lentils and rice to the onions. Add the buttermilk to moisten and bind the mixture. Season to taste with salt and pepper. Serve warm or at room temperature.

French Lentils in Mustard Sauce

Serves 4

French bistro-style cooking often features lentils as a side dish, and this is a lovely one to accompany any sort of meat or poultry. (It also makes a fine vegetarian main dish if you substitute vegetable stock for the chicken stock.) Use French green or black lentils, which hold their shape well. The dish gets better with age, so make it early in the day, if possible, and reheat before serving.

INGREDIENTS

- 1 cup French green or black lentils, picked over
- 4 cups water, plus more if needed
- 1 bay leaf
- 1 teaspoon chopped fresh thyme leaves or ½ teaspoon dried
- 3 tablespoons extra-virgin olive oil, butter, chicken fat, duck fat, goose fat, lard, or tallow
- 2 large shallots, thinly sliced
- 2 carrots, finely diced
- ½ cup dry white wine
- ½ cup poultry stock (page 107) or vegetable stock (page 37)
- 2 tablespoons Dijon mustard
- ½ cup coarsely chopped flat-leaf parsley
- Salt and freshly ground pepper

1. Combine the lentils, water, bay leaf, and thyme in a medium saucepan and bring to a boil over high heat. Cover, reduce the heat, and simmer until the lentils are tender, 25 to 30 minutes. Drain the lentils and return them to the saucepan; discard the bay leaf.

2. Meanwhile, heat the oil in a medium skillet over medium-high heat. Add the shallots and carrots and sauté until the carrots are softened, about 5 minutes. Add the wine to the skillet and bring to a boil. Cook, stirring, until reduced by half, about 2 minutes. Add the stock and the mustard. Boil, whisking constantly, for 1 minute. Remove from the heat. Stir into the lentils along with the parsley. Season to taste with salt and pepper. Serve hot.

Red Chile Beans

Serves 6

As with many bean dishes, the meat is optional but adds a really satisfying flavor that lifts the beans from side dish to main dish. Serve the beans plain, with flatbreads (page 330), with brown rice and a sprinkling of fresh cilantro, or folded into tacos along with your favorite taco fixings. The chile sauce (on the next page) doesn't take much time to make, but in a pinch you can substitute a can of commercial enchilada sauce; Hatch is a good brand.

INGREDIENTS

2 cups pinto beans, soaked overnight

8 cups water

1 onion, diced

2 bay leaves

1 smoked ham hock, or 4 ounces chopped salt pork (page 254) or bacon (page 253) (optional)

Red chile enchilada sauce (recipe follows)

Salt and freshly ground black pepper

1. Combine the beans with the water in a large saucepan. Add the onion, bay leaves, and ham hock (if using). Cover and bring to a boil. Then reduce the heat and simmer, partially covered, until the beans are very, very tender, 1½ to 2½ hours.

2. Drain the beans, reserving the cooking liquid and the ham hock (if using). Combine the beans with enchilada sauce and enough cooking liquid to cover the beans. Remove the meat from the ham hock (if using) and add to the beans. Taste and add salt and pepper if needed. Reheat and serve hot.

Red Chile Enchilada Sauce

Makes 1½ to 2 cups

I use this sauce a lot: for making enchiladas, for braising Mexican-style meats (page 310), and for flavoring beans. The chiles you use can be varied, but New Mexico chiles should form the basis of the sauce. I think the sauce is perfect (giving just a slight burn) with four New Mexico chiles, three ancho chiles, and one chipotle chile. Obviously, it is a good idea to limit the number of super-hot chiles you use, unless you and yours have a very high tolerance for spice. You can make large batches of this sauce and freeze the extra, or you can pressure-can the sauce (do not use a boiling-water bath) for 60 minutes for pints or 75 minutes for quarts.

INGREDIENTS

8 dried chiles, including at least 4 New Mexico red chiles

1 onion, quartered

4 garlic cloves, peeled and left whole

2 tablespoons lard, tallow, extra-virgin olive oil, or canola oil

½ teaspoon ground cumin

½ teaspoon dried oregano

1 cup poultry stock (page 107) or vegetable stock (page 37)

1 tablespoon apple cider vinegar

Salt and freshly ground black pepper

1. Rinse the chiles under running water. Combine the chiles in a saucepan with the onion and garlic and cover generously with water. Bring to a boil, then remove from the heat and cover. Let stand, covered, between ½ hour and 4 hours, until the chiles are soft.

2. Drain the chiles, onions, and garlic, reserving 1 cup of the soaking liquid. Pull the stems off the chiles and gently remove as many of the seeds as you can, being careful not to remove the delicate flesh also.

3. Put the chiles, onion, and garlic in a blender and pour in the reserved soaking liquid. Blend until puréed.

4. Pour into a strainer over a bowl and rub through, pressing out as much liquid as you can. Discard the solids (skin and seeds).

5. Heat the lard in a small saucepan over medium heat. Add the cumin and oregano and sauté for 1 to 2 minutes, until fragrant. Add the puréed chile mixture and stock. Bring to a boil, then reduce the heat and simmer for a few minutes. Add the vinegar. Taste and add salt and pepper as needed.

6. Use immediately or store in the refrigerator for up to 5 days.

Tuscan White Beans and Kale

Serves 8 to 10

The point of this dish is to slowly, slowly, slowly cook the beans and meat together, then wilt in the greens. Any tough cut of meat can be used. Use up to 3 pounds if the meat is mostly bone (pork neck, oxtail, trotters) or just 1 pound for anything meaty (country-style pork ribs, pork shank, beef short ribs). Kale is classic in this dish, but collards, cabbage, mustard greens, spinach, or Swiss chard can be used; adjust the cooking time as needed.

INGREDIENTS

2 cups cannellini beans, soaked overnight and drained

1–3 pounds any tough cut of pork or beef, with or without bones

4 cups poultry stock (page 107) or water

4 cups water

1 whole bulb garlic, cloves separated and peeled

1 large sprig rosemary or 1 teaspoon dried

1 large sprig sage or 1 teaspoon dried

1 teaspoon salt, plus more to taste

Freshly ground black pepper

1 large bunch kale or collard greens, stemmed, leaves chopped

Grilled or toasted bread, to serve

1. Combine the beans, pork, stock, water, garlic, rosemary, sage, and salt in a slow cooker. Set on high and cook for 6 hours, or until the beans are tender. (If you combine these ingredients in a saucepan and bring to a boil before transferring to the slow cooker, you can knock 1 to 2 hours off the cooking time.) Or combine these ingredients in a large Dutch oven, bring to a boil on the stovetop, then cover and bake at 250°F (120°C) for 4 to 6 hours. Season to taste with more salt, if needed, and pepper.

2. About 15 minutes before serving, reheat, if necessary. Stir in the kale and cook on high in a slow cooker or on top of the stove in a Dutch oven until the kale is wilted and tender, about 10 minutes.

3. To serve, place two slices of bread in each dish (shallow pasta bowls work well). Ladle the bean mixture on top.

Kale Salad with Catalina Dressing

Serves 4 to 6

Kale salads are an Internet phenomenon. Some enterprising cook posted his or her idea, other people followed, and now we all enjoy them. Early posters may have expressed their understanding that you had to massage the oil into the kale, or that it was the vinegar you had to massage with. But the reality is that any liquid or semiliquid dressing works as a lubricant for the rough handling that is required to break down the cell walls of kale. A hearty, robustly flavored dressing will work, but here's a tip: slightly limp, aging kale works best. So harvest your kale early in the day (at least) and leave it out at room temperature if you can. The dressing here is a classic for taco salads; it works with any type of salad you can imagine. A maple-soy vinaigrette (page 36) works equally well.

INGREDIENTS

DRESSING

½ cup ketchup

⅓ cup water

3 tablespoons red wine vinegar

2 tablespoons extra-virgin olive oil

2 tablespoons finely chopped onion

2 tablespoons sugar

2 garlic cloves, minced

Salt and freshly ground black pepper

SALAD

1 bunch kale, stemmed

1 cup nuts (walnuts, pecans, almonds), toasted

1. To make the dressing, combine the ketchup, water, vinegar, oil, onion, sugar, garlic, and salt and pepper to taste in a blender and process until smooth. Pour into a large bowl. Taste and adjust the seasonings.

2. Chop the kale leaves into thin ribbons and add to the bowl with the dressing. With your hands, toss the leaves with the dressing. Continue to toss and squeeze the kale leaves, rubbing and massaging them until the kale is tender and limp. This will take about 5 minutes, so keep at it — it's almost impossible to be too rough with it.

3. Toss in the nuts. The salad can be served immediately but will hold up for at least 1 day in the refrigerator.

CHAPTER 19

Poultry and Meat Dishes

Chicken Liver Mousse

Makes about 2 cups

The creamy, silken texture makes this pâté anything but rustic. Though it is traditionally made with chicken liver, it can also be made with duck or goose liver.

INGREDIENTS

1¼ pounds chicken, duck, or goose livers
½ cup butter
3 shallots, diced
½ cup cognac or brandy
¼ cup heavy cream
½ teaspoon dried thyme
¼–½ teaspoon salt
¼ teaspoon ground coriander
⅛ teaspoon freshly ground black pepper
Finely chopped fresh parsley, to serve
Crackers or sliced baguette, to serve

1. Trim the livers by removing any greenish or blackish spots and any fat and membranes. Cut into 1-inch pieces.

2. Melt ¼ cup of the butter over medium heat in a large skillet. Add the livers and shallots and sauté for 2 to 3 minutes, until the livers are browned on the outside but still rosy inside. Do not sear the livers; the skins should remain soft. Scrape into the bowl of a food processor.

3. Pour the cognac into the pan and boil it down rapidly until it has reduced by about half. Pour into the food processor.

4. Add the cream, thyme, salt (using the lesser amount if your butter is salted), coriander, and pepper. Process for several seconds until the liver is a mostly smooth paste. Melt the remaining ¼ cup butter and add to the food processor with the motor running.

5. Push the mousse through a fine sieve with a wooden spoon or silicone spatula to remove any solid bits.

6. Pack into a bowl or crock and chill for 2 to 3 hours, until the flavors have blended. To serve, sprinkle with the chopped parsley and serve with crackers or bread. Leftover mousse will keep for 3 to 4 days. Leftovers can be frozen, but they will need to be moistened with cream and stirred well when defrosted.

Any Liver Pâté

Serves 8 to 10

Liver from a large meat animal can be daunting. It's huge, it's dense, it's strongly flavored. Enjoying chicken liver is no guarantee that you will find other livers equally enticing. This recipe works because the strong flavors of the liver are balanced with wine, fruit, and balsamic vinegar.

INGREDIENTS

  4 pounds pork, beef, lamb, or venison liver
  4 cups milk
10 tablespoons butter
    Salt and freshly ground black pepper
  4 large shallots, thinly sliced
  4 garlic cloves, minced
  ½ cup red or white wine
  ¼ cup sherry
  2 teaspoons juniper berries
  1 teaspoon ground cardamom
  1 teaspoon dried oregano or thyme
  ¼ cup heavy cream
  ½ cup dried cherries
  2 tablespoons balsamic vinegar, or to taste

1. Trim the liver, removing all veins, ventricles, and grizzly bits. Chop into 2-inch pieces. Place in a bowl and rinse under cold running water until the water runs clear (it may run bloody at first). Drain well. Add the milk and soak the liver in the milk in the refrigerator for 12 hours, or overnight. Pat dry.

2. Melt 4 tablespoons of the butter in a large skillet over medium heat. Add the liver, season with salt and pepper, and cook until browned on the outside; it can still be pink in the middle. Remove from the pan with a slotted spoon and set aside.

3. Melt another 4 tablespoons of the butter in the skillet over medium heat. Add the shallots and garlic, season with salt and pepper, and sauté until softened, about 5 minutes.

4. Return the liver to the pan and add the wine, sherry, juniper berries, cardamom, and oregano. Cover partially with a lid and simmer until the liquid has reduced by two-thirds, about 15 minutes.

5. Remove from the heat and let cool for a few minutes. Scrape the mixture into a food processor and purée until smooth. With the machine running, add the remaining 2 tablespoons butter and process until blended. Then add the cream and continue to purée until smooth and creamy.

6. Pass the mixture through a fine-mesh strainer and discard the solid bits left in the strainer.

7. Combine the dried cherries and balsamic vinegar in a small cup, cover, and microwave on high for 1 minute. Add to the pâté. Season to taste with more salt and pepper or balsamic vinegar as needed. Pack in a crock and chill in the refrigerator for at least 4 hours before serving.

Coq au Vin

Serves 6

There is a reason this is such a classic dish — it is absolutely delicious, especially made with a real *coq* (rooster). You can find simpler recipes, but making the stock, marinating the bird, reducing the wine mixture, and cooking the bird slowly all add up to incomparable flavor — and are necessary steps with a tough old bird. Serve with steamed parsleyed potatoes or egg noodles and a loaf of good bread for sopping up the delicious gravy, and save any extra gravy to turn into soup with the addition of poultry stock and vegetables.

INGREDIENTS

BIRD
1 rooster or stewing hen, about 5 pounds

MARINADE
2 ribs celery or 1 celery root, chopped

1 carrot, chopped

4 garlic cloves, chopped

2 shallots, chopped

2 sprigs fresh thyme or 1 tablespoon dried

1 sprig fresh sage or 2 teaspoons dried

3 bay leaves

1 (750 ml) bottle red wine, such as Pinot Noir or French burgundy

STOCK
2 ribs celery or 1 celery root, chopped

1 carrot, chopped

1 onion, chopped

1 bunch flat-leaf or curly parsley

8 cups water

STEW
8 ounces salt pork (page 254), diced (or substitute bacon, page 253)

8 ounces mushrooms, sliced

1 pound pearl or boiling onions

2 ribs celery or 1 celery root, chopped

1 carrot, cubed

4 garlic cloves, sliced

1 cup all-purpose flour

¼ cup tomato purée or unseasoned tomato sauce

1. Cut the rooster into eight serving pieces (two wings, two thighs, two drumsticks, two breasts), plus the back and neck.

2. To make the marinade, combine the celery, carrot, garlic, shallots, thyme, sage, and bay leaves in large container. Add the wine and stir well. Put the rooster pieces (minus the back and neck) into the marinade and toss to make sure that all pieces are coated well. Cover and place in the refrigerator for 24 to 72 hours. (All of the pieces should be covered by the marinade.)

3. To make the stock, combine the back and neck in a saucepan with the celery, carrot, onion, and parsley. Add the water, bring to a boil, then reduce the heat and simmer until flavorful, about 4 hours. Let cool briefly, then strain out the solids and discard. Chill until needed.

4. When you are ready to start cooking, remove the rooster pieces from the marinade (they will be purple!), pat dry, and set aside. Pour the marinade and vegetables into a saucepan and cook over medium heat until the liquid has reduced by about half, about 15 minutes. Remove from the heat, strain into a bowl, and set aside the liquid.

5. Preheat the oven to 200°F (95°C).

6. Brown the salt pork in a large Dutch oven over medium heat until crisp, about 8 minutes. Remove the salt pork with a slotted spoon and drain on paper towels. Brown the rooster pieces in the rendered fat over medium heat; you may have to do this in batches. Remove the rooster pieces to a plate as they are browned.

7. Add the mushrooms, onions, celery, carrot, and garlic to the Dutch oven and sauté until the mushrooms are golden, about 10 minutes. Stir in ¼ cup of the flour and cook for about 3 minutes. Stir in the tomato purée, blending well. Add the reduced marinade and stir until well blended. Return the rooster pieces and salt pork to the pan and add enough stock to cover them. Bring to a boil, then cover and place in the oven.

8. Bake for about 6 hours, stirring occasionally, until the meat begins to fall off the bones or is very tender.

9. Remove from the heat and chill overnight.

10. The next day, skim the solid fat from the top of the stew. Warm the stew slowly over medium heat. When the gravy is liquid, taste and add salt and pepper as needed; the saltiness of the salt pork varies. If you'd like the gravy to be thicker, remove about 1 cup and stir ½ to ¾ cup of the remaining flour into it to form a smooth slurry. Bring the stew to a boil, then stir in the flour mixture and keep stirring until the gravy is thickened and smooth. Serve in bowls.

Bird and Biscuits

Serves 6

For my own family, by popular demand, I have replaced chicken pot pie with chicken and biscuits. The complaint about my pot pie, which I topped with biscuits rather than a crust, was that the biscuits absorbed too much moisture as they baked. When I baked the biscuits separately from the creamed chicken and vegetables, everyone was happy. When I started making sourdough biscuits (page 332), everyone was happier still.

The chicken can be leftovers from a roast, or it can be quickly prepared using split chicken breasts poached with some aromatic vegetables (onion, carrot, celery, or celery root) for about 45 minutes. Change the vegetables with the seasons. You can also easily substitute turkey or rabbit for the chicken.

INGREDIENTS

Sourdough biscuits (page 332) or baking powder biscuits (page 331)

4 cups fresh or frozen diced, sliced, or chopped vegetables

Salt and freshly ground black pepper

6 tablespoons butter, chicken fat, duck fat, or goose fat

2 shallots, minced, or 2 leeks, thinly sliced

2 garlic cloves, minced (optional)

6 tablespoons all-purpose unbleached flour

4 cups poultry stock (page 107)

4 cups chopped cooked chicken

1 tablespoon chopped fresh dill or 1 teaspoon dried thyme

1. Prepare the biscuits according to the directions on page 331 or page 332, up through step 3. Place in the refrigerator.

2. If you are using fresh root vegetables, place in a saucepan, cover with water, and add about 2 teaspoons salt. Bring to a boil, and boil until just tender, about 10 minutes. Drain. If you are using fresh summer vegetables, steam blanch over boiling water until tender (see page 160). If you are using frozen vegetables, remove from the freezer.

3. Preheat the oven to 450°F (230°C).

4. Heat the butter in a large saucepan over medium heat. Add the shallots and garlic (if using) and sauté until fragrant and limp, 3 to 5 minutes. Sprinkle in the flour and stir until all the flour is absorbed into the oil. Whisk in the stock and stir until thickened and smooth. Stir in the chicken, vegetables, and dill. Season with salt and pepper to taste. Bring to a simmer. Keep hot while you bake the biscuits.

5. Remove the biscuits from the refrigerator. Bake according to the recipe directions for 15 to 30 minutes, depending on the recipe, until the biscuits are golden.

6. To serve, split open one or two biscuits for each serving. Ladle the chicken and vegetable mixture over the biscuit halves. Serve immediately.

Red-Cooked Chicken (and More)

Serves 4 to 6

Red cooking should be a part of everyone's repertoire, especially if you are sometimes faced with tough cuts that need slow cooking. It is unbelievably delicious. Each time you make it, save the broth for the next batch. Strain it, then freeze it. The next time you make the dish, half the ingredients and the spices should be replenished. This same broth can be used for pork (especially pork belly, which is my favorite way to cook this cut), beef, chicken gizzards, tofu, and duck; the timing will have to be adjusted — just cook until tender. Also, meat should be cut into serving-size pieces before cooking. Red cooking is the home-style Chinese cooking you never get to experience in today's Americanized Chinese restaurants where General Tso's chicken reigns supreme. Serve with steamed greens and rice.

INGREDIENTS

- 4 cups water
- 1 cup soy sauce
- ½ cup honey, maple syrup, or brown sugar
- ½ cup Chinese rice wine or sake
- 6 garlic cloves
- 6 thin slices ginger
- 1 orange or tangerine peel
- 1 tablespoon Chinese five-spice powder
- 1 whole chicken (or any of the cuts mentioned above)
- Dark sesame oil
- Finely chopped cilantro, to serve
- Finely chopped scallions, white and green parts, to serve
- Hot cooked rice

1. Combine the water, soy sauce, honey, rice wine, garlic, ginger, orange peel, and five-spice powder in a large Dutch oven. Bring to a boil, then reduce the heat to low and let simmer for 5 minutes.

2. While the liquid simmers, rinse the chicken and remove any fat from the cavity and neck. Place the chicken in the red-cooking liquid, breast-side down, and simmer for 1 to 1½ hours, turning the chicken occasionally, until the chicken is tender and shows no red near the bone.

3. Turn off the heat and let the chicken cool in the liquid for 15 minutes.

4. Remove the chicken from the cooking liquid and set aside. Preheat the oven to 400°F (200°C).

5. Cut the chicken into small pieces, cutting through the bone. Arrange in a single layer, skin-side up, on a baking sheet. Drizzle with the sesame oil. Place in the hot oven for 10 minutes to make the skin crispy.

6. Meanwhile, skim the fat from the cooking liquid and bring to a boil.

7. To serve, place the chicken on a platter and sprinkle with cilantro and scallions. Pour the cooking liquid into a pitcher. Spoon the rice into individual bowls and pass the chicken and cooking liquid at the table.

Rabbit or Chicken Ragu with Rigatoni

Serves 6 to 8

The plumper the rabbit, the more tender its meat. This recipe is for the rabbit you suspect might be a little tough. It is also a good choice for chicken. For instructions on how to cut up a rabbit into serving-size pieces, see page 112.

INGREDIENTS

2 tablespoons extra-virgin olive oil

1 (2- to 3-pound) rabbit, cut into serving-size pieces, or 2–3 pounds chicken parts (preferably thighs), skinned, boned, and cubed

Salt and freshly ground black pepper

1 carrot, finely diced

2 ribs celery or 1 celery root, finely diced

1 onion, finely diced

1½ cups poultry stock (page 107)

1 cup medium-bodied red wine

2 cups canned diced tomatoes, with the juice

1 (6-ounce) can tomato paste

1 bulb garlic, cloves separated and coarsely chopped

2 bay leaves

1 tablespoon mixed dried Italian herbs

1 pound rigatoni

1 cup freshly grated Parmesan cheese, plus more for serving

1. Preheat the oven to 275°F (135°C) or set out a slow cooker.

2. Heat the oil in a Dutch oven or (if finishing in a slow cooker) a skillet over medium-high heat. Add the meat, season with salt and pepper, and brown, turning as needed, about 5 minutes. Remove the browned meat with a slotted spoon and keep warm. Add the carrot, celery, and onion, and sauté until the vegetables are softened, about 5 minutes.

3. Add the stock, stirring to loosen any browned bits. Bring to a boil, then decrease the heat. If using a Dutch oven, return the meat to the pot and stir in the wine, tomatoes, tomato paste, garlic, bay leaves, and Italian herbs. If using a slow cooker, transfer the hot stock to the slow cooker and add the meat, wine, tomatoes, tomato paste, garlic, bay leaves, and Italian herbs.

4. Cover the Dutch oven, place in the oven, and bake for 2 to 2½ hours, until the meat is completely tender and falling apart. Alternatively, cook in the slow cooker for 3 to 4 hours on high or 6 hours on low. Remove the bay leaves.

5. Cook the rigatoni in plenty of boiling salted water until al dente. Drain well, reserving 1 cup of the pasta cooking water.

6. Combine the pasta with the sauce and mix well. Add some of the pasta cooking water if the pasta seems dry (it may not need any). Stir in the Parmesan. Taste and adjust seasonings. Serve hot, passing the extra cheese at the table.

Mustard-Braised Rabbit or Chicken

Serves 4

This is a traditional French bistro dish, made with either rabbit or chicken, and it's so delicious that even people who generally avoid mustard (myself included) find it irresistible. It is wonderful served over mashed potatoes with steamed green beans or carrots. For instructions on how to cut up a chicken or rabbit, see pages 102 or 112, respectively.

INGREDIENTS

- ½ cup whole-grain Dijon mustard
- ½ teaspoon smoked paprika (or substitute sweet paprika)
- 1 teaspoon salt
- Freshly ground black pepper
- 1 (3-pound) rabbit or chicken, cut into serving-size pieces
- 1 cup (4 ounces) diced thick-cut bacon (page 253)
- 1 onion, diced
- 2 garlic cloves, minced
- 1 teaspoon fresh thyme leaves or ½ teaspoon dried
- Olive oil (optional)
- 1 cup white wine
- ½ cup poultry stock (page 107)
- 2 tablespoons crème fraîche, heavy cream, cultured buttermilk, or half-and-half
- Chopped fresh flat-leaf parsley, for garnish

1. Preheat the oven to 325°F (165°C).

2. Mix the mustard in a bowl with the paprika, salt, and a few generous grinds of black pepper. Toss the rabbit or chicken pieces in the mustard mix. If using chicken, lift the skin and rub some of the mustard mix underneath.

3. Heat a large Dutch oven over medium heat and add the bacon. Cook the bacon, stirring frequently, until it's cooked through and just starting to brown, about 5 minutes. Remove the bacon from the pan and drain on paper towels.

4. If there's more than about 2 tablespoons of bacon fat in the pan, pour off the extra, setting it aside. Add the onion and garlic to the pan and sauté until soft and translucent, about 3 minutes. Transfer to a bowl with a slotted spoon.

5. Return 1 to 2 tablespoons of the bacon fat to the pan or add 1 to 2 tablespoons olive oil. Add a single layer of rabbit or chicken pieces. (You will need to cook them in batches.) Cook until browned on both sides, about 5 minutes per side. As the pieces brown, transfer them to the bowl with the onion and continue browning the meat, adding more bacon fat or olive oil as needed, until all the meat is cooked.

6. Add the wine and stock to the pan, scraping the darkened bits off the bottom with a wooden spoon. Return the rabbit or chicken pieces to the pan along with the bacon and onion. Cover and bake until the meat is cooked through, 1 to 1¼ hours, turning the meat in the sauce a few times.

7. Remove the pot from the oven and stir in the crème fraîche. Sprinkle with the chopped parsley and serve.

Hoisin-Braised Chicken or Rabbit

Serves 4 to 6

This is a wonderful dish for so many reasons, starting with the flavor it imparts to the meat and the copious amount of sauce it makes for the rice. Beyond that, it is a wonderful fix-it-and-forget-it dish that can easily be made ahead, and it works perfectly in a meal of Chinese dishes when most of the other dishes are last-minute stir-fries. I like to serve this with steamed greens — regular broccoli or Chinese broccoli, green beans, kale, or baby bok choy. If you are handy with a cleaver, cut the chicken or rabbit into 2-inch pieces, even if it means whacking through the bone. If you prefer larger serving pieces, see page 102 or 112 for cutting a chicken or rabbit into serving-size pieces.

INGREDIENTS

About 1 cup cornstarch

2 tablespoons any vegetable oil or chicken fat

1 (3- to 4-pound) chicken or rabbit, cut into 6–8 pieces

3 garlic cloves, minced

1 (1-inch) piece ginger, minced

1 cup hoisin sauce

2 tablespoons soy sauce

2 tablespoons rice wine

Chopped fresh cilantro, to serve

Chopped scallions, white and green parts, to serve

1. Preheat the oven to 350°F (180°C). Put the cornstarch in a shallow bowl.

2. Heat the oil in a large skillet or wok over medium-high heat. One at a time, dredge the chicken or rabbit pieces in the cornstarch, shake off the excess, and add to the skillet. Continue adding pieces until the skillet is full without crowding. Brown the meat, turning as needed, and transfer to a Dutch oven. Continue until all the meat is browned.

3. Combine the garlic, ginger, hoisin sauce, soy sauce, and rice wine in a small bowl and mix well. Pour over the chicken. Cover the Dutch oven and braise in the oven until the chicken is tender, about 1½ hours.

4. Sprinkle the cilantro and scallions over the chicken and serve.

Herb-Roasted Rabbit and Potatoes

Serves 4

Because rabbit is so lean and without the skin that protects poultry, it dries out when roasted. A classic solution is to cover the rabbit with bacon, which bastes the meat as it cooks. Might as well roast some potatoes at the same time.

INGREDIENTS

1½ pounds potatoes, quartered or cut into eighths, depending on size

2 tablespoons olive oil

8 ounces bacon (page 253)

1 (3- to 4-pound) rabbit, cut into serving-size pieces (page 112), rinsed, and patted dry

6 shallots, halved or quartered, depending on size

1 tablespoon chopped fresh oregano or 1 teaspoon dried

1 tablespoon chopped fresh rosemary or 1 teaspoon dried

1 tablespoon chopped fresh thyme or 1 teaspoon dried

1 teaspoon freshly ground black pepper

1. Preheat the oven to 375°F (190°C).

2. Combine the potatoes and oil in a shallow roasting pan or baking dish big enough to hold the rabbit. Toss to coat. Bake for 30 minutes.

3. Meanwhile, dice half the bacon and sauté in a large skillet over medium heat just until the bacon renders its fat and becomes crisp, 6 to 8 minutes. Remove the bacon with a slotted spoon and set aside. In the fat that remains in the skillet, brown the rabbit, in batches if necessary, setting aside the pieces as they are browned. Reserve the pan drippings.

4. Remove the roasting pan from the oven. Using a pancake turner, flip the potatoes. Sprinkle the bacon and shallots over the potatoes. Arrange the rabbit in a single layer on top. Sprinkle with the oregano, rosemary, thyme, pepper, and reserved pan drippings. Bake for about 50 minutes, until a knife inserted near a bone in one of the larger pieces shows no redness remaining in the meat. Serve hot.

Wonton Soup

Serves 6 to 8

When it comes to chicken gizzards and hearts, people either love them or can't get beyond the chewy texture. Grinding up the gizzards reduces the chewiness, and who doesn't love wonton soup? The broth is simple to prepare, and the wontons may be easier to make than you might think. If this all strikes you as too much work (it isn't), use the broth as the basis of a Chinese noodle bowl and add cooked noodles, tofu, and more veggies. If you like, use the gizzard mixture to make tiny meatballs that you cook by simmering in the broth. And if gizzards really freak you out, substitute ground pork.

INGREDIENTS

SOUP

- 2 tablespoons chicken fat, lard, or any neutral-tasting vegetable oil
- 4–6 ounces any boneless cut of pork, cut into matchsticks
- 3 quarts chicken stock (page 107)
- 4 garlic cloves, minced
- 2 tablespoons rice wine
- 2 tablespoons soy sauce, or to taste
- 1 star anise

WONTONS

- 1 pound (about 2 cups) chicken gizzards and hearts
- 3 scallions, white and green parts, finely chopped
- 4 garlic cloves, minced
- 1 (½-inch) piece ginger, chopped
- Cornstarch
- About 40 wonton skins

GREENS

- 3–4 cups greens, chopped as needed (bok choy, Chinese cabbage, kale, spinach)
- 3 scallions, white and green parts, finely chopped

1. To make the soup, heat the fat in a soup pot over medium-high heat. Add the pork and sauté until browned, about 4 minutes. Add the stock, garlic, rice wine, soy sauce, and star anise. Bring to a boil, then reduce the heat and simmer for at least 30 minutes.

2. To make the wonton filling, trim the gizzards to remove the connective tissue between the lobes and any other gristle or fat. Chop coarsely. Combine in a food processor with the scallions, garlic, and ginger. Pulse until finely ground. Pulse some more. (Alternatively, grind in a meat grinder.) The finer the grind, the less chewy the meat.

3. Dust a large baking sheet with cornstarch and set out a shallow bowl of water. Work with a few wonton skins at a time, keeping the others covered with plastic wrap. Lay a wonton wrapper in the palm of your left hand (if you are right-handed) or on a clean cutting board. Place a generous teaspoon of filling in the middle of the wrapper. Moisten the edges of the wrapper with water and the tip of your finger. Fold the wrapper in half to form a triangle, pressing firmly on the edges to ensure a good seal. Wet the two side corners of the triangle, gently pull them together, and press firmly to seal. Set on the baking sheet. Continue until all the filling is used; you should be able to make 35 to 40 wontons.

4. To cook the wontons, bring a large pot of water to a boil. Line a baking sheet with parchment paper. Add half the wontons to the boiling water and boil *gently* for 4 to 5 minutes, until the filling is cooked through on a test wonton. With a spider strainer or a slotted spoon, lift the wontons out of the water and place on the lined baking sheet. Return the water to a boil and cook the remaining wontons in the same way.

5. Just before serving the soup, remove the star anise from the soup broth. Add the greens to the broth and let simmer until just wilted but still vividly green, 1 to 3 minutes. Place about 4 wontons in each soup bowl, ladle the soup over them, and serve.

Any Meat Stir-Fry with Vegetables

Serves 4 to 6

I make a lot of stir-fries, in part because I really like the convenience of a stir-fry and that a tough cut of meat, cut into thin matchsticks, can be cooked quickly and without fuss. It is important to have all the vegetables prepped and all the ingredients assembled before you start cooking. And don't forget to start cooking the rice first. All of the flavoring ingredients can be found in an Asian market; oyster sauce and black bean sauce (made from fermented soybeans) have very different flavors, so you can change things up if you want. The chili sauce is optional but recommended. You can prep your veggies while the meat is marinating.

INGREDIENTS

12–16 ounces boneless, skinless chicken, rabbit, goat, lamb, beef, or pork, sliced into matchsticks

4 tablespoons soy sauce

3 tablespoons Chinese oyster sauce or oyster-flavored sauce (depending on the brand) or Chinese black bean sauce

2 tablespoons rice wine or dry sherry

1 tablespoon sugar

2 teaspoons Asian sesame oil

3–4 garlic cloves, minced

1 (1-inch) piece fresh ginger, minced

1–2 teaspoons chili paste with garlic (optional)

3 tablespoons peanut or canola oil

1 onion, halved and cut into slivers, or 1 leek, white and tender green parts only, thinly sliced

4 cups chopped or diced firm vegetables (asparagus, baby corn, broccoli, carrots, snap beans, snap peas, snow peas), or shelled peas

8 cups slivered greens (bok choy, broccoli rabe, cabbage, Chinese cabbage, kale)

Hot cooked white rice, to serve

1. Combine the meat with 3 tablespoons of the soy sauce in a medium bowl, along with the oyster sauce, rice wine, sugar, sesame oil, garlic, ginger, and chili paste (if using). Set aside to marinate for about 15 minutes.

2. Heat a large wok or skillet over high heat. Add 1 tablespoon of the peanut oil and heat until very hot. Add the meat and its marinade and stir-fry, stirring constantly, until well browned, 4 to 6 minutes. With a silicone spatula, scrape out all the meat and sauce into a medium bowl and keep warm. Return the wok to high heat.

3. Heat another 1 tablespoon of the peanut oil in the wok over high heat until very hot. Add the onion and chopped vegetables and stir-fry until slightly softened, about 3 minutes. Add the remaining 1 tablespoon soy sauce, cover, and let the vegetables steam until tender-crisp, 2 to 4 minutes. Remove from the wok and add to the meat.

4. Return the wok to high heat and add the remaining 1 tablespoon peanut oil. Add the leafy greens and stir-fry for 3 minutes, until the vegetables are limp and somewhat tender. Return the meat and vegetables to the wok and toss to combine. Stir-fry until everything is heated through, about 1 minute more. Serve immediately with the hot rice.

Char Siu Pork

Serves 6

The marinade for Chinese barbecued pork is so delicious that just about any pork cut benefits from being cooked this way, though I have a preference for fattier cuts. Serve with white rice and steamed greens. Leftovers are delicious chopped and stuffed into steamed buns or sourdough biscuits (page 332); you can also stir-fry them with vegetables and serve over rice or noodles.

INGREDIENTS

- 2–3 pounds boneless or bone-in pork loin or shoulder chops, steaks, country-style ribs, or pork belly
- ¼ cup hoisin sauce
- 3 tablespoons honey or maple syrup
- 3 tablespoons soy sauce
- 1½ tablespoons rice wine or dry sherry
- 2 teaspoons Asian sesame oil
- 1 teaspoon Chinese five-spice powder
- 4 garlic cloves, minced

1. If you are working with chops, steaks, or a roast, cut the pork into strips about 6 inches long and 1½ inches thick. Pork belly can be cut into cubes. There will probably be some odd-sized pieces; just make sure they are all about the same thickness.

2. Combine the hoisin sauce, honey, soy sauce, rice wine, sesame oil, and five-spice powder in a large bowl or shallow baking dish. Mix in the garlic. Set aside 1 cup of the marinade to use as a baste. Add the pork to the marinade and toss to coat evenly, using tongs or a spatula. Cover with plastic wrap and refrigerate for as little as 1 hour or up to 12 hours, turning the pork a few times.

3. Preheat the oven to 475°F (245°C). Line a large baking sheet with aluminum foil and place a flat wire rack on the baking sheet.

4. Turn the pork in the marinade one more time to coat the pieces and then arrange on the wire rack, leaving as much space as possible between the pieces.

5. Roast, basting with the reserved marinade every 10 to 15 minutes, for 30 to 40 minutes. The pork is done when it looks glazed, is slightly charred, and registers about 160°F (71°C) on an instant-read meat thermometer. Depending on how crowded the baking sheet is, the meat may not cook evenly. Remove pieces as they become slightly charred and keep them warm while continuing to cook the remaining pieces. Let the meat rest for 10 minutes to finish cooking and seal in the juices before serving.

Variation: Chinese Barbecued Duck. Replace the pork with a 10- to 12-pound duck and roast as on page 110.

Pimenton-Crusted Pork Chops

Serves 4

The difference between a thick pasture-raised pork chop and a thin, cheap factory-raised pork chop is at least as great as the difference between homemade sourdough bread and squishy supermarket white bread. You'll get many meals of pork chops from a side of pork or a whole pig, so you might as well cook it right. The recipe below, influenced by J. Kenji López-Alt, managing culinary director of the website Serious Eats, involves both dry brining and reverse searing. The method is counterintuitive and requires some planning ahead, but, oh, is it good. Use the recipe as a road map, and make changes to the spices in the dry rub and the aromatics as you please.

INGREDIENTS

4 bone-in pork chops, cut 1½ inches thick

¼ cup kosher salt

3 tablespoons brown sugar

2 tablespoons pimenton (smoked Spanish paprika)

2 tablespoons lard or any vegetable oil

2 tablespoons butter

2 shallots, diced, or 1 onion

1 green or red bell pepper, diced (optional)

Handful of chopped fresh herbs (parsley, sage, rosemary, thyme), or 1 tablespoon dried

1. At least 8 hours and up to 24 hours before you plan to cook, rinse the pork chops and pat dry with paper towels. Set up wire racks on a rimmed baking sheet that will hold the chops in a single layer, and clear a space in the refrigerator.

2. Mix together the salt, brown sugar, and pimenton in a small bowl. Sprinkle the salt mix over the pork chops, generously covering the meat on all sides. Transfer the meat to the wire racks on the baking sheet and refrigerate, uncovered, for 8 to 24 hours.

3. When you are ready to cook, preheat the oven to 250°F (120°C). Place a temperature probe into the center of one of the pork chops and roast until the internal temperature reaches 115°F (45°C) for medium, about 35 minutes (remember to check the temperature in a few spots). If you don't have a probe and alarm, begin checking for the proper internal temperature with an instant-read thermometer after 25 minutes and keep checking until you reach 115°F (45°C). Remove from the oven.

4. Melt the lard in a large cast-iron skillet over high heat until very hot (preferably with a ventilation fan on). Place the pork chops in the skillet and sear on all sides, turning the chops with tongs, 1 to 2 minutes per side. (If necessary, do this in batches.) Add the butter, shallots, bell pepper (if using), and herbs to the skillet. Continue cooking, spooning the aromatics and pan juices on top of chops until browned on both sides and well crusted, about 2 minutes longer. Again, if necessary, do this in batches. Transfer the chops to serving plates and let rest for 3 to 5 minutes before serving.

Chorizo Skillet Supper

Serves 4

This is a dish we enjoy often, but it is especially good when it is made with homegrown, homemade ingredients. The only part I always outsource is the limes, but you can pick and choose your homemade ingredients, depending on your time and inclination. If you're using homemade flatbreads as your tortillas, they require a little resting time once the dough is made, so make them first.

INGREDIENTS

- 1 tablespoon extra-virgin olive oil
- 1 pound Mexican chorizo, homemade (page 261) or store-bought
- 1 green bell pepper, seeded and thinly sliced
- 1 red bell pepper, seeded and thinly sliced
- 1 large onion, halved and slivered
- 1 cup fresh or frozen corn
- ½ cup chopped fresh cilantro

TO SERVE

Homemade flatbreads (page 330) or 8–12 corn or wheat tortillas, warmed

Lime crema (recipe follows) or 1 lime, cut into wedges

Shredded lettuce (optional)

Salsa (optional)

1. Heat the oil in a large skillet over medium-high heat. Add the chorizo and cook until browned, about 8 minutes, crumbling the meat as it cooks. Remove from the skillet with a slotted spoon and keep warm.

2. Add about half the peppers and onion and sauté until limp, about 4 minutes. Remove from the skillet and add to the meat. Repeat with the remaining vegetables. (Do this in batches so the vegetables sauté, not steam.)

3. Return the meat and vegetables to the skillet. Stir in the corn and cilantro and continue to sauté until heated through, a few minutes. To serve, set out the meat and vegetables, flatbreads, lime crema, lettuce, and salsa, and let the diners assemble their own meals.

Lime Crema

Makes about 1⅔ cups

INGREDIENTS

- 1½ cups sour cream or crème fraîche
- 3 tablespoons fresh lime juice
- 1 teaspoon (packed) finely grated lime peel
- Pinch of salt

To make the lime crema, mix together the sour cream, lime juice, lime peel, and salt. Keep refrigerated.

Braised Meat, Mexican-Style

Serves 4 to 6

This meat can be enjoyed in all sorts of ways: atop rice, as an enchilada or taco filling, or as a topping for a modified taco salad (crumbled tortilla chips, salad greens, braised meat, chopped veggies, salsa, sour cream). You can easily make the red chile enchilada sauce in advance with dried red chiles (see page 291), or you can resort to a store-bought can (Hatch is a good brand). Either way, cook the meat slowly while you go about your busy day. Then return to the kitchen and set out the fixings for an easily assembled meal.

INGREDIENTS

- 1 tablespoon chili powder
- 1 tablespoon white or brown sugar
- 1 teaspoon ground cumin
- 1 teaspoon salt
- ½ teaspoon freshly ground black pepper
- 2-3 pounds any tough cut of meat suited for moist-heat cooking from the list on page 145
- 2 tablespoons lard, tallow, or extra-virgin olive oil
- ½ cup brown stock (page 142) or beef stock
- 1½-2 cups red chile enchilada sauce (page 291) or 1 (15-ounce) can store-bought red enchilada sauce
- 1 cup diced tomatoes with their juice (canned or fresh)
- ½ teaspoon ground chipotle powder, or 1 chipotle pepper in adobo sauce, minced (optional)
- 1 onion, sliced
- 1 green bell pepper, sliced (optional)
- 4 garlic cloves, minced

1. Preheat the oven to 275°F (135°C) or set out a slow cooker.

2. Mix together the chili powder, sugar, cumin, salt, and black pepper in a small bowl. Rub the spice mix into the meat, covering each side evenly.

3. Heat the lard in a large Dutch oven or skillet over medium-high heat. Add the meat and sear on each side until browned, 2 to 3 minutes per side. Transfer to a plate or the slow cooker.

4. Add the brown stock to the pan to deglaze, scraping up any browned bits from the bottom of the pan. Add the enchilada sauce, tomatoes, and chipotle (if using) and bring to a boil; then reduce the heat and simmer for 3 to 5 minutes, until the sauce has reduced and thickened slightly.

5. If braising in the oven, return the meat to the Dutch oven, along with the onion, bell pepper (if using), and garlic. If using the slow cooker, combine the onion, bell pepper (if using), and garlic with the meat in the slow cooker. Pour the sauce over all. Cover and bake in the oven for 3 to 4 hours, or in the slow cooker on low for 6 to 8 hours or on high for 3 to 4 hours. The meat is done when it is easily shredded with a fork.

6. Remove the meat and solids from the sauce. Strain the sauce into a tall measuring cup; allow the fat to rise to the surface and then remove it. Shred the beef with two forks. Return the meat and vegetables to the pan along with the sauce and reheat as needed.

Smoky-Sweet Slow-Cooked Ribs

Serves 3 to 4

Barbecued ribs are too good to limit to outdoor cooking. These ribs (beef or pork) are slowly braised in the oven or slow cooker, then finished to a sweet, crispy finish on the grill or under the broiler.

INGREDIENTS

RIBS

- 2 tablespoons maple syrup, honey, or apple cider syrup (page 82)
- 1 tablespoon chili powder
- 1 tablespoon smoked hot paprika
- 1 tablespoon salt
- 2 teaspoons garlic powder
- 1 teaspoon ground chipotle chile
- 1 teaspoon freshly ground black pepper
- ½ teaspoon ground ginger
- 4–5 pounds beef back ribs, 2 racks pork spareribs, or 3–4 pounds country-style pork ribs

BARBECUE SAUCE

- 1 tablespoon lard, tallow, or any vegetable oil
- ½ small onion, finely chopped
- 3 garlic cloves, finely chopped
- 1½ cups ketchup
- 6 tablespoons maple syrup, honey, or apple cider syrup (page 82)
- ¼ cup cider vinegar
- ¼ cup water
- 1 tablespoon soy sauce
- 2 chipotles in adobo sauce, finely chopped
- ¾ teaspoon freshly ground black pepper

1. Combine the maple syrup, chili powder, paprika, salt, garlic powder, chipotle chile, black pepper, and ginger in a large baking dish. Stir to combine. Add the ribs and evenly rub the spice mixture on all sides. Cover the dish and set aside to marinate for at least 1 hour at room temperature, or in the refrigerator for up to 24 hours.

2. Meanwhile, make the barbecue sauce. Melt the lard over medium heat until shimmering. Add the onion and garlic and cook, stirring occasionally, until softened, about 3 minutes. Stir in the ketchup, maple syrup, vinegar, water, soy sauce, chipotles, and black pepper. Bring to a simmer, then reduce the heat to low and continue to simmer, stirring occasionally, for 30 to 45 minutes.

3. Preheat the oven to 325°F (165°C). Put the ribs in a large roasting pan and pour half the sauce over, reserving the remaining sauce. Cover tightly with aluminum foil and cook until the ribs are tender and pulling away from the bones, 2 to 3 hours. The meat should read at least 185°F (85°C) on an instant-read thermometer.

4. Preheat the broiler or prepare a medium-hot fire in the grill. If using the broiler, line a broiler pan or baking sheet with aluminum foil (for cleanup, you'll thank me). Let the meat rest, covered, for 20 to 30 minutes.

5. To finish the ribs, place them on the prepared baking sheet or broiler pan, or on a plate to take out to the grill. Place the ribs under the broiler or on the grill. Broil or grill for 3 to 5 minutes, until the edges of the meat begin to burn, turning the ribs as needed. Serve hot, passing the reserved barbecue sauce on the side.

Wine-Braised Meat with Vegetables

Serves 6

Slow-cooked meat braised in tomatoes and wine makes a dish to be savored slowly, with red wine and candlelight. Your choice of meat is broad; basically any tough cut will benefit from this kind of slow cooking. (For a list of suggested meats for braising, see page 335.) My family loves this made with lamb shanks, pork shanks, and turkey drumsticks. Serve with mashed potatoes and a good bread for sopping up the delicious gravy.

INGREDIENTS

6 lamb shanks, center-cut beef shank bones, or turkey drumsticks; or 2 pork shanks; or 1–3 pounds any tough cut of meat suited for moist-heat cooking from the list on page 145

Salt and freshly ground black pepper

½ cup all-purpose flour

2 tablespoons olive oil

1 large onion, finely diced

2 carrots, finely diced

1 cup red wine

2 cups brown stock (page 142) or poultry stock (page 107)

2 cups canned or fresh diced tomatoes with juice

4 garlic cloves, minced

1 tablespoon fresh chopped rosemary or 2 teaspoons dried

1 tablespoon fresh thyme leaves or 2 teaspoons dried

2 bay leaves

4 cups chopped root vegetables (celery root, golden beets, parsnips, rutabagas, turnips), cut in ½-inch cubes (optional)

1. Preheat the oven to 300°F (150°C). Set out a large roasting pan or a large slow cooker.

2. Generously season the meat with salt and pepper, then dredge in the flour until evenly coated. Heat the oil in a large skillet over medium-high heat. Add the meat in a single layer and brown on all sides, about 5 minutes per side. You will have to do this in batches. Transfer the meat to the roasting pan or slow cooker.

3. Add the onion and carrots to the skillet, reduce the heat to medium, and sauté until softened, about 3 minutes.

4. Pour in the wine to deglaze all the browned bits. Bring to a boil, stirring, and cook until reduced by about a third. Pour into the roasting pan or slow cooker, along with the stock and tomatoes with their juice. Sprinkle with the garlic, rosemary, thyme, and bay leaves. Season with salt and pepper. Tightly cover the roasting pan with aluminum foil or secure the lid on the slow cooker.

5. Bake for 2 to 4 hours, slow-cook on high for 2 to 4 hours, or slow-cook on low for 6 to 8 hours, until the meat is tender. (A fork inserted into the meaty part will meet with little resistance on its way in or out.)

6. Add the root vegetables (if using), replace the cover, and continue baking or slow-cooking on high for 1 hour.

7. Remove and discard the bay leaves. Pour off the liquid into a gravy separator or tall glass container and let sit for about 10 minutes, to allow the fat to rise to the top. Skim off the fat and return the liquid to the meat and vegetables. Reheat as needed. Serve hot in large shallow bowls.

Note: This dish is excellent made a day in advance and is easily reheated. An added advantage of making it ahead is that it makes it easier to defat the liquid. The recipe is easily multiplied if you have a big enough roasting pan. If you like, you can skip the root vegetables and accompany the dish with a different vegetable, such as steamed green beans.

Herbed Lamburgers

Serves 4

This is a great dish for the summer, especially if you feel like grilling the burgers. But if you prefer, you can broil or pan-fry them. The herbs add moisture and flavor to the meat, so use whatever you have on hand or snip from the garden. Be generous, but don't fuss with measuring — more or less always works out. The tzatziki can be made up to 8 hours ahead. Oven fries (page 279) are the perfect accompaniment.

INGREDIENTS

2 garlic cloves

1 small onion, quartered, or 3 shallots, halved

Handful of mixed herbs (mint, thyme, rosemary, sage, parsley, basil, oregano)

1 pound ground lamb or goat (or substitute ground chicken, ground turkey, ground pork, or ground beef)

1 teaspoon salt

½ teaspoon freshly ground pepper

Homemade flatbreads (page 330), sour-dough biscuits (page 332), pita pockets, or hamburger buns

Tzatziki (page 276), to serve

Sliced tomatoes, optional

1. If you are grilling outdoors, prepare a medium-hot fire in the grill.

2. Combine the garlic, onion, and herbs in a food processor and process to make a paste. Transfer to a bowl. Add the meat, salt, and pepper, and mix with your hands until thoroughly blended. Form into 4 to 8 patties, depending on the size of your buns or flatbreads.

3. When the coals in the outdoor grill are covered with white ash, place the burgers on the grill. Alternatively, if you're using an indoor grill pan or cast-iron skillet, preheat over high heat. Grill the patties until cooked through, about 4 minutes per side for medium, turning once. (Adjust the timing as you like; I prefer medium-rare.)

4. Pass the burgers, bread, tzatziki, and tomatoes at the table and let everyone build their own burgers.

New England Boiled Dinner

Serves 4 to 6

Having corned a brisket (page 255), you might as well go all the way with a typical New England boiled dinner. The first printed recipe for this dish, which appeared in a 1936 edition of the Fannie Farmer's *Boston Cooking-School Cookbook* called for rutabagas, potatoes, carrots, and cabbage, as does this version, which cooks the beef in a slow oven for an extra-tender, fuss-free dinner. Substitute other vegetables as you please.

INGREDIENTS

4–5	pounds corned beef (page 255)
2	onions, chopped
2	tablespoons mixed pickling spices
3	thin-skinned potatoes, peeled and cubed
2	small carrots, cubed
1	small rutabaga, cubed
½	head large cabbage, cut into wedges
	Mustard, to serve

1. Preheat the oven to 225°F (110°C). Rinse the corned beef under cold running water.

2. Put the corned beef in a large roasting pan. Cover with water. Add the onions and pickling spices. Cover tightly with aluminum foil.

3. Bake for 5 to 6 hours, until the meat is tender when poked with a fork and registers 185°F (85°C). Let the meat cool in the cooking liquid for at least 15 minutes. Transfer the meat to a platter and cover with a tent of foil.

4. Put the potatoes, carrots, and rutabaga in a pot on top of the stove. Add enough cooking liquid from the roasting pan to completely cover the vegetables. Cover and bring to a boil; then reduce the heat and simmer for 20 minutes, until the vegetables are mostly tender. Add the cabbage and simmer for another 5 to 10 minutes, until all the vegetables are tender.

5. Use a slotted spoon to transfer the vegetables to a serving bowl. Cover and keep warm. Return the meat to the cooking liquid to reheat for about 5 minutes.

6. Slice the meat against the grain and serve with the vegetables, passing the mustard at the table.

Boiled Tongue with Mustard Sauce

Serves 6

If you are new to cooking tongue, here is a basic recipe you might enjoy. Tongues have an ick factor because they look like tongues. After cooking, you peel off the bumpy skin, which makes it a little less icky, but the shape is still distinctively tonguelike. Bring the tongue to the table sliced to completely eliminate any yuck factor. The mustard sauce is a lovely complement to the meat. Cow tongues vary in size from about 1½ pounds to 3½ pounds. If your tongue is on the small side, it will feed fewer people and may be ready to eat a little sooner.

INGREDIENTS

TONGUE

1 (3-pound) fresh beef tongue

1 large onion, quartered

6 garlic cloves, sliced

2 tablespoons mixed pickling spices

2 tablespoons salt

SAUCE

2 tablespoons butter, lard, or tallow

2 shallots, diced

2 tablespoons all-purpose flour

2 tablespoons whole-grain Dijon mustard

1 tablespoon chopped fresh dill or 1 teaspoon dried

1 tablespoon chopped fresh thyme or 1 teaspoon dried

1 teaspoon freshly ground black pepper

3 tablespoons crème fraîche or heavy cream

1. Rinse the tongue well with cold water and place in a deep 6- to 8-quart pot. Add cold water to cover by 3 inches. Add the onion, garlic, pickling spices, and salt. Cover and bring to a boil; then reduce the heat and simmer, partially covered, until the tongue is fork-tender, 2½ to 3 hours.

2. Transfer the tongue to a cutting board and strain the cooking liquid into a fat separator. When the tongue is cool enough to handle, peel off the skin and trim away any fat or gristle with a knife. Cover and keep the tongue warm while you make the sauce.

3. To make the sauce, melt the butter in a small saucepan over medium heat. Add the shallots and cook until softened, about 3 minutes. Stir in the flour and cook, stirring constantly, for about 1 minute. Pour in 1 cup of the reserved cooking liquid. Stir in the mustard, dill, thyme, and pepper. Simmer the sauce, whisking occasionally, until slightly thickened, 2 to 3 minutes. Stir in the crème fraîche and remove from the heat.

4. Cut the tongue into slices about ½ inch thick and serve with the sauce.

CHAPTER 20

Desserts and Baked Goods

Any-Frozen-Fruit Yogurt

Serves 4 to 6

I feel almost guilty calling this a recipe, since it is such an obvious way to whip up a delicious dessert. You can use any frozen fruits that started out soft and juicy, such as berries or peaches. A mixture of berries is particularly wonderful.

INGREDIENTS

4 cups frozen fruit, sweetened or unsweetened (do not thaw)

½ cup sugar (if the fruit was frozen unsweetened)

1 tablespoon lemon juice

1 cup plain yogurt

1. Combine the frozen fruit, sugar (if using), and lemon juice in a food processor and pulse until coarsely chopped. Add the yogurt and process until smooth and creamy, scraping down the sides of the bowl once or twice.

2. Serve immediately in dessert bowls or freeze for several hours until quite firm.

Simple Vanilla Custard

Serves 4

Everyone should have a simple stirred custard recipe handy, something you can whip up without even consulting the recipe after making it a few times. It is made of just egg yolks, milk, sugar, vanilla, and cornstarch. Omit the cornstarch, and it is a sauce you can pour on cake, the way the Brits do, or use as a base for ice cream. Increase the cornstarch, and you have pastry cream to fill cream puffs and éclairs, or to layer under fresh fruit in a tart. But follow the recipe below and you have a pudding that is superior to any mix, and a great way to use up extra milk and eggs.

INGREDIENTS

5 tablespoons sugar

3 tablespoons cornstarch

¼ teaspoon salt

3 egg yolks

2 cups milk

1 teaspoon vanilla extract

1. Whisk together the sugar, cornstarch, and salt in a small saucepan until well blended. Blend the yolks together in a small bowl until smooth.

2. Whisk the milk into the cornstarch mixture and bring to a boil over medium-high heat, stirring with a silicone spatula or wooden spoon to prevent scorching. The mixture should thicken as it comes to a boil.

3. Pour about a third of the mixture over the egg yolks to temper them, then pour the tempered yolks into the saucepan. Bring the mixture back to a simmer for about 30 seconds, then remove the pan from the heat. Stir in the vanilla.

4. Pour the custard into a bowl or individual serving cups and chill before serving.

Desserts That Start with Custard

Any number of desserts start with a simple vanilla custard. Here are a few ideas.

Fruit parfaits. Cool the custard for about 30 minutes. Then layer in wineglasses or glass parfait dishes with fresh or frozen fruit. Chill for an hour (the frozen fruit will defrost).

Granola parfait. Cool the custard for about 30 minutes. Soak your favorite dried fruit in warm water for 30 minutes, then drain. Layer the custard, granola, and fruit in wineglasses or glass parfait dishes. Chill for an hour before serving.

Fruit trifle. Cool the custard for about 30 minutes. Soak ladyfingers or sliced sponge cake with sherry. Layer the custard, cake, and fresh or frozen fruit in a bowl, preferably glass. End with whipped cream.

Fruit pudding. Make the custard and cool. Defrost some frozen fruit, or cut up some juicy summer fruit or berries, and sprinkle with sugar. Blend the fruit and juices with the custard and chill.

Peaches and cream. Peel, halve, and pit peaches. Sprinkle with brown sugar and run under the broiler for 1 to 2 minutes until the sugar caramelizes. Pour the custard into dessert bowls and top with the peaches.

Banana pudding. Make the custard. Mash up 2 bananas and stir into the pudding. Chill for at least 1 hour before serving.

Strawberry custard shortcake. Cool the custard, and serve with biscuits and strawberries in a sugar syrup.

Frozen Fruit Crisp

Serves 6 to 9

Wish you could keep the crisp in a juicy fruit crisp? It's easy: just bake the topping and filling separately. I came across this method for baking fruit crisps on the King Arthur Flour website, and it struck me as genius, especially when working with frozen fruits, which tend to be extra juicy. Baking the fruit without the topping tends to reduce the juiciness of the filling (which is a good thing in this case) and keeps the topping nice and crispy. ClearJel is the thickener of choice here. It is a modified cornstarch, and it thickens whether you are baking or freezing your pie fillings and should be stocked in your pantry. (For more on ClearJel and other thickeners, see page 51.)

INGREDIENTS

FILLING

3 tablespoons ClearJel

¾ cup granulated sugar

½ teaspoon salt

6 cups unsweetened frozen berries and/or peeled and diced peaches, nectarines, or cherries

2 tablespoons lemon juice

TOPPING

¾ cup unbleached all-purpose flour

¾ cup old-fashioned rolled oats

1 teaspoon ground cinnamon

½ teaspoon salt

½ teaspoon freshly grated nutmeg or ground ginger

6 tablespoons butter, diced, at room temperature

½ cup maple syrup, honey, apple cider syrup (page 82), or firmly packed brown sugar

Heavy cream, whipped cream, or ice cream, to serve

1. Preheat the oven to 350°F (180°C). Generously butter an 8-inch square baking dish. Line a baking sheet with parchment paper.

2. To make the filling, whisk together the ClearJel with the sugar and salt. Add the fruit and lemon juice. Spoon into the prepared pan.

3. To make the topping, combine the flour, oats, cinnamon, salt, and nutmeg in a medium bowl. Add the butter and mix with your fingertips until the mixture is crumbly. Stir in the maple syrup. (Alternatively, you can mix all the topping ingredients in a food processor.) Spread the topping evenly on the lined baking sheet.

4. Place both the fruit and topping in the oven. The fruit will bake for a total of 50 minutes, while the topping will bake for a total of 30 to 35 minutes. At the 15-minute mark, remove the topping from the oven and stir well. Bake for an additional 15 to 20 minutes, until the topping is a light golden brown. Remove it from the oven. Keep the fruit in the oven for another 15 to 20 minutes, until bubbling.

5. Remove the fruit from the oven and sprinkle the baked topping evenly over the hot fruit. Cool to lukewarm before serving in bowls. Add a splash of heavy cream, a dollop of whipped cream, or a scoop of ice cream if desired.

Any-Frozen-Berry Pie

Serves 8

Berries are probably the easiest summer fruit to freeze, and the fruit most likely to be forgotten about once frozen. Many people have told me they never freeze berries anymore because they end up not using them all. Well, frozen berries can be a problem, especially in pies, because without a little coaxing they can turn your pie to a soggy mess. A couple of tricks make this pie work really, really well. First, let the berries defrost, then collect the juices and reduce them on top of the stove (a trick from Rose Levy Beranbaum's book *The Pie and Pastry Bible*) before thickening with cornstarch. Second, bake the pie on the bottom rack of the oven on top of a preheated baking sheet to prevent a soggy bottom crust (and incidentally catch any drips). Third, use a lattice top crust to help evaporate more liquid. If your berries are frozen with sugar, adjust the amount of sugar in this recipe — or eliminate it entirely. Try this with peaches, too, but reduce the cornstarch a bit.

INGREDIENTS

6½ cups frozen mixed berries (blueberries, raspberries, sliced or quartered strawberries, blackberries)

1¼ cups sugar

½ cup cornstarch

Dough for 1 double-crust 10-inch pie (page 333)

1. Combine the berries and sugar in a large bowl and toss to mix. Let the berries defrost overnight in the refrigerator or for several hours at room temperature.

2. Preheat the oven to 425°F (220°C) with a baking sheet set on the bottom rack.

3. Pour the berries into a strainer or colander set over a small saucepan. Scrape out any undissolved sugar, too. You should have about 1¾ cups juice. Set aside ⅓ cup.

4. Bring the juices to a boil over medium-high heat and boil until reduced by half, about 10 minutes. Dissolve the cornstarch in the reserved berry juice and pour into the fruit juice. Continue to boil until the fruit juice clears and thickens, about 2 minutes. Remove from the heat and pour into the fruit in the bowl. Mix well.

5. Roll out half the pie dough, fit it into a 10-inch pie plate, and trim the overhang so that it falls 1 to 2 inches beyond the lip of the pan. Roll out the other half into a 12-inch round and cut into strips to make a lattice pie top.

6. Scrape the berry mixture into the pie shell. Weave the strips of dough over the filling to make a lattice top; trim the edges of the lattice strips flush with the bottom pie crust. Roll the bottom crust up over the ends of the lattice and crimp the dough to make an edge that stands up.

7. Bake on the baking sheet on the lowest rack of the oven for 20 minutes. Then decrease the oven temperature to 350°F (180°C) and continue baking for 40 minutes, until the top is golden brown and the filling is bubbling up through the slits. If parts of the crust begin to look too dark, cover these spots with patches of foil to protect them from burning. Cool the pie for at least 2 hours before serving.

Creamy Yogurt Fruit Pie

Serves 8

Combine yogurt and fruit in a pie shell, and you have an exceptional dessert that is so easy to make! The pie crust has to be baked and cooled in advance, and the yogurt must be made and drained in advance. It takes about 6 hours in the refrigerator for the yogurt to set up, but your active preparation time is pretty brief. Here's the really neat thing about this recipe: If you are feeling overwhelmed by all the yogurt you have, use more yogurt and less fruit. If fruit is in abundance but the yogurt is almost gone, tip the scales in the other direction. This pie will work for you!

INGREDIENTS

- 1½–2 cups plain yogurt or 1–1⅔ cups Greek-style plain yogurt
- 2–3 cups fresh, canned, or frozen and thawed berries, pitted cherries, or sliced, peeled peaches or nectarines
- ½ teaspoon vanilla extract or finely grated lemon zest
- ½ cup maple syrup or honey, plus more if needed (optional)
- 4 tablespoons cold water
- 1 envelope unflavored gelatin
- 1 baked and cooled 9-inch pie crust (page 333)

1. If you are not using Greek-style yogurt, put the yogurt in a strainer and let drain for about 30 minutes.

2. Combine the yogurt, fruit, and vanilla in a food processor. If the fruit is fresh, or if it was preserved without added sweetener, add the maple syrup. Process until smooth. Taste and add maple syrup, if needed. Because the pie will be served chilled, the filling should be quite sweet.

3. Bring a couple of inches of water to a simmer in a saucepan. Meanwhile, add the 4 tablespoons cold water to a bowl of a size that will sit on top of the saucepan without falling in. Sprinkle the gelatin over the water in the bowl and let it "bloom," or soften, for 2 minutes.

4. Set the bowl of softened gelatin over the barely simmering water in the saucepan and heat, stirring constantly, until the gelatin is completely melted. With the food processor running, pour in the gelatin mixture and process with the yogurt and fruit until completely blended in.

5. Scrape the mixture into the prepared pie shell. Refrigerate until completely set, at least 6 hours.

Fresh Fruit Tart

Serves 8

Fresh fruit tarts, assembled with care, can be more than a sum of their parts — or not, if you've ever been disappointed by a bakery tart that was much prettier than it was tasty. A classic French fruit tart is obviously inspired by just the kinds of farm-fresh ingredients you are most likely to raise yourself. The crust is little more than flour and butter (or lard), the filling is made from eggs and milk, the topping is whatever fruit you have on hand, and the glaze is made from last season's jelly or maple syrup. I added a few touches, like a little jam under the pastry cream, to guarantee the farm-fresh flavor.

INGREDIENTS

PASTRY CREAM

¾ cup milk or cream

¼ cup sugar

2 tablespoons all-purpose unbleached flour

¼ teaspoon salt

2 egg yolks

½ teaspoon vanilla extract

TART

About 2 cups berries or 1–2 pounds fresh fruit

2 tablespoons fruit jam

1 baked and cooled 9-inch pie crust (page 333)

¼ cup fruit jelly or 2 tablespoons fruit jam, heated and strained

1. To make the pastry cream, scald the milk in a small saucepan over medium heat until you see steam rising and small bubbles forming. In a bowl, whisk together the sugar, flour, and salt. Add the egg yolks and whisk to form a thick paste. Slowly pour the hot milk into the egg-yolk mixture, whisking to combine. Pour it all back into the saucepan and place over medium heat. Stirring constantly, cook until the mixture thickens and just barely comes to a boil. Remove from the heat. If you like, strain the pastry cream through a fine-mesh strainer — you may have to push it through with a wooden spoon — to eliminate any lumps. Stir in the vanilla and let cool.

2. To prepare the fruit, wash and peel as needed. Slice as desired.

3. Spread the jam in the tart shell. Smooth the pastry cream over the jam. Arrange the fruit over the pastry cream to completely cover the filling. Small berries, such as blueberries and raspberries, can be scattered over the filling. Slice any large berries, such as strawberries. Place sliced fruit in concentric circles, with each slice resting on the previous one so that none of the pastry cream shows through.

4. Melt the jelly until liquid and brush over the fruit. Chill the tart for at least 30 minutes before serving. Tarts are best served on the day they are made.

Variation: Instead of making the pastry cream, use a cream cheese filling. Combine 4 ounces of room-temperature cream cheese with ½ cup confectioner's sugar, 1 teaspoon finely grated lemon zest, and 1 tablespoon lemon juice in a food processor. Process until smooth.

Nutty Sticky Buns

Makes 12 large buns

Sticky buns have long been a holiday tradition at my house, but it is only recently that I revised the dough to use my sourdough starter. With the sourdough, the buns stay soft and moist longer (not that these last very long with my family around anyway).

INGREDIENTS

DOUGH

4 eggs

1½ cups sourdough starter (page 61)

½ cup melted butter

1 teaspoon vanilla extract

About 4 cups unbleached all-purpose flour

¼ cup granulated sugar

1 teaspoon instant active dry yeast

2 teaspoons salt

GLAZE

¾ cup butter

¼ cup packed light or dark brown sugar

1 cup maple syrup or honey

FILLING

1 cup finely chopped nuts (almonds, hazelnuts, pecans, or walnuts)

½ cup packed light or dark brown sugar

1½ teaspoons ground cinnamon

¼ teaspoon freshly grated nutmeg

2 tablespoons butter

2 tablespoons maple syrup or honey

1. To make the dough, beat the eggs in a large bowl until well blended. Stir in the sourdough starter, butter, and vanilla. Add 1 cup of the flour, the granulated sugar, and the yeast. Beat until smooth. Add another 1 cup flour and the salt, and mix in. Add about a cup of the remaining flour, enough to make a smooth, soft dough, using your hands to knead in the flour when the dough becomes too stiff to stir.

2. Flour a work surface with ¼ cup flour. Turn the dough out onto the floured surface and knead until the dough is springy and elastic, about 5 minutes, adding the remaining ¼ cup flour if needed. Place the dough in a large greased bowl, cover with a damp cloth, and let rise in a warm place until doubled in size, about 3 hours.

3. To begin the glaze, melt ¼ cup of the butter and spread generously inside a 9- by 13-inch baking pan. Sprinkle with the brown sugar and set aside.

4. Punch down the dough. Place on a lightly floured work surface. Pat out the dough to form a rectangle approximately 18 inches by 12 inches.

5. To make the filling, mix together the nuts, brown sugar, cinnamon, and nutmeg in a small bowl. Heat the 2 tablespoons butter and 2 tablespoons maple syrup together until the butter is melted.

6. Brush the butter-syrup mixture onto the dough, leaving a ½-inch border on the long sides. Sprinkle the filling mixture on top, leaving a ½-inch border on the long sides, and press in with the rolling pin or your hands. Roll up the dough into a tight log, starting at one of the long sides. Cut into 1½-inch slices and place cut-side down in the prepared pan. Cover and let rise until it has risen by about 50 percent, 15 to 30 minutes.

7. Meanwhile, preheat the oven to 375°F (190°C).

8. When the buns have risen by half, put the pan in the oven. When they have baked for 15 minutes, begin making the rest of the glaze: Combine the remaining ½ cup butter and 1 cup maple syrup in a small saucepan. Boil for 5 minutes over medium heat. When the buns have baked for 20 to 25 minutes and the tops are golden, remove the pan from the oven and place on a baking sheet (to avoid spills). Separate the buns with a spatula or rounded knife. Spoon the maple syrup glaze evenly over the top, allowing the syrup to flow between the buns. Return the pan to the oven for 5 minutes to caramelize the syrup.

9. Remove from the oven and immediately invert the buns onto a rimmed baking sheet. Let cool for 20 minutes before serving.

Baklava

Makes 36 pieces

Throughout southern Europe and western Asia (the old Ottoman Empire), you will find versions of baklava, and much disagreement about its origins. The nuts will vary, the spicing will vary, even the method of layering the phyllo pastry and nuts will vary, but the honey syrup is always present. To me, the best-tasting baklava recipes are those that were developed in areas where honey was the predominant sweetener, like this one.

INGREDIENTS

- 2½ cups sliced almonds, walnut halves, pistachios, hazelnuts, or a mixture
- ½ cup sugar
- 1 teaspoon ground cinnamon
- 1 cup butter, melted
- 1 pound phyllo pastry, thawed if frozen
- 1 cup honey
- ⅔ cup water
- 2 tablespoons fresh lemon juice
- 1 (2-inch) piece lemon zest
- 4 cardamom pods
- 1 cinnamon stick

1. Preheat the oven to 325°F (165°C).

2. Spread out the nuts in a single layer on a large baking sheet. Toast in the oven for 10 to 15 minutes, until very lightly browned and fragrant. Cool for a few minutes.

3. Combine the nuts, sugar, and cinnamon in a food processor and process until finely chopped.

4. Brush a 9- by 13-inch baking pan with some of the butter. Working one sheet at a time, layer about 10 phyllo sheets in the pan, brushing each sheet evenly with melted butter. Allow the sheets to drape over the edge of the pan, if necessary. Keep unused sheets covered with plastic wrap while assembling the baklava to prevent them from drying out.

5. Sprinkle one-third of the nut mixture (about 1 cup) evenly over the buttered phyllo. Layer another 10 sheets of phyllo, one sheet at a time, over the nut mixture, brushing each sheet evenly with butter. Sprinkle with one-third of the nut mixture. Repeat with another 10 sheets of buttered phyllo and the remaining nut mixture. Cover with the remaining phyllo sheets, brushing each sheet with butter before laying on the next sheet. Fold over any overhanging edges of the phyllo. Slice on the diagonal to make 2-inch diamonds, cutting completely through all the layers.

6. Bake until crisp and golden, 40 to 45 minutes.

7. Meanwhile, combine the honey, water, lemon juice, lemon zest, cardamom pods, and cinnamon stick in a small saucepan. Bring to a boil, then reduce the heat and simmer while the baklava bakes.

8. Remove the baklava from the oven. Remove the lemon zest, cardamom pods, and cinnamon stick from the honey syrup with a slotted spoon. Pour the warm honey syrup evenly over the baklava. Cool completely before serving.

Orange-Scented Polenta Honey Cake

Serves 12

Like many other honey cakes, this one continues to stay moist and improve in flavor over the course of a few hours or even a day. Polenta — or stone-ground cornmeal — gives the cake its distinctive gritty texture.

INGREDIENTS

- 1½ cups butter, softened
- ½ cup honey, warmed
- 3 eggs
- 2 cups unbleached all-purpose flour
- ¾ cup polenta or stone-ground cornmeal
- 1½ teaspoons baking powder
- ½ teaspoon baking soda
- ½ teaspoon salt
- Finely grated zest of 2 oranges
- ½ cup freshly squeezed orange juice

1. Preheat the oven to 350°F (180°C). Butter an 8-inch round cake pan.

2. Beat the butter and honey together until well blended. Beat in the eggs one at a time. In a separate bowl, combine the flour, polenta, baking powder, baking soda, salt, and orange zest.

3. Beat the dry ingredients into the wet ones in three parts, alternating with the orange juice. Scrape the batter into the prepared pan. Bake for 45 to 50 minutes, until the edges begin to pull away from the pan and the middle is set. Let cool before serving.

Creamy Rice Pudding

Serves 4 to 6

Rice pudding is the epitome of thrifty home-style cooking (what the French call *la cuisine de bonne femme*), especially in rural areas where milk and eggs are in abundance and no food is wasted. Since this describes the typical backyard homestead kitchen, rice pudding should be on the menu frequently. How to overcome the dry, gritty texture of leftover rice, which often ruins a good rice pudding? Simmer the rice in milk first.

INGREDIENTS

2 cups leftover cooked rice

4 cups whole milk

½ teaspoon salt (if rice was cooked without salt)

4 egg yolks

½ cup sugar

1 teaspoon vanilla extract

1. Combine the rice, milk, and salt (if needed) in a large heavy saucepan over medium heat. Slowly bring the milk almost to a boil, stirring frequently to prevent scorching.

2. In between stirring the milk, combine the egg yolks and sugar in a bowl and whisk until well blended.

3. Test a grain of rice. If it is pudding-soft, then proceed with the recipe. Otherwise, continue to stir over medium heat until the rice is fully softened.

4. Slowly add about 2 cups of the milk-and-rice mixture to the egg mixture, stirring constantly, to temper the eggs and prevent them from curdling. Pour the tempered eggs into the pot with the milk and bring to a boil, stirring constantly, until the mixture has thickened and coats the back of the spoon. You should be able to run your finger through the velvety coating on the back of the spoon to leave a distinct trail.

5. Stir in the vanilla. Transfer to a bowl and lay a sheet of plastic wrap directly on the pudding's surface, if desired, to prevent a skin from forming. Serve warm, at room temperature, or chilled.

Black Forest Ricotta Mousse

Serves 8

Who can resist the combination of chocolate and cherries? Not me, certainly. If you don't have both ricotta and mascarpone on hand, you can swap the 1 cup mascarpone for another cup of ricotta. And raspberries can replace the cherries, in which case framboise can replace the kirsch.

INGREDIENTS

4 cups pitted sour cherries, fresh or frozen

1½ cups sugar

3 tablespoons kirsch or other cherry liqueur

½ teaspoon ground cinnamon

4 ounces dark chocolate, chopped

4 ounces unsweetened chocolate, chopped

3 tablespoons water

1 envelope powdered unflavored gelatin

2 cups ricotta (page 241)

1 cup mascarpone

Whipped cream and shaved dark chocolate, to serve (optional)

1. Combine the cherries with the sugar, kirsch, and cinnamon in a small saucepan over low heat. Cook until the sugar melts and the cherries release some juice, about 10 minutes. Stir occasionally.

2. Meanwhile, combine the dark chocolate and unsweetened chocolate in a microwave-safe bowl and microwave in 30-second bursts until the chocolate is melted. Set aside to cool.

3. Measure the water into a small bowl. Sprinkle the gelatin over the water and let soften for 5 minutes. Pour into the cherry mixture, increase the heat, and cook, stirring, until the gelatin completely dissolves. Remove from the heat and let cool.

4. Purée the ricotta in a food processor until smooth. Add the mascarpone and melted chocolate and purée until smooth. Transfer to a large bowl. Fold in the cherry mixture.

5. Chill for at least 4 hours, or overnight, before serving. If desired, top each serving with whipped cream and/or shaved dark chocolate.

Everyday Flatbreads

Makes 8 flatbreads

These simple-to-make flatbreads resemble flour tortillas, but don't limit yourself to serving them only with Tex-Mex foods. They can be used to wrap everything from hummus to Indian lentils to lamb burgers to chicken salad. What they are good for is making a humble meal special. The secret to the ease of making these flatbreads is the lard. You can substitute another solid shortening, such as butter, tallow, or coconut oil. But don't even think of using a vegetable oil; it just makes the rolling-out process too darn hard.

INGREDIENTS

2 cups unbleached all-purpose flour, plus more as needed

1 teaspoon salt

¼ cup lard

Scant ⅔ cup warm (98°–100°F/37°–38°C) water

1. Mix the flour and salt in a food processor. Add the lard and process until completely mixed in. Add the water and continue processing until the dough forms a ball. If the dough is tacky, knead in a little more flour, a tablespoon at a time (and add as little as possible). Cover and let rest on your counter for at least 30 minutes and up to 60 minutes.

2. Divide the dough into 8 even-size pieces and roll each into a ball. Working with one at a time, roll out each dough ball to form a circle, making it as thin, round, and even in thickness as you can. Stack between pieces of waxed paper or parchment paper. (You can fold up the papers when you're done and reuse them the next time you make these flatbreads.)

3. Heat a dry griddle or large cast-iron skillet over high heat until hot. Cook the flatbreads one at a time for about 30 seconds on each side. There should be some dark brown (not burnt!) spots on each side to indicate when a flatbread is done.

4. Stack the flatbreads on a plate as you continue to cook them all. These are best if used immediately. If necessary, you can store them, wrapped in paper towels in a resealable plastic bag in the refrigerator; reheat them for a few seconds in a skillet before serving.

Note: You can substitute whole-wheat flour for a portion of the white flour in these flatbreads, but be sparing. Whole wheat makes the dough more difficult to roll out, more tough in texture, and more like cardboard on the second day.

Baking Powder Biscuits

Makes 12 biscuits

Biscuits can make a meal. Anytime you have leftover chicken, turkey, or rabbit, consider making "bird and biscuits" (see page 298). Anytime you want a quick fruit dessert and have whipped cream on hand, make biscuits for shortbread. Indeed, biscuits are so useful that I've included two recipes, this one with baking powder for leavening and another one with sourdough on the next page. Both are mixed by hand so that, as the biscuits bake, the irregular pieces of fat in the dough generate steam and create the flaky layers that make biscuits extra special. But if you are in a hurry, you can always mix the dough in a food processor (see the note below).

INGREDIENTS

3 cups unbleached all-purpose flour

2 tablespoons baking powder

1½ teaspoons salt

⅔ cup lard or butter, cut into very small pieces

1 cup buttermilk

1. Preheat the oven to 450°F (230°C) with an oven rack in the middle of the oven. For ease of cleanup, line a sheet pan with parchment paper or a silicone baking mat.

2. Combine the flour, baking powder, and salt in a bowl. Add the lard and mix it in with two knives or a pastry blender, or rub it in with your fingers, until the mixture resembles coarse sand with some larger pieces. Pour in the buttermilk and blend with a fork.

3. Turn the dough out onto a floured surface. Handling it as little as possible, pat out the dough into a rectangle and fold in the sides. Pat out again to a thickness of about 1 inch. Cut into 3-inch rounds. By gathering the scraps and patting out again, you should get 12 biscuits.

4. Bake for 15 to 18 minutes, until golden brown. Serve as soon after baking as possible. Biscuits are best on the day they are made, but day-old biscuits are delicious toasted.

Note: Biscuits are really easy to make with a food processor, but the texture will be less tender and flaky. Combine the flour, baking powder, and salt in a food processor. Add the lard and process until the mixture resembles coarse crumbs. Pour in the buttermilk and process to make a soft dough.

Sourdough Biscuits

Makes 9 to 12 biscuits

The secret to great texture in a biscuit is to use lard and mix it all by hand. The secret to great flavor in a biscuit is sourdough. If you like, tray-freeze unbaked biscuits, slip into a bag when frozen, and bake as needed, popping them into the oven still frozen; they may need a few extra minutes to bake, and they won't rise quite as high as fresh biscuits, but they are still a wonderful convenience.

INGREDIENTS

SOURDOUGH
Sourdough starter (page 61)
1 cup unbleached all-purpose or bread flour
1 cup water

BISCUITS
2½ cups all-purpose flour
1 tablespoon sugar
1 tablespoon salt
½ cup lard or butter, chilled and diced
Milk (optional)

1. At least 4 hours, and up to 12 hours, before you plan to bake, feed your sourdough starter with the flour and water. Mix well and leave at room temperature.

2. When you are ready to bake, combine the flour, sugar, and salt in a large bowl. Rub in the lard with your fingers until the mixture resembles coarse sand with some larger pieces. Stir in 2 cups of the sourdough starter and knead in the bowl to form a ball, making sure all the flour is incorporated. Try your best to incorporate all the flour, but if needed, add a little milk, 1 teaspoon at a time.

3. Turn the dough out onto a floured surface. Handling it as little as possible, pat out the dough into a rectangle and fold in the sides. Pat out again and fold in the sides. Pat out again to a thickness of about 1 inch and cut the dough into 3-inch rounds. Place on a baking sheet lined with parchment paper. Gather the scraps together, pat out, and cut all into rounds.

4. Preheat the oven to 450°F (230°C).

5. Brush the tops of the biscuits with milk. Bake for 30 minutes, until golden brown. These are best served warm, but day-old biscuits (if they last that long!) are delicious toasted.

Basic Pie Pastry

Makes 1 double or 2 single crusts for a 9- or 10-inch pie

Lard makes a flakier pie crust, but there is nothing wrong with a butter crust.

INGREDIENTS

- 2 cups all-purpose unbleached flour
- 1 teaspoon salt
- ⅔ cup lard or butter
- 6-7 tablespoons cold water

1. Stir together the flour and salt. Cut the lard into the flour with a pastry blender or two knives until the mixture resembles coarse crumbs. Sprinkle the water over the flour mixture and stir together. Press the mixture into two disks, wrap in plastic wrap, and refrigerate for 30 minutes.

2. On a lightly floured surface, roll out one disk of dough, working from the center outward in all directions until you have a 12-inch round. Fold the dough in half and ease into the pie pan with the fold in the center. Unfold the dough and trim to the edge of the pie pan.

3. Fill the pie as directed in your recipe.

4. Roll out the second disk of dough in the same manner. To use it for a top crust, roll out the dough into a circle just an inch or so wider than you'll need to cover the pie. Lay it over the filled pie. Trim the dough to ½ inch beyond the edge of the pie plate all around. Fold the extra pastry under the bottom pastry. Crimp the edges. Prick holes in the top pastry in several places to allow steam to escape.

5. Bake the pie as directed in the recipe.

To bake an unfilled single crust: Preheat the oven to 450°F (230°C). Fit the dough circle into the pie pan as directed above, and trim and crimp the edges, pressing the edges against the rim of the pie pan to prevent slumping. Prick the dough with a fork, covering the surface with tiny holes. Bake for 10 to 15 minutes, until browned.

APPENDIX
Basic Cooking Methods

COOKING LESSONS FOR KIDS are pretty common these days, but most of us learn simply by watching and helping out. Apparently, I learned enough just hanging out in my mother's kitchen to be able to cook when I had my first apartment. I never taught my kids how to cook the way I taught them how to drive. But I did set them up on the counter when they were little so they could "help" me. And I did require that they cook the occasional meal of their choosing, starting when they were 10 years old or so. When it comes to cooking, most of us absorb enough to get by — until we start following recipes that use unfamiliar language.

All cooking involves a combination of a few basic techniques. I've tucked this information into the back of the book just in case you need a little explanation of some of the language in the recipes and tables. You will find recipes throughout the book and especially in part 3 that rely on many of the following cooking methods.

Aromatics: Vegetables or herbs used to impart flavor. Typically, finely chopped carrots, celery, garlic, onions, parsley, and/or shallots are used as aromatics at the start of making a braise, soup, or sauce.

Bake: A dry-heat cooking method that mostly aims for a consistent and even texture throughout the baked item. It is quite similar to roasting, the difference being that we generally "bake" breads, cakes, and casseroles, but we "roast" meats and vegetables. In the old days, roasting was done on a spit over a fire. Today's roasting is done in the oven, which makes it pretty similar to baking.

Barbecue: To cook over the very low, indirect heat of a charcoal or wood fire, where the temperature is maintained between 200°F and 275°F (93°C and 135°C) for long periods of time. Tough and fatty cuts, including brisket, pork shoulder, pork spareribs, beef ribs, and whole lamb shoulders, are well suited for barbecuing.

Blanch: To partially cook in a boiling liquid, usually water. Any food can be blanched, but it is a technique most commonly used with vegetables. Working in small batches (no more than 1 pound), you plunge the vegetables into boiling water and cook them just briefly, usually 30 to 60 seconds. Then you lift out the vegetables and drop them into ice water to stop the cooking.

Vegetables are almost always blanched before being frozen or dried; the blanching sets their color and destroys the enzymes that would otherwise continue to ripen them. Sometimes vegetables are blanched as a do-ahead step. For example, you could blanch a vegetable in the morning, then quickly sauté it in butter or olive oil to finish cooking the vegetable for dinner.

Peaches and tomatoes are blanched to make it easier to remove their skins. Bones are sometimes blanched to remove impurities before they're used to make stock. Chicken feet are blanched to make peeling easier. Blanching times vary by ingredient.

Boil: To cook in boiling liquid, or to bring a liquid to boiling (212°F/100°C) so that the liquid is in motion, with bubbles rising to the surface and roiling the liquid.

In the case of vegetables, it means cooking in boiling, salted liquid, usually water, until tender. Most green vegetables are added to already boiling water; however, root vegetables and potatoes should be started in cold water and boiled gently. Water-soluble vitamins are leached into the cooking water when vegetables are boiled. Boiling is not recommended for high-sulfur vegetables such as cabbage and Brussels sprouts.

Pasta is one of the few foods that should be cooked at a rapid boil. When cooking meats and dried beans, you want to use a gentle boil, or even a simmer.

Boiling can be used to reduce a liquid (via evaporation). Jams and jellies, for example, are boiled to reduce their liquid content and concentrate their flavor. Maple sap and cider are boiled to reduce the liquid and concentrate the sugars.

Braise: To brown in oil or fat (butter, chicken fat, duck or goose fat, lard, tallow, or bacon grease), then cook, covered, in a small amount of liquid (stock, wine, cream, water). This is the very best method for cooking tough cuts of meat and old birds. It is a terrific way to cook vegetables, especially when you are feeling bored with your usual steamed flavors. The slow cooking can be done in a Dutch oven over a low flame or in a low oven or in a slow cooker.

When braising vegetables, after they become tender, if they are sitting in liquid, remove them from the cooking liquid with a slotted spoon and set aside. Then boil the cooking liquid to reduce it to a glaze or a sauce. Flavor the sauce with lemon juice, garlic, mustard, Parmesan, and fresh or dried herbs, and return the vegetables to the seasoned sauce. Of all the cooking methods, this has the potential to add the most flavor.

After meat or fowl has braised, remove the meat from the cooking liquid and let the fat rise to the surface of the liquid. Then skim it off. If you have the time, cool the cooking liquid in the refrigerator; the fat will harden and then be very easy to remove. If the cooking liquid is very thin, boil it to reduce it to a better consistency. Before serving, reheat the meat or fowl in the sauce. Good cuts for braising include any beef cut from the round or chuck, any pork from the leg or shoulder, and any lamb from the shoulder. All poultry can be braised.

Broil: To cook under an intense direct heat. Tender cuts of meat are all suited to broiling, especially beef steaks cut ¾ inch to 2 inches thick, lamb chops, burgers, and kabobs. For best results, preheat the broiler before putting the meat under it. Let the meat rest for 5 to 15 minutes after broiling to reabsorb its juices.

Deep-fry: To cook in enough hot oil or fat to cover whatever you're cooking. Generally you will need 4 to 8 inches of fat or oil, and the fat or oil is usually heated to around 365°F (185°C). The food is often dipped first in flour, then in a wash of buttermilk or eggs and milk, then in seasoned crumbs. Or it can be dipped in flour, then batter. Avoid adding too much food to the hot oil at once, so the oil temperature is not significantly lowered, which would result in greasy food. Generally, the fried food should be drained on paper towels or brown paper to absorb any excess oil. Once you're done frying, the oil can be filtered through a paper coffee filter and reused a couple of times.

Dry heat: In terms of meat, dry-heat cooking means broiling, grilling, pan-searing, and roasting. Tender cuts cooked by dry-heat methods are at their best cooked until rare or medium-rare. Tender beef cuts, such as steaks, rib roasts, sirloin, and top round, can all be cooked by dry heat. Almost all pork cuts can be cooked by dry heat, except the shanks, hocks, neck, and shoulder. Almost all parts of a lamb can be cooked by dry heat, except for the shanks and neck. All ground meats and sausages can be cooked by dry-heat methods.

Grill: To cook over an open flame, usually gas, charcoal, or wood. Generally, vegetables and small pieces of meat, fish, or fowl are grilled over direct heat — that is, directly over the flames. Cuts of meat suited to direct-heat grilling include burgers, kabobs, steaks, chops, and sausages.

Indirect grilling means that the flames are on one side of the grill, but the food is on the other side of the grill, with a drip pan underneath to catch the dripping fats. Indirect grilling is done with the grill cover on. Good cuts of meat for indirect grilling include chicken, pork shoulder, and leg of lamb.

When you're grilling vegetables, you may opt to use a vegetable grill plate, a flat piece of metal with open holes that allows the vegetables to cook without falling through the grate. Generally, vegetables are slicked with oil or a marinade to prevent them from drying out. The high heat of the grill gives the vegetables a slight char, indicating that the natural sugars in the vegetable have caramelized, and their flavor is enhanced by a slight smokiness from the grill. For best results, do not cover the grill when cooking vegetables. (Covering the grill traps smoke and steam, which results in a greasy film on the vegetables, especially in grills that are also used to cook meat.)

You can estimate the grill temperature by how long you can hold a hand 4 to 5 inches above the grill:

➤ 2 to 3 seconds: hot (450°–650°F/230°–343°C); good for steaks and chops (watch carefully!)
➤ 4 to 5 seconds: medium-hot (375°–450°F/190°–230°C); good for vegetables, burgers, fish
➤ 6 to 7 seconds: medium (325°–375°F/163°–190°C); good for indirect cooking of chickens, turkeys, roasts
➤ 8 to 10 seconds: medium-low (250°–325°F/121°–165°C); good for warming breads, reheating

Moist heat: With respect to meat, moist-heat cooking usually means braising or stewing, but it can include poaching or boiling as well. Cuts of meat suited for moist-heat cooking are generally tough, with a lot of connective tissue. The meat is cooked until well done.

Pan-fry: To cook in a small amount of oil or fat (butter, lard, chicken fat, duck or goose fat, tallow, or bacon grease) over medium to medium-high heat until browned on all sides and cooked through. It differs from sautéing in that the food is not stirred or moved around as it cooks. It is a good idea to use a heavy pan and to preheat the cooking oil or fat along with the pan before adding the food. Foods that are pan-fried can be dipped in a batter or coating, but it isn't necessary. It is important not to overcrowd the pan, so the food sears and doesn't steam.

Pan-sear: To cook food in a very, very hot skillet over high heat. This method is suited for tender cuts of meat, such as steaks, pork chops, and lamb chops. The skillet can have a flat or ridged surface and should be quite heavy. Oil can be used to grease the pan, or not. For best results, preheat the pan until it is very hot before adding the meat, and do not crowd the pan. Meats should rest for 5 to 15 minutes after pan-searing to reabsorb the juices.

Poach: To simmer (not boil!) in just enough liquid to cover. Delicate foods like fish, eggs, and fruit are often poached, which allows them to be cooked without falling apart.

Pot roast: A piece of meat braised in the oven, cooked low and slow in an aromatic liquid.

Reduce: To boil a liquid to concentrate the flavors and make thicker in consistency. Pan juices are often reduced, sometimes with the addition of wine, to make a simple sauce or gravy for meat.

Reverse sear: To partially roast meat in a very low oven until almost done and then quickly sear it on the stovetop in a very hot skillet to add an attractive color and tasty crust on the meat.

Roast: To cook with dry oven heat. The temperature will vary depending on what you're roasting. Spatchcocked chicken should be roasted at 450°F (230°C). Slow roasting at 250°F to 275°F (120°C to 135°C) is good for all beef cut from the chuck or the round — tough cuts of meat. Slow-roasted cuts from the round can be cooked until rare, then thin-sliced for sandwiches. High-temperature roasting at 450°F (230°C) or higher can be used with very tender meats such as beef tenderloin, strip steak, prime rib, lamb loin, and rack of lamb. Moderate-temperature roasting at 300°F to 350°F (150°C to 180°C) is best for smaller and leaner roasts, such as pork tenderloin, beef sirloin, or leg of lamb.

Vegetables are best roasted quickly in a hot oven, at 425°F to 450°F (220°C to 230°C). Generally, it is best to slick the vegetables with oil and cook on a sheet pan or roasting pan with low sides. Vegetables roast most evenly when all are cut to the same size and aren't crowded on the pan. Smaller cubes roast more quickly and evenly than larger pieces. Root vegetables are particularly enhanced by roasting. After roasting, a drizzle of pomegranate molasses, balsamic vinegar, or maple syrup and/or a sprinkle of coarse salt will enhance the flavor.

Sauté: To cook in a small amount of oil or fat (butter, lard, chicken fat, duck or goose fat, tallow, or bacon grease) over medium to medium-high heat until browned on all sides. Sautéing differs from pan-frying in that the food is occasionally stirred or moved around as it cooks — don't stir too much or the food will never brown. As with pan-frying, it is important to avoid overcrowding the pan, which will cause the food to steam instead of sear.

Simmer: To cook in a liquid that is just below the boiling point, at 180°F to 190°F (82°C to 88°C). Unlike boiling, where the gases are rising so rapidly that the cooking liquid is in motion, simmering means that a bubble will break the surface of the liquid every few seconds. Simmering cooks food gently and slowly.

If the food is simmered in just enough water to cover it, the process is often called poaching. And although we call some meats boiled — like corned beef and cabbage — meats should be simmered if you want them to be moist and fork-tender. Boiled meats are often dry and tough. Stocks are simmered so the fat and proteins released by any cooking meat or bones float to the top, where they can be skimmed off instead of being churned back in, which can make the stock cloudy and greasy.

Steam: To cook, covered, in a perforated basket over a small amount of boiling water. Delicate or young spring and summer vegetables such as asparagus, peas, and young green beans are good candidates for steaming — no flavor is added, but none is lost.

Stew: As with braising, in stewing the meat is browned and then cooked in an aromatic liquid. The difference lies in the quantity of liquid. For stewing, the meat is covered in liquid. When the meat is almost done, vegetables can be added to cook in the gravy. To thicken the liquid, the meat should be dredged in seasoned flour (salt, pepper, and whatever herbs you choose) before browning. If the stew is still thin after cooking, the meat and vegetables can be scooped out with a slotted spoon and the gravy boiled until reduced. Alternatively, a slurry of a few tablespoons flour dissolved in cool water can be added; then the liquid should be brought to a boil.

Stir-fry: To cook in a wok or skillet, over high heat, moving the ingredients around. To stir-fry well requires very high heat. Preheat a wok or large skillet; then add the oil. To compensate for the fact that home stoves do not generate enough heat, stir-fry small amounts at a time, transferring the food to a bowl to keep warm before adding the next ingredient. Stir-fried meat can be from either tough or tender cuts, as long as the pieces are cut into thin matchsticks.

Resources

IT TAKES A COMMUNITY to build a thriving homesteading culture. This includes farmers, writers, and friends.

Books

When I need expert information, I often turn to books, the collective wisdom of those who came before me and those who are solving problems in their own ways. I am proud to be published by Storey Publishing, and many of the books I have relied on over the years have been published by Storey. Here's a list of some of the books I have referred to, and continue to refer to.

Aidells, Bruce, and Denis Kelly. *The Complete Meat Cookbook.* Houghton Mifflin, 1998.

Andress, Elizabeth, and Judy Harrison. *So Easy to Preserve.* University of Georgia Cooperative Extension Service, 5th ed., 2006.

Bubel, Mike, and Nancy Bubel. *Root Cellaring: Natural Cold Storage of Fruits & Vegetables.* Storey Publishing, 1991.

Carroll, Ricki. *Home Cheese Making: Recipes for 75 Homemade Cheeses,* 3rd ed. Storey Publishing, 2002.

Danforth, Adam. *Butchering Beef.* Storey Publishing, 2014.

———. *Butchering Poultry, Rabbit, Lamb, Goat, Pork.* Storey Publishing, 2014.

Farrell-Kingsley, Kathy. *The Home Creamery.* Storey Publishing, 2008.

Krasner, Deborah. *Good Meat: The Complete Guide to Sourcing and Cooking Sustainable Meat.* Stewart, Tabori & Chang, 2010.

Peery, Susan Mahnke, and Charles G. Reavis. *Home Sausage Making: How-to Techniques for Making and Enjoying 100 Sausages at Home,* 3rd ed. Storey Publishing, 2003.

Ruhlman, Michael, and Brian Polcyn. *Charcuterie: The Craft of Salting, Smoking, and Curing,* rev. ed. W. W. Norton, 2013.

Ward, Cole, with Karen Coshof. *The Gourmet Butcher's Guide to Meat: How to Source It Ethically, Cut It Professionally, and Prepare It Properly.* Chelsea Green, 2014.

Websites

Sometimes it seems easier to type a query into Google than to sit down with a book and find the answer you need. But user beware! There's a lot of bad information out there, as well as some great sources. These websites have never let me down.

King Arthur Flour
www.kingarthurflour.com
Has excellent, well-tested recipes for all manner of baked goods, well-respected (and tested) information on all aspects of working with grains and flours, and very good products, with excellent customer service.

National Center for Home Food Preservation
http://nchfp.uga.edu
The best source for current research-based recommendations for most methods of home food preservation.

New England Cheesemaking Supply Company
www.cheesemaking.com
Everything you need to make cheese, yogurt, and other dairy products, including equipment, supplies, and expertise.

PickYourOwn.org
www.pickyourown.org
Good information on preserving fruits and vegetables, as well as equipment and supplies.

Serious Eats
www.seriouseats.com
The "Food Lab" pages have some of the best science-based cooking information I've ever read.

Sugar Mountain Farm
http://sugarmtnfarm.com
The website of Walter Jeffries and Sugar Mountain Farm, a small sustainable family farm in Vermont. They raise and sell pastured pork, sheep, geese, ducks, and chickens — and they blog about it.

Metric Conversion Charts

Unless you have finely calibrated measuring equipment, conversions between U.S. and metric measurements will be somewhat inexact. It's important to convert the measurements for all of the ingredients in a recipe to maintain the same proportions as the original.

General Formula for Metric Conversion	
Ounces to grams	multiply ounces by 28.35
Grams to ounces	multiply grams by 0.035
Pounds to grams	multiply pounds by 453.5
Pounds to kilograms	multiply pounds by 0.45
Cups to liters	multiply cups by 0.24
Fahrenheit to Celsius	subtract 32 from Fahrenheit temperature, multiply by 5, then divide by 9
Celsius to Fahrenheit	multiply Celsius temperature by 9, divide by 5, then add 32

Approximate Equivalents by Volume	
U.S.	Metric
1 teaspoon	5 milliliters
1 tablespoon	15 milliliters
¼ cup	60 milliliters
½ cup	120 milliliters
1 cup	230 milliliters
1¼ cups	300 milliliters
1½ cups	360 milliliters
2 cups	460 milliliters
2½ cups	600 milliliters
3 cups	700 milliliters
4 cups (1 quart)	0.95 liter
1.06 quarts	1 liter
4 quarts (1 gallon)	3.8 liters

Approximate Equivalents by Weight			
U.S.	Metric	Metric	U.S.
¼ ounce	7 grams	1 gram	0.035 ounce
½ ounce	14 grams	50 grams	1.75 ounces
1 ounce	28 grams	100 grams	3.5 ounces
1¼ ounces	35 grams	250 grams	8.75 ounces
1½ ounces	40 grams	500 grams	1.1 pounds
2½ ounces	70 grams	1 kilogram	2.2 pounds
4 ounces	112 grams		
5 ounces	140 grams		
8 ounces	228 grams		
10 ounces	280 grams		
15 ounces	425 grams		
16 ounces (1 pound)	454 grams		

Index

Page numbers in *italic* indicate illustrations; page numbers in **bold** indicate charts.

gravy, 142
poultry, 106–7, *106*, *107*
greens, 304–5. *See also* collard greens; kale; lettuce;
spinach; Swiss chard
cold storage and, 152, *152*
collard, 20
washing, 24
greens, recipes
Any Meat Stir-Fry with Vegetables, 306
Cheese Tortelloni on a Bed of Greens, 285
Wonton Soup, 304–5
gribenes, 100
grinder, 257, *257*
guinea fowl, 84, **91**, 92
roasting, 103–4, *104*

H

ham, 129–130
ham recipes
Red Chile Beans, 290
harvesting
fruits, 39
vegetables, 15
headcheese, 128
headspace, 174–75
health, animal fats and, 137
heart, *136*
poultry, 97, *97*, 109
herb(s), 31. *See also specific type*
curing and, 251
freezing, 163
in omelet fillings, 89
for pickling, 205
herb recipes
Cheese Tortelloni on a Bed of Greens, 285
Herbed Lamburgers, 314
Herb-Roasted Rabbit and Potatoes, 303
Oven-Baked French Fries, 279
Hoisin-Braised Chicken or Rabbit, 302
Hollandaise, Easy, 34
Home-Cured Bacon, 253
Red Chile Beans, 290
Home-Cured Corned Beef, 255
Homemade Fruit Liqueur, 53
Homemade Liquid Pectin, 229
homestead diet, 137
honey
about, 74
extracting, 74–75, *74*, *75*
infants and, 75
pairing cheese and, 80

storage of, 76
honey recipes
Baklava, 326
Orange-Scented Polenta Honey Cake, 327
honing steel, 13, *13*
hydrometers/test cups, 77, *77*

I

immersion blender, 7
innards, edible, 97, *97*
insect control, natural, 55
insulated coolers, 6, *6*

J

jam. *See* preserves
jar(s)
canning, 173, *173*, *174*
lids for, 173, *173*, 176, *176*
Mason, 155, *155*
sterilizing, 117, 176
jar lifter, 174, 183, *183*
jar rack, 173, 177, *177*
jellies. *See* preserves
jelly bag, 221, *221*, 225
jerky, making, 199–201
meat choice and, 199
step-by-step, 199–200, *199*, *200*
jerky recipes
Spicy Beef Jerky, 201
Jerusalem artichokes, 23
jostaberries, 43

K

kale, 23
kale recipes
Cheese Tortelloni on a Bed of Greens, 285
Kale, Carrot, and Apple Ferment, 215
Kale Salad with Catalina Dressing, 293
Seasoned Kale Chips, 194
Tuscan White Beans and Kale, 292
kidney, *136*
kimchi(s)
making, 216–17
step-by-step, 212–13, *213*
kimchi recipes
Mild Kimchi, 217
kitchen scale, 6, *6*
kitchen tools, 7

S

safety issues
  botulism, 75, 171, 172
  curing meats, 247–48
sage, 31
Salad with Catalina Dressing, Kale, 293
salmon, Gravlax, 252, 252
salsas, 208
salsify, 28
salt
  cheese, 237
  in history, 250
  Kosher, 249–250
  pickling and, 204–5
salt brine, 207
Salt-Cured Dilly Beans, 216
Salt Pork, 254
  Coq au Vin, 296–97
  Red Chile Beans, 290
  Spaghetti Carbonara, 271
sanitizing, 13–14
  cheesemaking and, 230
  jars, sterilizing, 117
sauce(s). *See also* mustard sauce
  fruit, 52
  pan, 142, 143–44
  for vegetable dishes, 32
sauce recipes
  Aioli, 33
  Applesauce, 52
  Barbecue Sauce, 311
  Cheese Sauce, Basic, 34
  Hollandaise, Easy, 34
  Pesto, 35
  Red Chile Enchilada Sauce, 291
sauerkraut, 212–13
sausage(s)/sausage making, 255–261
  cured, 256
  curing, 260
  equipment for, 257, 257
  fresh, 255–56
  German-style sausage, 256
  ingredients for, 256
  patties, making, 260
  smoked, 256
  step-by-step, 258–59, 258, 259
  types of, 255–56
sausage recipes
  Bulk Fresh Mexican Chorizo Sausage, 261
  Bulk Hot or Sweet Italian Sausage, 260
  Chorizo Skillet Supper, 309

sausage stuffer, 257, 257
scale, kitchen, 6, 6
schmaltz, 100
scorzonera, 28
screwbands, 173, 177, 187, 187
searing, reverse, 141–42
searing dry heat, 145
Seasoned Kale Chips, 194
Shakshuka, 269
shallots, 25
  cold storage and, 148
sheet test, 222, 222
shoulder
  lamb, 123
  pork, 128–29
Simple Vanilla Custard, 318
sirloin, beef, 131
Skillet Supper, Chorizo, 309
slow cooker, 7, 226, 226, 233
Slow Food USA, 81
Slow-Rise Sourdough Pizza, 283
small equipment, 4–6, 4, 5, 6
smoked sausage, 256
Smoky-Sweet Slow-Cooked Ribs, 311
solar dehydrators, 190, 190
sorghum syrup, 81
soup(s), making vegetable, 37
soup recipes
  Cream of Any Vegetable Soup, 38
  Gazpacho, 275
  Tomato-Vegetable Soup, 274
  Wonton Soup, 304–5
sour cream
  freezing, 167
sour cream recipes
  Lime Crema, 309
sourdough
  no-knead, 63–64
  sourness and, 63
Sourdough Biscuits, 332
  Bird and Biscuits, 298
sourdough starter
  about, 61
  feeding your, 62
  growing, from cup of, 63
  math, 62
  metals and, 62
  neglected, reviving, 62–63
  recipe for, 61
sourdough starter recipes
  Nutty Sticky Buns, 324–25
  Slow-Rise Sourdough Pizza, 283

THE
BACKYARD HOMESTEAD
Series

Put your backyard to work with the definitive, bestselling Backyard Homestead series — it doesn't get more local than this. Rural, urban, and suburban residents alike can be more self-reliant and productive with in-depth guidance on homesteading, essential projects for equipping your homestead and building backyard structures, and comprehensive DIY guides to raising livestock and preparing and preserving your homegrown bounty. Live sustainably and independently and thrive in your own backyard for years to come.

The Backyard Homestead
edited by Carleen Madigan

368 pages. Paper.
ISBN 978-1-60342-138-6.

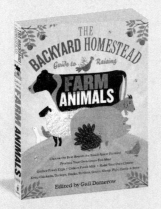

The Backyard Homestead Guide to Raising Farm Animals
edited by Gail Damerow

360 pages. Paper.
ISBN 978-1-60342-969-6.

The Backyard Homestead Book of Building Projects
by Spike Carlsen

296 pages. Paper.
ISBN 978-1-61212-085-0.

Also by Andrea Chesman

Complement your country kitchen skills with more books from
experienced homesteader and recipe writer Andrea Chesman. Bring out the best in your
garden-fresh summer vegetables, then eat heartily through the winter and into spring with
delicious recipes for root vegetables and methods for pickling and preserving your harvest.

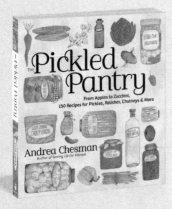

The Pickled Pantry

Preserve your own homegrown feast
with 150 delicious recipes for salsa,
relishes, fermented pickles, chutneys,
and much more. Put up everything
from asparagus to rhubarb and
cabbage to pineapple with Andrea
Chesman's expert advice.

304 pages. Paper.
ISBN 978-1-60342-562-9.

Recipes from the Root Cellar

A collection of more than 250 recipes
for winter kitchen produce — jewel-
toned root vegetables, hardy greens,
sweet winter squashes, and potatoes
of every kind.

400 pages. Paper.
ISBN 978-1-60342-545-2.

Serving Up the Harvest

A collection of 175 recipes to bring
out the best in garden-fresh vegetables, with 14 master recipes that can
accommodate whatever happens to
be in your produce basket.

512 pages. Paper.
ISBN 978-1-58017-663-7.

These and other books from Storey Publishing are available
wherever quality books are sold or by calling 1-800-441-5700.
Visit us at www.storey.com or sign up for our newsletter
at www.storey.com/signup.